BUSINESS COMMUNICATION READER

J. HAROLD JANIS

Professor of Business Writing
New York University

HARPER & BROTHERS,
PUBLISHERS, NEW YORK

Library of Congress catalog card number: 58-8357

Contents

Preface

To the businessman and prospective businessman this book offers an acquaintance with good writing about business, professional help in developing his own communication skills, and some rewarding reading on the business culture—all brought together in a single, conveniently arranged volume.

I believe this anthology will be helpful and interesting to anyone who wishes to explore it on his own. On the other hand, the book arose from the needs of the communication courses for business majors, and I have kept the college student and teacher in mind throughout.

This is a time of healthy experimentation in the teaching of communication skills on the college level. For me, the writing problems of the business administration student have held particular interest. As a result of my teaching experience in both business writing courses and the traditional freshman composition course, I have felt that the two ought to be drawn more closely together. This view is in keeping with the trend, endorsed by business itself, to broaden the base of collegiate education for business.

After considering the means by which to enlarge the scope of the business writing course, I reached the conclusion that a book of this nature would do the job best. It requires the teacher to give up none of his hard-learned methods and basic texts; yet it puts in his hands and in the hands of his students certain raw materials that give a new dimension to the concept of business writing. What, specifically, have I tried to do?

Since reading is the best introduction to writing that I know, I have tried to make this a book that invites reading. The selections are varied and should appeal to anyone who professes an interest in business. They range in subject matter from Adam Smith's discourse on the making of pins to the history of radio commercials; from the life of the earliest do-it-yourself Americans to the introduction of the Model T—and automation; from advice on how to be an employee to the romance of figures.

Beyond providing good reading, though, I have had several more pertinent aims. One of these is to put before students of business communication some ideas on communication itself, at the same time stressing the interrelationship of all the communication media. Thus I have included articles on letter writing, report writing, reading, speaking, advertising, publicity, business journalism, and human relations. These, extracted mainly from business sources, are intended to supplement the often more formal treatments in the standard texts. In themselves, they constitute a small but select library on business communication.

Another aim is to provide examples of business writing, including writing about business, culled from such diverse sources as newspapers and magazines, books, speeches, and Congressional testimony, and from reports, bulletins, manuals, and brochures issued by business. Many of these are materials not ordinarily available in textbooks. They afford a showcase of many kinds of good writing for study and emulation.

Still another purpose I have kept in mind in selecting these readings is to give future business executives some orientation in the world for which they are headed. As many of the readings suggest, experience no longer provides—if it ever did—the surest road to success. The college graduate entering business today needs, far more than experience, an understanding of some of the history and culture of business and an awareness of the interplay of its many functions. By bringing together selections on a wide variety of subjects related to business, I hope to encourage further study and to stimulate some of the enthusiasm for business that success in business requires.

With all these aims, this book would still not fulfill my ambitions for it if it did not include a large number of writing exercises relating to or suggested by the readings. Most of the exercises require no formal research beyond the readings themselves. Some require library or other types of investigation. Among the writing projects are very short pieces, including definitions and summary paragraphs, and such longer exercises as letters, themes, reports, and answers to discussion questions. Knowing that there is available elsewhere an amplitude of technical projects in letter and report writing, I have devised the present exercises with a view to variety and to the general development of the student's powers of expression. In any case, the exercises are merely suggestive, and the teacher will no doubt think of many more as he reads the selections. Indeed, one of the values of such an anthology is that it provides innumerable avenues for the teacher's own inventiveness.

As with the readings, I believe the exercises will prove interesting as well as instructive. Many extend the subject of a reading into the college environment. These and others give the student a needed outlet for his creative urges. On the other hand, most of the exercises are anchored in the bedrock of the readings themselves and challenge the student to summarize, analyze, criticize, emulate, and adapt. If the student's write-as-I-please impulses are in these instances kept in check, the plan is deliberate. For I believe that any purposeful writing—outside of the purely creative—is usually circumscribed by requirements beyond the control of the writer. That observation applies to most college writing, and it applies even more to writing for business.

Of course, this book could not have been compiled without the help of a great many people, especially the authors and publishers represented in its pages. Although acknowledgments are made in the footnotes, they do not begin to discharge my indebtedness. Let me therefore express my gratitude here. Without exception, everyone of whom I requested permission to use material was generous and gracious.

Among my colleagues I also received much help for which I should like to declare my thanks. Dean Thomas L. Norton has for a long time been interested in finding the means to improve the writing skills of business students. It was his encouragement that helped me decide to undertake this book. His wide reading also led me to many sources of material I might easily have overlooked. Professor A. Earl Manville, chairman of the Department of Business Writing and Speaking, has been my mentor since my undergraduate days. His advice has been of immense help to me. I am also indebted to Professor Edward J. Kilduff who, over the years, has given me the opportunity to work with him and to learn much from him. Another colleague, Professor Lawrence D. Brennan, gave me many valuable leads and suggestions. Other suggestions were made by Mr. George Thomas and Mr. Norman Wesley.

J. HAROLD JANIS

New York University
February, 1958

BUSINESS COMMUNICATION READER

1

PREPARING FOR BUSINESS LEADERSHIP

It was in 1908 that banker Henry Clews wrote: "As the college curriculum and training stand at present, the ordinary course is not generally calculated to make a good businessman. It is erroneously regarded by some people as a kind of substitute for business training in the earlier years of a young man's life. There could be no greater mistake in the beginning of a business career. It is in many instances not only a hindrance, but absolutely fatal to success."

The fact that Henry Clews had an LL.D. and made a huge success in business is perhaps irrelevant. What is not irrelevant is that the business world has grown bigger and more complex since his time. The self-made man is a vanishing race. Advances in the physical and social sciences and the application of these advances to business and industry have put a premium on the kind of education that can be obtained only in college classrooms, libraries, and laboratories. Experience is still important for success, but not more so than technical knowledge, broad understanding of the forces that control people and processes, and the ability to organize and direct the activities of others. Growing emphasis is also being placed on the businessman as a whole human being. As such, he must seek fulfillment not only in the market place, but also in his home, his hobbies, and his cultural pursuits.

In this section, the reader will find a variety of views on the subject of business success, from the philosophic to the immediately practical.

THE GREAT HUNT FOR EDUCATED TALENT
John W. Gardner

"It is now the employers, not the young men, who have their hats in their hands." The president of the Carnegie Corporation of New York tells what the shortage of educated talent promises for the uncommon man.

Everyone is familiar with the hopelessly difficult plight of the young graduate of a technical institution. On the day he finishes college he may be forced to make a painful choice among the fat salaries offered him by dozens of corporations. Without experience he can command from $360 to $500 a month. He sorts out the firms that compete for his favors.

"We don't screen them," an official of one of the great industrial firms has said: "they screen us."

Not everyone, however, realizes that the talent hunt extends far beyond technicians and engineers. We are, it is plain, in the midst of a revolution in society's attitude toward talent. For the first time in history men and women of high ability and advanced training are not merely finding a market for their gifts; they are being pursued, flattered, and fought over. Never in the history of America have so many people spent so much money in search of talent. Never before have educators worked so hard trying to identify gifted youngsters, and, when they have found them, tried so conscientiously to nurture their abilities.

Throughout the ages human societies have always been extravagantly wasteful of talent. Today we can no longer afford to be. Among the historic changes which have marked our era this may in the long run prove to be one of the most profound.

If you are in any doubt that the search for the uncommon man is in full swing, ask the nearest executive what he is doing to find good men. Last year General Electric had recruiting teams on two hundred campuses. Great law firms that twenty years ago waited regally for bright law-school graduates to knock at their doors, now match wits with other firms to entice the young to their paneled offices. Government agencies comb the colleges for promising young men and women. You no longer hear the anecdotes about the cocky, impractical college graduate who came on the job bursting with confidence and muffed every assignment. It is now the employers, not the young men, who have their hats in their hands.

Both groups have what is certainly an absurd faith in the utility of a college degree. ("Business," says the Na-

From *Harper's Magazine*, January, 1957. Reprinted by permission.

tional Manpower Council, "strongly prefers the college graduate.") But there is nothing absurd about the fact that the world of work needs educated talent and is willing to pay handsomely for it.

Twenty years ago the old and distinguished institutions of higher learning thought their only responsibility was to act as coolly as possible toward applicants; now they scour the nation for superior students. $55,000,000 in scholarship programs helps them to attract and train talented young people, and the colleges and universities are aware that virtually the total future leadership of our society—political, cultural, industrial, technical, professional, educational, and agricultural—has become their province. Indeed, one of the most important consequences of the rise of educated talent is the wholly new position of the colleges and universities in our national life. As the cradle of our national leadership, their role is increasingly weighty and powerful.

The great talent hunt is not without its problems. It is bound to change the nature of some of our institutions and strain others. Let us assess the forces that have led to the hunt, see how it is being conducted, and try to predict its future course.

The nature of our life and times provides the background for the talent hunt, and the demand runs far deeper than the much advertised shortages of the moment. The problem created by the low birth rate of the 1930's is part of the present difficulty. This will pass. Some of our current shortages are a direct result of our intensive military research and development. This may or may not pass.

But there is a far deeper current that has been running for centuries and is now growing into a great wave. Our present demand for talent is not, as some people insist, a mere by-product of prosperity. It is the nature of our society that has churned up the wave of demand—the rapid rate of our technical innovation and the social complexities that have come in its wake. We are only beginning to understand that one of the marks of a modern complex society is an insatiable appetite for educated talent. It is not just technologists and scientists that we need. We desperately need gifted teachers, professional men, scholars, critics, and seers.

THE MAN WITH THE DEGREE

But let us go back a generation and more and see what has happened to change the American attitude toward talent, and why.

As few as fifty years ago the only fields that *required* advanced training were medicine, law, the ministry, and the scholarly fields. Only a tiny number of leaders in other fields could boast college degrees. Today the "man with a degree" is taking over every central and significant activity in our society.

The figures are revealing. Since the turn of the century, the population has nearly doubled, but the number of bachelor's and first professional degrees has multiplied about eleven times, and the number of doctoral degrees about twenty-two times. A look at the eighty years between 1870 and 1950 reveals that the number of professional workers has grown three and a half times faster than the population, and three times faster than the labor force generally.

The most dramatic change has, as you might expect, taken place in science and technology. In 1870 scientists and engineers were so little in demand that they represented only 3 per cent of professional men. Now they constitute 20 per cent. In 1870 a scientist, engineer, or technician was only one worker in 1,100. In 1950 he was one in sixty.

It is not so easy to measure the demand for high ability and advanced training in managerial and administrative jobs, but there is not the slightest question that business and industry now recruit their top leaders from the ranks of highly educated men.

"Education," says Lloyd Warner, who recently completed a study of business leadership, "has become the royal road to positions of power and prestige in American business and industry."

One needs only to look at the astonishing rise of professional schools of business to confirm this observation.

Roughly two-thirds of American college graduates already take their degrees in some form of professional education. The old-line professions such as law and medicine have vastly strengthened their position in the past half-century. They have raised standards of professional training, and have learned effective ways of advancing their own professional interests. Fields such as teaching and engineering, which were not universally recognized as professional fields fifty years ago, are now well established in that category. Meanwhile, newer fields such as social work and accountancy are energetically raising their standards, strengthening their associations, and demanding full professional status.

And the professions are playing an increasingly important role in public administration at all levels—federal, state, and local. The highly trained man now sits behind a government desk, not just as an "expert" in statistics or economics, but—for better or worse—as an administrator of public affairs.

This growth of the professions is a striking social development. If the present trend continues, it is quite possible that within a few years a very high proportion of all educated talent will be professionalized.

As the demand for educated talent has grown, so, of course, have the prominence and influence of our educational institutions. The college population has increased more than fifty times since 1870 and there is reason to believe that it will at least double and possibly triple in the next twenty years. While the number of schoolteachers has doubled since 1910, the number of college teachers has multiplied ten times. Higher education is now available in more than 1,800 institutions scattered over the face of the nation. In 1952 the physical plant and plant funds of these institutions were valued at 9.7 billion dollars. Anyone who thinks he has kept abreast of the tremendous growth of higher education might try naming the thirty-eight American universities with enrollments of over 10,000 students. Few well-informed Americans could name even half of these giant institutions.

But size and numbers tell only a small part of the story. The colleges and universities have rooted themselves in important and little recognized ways in our national and international life. Everyone links the names Salk and Enders with the polio vaccine, but few go on to think of their home bases, the universities of Pittsburgh and Harvard. The engineering professors are at home in industrial plants near their campuses. A university's agricultural specialists advise farmers throughout the state. Those universities that are working on defense contracts for the federal government have developed gargantuan research laboratories—like Berkeley's radiation lab and its cyclotron—and expend hundreds of millions of public dollars a year.

Outside our borders, experts from American universities are conducting projects in nearly every country of the free world. Anyone who travels in the far places of the world today is accustomed to the fact that no matter how remote the village or countryside, he may encounter an engineer from Purdue, or a public health expert from Johns Hopkins, or an anthropologist from Cornell, or an agricultural expert from the University of Maryland. In Bonn he will find a former president of Harvard serving as American Ambassador. Men from our universities are advising foreign governments, working devotedly for our own government, carrying on fundamental research, applying new discoveries, and in endless ways affecting the shape of the future.

There is no question that our colleges and universities have achieved remarkable prestige, and that they are being given tasks of unprecedented range and importance. Furthermore, they hold the key to professionalization. When the members of any occupation want professional status they start by trying to establish courses in their field in the college curriculum. As Robert Merton has pointed out, the universities play a central role in establishing the legitimacy of a new profession—from hotel management to forestry. And in the process they establish standards of training, of professional practice and values which will govern future professionals.

The demand for talent is now so familiar to us that it seems wholly unremarkable. Yet it is a profound change in human affairs. Throughout history, mankind has given only a very few of its gifted individuals the chance to develop their gifts. Generally speaking, those individuals whose talents have been discovered and cultivated have been like chance out-croppings of precious rock; the great reserves of human talent have lain all undiscovered below.

Without the major changes in social organization that followed the Industrial Revolution the present role of educated talent would not have been possible. Almost all societies before the Industrial Revolution were "societies of status," in which what counted was not *what a man could accomplish*, but *who he was*.

DO WE REALLY VALUE EXCELLENCE?

The American people, spurred by religious, political, and social views which laid enormous emphasis upon individual opportunity, moved farther and faster than any other nation in rejecting this kind of status society. In the United States, to an unprecedented degree, the individual's social role has come to be determined not by *who he is* but by *what he can accomplish*.

A society which has done away with the distinctions of a status system, however, has not just by so doing solved the problem of dealing with human differences. It still must decide what its attitude will be toward *excellence*, and this is something about which we have never quite made up our minds. In some matters we seem unstintingly committed to recognize excellence, to cherish high standards of quality and, in the words of William James, "to disesteem what is cheap, trashy, and impermanent." But in others we enshrine the mediocre, fear and scorn superior performance, and tie down every Gulliver who appears.

A tension between these conflicting views is inherent in our thinking and way of life; only recently has necessity swung the balance markedly toward the preferment of excellence.

Some people, particularly in the academic world, have been worried by what they believe to be popular hostility to people of high ability and advanced training. Such "anti-intellectualism" does exist in some measure, but it is not a major factor in the future of educated talent in the United

States. The forces which have made for acceptance and assimilation of educated talent have been so overpowering that they have swept all opposition before them. It is the rule rather than the exception that our society has accepted, encouraged, nurtured, and even coddled the man of gifts and training.

REWARDS AND HAZARDS

What are some of the consequences of the new position that educated talent has achieved?

One is already obvious: We shall give far more attention to the development of human capacities than we have in the past. Stung by grave shortages in various fields, we have already started the search for gifted youngsters. Sooner or later we shall have to find more adequate ways to educate the ones we find.

We will also have to try to salvage the able youngsters who are now lost to higher education—those who are prevented by financial need and inadequate motivation from continuing their education. We will have to find a way to give the gifted student active guidance at elementary and high-school levels to show him (and his parents) the potentialities which he has for further education. We will have to increase scholarship assistance for needy young people. In these and innumerable other ways we shall have to discover and make full use of all the sources of talent in the population.

Far more intense competition in the educational system will also result from the new position of educated talent. The cash value that the world attaches to a college degree cannot escape the notice of youth.

Youth knows, for example, that the armed services recognize a college degree as a good signal that a young man is potential officer material. They are also aware of the value which the world

attaches to high grades. The recruiting teams who appear on the campus each year to interview the "top quarter" or "top half" of the class have left an indelible impression on many a sophomore and junior.

This intensified competition is going to extend even farther down the line and will make itself felt in all of our schools. The never-ending talent hunt, the incessant testing programs, and the emphasis upon achievement are bound to point up individual differences in youngsters at very early age levels. The consequences of this are by no means wholly attractive. Indeed, in some respects they make one shudder. We can only hope that ways will be found to soften the edge of competition and minimize harsh comparisons. We must hope, too, that we shall have the wisdom to avoid a tyranny of the aptitude tester.

The rise of trained talent will greatly increase the emphasis on the importance of graduate training. Higher levels of expertness will be identified with advanced degrees.

Although the total plant for higher education is vast in size, facilities for graduate training are still very limited. In 1950, there were 148 American institutions of higher education offering programs that lead to the Ph.D. And a surprisingly small fraction of these carries the major burden of training our professional, scholarly, scientific, and technical leaders. Of the 3,000 physicists with doctoral degrees listed in the 1949 edition of *American Men of Science*, 85 per cent received their degrees from one or another of thirty-three leading institutions. In other words, the tremendously important national job of training our highest echelons of professional, scientific, and scholarly talent falls to a very small group of first-line institutions.

We are bound to see more and

greater emphasis upon specialization. This poses a familiar dilemma. The tremendous rewards for specialization encourage narrow training; and for certain purposes of science, business, and government, this is useful. But a world of ever-ramifying specialties soon cries out for generalists. Someone must be able to see beyond his immediate job and be able to cope with the larger relationships.

With this in mind, the most forward-looking of our colleges and universities are making active efforts to ensure that every specialist will build his specialty on a base of general education so that he will have some flexibility and breadth as a background for specializing. What the future is going to demand is specialists who are capable of functioning as generalists.

There are other reasons for avoiding narrow specialization. The youngster who trains himself as a narrow specialist, in the belief that there will always be a demand for his specialty, may be in for a nasty jolt. Our world changes so rapidly that no one can promise that today's specialty will be needed tomorrow. The way in which a group of specialists is required to function may change overnight and the demand for them may disappear; a new professional field may take over the functions of an older one; skills that have been acquired by long hard work may be out of date in a decade. To be safe a man

must have professional training that is broad and flexible enough so that he can survive the ups and downs of demand and adapt himself to changing situations. If he has such breadth and flexibility, a highly trained man can look to the future with considerable confidence.

There are, as I have mentioned, those who fear that the present educational boom is wholly a product of the economic boom. They are afraid that our heavy college enrollments could not survive a setback in the economy. It seems to me that this fear is unwarranted. During the Depression of the 1930's, college and graduate school enrollments did not drop. They rose. The yearly expenditure for scientific research and development more than doubled during that decade.

This is not to say that the educated man enjoys a pleasant invulnerability to economic setbacks, but men of high ability and advanced training will probably suffer less than any other sector of society from hard times. It would be foolish to say that they will not suffer at all. As a matter of fact the data at hand indicate that the college man outstrips the non-college man with astonishing ease in every measure of worldly success. Taking good times and bad, he is more apt to be employed, gets better jobs, earns more money, and gets ahead faster. . . .

WHAT DO COLLEGE GRADES PREDICT?
Richard W. Husband

"Do we really value excellence?" The question dealt with in the preceding article is again answered affirmatively in this statistical study of the Class of '26, Dartmouth. Dr. Husband is Professor of Industrial Psychology at Florida State University.

As an industrial psychologist who has trained students for business, and as a onetime member of the industrial relations department of a large corporation who has hired them, I have long wanted to discover if it might be possible to predict from a man's record of achievement in college how successful he would be two or three decades hence. Certainly, it is not unique to survey a college class; it's often done for twenty-fifth and other reunions. However, the surveys that I have seen are largely, if not wholly, chatty and personal, dealing with wife and children, beer and poker, church and politics, sometimes with a brief tabulation of vocations and perhaps incomes.

My idea was to take my own class of Dartmouth 1926 and attempt to correlate their 1956 status with how they did in grades and extracurricular activities when they were in college. The senior yearbook provided a record of their athletic and extracurricular activities, and the college administration furnished me with records of their grades and their intelligence scores. Then, after consultation with class-

mates, professional associates, and personnel men, I worked up a four-page questionnaire covering, among other things, the alumnus' subsequent education, if any; job history, income; civic, social, professional associations, and hobbies.

The questionnaires were mailed in June, 1956, thirty years to the week after graduation, to every one of nearly 500 men, graduates and non-graduates, in the class of 1926. Almost immediately, 150 replies came in. I followed up with three more mailings, the last consisting of postcards with such personal touches as "I particularly want to hear from you in view of your high scholastic average," or "Too few track men have replied; how about helping us along?" Eventually 275 of 368 graduates replied, a 75 per cent return. Interestingly, virtually every graduate who could be said to have made an excellent undergraduate record—whether in grades, sports, leadership, or any other activity—replied. A check of the non-respondents showed that in grades and extracurricular activity they were slightly below class average, and

Reprinted by Special Permission from the June, 1957, issue of Fortune Magazine; © by Time Inc.

most of them were missing from the lists of donors to the Alumni Fund.

Median income, the replies indicated, is $14,950. Eighty-five men (31 per cent) earn over $20,000. (I wish now I had included at least one higher category, say, "Over $50,000.") Here is how incomes correlated with college grades:

Grade point average	Number	Median income
1.50–1.69	17	$10,625
D 1.70–1.89	49	14,250
1.90–2.09	36	15,625
2.10–2.29	31	14,375
2.30–2.49	50	14,680
C 2.50–2.69	19	14,375
2.70–2.89	24	15,000
2.90–3.09	17	13,125
B 3.10–3.29	11	16,250
3.30+	14	20,000 plus

Trends appear only at the two extremes. First, we see that those who barely graduated have definitely lower than average earnings at present. At the other end of the scale, the two top groups show a definite rise in income. Contrary to the stereotype that the Phi Bete becomes a low-salaried intellectual, of the twenty-two awarded Phi Beta Kappa, thirteen are earning over $20,000.* Only five entered scholarly work, four as college teachers and one in research. Six became lawyers; virtually all the rest are in business.

As a further check, I compared the scores of the intelligence tests the men had taken as college freshmen with their present earnings. Three facts

* A study done by Donald Bridgman of the Bell Telephone Co. in 1930 shows a similar relationship. Employees whose grades were in the top tenth of their graduating class had earnings, thirty years later, 60 per cent above the median of all college graduates of that length of service within that company. At the other extreme, those from the lowest third had earnings of just 80 per cent of the median.

emerged: (1) Those lowest in the scale have not done so well. (2) The very highest fall off in earnings. One reason: the men who went into scholastic work were likely to be men with exceptionally high intelligence scores. (3) For the bulk of the men between the two extremes, no special trends appear.

A comparison of income with the men's major at college revealed that as a group those who chose the Tuck School (business) or economics have the highest median income: $16,800. Social-science majors are next; many of the businessmen specialized within that area. Third were men in basic science, chiefly the pre-medics. Cultural majors (English, languages, art, philosophy) ranked lowest; their present income is nearly $1,500 below the class median.

Most striking was the relationship between extracurricular activities and incomes. The more activities, the higher the present income.

No extracurricular activities	78 men	$13,840 plus
Slight participation	126 "	$14,220
Wide participation	46 "	$15,625
Outstanding success	16 "	$20,000 plus

Fraternity membership was another factor. Non-fraternity men now earn $11,250; fraternity men, $15,235.

IT PAYS TO EXERCISE

Fiction is full of stories of the All-American who turns out to be a complete bum. How about this? John R. Tunis, making a follow-up study of his own Harvard 1911 at the time of its twenty-fifth reunion in 1936, seemed to confirm this belief when he reported that high-scholarship men had highest earnings, the athletes the lowest. In the case of Dartmouth '26, however, the athletes have done very well for themselves.

No athletics	194	men	$14,280
1926 numerals only	18	"	$15,000
"D" letter	24	"	$18,575
2 letters	9	"	$17,500

Twenty-five per cent of those now rated as outstanding made a team at college. Conversely, of the twenty-four men in the class who made a team, only three are rated as having had a poor or mediocre career, thirteen are rated as good, and eight as outstanding.

Men who had been editors or top staff members of literary or musical organizations at college now average $16,250, versus the class median of slightly under $15,000. Those who had been "privates" in these organizations average a few hundred above the median.

Higher yet is the income of the leaders in campus "political" activities; men who had belonged to two or more leadership organizations (this would include most of the class officers) rank very high in present income.

No activity	185	men	$14,250
One	43	"	$14,583
Two or more	38	"	$20,000 plus

In demonstrating the relationship between extracurricular participation and income, I have not, of course, demonstrated cause and effect. Whether participation developed the traits that have created vocational success is impossible to determine. What seems probable is that effective work habits, broad interests and enthusiasms, and desire to succeed are what bred success at two stages of life.

Since recruiters look for a balance of qualities, I attempted to match classroom and outside-activity records to derive an all-around rating of college achievement. The results give support

to the recruiter who says he would like to employ the B student who has some outside activities.

College scholarship poor and little or no extracurricular	$16,667
Fair in either or both combined	$13,889
Average in combined rating	$14,422
Top quarter in both, or outstanding in one and at least above average in other	$19,603

The above-average income of the "poor" group is puzzling; the number of cases was small, however, and virtually everyone in this category went into a financially profitable occupation.

THE WELL ROUNDED

I next compared the men's careers at college with their general success since then. I used two indexes of success: (1) Income. (2) An index based on how well a man has done in his profession with respect to estimated opportunities. I felt this second index advisable because of the charge that cash is not the sole measure of success; earning opportunities, furthermore, are far greater in some fields than in others.

Of the seven men judged to have had poor success in their vocations only one had even an average undergraduate record. The rest barely graduated and had little outside activity. One step higher are those who have had only mediocre success; 70 per cent of these had mediocre (fair or poor) college records also. Going further up the scale of success, one observes that it is easier to predict mediocrity than success. This is probably so because any one crucial failing can produce mediocrity, while all factors have to be favorable for success. Of the thirty-two now rated as outstanding successes, half did have highly superior college records, but ten had only average grades, and six had only fair or poor grades.

THE "LATE BLOOMER"

Just as we have stories of the big wheel in college who becomes a bum, so we also have fiction about the college nonentity who returns to reunion in a Rolls-Royce. I found fifty cases of the "late bloomer": men whose grade-point average was below C and who had engaged in little or no outside activities, and yet who at middle age report earnings better than the class median. Their rank on the intelligence test was only a trifle higher than their relative classroom standing, so the special success of this group was not due to any hidden intellectual talents. We must, then, look for personality factors. Since their extracurricular participation was scanty, a recruiter could hardly have detected predictive factors outside the classroom. The majority majored in a practical area, but in this they were not significantly different from the class as a whole.

Now here is an interesting figure. Despite their lower than average grades at Dartmouth, two-thirds of the late bloomers took further education after Dartmouth. Almost a third earned some advanced degree.

Much of this reversal between undergraduate performance and present income is contributed by the M.D.'s. The majority of them had quite poor undergraduate records; they averaged scarcely above a straight C. It is difficult to interpret the significance of this. It may suggest that medicine is so lucrative now that persons of only mediocre college aptitude can achieve high earnings.

In general, I must admit that I can find no significant factor to explain the late bloomers. Perhaps there is just no way of identifying by springtime of senior year which people heretofore mediocre will eventually become howling successes. The familiar laws of probability will have to be used. We know from our data that the prominent undergraduate, whether this prominence is in scholarship, outside activities, or campus politics, almost always becomes a real success. So it may just remain unfortunate for industry, and even more for the man himself as a job seeker, that the late bloomer is the long shot who does come through once in a while, but who at time of possible hiring is difficult or impossible to identify.

THE MEN OF DISTINCTION

I made a special check of men who were judged by others to have been outstanding as undergraduates; second, of men judged as outstanding successes today. Without exception, the fifteen undergraduate leaders have made either superior or excellent records in the world; of the fifteen men judged outstanding today, all but four had fine college records thirty years previously— scholastically, extracurricularly, and socially. In both groups, 40 per cent have held five or more jobs since graduation.

Fifteen of Dartmouth '26 are in Who's Who. Nine are in scholarly work of some sort, which accounts for a very atypical distribution; seven earn over $20,000, the other eight in the neighborhood of $8,000 to $10,000. As expected, as students they earned high grades; but it is significant to add that eleven of the fifteen had engaged in three or more extracurricular activities, nine were on athletic squads, and eight had records as class officers or in organizations honoring leadership qualities.

The non-graduates furnished somewhat surprising statistics. Of the thirty-four of about 120 non-grads who replied to the questionnaire, about a quarter had been "separated" and the majority were well behind the average necessary to graduate. But several turned out to be "late bloomers"; one earned a Ph.D., a second a Phi Beta Kappa key elsewhere, and four more got bachelors' degrees. One is an M.D., and four have law degrees. Median earnings of this group are $16,875. I doubt whether such a small sample is typical, however; the high median income suggests that those who replied may be mainly those who have done well and are proud to show that they have succeeded without being handed a Dartmouth sheepskin.

PLAY THE AVERAGES

The practical-minded reader will want an interpretation. Just what do all these data mean to the personnel man? Should he, for example, look harder for the "late bloomers"? In many ways selecting men for employment is like betting on a horse race; if you bet on the favorite you will win most of the time, and if you bet on a long shot you will only occasionally collect.

In a horse race, the favorite has such small odds that you won't win much, but if the long shot comes in you will win a large sum. But in the employment situation each winner pays approximately the same profit, and the costs of betting—that is, of recruiting and training—are the same for the favorite as the long shot. So if we can predict that one man has, let us say, seven chances out of ten of becoming a top supervisor, we will be right more than twice as often as we will be wrong. But if he has only two or three chances out of ten of rising above mediocrity, we are making a risky gamble—and without the possible large reward that the long shot in the horse race pays.

I would suggest, then, that one look for the man in the top quarter of his class—the top quarter in almost anything: scholarship, campus politics, sports, or any other extracurricular activity. Actually, *it does not seem to make much difference in what field, or fields, he made his mark.* Together or singly, in sum, grades and extracurricular activity furnish an excellent predictor of later success.

Let me acknowledge that my data cover just one class in a single liberal-arts college in New England. Whether the conclusions would apply to a state university, an engineering school, or a midwestern or Pacific Coast college, I cannot say. But this type of investigation could bear duplicating in other colleges. Large corporations might also see how graduates with various degrees and types of college records have progressed within the company.

HOW TO BE AN EMPLOYEE

Peter F. Drucker

Big company or small? Routine work or something chancier? Start at the bottom or try the trapeze? Quit—or be fired? In this suggested commencement address a well-known business writer and consultant delivers some truths that Every Young College Graduate Should Know—and, according to *Fortune*, won't be taught at school. Dr. Drucker holds the title of Professor of Management at New York University's Graduate School of Business Administration. One of his best known works is *The Practice of Management*.

Most of you graduating today will be employees all your working life, working for somebody else and for a pay check. And so will most, if not all, of the thousands of other young Americans graduating this year in all the other schools and colleges across the country.

Ours has become a society of employees. A hundred years or so ago only one out of every five Americans at work was employed, i.e., worked for somebody else. Today only one out of five is not employed but working for himself. And where fifty years ago "being employed" meant working as a factory laborer or as a farmhand, the employee of today is increasingly a middle-class person with a substantial formal education, holding a professional or management job requiring intellectual and technical skills. Indeed, two things have characterized American society during these last fifty years: the middle and upper classes have become employees; and middle-class and upper-class employees have been the fastest-growing groups in our working population—growing so fast that the industrial worker, that oldest child of the Industrial Revolution, has been losing in numerical importance despite the expansion of industrial production.

This is one of the most profound social changes any country has ever undergone. It is, however, a perhaps even greater change for the individual young man about to start. Whatever he does, in all likelihood he will do it as an employee; wherever he aims, he will have to try to reach it through being an employee.

Yet you will find little if anything written on what it is to be an employee. You can find a great deal of very dubious advice on how to get a job or how to get a promotion. You can also find a good deal on work in a chosen field, whether it be metallurgy or salesmanship, the machinist's trade or bookkeeping. Every one of these trades requires different skills, sets dif-

Reprinted by Special Permission from the May, 1952, issue of Fortune Magazine; © by Time Inc.

ferent standards, and requires a different preparation. Yet they all have employeeship in common. And increasingly, especially in the large business or in government, employeeship is more important to success than the special professional knowledge or skill. Certainly more people fail because they do not know the requirements of being an employee than because they do not adequately possess the skills of their trade; the higher you climb the ladder, the more you get into administrative or executive work, the greater the emphasis on ability to work within the organization rather than on technical competence or professional knowledge.

Being an employee is thus the one common characteristic of most careers today. The special profession or skill is visible and clearly defined; and a well-laid-out sequence of courses, degrees, and jobs leads into it. But being an employee is the foundation. And it is much more difficult to prepare for it. Yet there is no recorded information on the art of being an employee.

THE BASIC SKILL

The first question we might ask is: what can you learn in college that will help you in being an employee? The schools teach a great many things of value to the future accountant, the future doctor, or the future electrician. Do they also teach anything of value to the future employee? The answer is: "Yes—they teach the one thing that it is perhaps most valuable for the future employee to know. But very few students bother to learn it."

This one basic skill is the ability to organize and express ideas in writing and in speaking.

As an employee you work with and through other people. This means that your success as an employee—and I am talking of much more here than getting promoted—will depend on your ability to communicate with people and to present your own thoughts and ideas to them so they will both understand what you are driving at and be persuaded. The letter, the report or memorandum, the ten-minute spoken "presentation" to a committee are basic tools of the employee.

If you work as a soda jerker you will, of course, not need much skill in expressing yourself to be effective. If you work on a machine your ability to express yourself will be of little importance. But as soon as you move one step up from the bottom, your effectiveness depends on your ability to reach others through the spoken or the written word. And the further away your job is from manual work, the larger the organization of which you are an employee, the more important it will be that you know how to convey your thoughts in writing or speaking. In the very large organization, whether it is the government, the large business corporation, or the Army, this ability to express oneself is perhaps the most important of all the skills a man can possess.

Of course, skill in expression is not enough by itself. You must have something to say in the first place. The popular picture of the engineer, for instance, is that of a man who works with a slide rule, T square, and compass. And engineering students reflect this picture in their attitude toward the written word as something quite irrelevant to their jobs. But the effectiveness of the engineer—and with it his usefulness—depends as much on his ability to make other people understand his work as it does on the quality of the work itself.

Expressing one's thoughts is one skill that the school can really teach, especially to people born without natural writing or speaking talent. Many other skills can be learned later—in this country there are literally thousands of places that offer training to adult people at work. But the foundations for skill in expression have to be laid early: an interest in and an ear for language; experience in organizing ideas and data, in brushing aside the irrelevant, in wedding outward form and inner content into one structure; and above all, the habit of verbal expression. If you do not lay these foundations during your school years, you may never have an opportunity again.

If you were to ask me what strictly vocational courses there are in the typical college curriculum, my answer—now that the good old habit of the "theme a day" has virtually disappeared —would be: the writing of poetry and the writing of short stories. Not that I expect many of you to become poets or short-story writers—far from it. But these two courses offer the easiest way to obtain some skill in expression. They force one to be economical with language. They force one to organize thought. They demand of one that he give meaning to every word. They train the ear for language, its meaning, its precision, its overtones—and its pitfalls. Above all they force one to write.

I know very well that the typical employer does not understand this as yet, and that he may look with suspicion on a young college graduate who has majored, let us say, in short-story writing. But the same employer will complain —and with good reason—that the young men whom he hires when they get out of college do not know how to write a simple report, do not know how to tell a simple story, and are in fact virtually illiterate. And he will conclude—rightly—that the young men are not really effective, and certainly not employees who are likely to go very far.

The next question to ask is: what kind of employee should you be? Pay no attention to what other people tell you. This is one question only you can answer. It involves a choice in four areas—a choice you alone can make, and one you cannot easily duck. But to make the choice you must first have tested yourself in the world of jobs for some time.

Here are the four decisions—first in brief outline, then in more detail:

1) Do you belong in a job calling primarily for faithfulness in the performance of routine work and promising security? Or do you belong in a job that offers a challenge to imagination and ingenuity—with the attendant penalty for failure?

2) Do you belong in a large organization or in a small organization? Do you work better through channels or through direct contacts? Do you enjoy more being a small cog in a big and powerful machine or a big wheel in a small machine?

3) Should you start at the bottom and try to work your way up, or should you try to start near the top? On the lowest rung of the promotional ladder, with its solid and safe footing but also with a very long climb ahead? Or on the aerial trapeze of "a management trainee," or some other staff position close to management?

4) Finally, are you going to be more effective and happy as a specialist or as a "generalist," that is, in an administrative job?

Let me spell out what each of these four decisions involves:

1. IS "SECURITY" FOR YOU?

The decision between secure routine work and insecure work challenging the imagination and ingenuity is the one decision most people find easiest to make. You know very soon what kind of person you are. Do you find real satisfaction in the precision, order, and system of a clearly laid-out job? Do you prefer the security not only of knowing what your work is today and what it is going to be tomorrow, but also security in your job, in your relationship to the people above, below, and next to you, and economic security? Or are you one of those people who tend to grow impatient with anything that looks like a "routine" job? These people are usually able to live in a confused situation in which their relations to the people around them are neither clear nor stable. And they tend to pay less attention to economic security, find it not too upsetting to change jobs, etc.

There is, of course, no such black-and-white distinction between people. The man who can do only painstaking detail work and has no imagination is not much good for anything. Neither is the self-styled "genius" who has nothing but grandiose ideas and no capacity for rigorous application to detail. But in practically everybody I have ever met there is a decided leaning one way or the other.

The difference is one of basic personality. It is not too much affected by a man's experiences; he is likely to be born with the one or the other. The need for economic security is often as not an outgrowth of a need for psychological security rather than a phenomenon of its own. But precisely because the difference is one of basic temperament, the analysis of what kind of temperament you possess is so vital. A man might be happy in work for which he has little *aptitude*; he might be quite successful in it. But he can be neither happy nor successful in a job for which he is *temperamentally* unfitted.

You hear a great many complaints today about the excessive security-consciousness of our young people. My complaint is the opposite: in the large organizations especially there are not enough job opportunities for those young people who need challenge and risk. Jobs in which there is greater emphasis on conscientious performance of well-organized duties rather than on imagination—especially for the beginner—are to be found, for instance, in the inside jobs in banking or insurance, which normally offer great job security but not rapid promotion or large pay. The same is true of most government work, of the railroad industry, particularly in the clerical and engineering branches, and of most public utilities. The bookkeeping and accounting areas, especially in the larger companies, are generally of this type too—though a successful comptroller is an accountant with great management and business imagination.

At the other extreme are such areas as buying, selling, and advertising, in which the emphasis is on adaptability, on imagination, and on a desire to do new and different things. In those areas, by and large, there is little security, either personal or economic. The rewards, however, are high and come more rapidly. Major premium on imagination—though of a different kind and coupled with dogged persistence on details—prevails in most research and engineering work. Jobs in production, as supervisor or executive, also demand much adaptability and imagination.

Contrary to popular belief, very small business requires, above all, close attention to daily routine. Running a neighborhood drugstore or a small grocery, or being a toy jobber, is largely attention to details. But in very small business there is also room for quite a few people of the other personality type—the innovator or imaginer. If successful, a man of this type soon ceases to be in a very small business. For the real innovator there is, still, no more promising opportunity in this country than that of building a large out of a very small business.

2. BIG COMPANY OR SMALL?

Almost as important is the decision between working for a large and for a small organization. The difference is perhaps not so great as that between the secure, routine job and the insecure, imaginative job; but the wrong decision can be equally serious.

There are two basic differences between the large and the small enterprise. In the small enterprise you operate primarily through personal contacts. In the large enterprise you have established "policies," "channels" of organization, and fairly rigid procedures. In the small enterprise you have, moreover, immediate effectiveness in a very small area. You can see the effect of your work and of your decisions right away, once you are a little bit above the ground floor. In the large enterprise even the man at the top is only a cog in a big machine. To be sure, his actions affect a much greater area than the actions and decisions of the man in the small organization, but his effectiveness is remote, indirect, and elusive. In a small and even in a middle-sized business you are normally exposed to all kinds of experiences, and expected to do a great many things without too much help or guidance. In the large organization you are normally taught one thing thoroughly. In the small one the danger is of becoming a jack-of-all-trades and master of none. In the large one it is of becoming the man who knows more and more about less and less.

There is one other important thing to consider: do you derive a deep sense of satisfaction from being a member of a well-known organization—General Motors, the Bell Telephone System,

the government? Or is it more important to you to be a well-known and important figure within your own small pond? There is a basic difference between the satisfaction that comes from being a member of a large, powerful, and generally known organization, and the one that comes from being a member of a family; between impersonal grandeur and personal—often much too personal—intimacy; between life in a small cubicle on the top floor of a skyscraper and life in a crossroads gas station.

3. START AT THE BOTTOM, OR . . . ?

You may well think it absurd to say that anyone has a choice between beginning at the bottom and beginning near the top. And indeed I do not mean that you have any choice between beginner's jobs and, let us say, a vice presidency at General Electric. But you do have a choice between a position at the bottom of the hierarchy and a staff position that is outside the hierarchy but in view of the top. It is an important choice.

In every organization, even the smallest, there are positions that, while subordinate, modestly paid, and usually filled with young and beginning employees, nonetheless are not at the bottom. There are positions as assistant to one of the bosses; there are positions as private secretary; there are liaison positions for various departments; and there are positions in staff capacities, in industrial engineering, in cost accounting, in personnel, etc. Every one of these gives a view of the whole rather than of only one small area. Every one of them normally brings the holder into the deliberations and discussions of the people at the top, if only as a silent audience or perhaps only as an errand boy. Every one of these positions is a position "near the top," however humble and badly paid it may be.

On the other hand the great majority of beginner's jobs are at the bottom, where you begin in a department or in a line of work in the lowest-paid and simplest function, and where you are expected to work your way up as you acquire more skill and more judgment.

Different people belong in these two kinds of jobs. In the first place, the job "near the top" is insecure. You are exposed to public view. Your position is ambiguous; by yourself you are a nobody—but you reflect the boss's status; in a relatively short time you may even speak for the boss. You may have real power and influence. In today's business and government organization the hand that writes the memo rules the committee; and the young staff man usually writes the memos, or at least the first draft. But for that very reason everybody is jealous of you. You are a youngster who has been admitted to the company of his betters, and is therefore expected to show unusual ability and above all unusual discretion and judgment. Good performance in such a position is often the key to rapid advancement. But to fall down may mean the end of all hopes of ever getting anywhere within the organization.

At the bottom, on the other hand, there are very few opportunities for making serious mistakes. You are amply protected by the whole apparatus of authority. The job itself is normally simple, requiring little judgment, discretion, or initiative. Even excellent performance in such a job is unlikely to speed promotion. But one also has to fall down in a rather spectacular fashion for it to be noticed by anyone but one's immediate superior.

4. SPECIALIST OR "GENERALIST"?

There are a great many careers in which the increasing emphasis is on specialization. You find these careers in engineering and in accounting, in production, in statistical work, and in teaching. But there is an increasing demand for people who are able to take in a great area at a glance, people who perhaps do not know too much about any one field—though one should always have one area of real competence. There is, in other words, a demand for people who are capable of seeing the forest rather than the trees, of making over-all judgments. And these "generalists" are particularly needed for administrative positions, where it is their job to see that other people do the work, where they have to plan for other people, to organize other people's work, to initiate it and appraise it.

The specialist understands one field; his concern is with technique, tools, media. He is a "trained" man; and his educational background is properly technical or professional. The generalist —and especially the administrator— deals with people; his concern is with leadership, with planning, with direction giving, and with coordination. He is an "educated" man; and the humanities are his strongest foundation. Very rarely is a specialist capable of being an administrator. And very rarely is a good generalist also a good specialist in a particular field. Any organization needs both kinds of people, though different organizations need them in different ratios. It is your job to find out, during your apprenticeship, into which of those two job categories you fit, and to plan your career accordingly.

Your first job may turn out to be the right job for you—but this is pure accident. Certainly you should not change jobs constantly or people will become suspicious—rightly—of your ability to hold any job. At the same time you must not look upon the first job as the final job; it is primarily a training job, an opportunity to analyze yourself and your fitness for being an employee.

THE IMPORTANCE OF BEING FIRED

In fact there is a great deal to be said for being fired from the first job. One reason is that it is rarely an advantage to have started as an office boy in the organization; far too many people will still consider you a "green kid" after you have been there for twenty-five years. But the major reason is that getting fired from the first job is the least painful and the least damaging way to learn how to take a setback. And whom the Lord loveth he teacheth early how to take a setback.

Nobody has ever lived, I daresay, who has not gone through a period when everything seemed to have collapsed and when years of work and life seemed to have gone up in smoke. No one can be spared this experience; but one can be prepared for it. The man who has been through earlier setbacks has learned that the world has not come to an end because he lost his job —not even in a depression. He has learned that he will somehow survive. He has learned, above all, that the way to behave in such a setback is not to collapse himself. But the man who comes up against it for the first time when he is forty-five is quite likely to collapse for good. For the things that people are apt to do when they receive the first nasty blow may destroy a mature man with a family, whereas a youth of twenty-five bounces right back.

Obviously you cannot contrive to get yourself fired. But you can always quit. And it is perhaps even more important to have quit once than to have been fired once. The man who walks out on his own volition acquires an inner independence that he will never quite lose.

WHEN TO QUIT

To know when to quit is therefore one of the most important things— particularly for the beginner. For on the whole young people have a tendency to hang on to the first job long beyond the time when they should have quit for their own good.

One should quit when self-analysis shows that the job is the wrong job— that, say, it does not give the security and routine one requires, that it is a small-company rather than a big-organization job, that it is at the bottom rather than near the top, a specialist's rather than a generalist's job, etc. One should quit if the job demands behavior one considers morally indefensible, or if the whole atmosphere of the place is morally corrupting—if, for instance, only yes men and flatterers are tolerated.

One should also quit if the job does not offer the training one needs either in a specialty or in administration and the view of the whole. The beginner not only has a right to expect training from his first five or ten years in a job; he has an obligation to get as much training as possible. A job in which young people are not given real training—though, of course, the training need not be a formal "training program"—does not measure up to what they have a right and a duty to expect.

But the most common reason why one should quit is the absence of promotional opportunities in the organization. That is a compelling reason.

I do not believe that chance of promotion is the essence of a job. In fact there is no surer way to kill a job and one's own usefulness in it than to consider it as but one rung in the promotional ladder rather than as a job in itself that deserves serious effort and will return satisfaction, a sense of accomplishment, and pride. And one can be an important and respected member of an organization without ever having received a promotion; there are such people in practically every office. But the organization itself must offer fair promotional opportunities. Otherwise it stagnates, becomes corrupted, and in turn corrupts. The absence of promotional opportunities is demoralizing. And the sooner one gets out of a demoralizing situation, the better. There are three situations to watch out for:

The entire group may be so young that for years there will be no vacancies. That was a fairly common situation in business a few years back, as a result of the depression. Middle and lower management ranks in many companies were solidly filled with men in their forties and early fifties—men who were far too young to be retired but who had grown too old, during the bleak days of the Thirties, to be promotable themselves. As a result the people under them were bottled up; for it is a rare organization that will promote a young man around his older superior. If you find yourself caught in such a situation, get out fast. If you wait it will defeat you.

Another situation without promotional opportunities is one in which the group ahead of you is uniformly old—so old that it will have to be replaced long before you will be considered ready to move up. Stay away from organizations that have a uniform age structure throughout their executive group—old or young. The only organization that offers fair promotional opportunities is one in which there is a balance of ages.

WHO GETS PROMOTED?

And finally there is the situation in which all promotions go to members of a particular group—to which you do not belong. Some chemical companies, for instance, require a master's degree in chemistry for just about any job above sweeper. Some companies promote only engineering graduates, some government agencies only people who majored in economics, some railroads only male stenographers, some British insurance companies only members of the actuaries' association. Or all the good jobs may be reserved for members of the family. There may be adequate promotional opportunities in such an organization—but not for you.

On the whole there are proportionately more opportunities in the big organization than in the small one. But there is very real danger of getting lost in the big organization—whereas you are always visible in the small one. A young man should therefore stay in a large organization only if it has a definite promotional program which ensures that he will be considered and looked at. This may take several forms: it may be a formal appraisal and development program: it may be automatic promotion by seniority as in the prewar Army; it may be an organization structure that actually makes out of the one big enterprise a number of small organizations in which everybody is again clearly visible (the technical term for this is "decentralization").

But techniques do not concern us here. What matters is that there should be both adequate opportunities and fair assurance that you will be eligible and considered for promotion. Let me repeat: to be promoted is not essential, either to happiness or to usefulness. To be considered for promotion is.

YOUR LIFE OFF THE JOB

I have only one more thing to say: to be an employee it is not enough that the job be right and that you be right for the job. It is also necessary that you have a meaningful life outside the job.

I am talking of having a genuine interest in something in which you, on your own, can be, if not a master, at least an amateur expert. This something may be botany, or the history of your county, or chamber music, cabinetmaking, Christmas-tree growing, or a thousand other things. But it is important in this "employee society" of ours to have a genuine interest outside of the job and to be serious about it.

I am not, as you might suspect, thinking of something that will keep you alive and interested during your retirement. I am speaking of keeping yourself alive, interested, and happy during your working life, and of a permanent source of self-respect and standing in the community outside and beyond your job. You will need such an interest when you hit the forties, that period in which most of us come to realize that we will never reach the goals we have set ourselves when younger—whether these are goals of achievement or of worldly success. You will need it because you should have one area in which you yourself impose standards of performance on your own work. Finally, you need it because you will find recognition and acceptance by other people working in the field, whether professional or amateur, as individuals rather than as members of an organization and as employees.

This is heretical philosophy these days when so many companies believe that the best employee is the man who lives, drinks, eats, and sleeps job and company. In actual experience those people who have no life outside their jobs are not the really successful people, not even from the viewpoint of the company. I have seen far too many of them shoot up like a rocket, because they had no interests except the job; but they also come down like the rocket's burned-out stick. The man who will make the greatest contribution to his company is the mature person—and you cannot have maturity if you have no life or interest outside the job. Our large companies are beginning to understand this. That so many of them encourage people to have "outside interests" or to develop "hobbies" as a preparation for retirement is the first sign of a change toward a more intelligent attitude. But quite apart from the self-interest of the employer, your own interest as an employee demands that you develop a major outside interest. It will make you happier, it will make you more effective, it will give you resistance against the setbacks and the blows that are the lot of everyone; and it will make you a more effective, a more successful, and a more mature employee.

You have no doubt realized that I have not really talked about how to be an employee. I have talked about what to know before becoming an employee —which is something quite different. Perhaps "how to be an employee" can be learned only by being one. But one thing can be said. Being an employee means working with people; it means living and working in a society. Intelligence, in the last analysis, is therefore not the most important quality. What is decisive is character and integrity. If you work on your own, intelligence and ability may be sufficient. If you work with people you are going to fail unless you also have basic integrity. And integrity—character—is the one thing most, if not all, employers consider first.

There are many skills you might learn to be an employee, many abilities that are required. But fundamentally the one quality demanded of you will not be skill, knowledge, or talent, but character.

THE CULTURE OF THE BUSINESSMAN

Crawford H. Greenewalt

"The time has long since come to end the graceless war which has raged for more than 100 years between the businessman and the scholar: hoary and insulting expletives like 'Babbitt,' 'Podsnap,' 'egghead,' and 'bohemian' have long outlived their proper targets." Supporting this thesis of the editors of *The Saturday Review*, the president of E. I. du Pont de Nemours and Company argues that there is no incompatibility between commerce and culture and suggests that businessmen follow the commands of their intellectual tastes and capacities throughout their lives.

In the relationship of education to business we observe today a fine state of paradox. On the one hand, the emphasis which most business places upon a college degree is so great that one can almost visualize the time when even the office boy will have his baccalaureate. On the other hand, we seem to preserve the belief that some deep intellectual chasm separates the businessman from other products of the university system.

Not long ago a young English professor was speaking of a collection of letters written by a Boston businessman back in the 1840's. He expressed amazement that this gentleman and some of his commercial confreres were members of a club which had numbered among its principal ornaments Mr. Ralph Waldo Emerson.

"Imagine Emerson hobnobbing with some of our modern business people!" he remarked morosely.

Well, I don't know. I have a feeling that Mr. Emerson might do worse, and

I get a little weary of the notion that business people are quite the Philistines that many seem to think. For some reason, we tend in this country to characterize vocations by stereotypes, none too flattering but nonetheless deeply imbedded in the national conscience. In this cast of characters the businessman comes on stage as a crass and uncouth person complete with top hat, paunch, and large watch chain, scoffing at all cultural pretensions and unmindful of all save gain. It is not a pleasant conception and no more truthful or less unpleasant than our other stereotypes—the absentminded professor in his ivory tower, the drunken reporter, the longhaired musician, the toolless plumber, or the interfering mother-in-law, to name a few.

I've known a great many business people. My own impression is that it would be impossible to crystallize a "typical" example out of the lot and, what's more, a completely pointless exercise. I know businessmen who are

From *The Saturday Review*, January 19, 1957. Reprinted by permission.

bores, some who lack the social graces, some who are dull companions, and some whose intellectual interest is limited to the business that engages them. On the other hand, I know some who are learned men of vast and unremitting scholarship, some with the sensitivity of poets, and some with the patient calm of saints. I know a number whose knowledge and feeling for music is as sophisticated as any. I know one who is an authority on Browning, another who is a Greek scholar, and another who has as profound an appreciation of the pre-Raphaelites as Ruskin's.

It sometimes seems to shock academic peoples to learn that there are business people who are reasonably literate. Here I imply no special offense, for business people are sometimes just as amazed to find a professor who is not a starry-eyed dreamer.

But of the two, I think the academic view is a bit more condescending. Some years ago I met a historian who was stunned to find that I had read Gibbon. He had, clearly, been taken in by the folklore and had generalized freely from the stock caricature of the business type. The truth is, of course, that business is made up of people with all kinds of backgrounds, all kinds of motivations, and all kinds of tastes, just as in any other form of human endeavor. Businessmen, in short, are not ambulatory balance sheets and profit statements, but perfectly normal human beings, subject to whatever strengths, frailties, and limitations characterize man on this earth. They represent a cross-section of society —the brilliant and the dull, the generous and the grasping, the expansive and the petty, the sensitive and the crass, the good and the bad. They are ordinary people grouped together in organizations designed to complement the weakness of one with the strength of another, tempering the exuberance of the young with the caution of the more mature, the poetic soarings of one mind with the counting-house realism of another.

I find it hard to believe that business would draw all its people from the culturally disenfranchised. I am inclined to think that the group of people comprising business management has pretty much the same proportion of good, bad, and indifferent mental qualities as any other. Men elect to enter the field of business just as they may choose some other vocation—the law or journalism or the clergy or teaching—sometimes through a leaning or predilection, more often through pure chance.

There is, in fact, considerable mobility between vocations. I, for one, started out as a scientist and wound up, for various reasons—not wholly voluntary—working at a desk instead of a laboratory bench. Several promising engineers and administrators have left us for the ministry or for teaching. We have a few who have reversed the procedure.

So, if we can concede that people in the main have decent, honorable, and reasonable standards of taste and behavior, I think we can say that those in the business world average out at about the same level as any other. Any disfigurement which society may suffer will come from man himself, not from the particular vocation to which he devotes his time.

Any group of people necessarily represents an approach to a common denominator, and it is probably true that even individually they tend to conform somewhat to the general pattern. Many have pointed out—I among them—the danger of engulfing our original thinkers in a tide of mediocrity. It is a very real danger. But I cannot see that conformity is any more prevalent or any more exacting in the business field than it is in any other.

Conformity is not a special characteristic of business; it is a characteristic of all organizations of whatever nature. I am inclined to think that, man for man, the large business unit provides greater opportunities for individuality and requires less in the way of conformity than other institutions of comparable size—the government service, say, or the academic world, or certainly the military.

I realize that it is popular to regard the large business unit as a machine in which human tolerances are held within precise limits and some All-Seeing Eye charts the manners, dress, and political views of each candidate for advancement. One of the magazines devoted to business has the curious conviction that the wives of business executives are screened critically as part of the criteria for promotion.

All this of course is pure fiction at least according to our experience. The Gray Flannel Suit is a pretty superficial symbol after all (I don't own one), and among my most valued associates taste in dress covers a pretty broad pattern. The same goes for personal habits and enthusiasms. As for wives, I can report that among my close co-workers there are a number whose ladies I have never seen.

It is not conformity in the outward signs which represents the danger; it is conformity in thought and in thinking. And on this level I suspect that business is less constrained than other ways of life. To cite an extreme, consider the monolithic unanimity of conviction demanded by the Communist Party. Members may, presumably, dress as they please, grow whiskers, or cultivate strange personal habits, but their views on everything are rigidly prescribed.

Assuming that education's objective is to cultivate the soil of human thought, its place in business is the same as its place in any other field of human endeavor. The man of talent who turns to business for a career will find just as much in the way of creative opportunity as he would in any other field.

The stake of business in education is as obvious as it is large, but it is a general, not a specialized, stake. We hear much these days about the shortage of technically trained people. Since business organizations employ a large percentage of those trained in the scientific disciplines, an area of conflict appears to develop in the feeling that the aims of the liberal arts and the social sciences are incompatible with those of the physical sciences. The educators themselves join the fracas, some holding that the engineers and scientists are impatient with the humanities, others contending that the student of the liberal arts might well concern himself with the realities of the physical world.

Well, there is something to be said on both sides. Yet it is, of course, ridiculous to assume that there should be any real incompatibility between technology or industrial development and the scholarly pursuit of learning. Much of the support for the establishment of colleges and universities of all inclinations has come, in one way or another, out of our industrial growth. Much of the cultural development, particularly that which has brought a high level of cultural opportunity to the people as a whole, resulted from institutions set up and endowed by businessmen who wished to share the rewards of their enterprise with the general public. Art galleries, libraries, historic restorations, public parks and gardens, museums, and many other such institutions offer testimony today to the public-spirited benefactions of men who were successful in the business and industrial field. In fact, I would say that American businessmen have been patrons of the arts and humanities to an even greater extent than they have been patrons of the sciences.

As many have pointed out, business must share part of the responsibility for keeping our colleges on a strong financial basis. Much is being done in this direction, and more will be done ultimately. But I confess to some irritation with the nomenclature which associates "education" so intimately and so exclusively with the university. This view seems to accept a rather shocking series of premises: First, that a university graduate is necessarily educated; second, that all non-graduates are necessarily uneducated; and third, that the educational process ends with the diploma.

Each of these assumptions, of course, is nonsense. The proper concept of a university, as many have described it, is simply that of a catalogue which sets forth the areas of human thought and indicates the avenues through which each may be explored. After that it is up to the individual. He may go as far along the road as his personal taste and capacities dictate.

How many of us can look back upon the day we became college graduates and say that, on that day, we were educated people? I am sure I cannot, and I know few who can. An education is not a single entity, developed in a few semesters of study and delivered with our diploma—it is a never-ending process built up over years of exposure and experience. How well we are educated, it seems to me, is simply a matter of how well we have adjusted ourselves to our lives and our environment, whether we have enlarged our

horizons or have been content to vegetate within a narrow valley.

Most, if not all, of the interests which broaden and enrich our lives and our careers are developed long after we have left college. One of my own interests, as I have noted, is Roman history, yet at graduation I could have identified neither Tacitus nor Diocletian. My fancy for serious music was not developed in college; in those days, I listened respectfully to "Whispering" and "Avalon," like everybody else. I've been running a hard race for many years against the list of books and authors I hope eventually to know; I caught up with Thackeray only last year.

There are, of course, young men who enter the business world and become so engrossed in immediate affairs that they ignore all else. They live in a narrow cell of their own making; the world looks at them and deplores their lack of culture. But this process is by no means exclusive to business; we see it at work in every other element of life. We see professors of history with few interests outside the period and the area of their own parochial specialty. We see artists indifferent to everything but their canvases; physicians who are lost outside medicine; lawyers unlearned in all save law.

Too often, I fear, we criticize the one-dimensional businessman while somehow finding excuses or even applause for the one-dimensional professor or artist or scientist. Yet I find it hard to differentiate. The narrow cell has the same walls and the same limitations whether it is an office, a laboratory, a studio, or a classroom.

Is there anything about the business process itself to make a difference? I cannot agree that there is. I cannot see that there is anything to make commercial institutions less worthy or less desirable or less ennobling of their participants than other institutions or other professions. If we were called upon to recreate a primitive society on a desert island, with each of us contributing his special skill to the community enterprise, there would be no reason to regard the man who made shoes in a less useful or less flattering light than the man who made poetry or sermons, or even laws. The fact that we today identify shoes as a commercial venture and others as cultural or spiritual or professional does not change the basic nature of any.

No, education is not the province of any one group or any one type of activity. One does not automatically become cultured in one trade and uncultured in another. All of us have our own specialties—otherwise we become mere dilettantes. Every tree must have its trunk, but it can put out branches in profusion, and the branches will spread and intertwine with one another to produce the whole speci-

men. And the purpose of education must be to encourage that growth.

Despite our mass attendance at college and our mass exposure to culture, education remains an individual achievement. I am afraid the emphasis, in education as elsewhere, has been in recent years on the group, with the tendency to obscure the star in the constellation, the soloist in the ensemble. Yet it will always be true, I am sure, that the individual will provide the basis for progress. Self-direction is difficult; it is frustrating and often downright unfashionable. Men of uncommon endowment will always represent a minority group within the ranks of society, subject to all the sanctions and discriminations which minorities have always suffered. But it is the uncommon man who will achieve the goal of a true education. For, short of a personal and highly individualistic effort, there is no other way to acquire an education at all.

HOW TO LAND YOUR JOB

National Association of Manufacturers

All the young businessman's resources—and resourcefulness—find expression when he applies for his first job. Where shall he go? What shall he say? This brief article is the distillation of the experience of both applicants and employers.

So you want a job! Your formal education is about to be completed. Perhaps you have been impatient to get out of the classroom and find out what the work-a-day world is really like. You want that comfortable feeling of independence that comes from having your own money in your pocket and not depending on Dad any longer.

Good! But don't rush out to get the first job you hear about. Stop and think a minute—or you may find your high hopes quickly dashed. If you wanted to win a football game, you would need to plan your strategy in advance. You'd carefully work out several plays you thought would work, then you'd try them out in practice. The same thing is true in applying for a job. You'll have some preliminary planning to do.

Before you begin, you must rearrange your thinking. Up to now you have thought of your qualifications and training largely in terms of what they would mean to you. Now you must think about selling yourself. You must think in terms of your value to your prospective employer. He doesn't owe you a job. It's up to you to prove that

he needs you just as much as you need the work.

Your job campaign will include three main parts:
1. The Application
2. The Interview
3. The Follow-Up

Each is important to make your efforts count for the most. And it is here that the planning you have done, up to now, begins to pay off.

THE APPLICATION

Do you know how to fill out an application blank so that it will present what you have to offer in the best possible light? Ask for copies from several firms and practice filling them out. Read the directions carefully and follow them exactly. Answer all questions honestly and completely. Be neat and accurate.

Include any brief or part-time jobs you have held. They show that you have already had some work experience.

You will need the names of at least three people as references. See your principal or teacher and others, such as your pastor or club leader, who know

From *Your Future Is What You Make It*. Reprinted by courtesy of the National Association of Manufacturers.

your character and abilities. Your employer will wish to check their opinions against his own judgment. Tell each one how you wish to use his name, obtain his permission to mention him and find out where he wants such inquiries addressed.

It will be well to know in advance why you wish to work for a particular company. You may be asked this either on your application blank or in your interview. Talk with someone else who does work for the company or read about it in the newspapers or trade journals so that you won't be "talking in the dark." Most companies are especially proud that their employees consider their plant a "good place to work."

In general, it is probably better to apply for work in person. But some employers require a letter of application. In other cases, it may be desirable to write one. If possible, find out the name of the man who does the employing and whether it is better to call on him or write to him. In every case, writing such a letter will be of help to you in organizing your own sales talk. In doing so, you will necessarily think over the job in terms of what you have to offer.

In putting down your training and abilities, word your letter to show what you can do for the employer. List courses, hobbies and extracurricular activities which will help you in the work. Summarize your scholastic and attendance record. If you were an honor student or member of an honor society, mention it. But don't expect to ride through on school honors alone. Cite any project you have carried out successfully, showing your initiative and willingness to take responsibility. If you have conducted your own small business, tell about it briefly.

Organize all this material in logical, readable order. Place first those things which you believe will be most important to your employers. Be specific about the kind of work you want to do. Type the letter, if possible. Conclude it with a statement that you would appreciate the opportunity to apply in person.

After mailing your letter, allow a reasonable time for an answer before calling to ask for an appointment. Ask the employer's secretary courteously for a definite time when you can discuss the matter further. Don't insist on this as a right. But assume that you have something to offer and that he will want to see you.

In the event that he may be out-of-town or otherwise unavailable, ask for a definite time when you may telephone again. Then follow this up with a letter of regret that he was not available. Express the hope that by the date you are to call him back his schedule will permit him to give you a few minutes of his time. If you make a date to call back, do so promptly. Be persistent but courteous.

THE INTERVIEW

Personal appearance is important when you have your interview with your prospective employer. You'll feel more at home if you are dressed neatly for the occasion. You'll make a better first impression, too. But don't overdress for the job you are seeking.

Take with you a filled-out copy of the application blank. Your first one could be misplaced. You might also take a letter of application to organize your selling talk.

When you enter the office, don't act like either a tornado or a timid mouse. Don't slouch or disturb others by entering noisily. You are there for business. You have something to sell— yourself—a product in which you believe, because you have done your best to prepare yourself.

State your business to the reception-ist briefly and to the point. When you are ushered into the office of the inter-viewer, let him set the tone of the interview. Be alert and friendly. Be prepared for personal questions, such as: "What is your father's occupation?" or "Do you have to work?" The inter-viewer is trying to get a better picture of you in his mind.

Most speakers, even the best of them, find that there is always an initial nervousness when they start to address an audience. It is the same with an interview. You'll feel more acquainted and at home after a few moments. But don't let this lead you into relaxing your courtesy. A word of caution to smokers: Don't smoke, un-less invited. And don't waste the inter-viewer's time by straying from the sub-ject.

The employer should be permitted to direct the conversation. But when he gives you the opportunity, you should be prepared to inform him why you believe that you are going to make him a valued employee. Honestly and sincerely, without bragging, you may be able to sell him indirectly on the idea that you're just the man or woman for whom he has been looking.

Here are two suggestions:

- Call attention to any of your special qualifications he may have overlooked.
- Ask about training courses offered by the company.

If you are just out of school, without previous experience, expect to start at the bottom. Most presidents of com-panies started there. You have to learn from the beginning sometime. You wouldn't take advanced algebra until you had passed the elementary course. At this stage, experience and training are more valuable to you than the size of your wages.

If the employer indicates that he cannot make a decision at that moment but may have something later, try courteously to find out how soon he expects this to be. If this particular company is your first choice, tell him so. But if there is another job open to you, ask his advice about committing yourself to other employment in the meantime.

In any case, you may want to ask his advice and counsel in your job hunting. He'll be glad to help you if he can.

THE FOLLOW-UP

If you are not hired on the first try, don't be discouraged. Try to leave the door open for further consideration later. Then follow up by interview, phone call or letter. *But don't depend on one cartridge in your job-hunting gun.* Investigate several jobs.

One thing always to remember is: *Keep your contacts alive.* In job hunt-ing you will make acquaintances and friends. Try not to lose them. By per-sonal word or letter, keep them re-minded of you.

Another point: Drop thank-you notes to the people you used as refer-ences. They took time and trouble in your behalf. It would be a good idea also to drop a note of thanks for the time he gave you to the employer who didn't hire you. He might again have a good spot for someone like you. You'll want him to remember you favorably when that time comes.

THE VICK SCHOOL OF APPLIED MERCHANDISING
William H. Whyte, Jr.

Here the legend of the intrepid salesman is entertainingly authenticated by a thoughtful business writer who is also assistant managing editor of *Fortune* Magazine. Mr. Whyte is genuinely concerned over the extent to which the carefully nurtured "organization man" has taken the place of the free-wheeling enterpriser.

It was a school—the Vick School of Applied Merchandising, they called it. The idea, as it was presented to job-hunting seniors at the time, was that those who were chosen were not going off to a job, but to a postgraduate training institution set up by a farsighted management. In September, some thirty graduates would gather from different colleges to start a year's study in modern merchandising. There would be a spell of classroom work in New York, a continuing course in advertising, and, most important, eleven months of field study under the supervision of veteran students of merchandising and distribution. Theoretically, we should be charged a tuition, for though we understood we would do some work in connection with our studies, the company explained that its expenses far outweighed what incidental services we would perform. This notwithstanding, it was going to give us a salary of $75 a month and all traveling expenses. It would also, for reasons I was later to learn were substantial, give us an extra $25 a month to be held in escrow until the end of the course.

Let me now point out the first distinction between the Vick program and the more current type. It was not executive training or even junior-executive training. Vick's did argue that the program would help produce the leaders of tomorrow, and prominent on the walls of the office was a framed picture of a captain at the wheel, with a statement by the president that the greatest duty of management was to bring along younger men. This notwithstanding, the question of whether or not any of us would one day be executives was considered a matter that could very easily be deferred. The training was directed almost entirely to the immediate job. The only exception was an International Correspondence Schools course in advertising, one of the main virtues of which, I always felt, was to keep us so occupied during the week ends that we wouldn't have time to think about our situation.

The formal schooling we got was of the briefest character. During our four

From *The Organization Man* by William H. Whyte, Jr., Copyright, © 1956 by William H. Whyte, Jr. Reprinted by permission of Simon and Schuster, Inc.

weeks in New York, we learned of Richardson's discovery of VapoRub, spent a day watching the VapoRub being mixed, and went through a battery of tests the company was fooling around with to find the Vick's type. Most of the time we spent in memorizing list prices, sales spiels, counters to objections, and the prices and techniques of Plough, Inc., whose Penetro line was one of Vick's most troublesome competitors. There was no talk about the social responsibilities of business or the broad view that I can remember, and I'm quite sure the phrase *human relations* never came up at all.

What management philosophy we did get was brief and to the point. Shortly before we were to set out from New York, the president, Mr. H. S. Richardson, took us up to the Cloud Club atop the Chrysler Building. The symbolism did not escape us. As we looked from this executive eyrie down on the skyscraper spires below, Golconda stretched out before us. One day, we gathered, some of us would be coming back up again—and not as temporary guests either. Some would not. The race would be to the swiftest.

Over coffee Mr. Richardson drove home to us the kind of philosophy that would get us back up. He posed a hypothetical problem. Suppose, he said, that you are a manufacturer and for years a small firm has been making paper cartons for your product. He has specialized so much to service you, as a matter of fact, that that's all he does make. He is utterly dependent on your business. For years the relationship has continued to be eminently satisfactory to both parties. But then one day another man walks in and says he will make the boxes for you cheaper. What do you do?

He bade each one of us in turn to answer.

But *how much* cheaper? we asked.

How much time could we give the old supplier to match the new bid? Mr. Richardson became impatient. There was only one decision. Either you were a businessman or you were not a businessman. The new man, obviously, should get the contract. Mr. Richardson, who had strong views on the necessity of holding to the old American virtues, advised us emphatically against letting sentimentality obscure fundamentals. Business was survival of the fittest, he indicated, and we would soon learn the fact.

He was as good as his word. The Vick curriculum was just that—survival of the fittest. In the newer type of programs, companies will indeed fire incompetents, but a man joins with the idea that the company intends to keep him, and this is the company's wish also. The Vick School, however, was frankly based on the principle of elimination. It wouldn't make any difference how wonderful all of us might turn out to be; of the thirty-eight who sat there in the Cloud Club, the rules of the game dictated that only six or seven of us would be asked to stay with Vick. The rest would graduate to make way for the next batch of students.

Another difference between Vick's approach and that now more characteristic became very evident as soon as we arrived in the field. While the work, as the company said, was educational, it was in no sense make-work. Within a few days of our session at the Cloud Club, we were dispatched to the hinterland—in my case, the hill country of eastern Kentucky. Each of us was given a panel delivery truck, a full supply of signs, a ladder, a stock of samples, and an order pad. After several days under the eye of a senior salesman, we were each assigned a string of counties and left to shift for ourselves.

The merchandising was nothing if not applied. To take a typical day of any one of us, we would rise at 6:00 or 6:30 in some bleak boarding house or run-down hotel and after a greasy breakfast set off to squeeze in some advertising practice before the first call. This consisted of bostitching a quota of large fiber signs on barns and clamping smaller metal ones to telephone poles and trees by hog rings. By eight, we would have arrived at a general store for our exercise in merchandising. Our assignment was to persuade the dealer to take a year's supply all at once, or, preferably, more than a year's supply, so that he would have no money or shelf space left for other brands. After the sale, or no-sale, we would turn to market research and note down the amount sold him by "chiseling" competitors (i.e., competitors; there was no acknowledgement on our report blanks of any other kind).

Next we did some sampling work: "Tilt your head back, Mr. Jones," we would suddenly say to the dealer. For a brief second he would obey and we would quickly shoot a whopping dropperful of Vatronol up his nose. His eyes smarting from the sting, the dealer would smile with simple pleasure. Turning to the loungers by the stove, he would tell them to let the drummer fella give them some of that stuff. After the messy job was done, we plastered the place with cardboard signs, and left. Then, some more signposting in barnyards, and ten or twelve miles of mud road to the next call. So, on through the day, the routine was repeated until at length, long after dark, we would get back to our lodgings in time for dinner—and two hours' work on our report forms.

The acquisition of a proper frame of mind toward all this was a slow process. The faded yellow second sheets of our daily report book tell the story. At first, utter demoralization. Day after day, the

number of calls would be a skimpy eight or nine, and the number of sales sometimes zero. But it was never our fault. In the large space left for explanations, we would affect a cheerful humor—the gay adventurer in the provinces—but this pathetic bravado could not mask a recurrent note of despair.*

To all these bids for sympathy, the home office was adamantine. The weekly letter written to each trainee would start with some perfunctory remarks that it was too bad about the clutch breaking down, the cut knee, and so on. But this spurious sympathy did not conceal a strong preoccupation with results, and lest we miss the point we were told of comrades who would no longer be with us. We too are sorry about those absent dealers, the office would say. Perhaps if you got up earlier in the morning?

As the office sensed quite correctly from my daily reports, I was growing sorry for myself. I used to read timetables at night, and often in the evening I would somehow find myself by the C & O tracks when the George Washington swept by, its steamy windows a reminder of civilization left behind. I was also sorry for many of the storekeepers, most of whom existed on a precarious credit relationship with

* I quote some entries from my own daily report forms: "They use 'dry' creek beds for roads in this country. 'Dry!' Ha! Ha! . . . Sorry about making only four calls today, but I had to go over to Ervine to pick up a drop shipment of ¾ tins and my clutch broke down. . . . Everybody's on WPA in this county. Met only one dealer who sold more than a couple dozen VR a year. Ah, well, it's all in the game! . . . Bostitched my left thumb to a barn this morning and couldn't pick up my first call until after lunch. . . . The local brick plant here is shut down and nobody's buying anything. . . . Five, count 'em, five absent dealers in a row. . . . Sorry about the $20.85 but the clutch broke down again. . . ."

wholesalers, and as a consequence I sold them very little of anything.

The company sent its head training supervisor to see if anything could be salvaged. After several days with me, this old veteran of the road told me he knew what was the matter. It wasn't so much my routine, wretched as this was. It was my state of mind. "Fella," he told me, "you will never sell anybody anything until you learn one simple thing. The man on the other side of the counter is the *enemy*."

It was a gladiators' school we were in. Selling may be no less competitive now, but in the Vick program, strife was honored far more openly than today's climate would permit. Combat was the ideal—combat with the dealer, combat with the "chiseling competitors," and combat with each other. There was some talk about "the team," but it was highly abstract. Our success depended entirely on beating our fellow students, and while we got along when we met for occasional sales meetings the camaraderie was quite extracurricular.

Slowly, as our sales-to-calls ratios crept up, we gained in rapacity. Somewhere along the line, by accident or skill, each of us finally manipulated a person into doing what we wanted him to do. Innocence was lost, and by the end of six months, with the pack down to about twenty-three men, we were fairly ravening for the home stretch back to the Cloud Club. At this point, the company took us off general store and grocery work and turned us loose in the rich drugstore territory.

The advice of the old salesman now became invaluable. While he had a distaste for any kind of dealer, with druggists he was implacably combative. He was one of the most decent and kindly men I have ever met, but when he gave us pep talks about this enemy ahead of us, he spoke with great intensity. Some druggists were good enough fellows, he told us (i.e., successful ones who bought big deals), but the tough ones were a mean, servile crew; they would insult you, keep you waiting while they pretended to fill prescriptions, lie to you about their inventory, whine at anything less than a 300 per cent markup, and switch their customers to chiseling competitors.

The old salesman would bring us together in batches for several days of demonstration. It was a tremendous experience for us, for though he seemed outwardly a phlegmatic man, we knew him for the artist he was. Outside the store he was jumpy and sometimes perspired, but once inside, he was composed to the point of apparent boredom. He rarely smiled, almost never opened with a joke. His demeanor seemed to say, I am a busy man and you are damned lucky I have stopped by your miserable store. Sometimes, if the druggist was unusually insolent, he would blow cigar smoke at his face. "Can't sell it if you don't have it," he would say contemptuously, and then, rather pleased with himself, glance back at us, loitering in the wings, to see if we had marked that.

Only old pros like himself could get away with that, he told us in the postmortem sessions, but there were lots of little tricks we could pick up. As we gathered around him, like Fagin's brood, he would demonstrate how to watch for the victim's shoulders to relax before throwing the clincher; how to pick up the one-size jar of a competitive line that had an especially thick glass bottom and chuckle knowingly; how to feign suppressed worry that maybe the deal was too big for "the smaller druggist like yourself" to take; how to disarm the nervous druggist by fumbling and dropping a pencil.

No mercy, he would tell us; give the devils no mercy.

We couldn't either. As the acid test of our gall the company now challenged us to see how many drugstores we could desecrate with "flange" signs. By all the standards of the trade this sign-posting should have been an impossible task. Almost every "chiseling competitor" would give the druggist at least five dollars to let him put up a sign; we could not offer the druggist a nickel. Our signs, furthermore, were not the usual cardboard kind the druggist could throw away after we had left. They were of metal, they were hideous, and they were to be screwed to the druggists' cherished oak cabinets.

The trick was in the timing. When we were in peak form the procedure went like this: Just after the druggist had signed the order, his shoulders would subside, and this would signal a fleeting period of mutual bonhomie. "New fella, aren't you?" the druggist was likely to say, relaxing. This was his mistake. As soon as we judged the good will to be at full flood, we would ask him if he had a ladder. (There was a ladder out in the car, but the fuss of fetching it would have broken the mood.) The druggist's train of thought would not at that moment connect the request with what was to follow, and he would good-naturedly dispatch someone to bring out a ladder. After another moment of chatter, we would make way for the waiting customer who would engage the druggist's attention. Then, forthrightly, we would slap the ladder up against a spot we had previously reconnoitered. "Just going to get this sign up for you," we would say, as if doing him the greatest favor in the world. He would nod absent-mindedly. Then up the ladder we

would go; a few quick turns of the awl, place the bracket in position, and then, the automatic screw driver. Bang! bang! Down went the sign. (If the druggist had been unusually mean, we could break the thread of the screw for good measure.) Then down with the ladder, shift it over to the second spot, and up again.

About this time the druggist would start looking up a little unhappily, but the good will, while ebbing, was still enough to inhibit him from action. He felt sorry for us. Imagine that young man thinking those signs are good looking! Just as he would be about to mumble something about one sign being enough, we would hold up the second one. It had a picture on it of a woman squirting nose drops up her nostrils. We would leer fatuously at it. "Just going to lay this blonde on the top of the cabinet for you, Mr. Jones," we would say, winking. We were giants in those days.

I suppose I should be ashamed, but I must confess I'm really not, and to this day when I enter a drugstore I sometimes fancy the sound of the awl biting irretrievably into the druggist's limed oak. I think the reader will understand, of course, that I am not holding up the Vick School of Applied Merchandising as an ideal model, yet I must add, in all fairness to Vick, that most of us were grateful for the experience. When we get together periodically (we have an informal alumni association), we wallow in talk about how they really separated the men from the boys then, etc. It was truly an experience, and if we shudder to recall the things we did, we must admit that as a cram course in reality it was extraordinarily efficient.

Exercises

"The Great Hunt for Educated Talent," by John W. Gardner

1. Express in a paragraph the idea of this article.
2. Write a 300-word summary of Mr. Gardner's position.
3. Write an original theme on the subject of "generalist" vs. "specialist." Be sure to define your terms. (See also Peter F. Drucker's treatment of the subject in "How to Be an Employee," pp. 19–20.)
4. From the financial pages of your newspaper or some other source, obtain the names of ten men who head large American corporations. After consulting their respective biographies in *Who's Who in America*, write a theme discussing their educational background, keeping in mind what Mr. Gardner has said about education as the road to power and prestige.
5. Using ideas in this article, write in your own words a theme entitled, "Wanted—the Uncommon Man."
6. Write a theme on one of the following subjects:
a. What Kind of Professional Education for Business?
b. How to Cultivate a Scholar
c. The Present Market for College Graduates
7. Explain what the great hunt for educated talent means to you.
8. The following words appear in this article: nurture, invulnerability, innovation, anti-intellectualism, unstintingly, motivation, echelons, potential. Define each term, and use each correctly in a sentence or short paragraph of your own composition.

"What Do College Grades Predict?" by Richard W. Husband

1. Using the data in this article as a starting point, write a theme on one of the following topics:
a. The Value of Extracurricular Activities for Future Business Success
b. How to Earn $20,000 a Year
c. The Plight of the Cultural Majors
d. Advice to Personnel Recruiters
2. Drawing ideas from both this article and the preceding one, and giving credit to the respective sources, write a theme entitled, "Do We Really Value Excellence?"
3. Write a paragraph incorporating all the data in the first table under the heading, "It Pays to Exercise." Be sure the paragraph has a topic sentence or conclusion, or both.
4. The author uses the term "median income" in his first table. In a paragraph, explain the meaning of the term and provide your own examples.
5. Write a memorandum addressed to the personnel director of a large company, assumedly at his request, digesting the information in this article.
6. Write a letter to *Fortune* (9 Rockefeller Plaza, New York 20, N.Y.) asking whether reprints of this article are available. You would like to have 25 copies for distribution to members of your composition class who want to discuss the topic.

"How to Be an Employee," by Peter F. Drucker

1. Write a theme in which you support the author's statement that the one basic skill in business is the ability to organize and express ideas in writing and in speaking. See "Why Study English?" in Section 2 for additional help.

2. Taking your cue from Mr. Drucker's statement that "Most of you graduating today will be employees all your life," write a light theme entitled, "Am I Doomed to Be an Employee?"

3. Combining your ideas and experience with the ideas of Mr. Drucker, write a theme on one of the following topics:
   a. English and I
   b. My Experience as a Public Speaker
   c. Give Me Job Security
   d. How Valuable Is Initiative in Business?
   e. Why I'd Like to Work for a Large (or Small) Company
   f. I'd Like to Start Near the Top
   g. The Job I'd Like to Have
   h. They Fired Me!
   i. I Quit My Job
   j. My Hobby
   k. Off-Job Interests I'd Like to Cultivate

4. Compare Mr. Drucker's remarks about "specialists" and "generalists" with those of Mr. Gardner in "The Great Hunt for Educated Talent" at the beginning of this section.

5. Write a theme on nepotism in business. Be sure you understand the word *nepotism* before you write. Mr. Drucker does not use the word but refers to the practice under the subheading "Who Gets Promoted?"

6. In a paragraph explain what you think the author means when he says, "To be promoted is not essential, either to happiness or usefulness. To be considered for promotion is." You may get some ideas from "Human Relations" in Section 4.

"The Culture of the Businessman," by Crawford H. Greenewalt

1. Write a 300-word synopsis of this article.

2. Using Mr. Greenewalt as your subject, write a theme entitled, "A Cultured Businessman." You may get additional material from Mr. Greenewalt's biography in *Who's Who in America.*

3. Drawing inspiration from Mr. Greenewalt, write a theme on one of the following topics:
   a. Businessmen—Cultured and Otherwise
   b. Need Culture Stop with College?
   c. Education—an Individual Achievement
   d. The Uncommon Man in Business
   e. Business and Conformity

4. Still harking back to the author's theme, write an informal essay on one of the following topics:
   a. I Try Culture
   b. Some Books I Have Recently Read on My Own
   c. Pleasures of the Art Museum
   d. How I Learned to Paint (or Draw or Sculpture)
   e. What the Library Means to Me
   f. I Visit the Living Theater

"How to Land Your Job," National Association of Manufacturers

1. When Tom Rath of *The Man in the Gray Flannel Suit* (see Section 8) applies for a job, he is placed alone in a room with a typewriter and given an hour to write an autobiography, which he is told to end with the completion of

the sentence, "The most important thing about me is. . . ." Write an autobiography ending in the same way. Give yourself exactly an hour.

2. Choose a company you would like to work for. After finding out something about it, write a theme on "Why I'd Like to Work for—," mentioning the company's name.

3. Write a theme entitled, "Why I'd Make a Good—." Fill in a job title.

4. Find a help-wanted advertisement that describes a full-time, part-time, or summer job that you can fill with your present qualifications, and paste the advertisement at the top of your theme paper. Then under it write a letter applying for the position.

5. Write a letter to a prospective employer of your own choosing, applying for a full-time, part-time, or summer job. Use facts only.

6. Write a concise outline or résumé of your qualifications for employment. It should contain your name, address, and telephone number at the top, a statement of the kind of job you want, and a matter-of-fact summary of your education, previous experience, other qualifications, and references. The résumé should not be longer than a single typewritten page. Many employers ask that such a data sheet be submitted as part of the job application.

7. Write in dialogue a report of an imaginary interview between you and a prospective employer. Stick to the facts about yourself.

8. Suppose, in your interview with a prospective employer, the following questions were asked. Answer each in not more than a paragraph.

  a. What salary do you want? (Avoid naming a specific figure.)
  b. Why do you think we ought to hire you?
  c. Why are you looking for work?
  d. What's your school record?
  e. Do you have any references?

9. Write a "thank you" note to a prospective employer who, you may assume, has interviewed you this morning for the job mentioned in Exercise 4 above and who has told you that he has several other candidates to see before reaching a decision.

10. Write a follow-up letter to an interviewer at an employment agency (or at your college placement bureau) two weeks after he has accepted your job application. You have heard nothing from him since.

"The Vick School of Applied Merchandising," by William H. Whyte, Jr.

1. Describe in your own words the philosophy of the Vick School of Applied Merchandising.

2. Do you know any parallels to the Vick School? If so, write a description of it in the vein of Mr. Whyte.

3. Under the title, "The Survival of the Fittest," write a not-too-serious piece relating to your college experience.

4. Mr. Whyte refers to the "current type" of executive, explaining him by such terms as "junior-executive training," "the broad view," and "human relations." From experience, reading, or hearsay, describe the modern antithesis to the training of the Vick School of Applied Merchandising. You may, if you wish, draw on Mr. Whyte's full exposition in *The Organization Man* or from any of the other readings in this section or in Section 4.

5. Write a light theme, "Are We Getting Soft?" lamenting the passing of the methods here described.

6. Describe an imaginary present-day meeting of the "alumni association" of the Vick School of Applied Merchandising.

7. Write a theme about your first job experience, with emphasis on the management's philosophy of training.

8. Write a theme entitled, "The Most Interesting Job I Ever Had."

9. Mr. Whyte uses the following words: adamantine, spurious, bostitching, rapacity, phlegmatic, inhibit, reconnoitered, eyrie, combative, camaraderie. Look up the pronunciation and meaning of each word in your dictionary. Then use each word correctly in a sentence or short paragraph of your own composition.

2

Developing Communication Skills

Anyone who wants to get ahead in business is so dependent on the impressions he makes on others that proficiency in speaking and writing quickly becomes a most important asset. In recent years businessmen have been devoting more and more attention to the communication skills of both their employees and themselves. At first their interest was centered on business correspondence. Soon it was also directed to the writing of memorandums and reports, to public speaking, conference techniques, and person-to-person communication. Today the rapid multiplication of the written word in business has prompted many executives to seek ways to sharpen their reading speed and comprehension. Interest in the human relations aspects of communication has led them also to studies of the meaningfulness of words and awakened them to the art of "listening."

The readings in this section (with the possible exception of Shepherd Mead's gay contribution) have been chosen for their practical value to everyone in business who writes, speaks, reads, and hears. Pieces dealing more specifically with the selection and effective use of words will be found in Section 3.

WHY STUDY ENGLISH?

Dwight Van Avery

Starting with a quotation on the value of good English from Peter F. Drucker's "How to Be an Employee" (see p. 14), Mr. Van Avery here adds a big company's views to a much discussed subject. The author is a member of the General Electric Educational Relations Staff.

If what Peter Drucker says is true, and we believe it is, you had better do something about your English.

Mr. Drucker wrote an article for the May, 1952, *Fortune* called "How to Be an Employee." He said that the ability to express ideas in writing and in speaking heads the list of requirements for success.

"As soon as you move one step up from the bottom, your effectiveness depends on your ability to reach others through the spoken or written word. And the further away your job is from manual work, the larger the organization of which you are an employee, the more important it will be that you know how to convey your thoughts in writing or speaking. In the very large organizations, whether it is the government, the large business corporation, or the Army, this ability to express oneself is perhaps the most important of all the skills a man can possess."

It pleases us at General Electric to go on record as supporters of Mr. Drucker's statement. We know, of course, that there are many skills and personal qualifications leading to success. There is no doubt in our minds,

for example, that you should have a genuine desire to exchange your best efforts in your employer's behalf for the chance to tackle increasingly more important, more challenging, and more rewarding assignments. We think that you should be able to look a fellow employee, including your boss, in the eye; that you should be reasonably neat and clean.

But right now we have much to say about English.

The top engineer upstairs is on the telephone. He says to us: "Right before my eyes is a brief report made out by one of our young engineers. I have to guess what the fellow is driving at. I'm no English shark, but I find myself getting a little angry when I see four sentences tied together into one with commas. He has *principle* for *principal*, and he has also misspelled *accommodate* and *Cincinnati*. What if some of this fellow's bad sentences get into the hands of our customers?"

We sympathize, and we say somewhat lamely that it's up to him to suggest that the fellow hire a tutor.

The top engineer is wound up. "At

Reprinted by permission of the General Electric Company.

43

the last meeting of our Association, representatives of all the major companies complained about the way their younger men were putting down their words—and futures—on paper. Can't someone tell us what to do?"

We reach for an answer.

"When boys and girls began avoiding mathematics like the plague," we remind him, "we began printing facts. It is now our duty and privilege to beat the drums for English! Our motives are partly selfish, because we want American business to succeed even more than it has in the past. But our motive is more than self-interest. We know because we rub shoulders with people, at work and in the community, that a solid background in English is prerequisite to happiness and well-being. Without a reasonably good command of English—as a means of communication—and without knowledge of what the best minds of all time have put into print, we are not educated for personal happiness, apart from the job, or for personal success in the exciting business of making a living."

"But I thought all boys and girls took English in high school and college?"

"Yes, they have put in their time. Their teachers have spread the feast, but some of them haven't been very hungry. Perhaps they will listen to us. Their teachers can tell them a thousand times that English is important, but they will say, 'Teacher means well, but she's trying to sell us on the importance of her subject.' Perhaps when a manufacturer of turbines, generators, jet engines, lamps, room air coolers, toasters, refrigerators, and 200,000 other electrical products says English is of tremendous importance, they will listen. After all, English is almost as important as math in our business, isn't it?"

The engineer's answer is deliberately emphatic: "Change the word *almost* to *just*, and, brother, you've said a mouthful! Tell them that English is important to them—and to us—because very soon their ability to read and to know and to remember what they have read, and to speak and to write well, will make all the difference, whether they and we or some other company of their career choice will succeed together."

At one time or another, all of us try our hand at writing.

A group of engineers applies the new principle to the development of a revolutionary type of gadget. The results of this effort are summed up in a typewritten report to the head of their department. The report is then mimeographed for the benefit of others in the organization.

The company prepares to put the new product on the market. Writers prepare literature describing its virtues, or explaining how to use it and keep it in working order.

This is indeed useful writing. No piece of company business can begin, progress, and achieve its purpose without the use of words. Writing, together with reading, is as much an integral part of the electrical manufacturing business (or any business) as your bones are part of your body.

Every day in your future you will be called upon to speak and write, and when you open your mouth, or write a letter or report, you will be advertising your progress and your potential worth.

Here is a verbatim extract from a laboratory notebook:

"Curt flew into the cloud, and I started the dispenser in operation. I dropped about three pounds (of dry ice) and then swung around and headed south.

"About this time I looked toward the rear and was thrilled to see long streamers of snow falling from the base of the cloud through which we had just passed. I shouted to Curt to swing around, and as we did so we passed through a mass of glistening snow crystals! We made another run though a dense portion of the unseeded cloud, during which time I dispensed about three more pounds of crushed dry ice . . . This was done by opening the window and letting the suction of the passing air remove it. We then swung west of the cloud and observed draperies of snow which seemed to hang for 2–3000 feet below us and noted the cloud drying up rapidly, very similar to what we observe in the cold box in the laboratory . . . While still in the clouds as we saw the glinting crystals all over, I turned to Curt, and we shook hands as I said, 'We *did* it!' Needless to say, we were quite excited."

This extract is from the laboratory notebook of Vincent J. Schaefer. It is of historical significance because it describes the first artificial snow making outside the General Electric Research Laboratory. Without such record, other men could not have understood the purpose, procedure, and effect; would not have had a starting point from which to take off on their own investigations.

Since its beginning in 1900, the Research Laboratory has published nearly 2000 papers in technical journals, and these have recorded new facts, new basic discoveries, and new theories. Many are recognized the world over as classics, and are cited as authoritative references in their fields. Some opened up wholly new fields for exploration. Others cast new light on known phenomena. Some disclosed new tools for research.

But the recording of ideas and facts is not confined only to the engineering and scientific laboratories. Each year, thousands of General Electric mechanics, stenographers, accountants, and others write down their suggestions for improving company products and procedures. To each whose suggestion is adopted is given a certain amount of money, but we suspect that the real gain—for company and employee—is the focusing of attention upon those persons who can think of a better way and who can tell about it with words on paper.

We thought little of it at the time, but one night several of us were visiting over the back fence, and a college boy, home for the summer, joined us. He told us how he was enjoying his summer job as helper on a General Electric truck. We asked him who his boss was and how he liked him. He gave us the name and said, simply, "I like him very much. He is a well-spoken man." We think that you, too, if you will stop to think, prefer well-spoken men and women.

You will probably grant that General Electric knows a thing or two about its various specialties, but you may question whether our expertness extends to the English part of the education field. Let's get off the hook directly: your English teacher has probably forgotten more about the teaching of English than we will ever know. As a matter of fact, if someday your employer finds you wobbly in English, he will be critical of you, not some long-suffering teacher or parent.

One of our business colleagues, who would hate us if we gave away his name, has an interesting background. Early in his growing-up years, he dropped schooling so he could earn enough money to buy a Stutz roadster. Eight years later, after working in a shoe factory, another powerful desire took possession of him. He wanted a Harvard degree. For one year he studied all the specified high school subjects; he read everything he could lay his hands on. Then he took all the required high school examinations and passed them with an average of 95 per cent. At Harvard, he kept on reading everything he could squeeze into four years' time. To make a long story short, he's now doing better than all right.

Attitude makes all the difference!

If you are one of those "dese" and "dose" guys, and if it "don't make no sense" to you that your school and your employer "wants" you to become a literate person, all the teaching skill and the modern facilities can't win you over.

Did you ever hear of a mental block? It's a massive barrier in your mind, but like the Maginot Line, it can be penetrated.

That block may be mathematics or history or spelling or perhaps a feeling that no one likes you or something else. Do you remember how you learned to swim? You had flailed the water and sunk like a stone. But then a fortunate stroke propelled you forward, and now it doesn't occur to you when you dive off the board that you may not be able to swim to shore.

Too, your mind may be blocked because you imagine all well-read, literate persons are precious, prissy characters who go around spouting Shakespeare. There may be a few of those people, but that is not Shakespeare's fault. We are just realistic enough to believe that some of the master poet's gracious writing style will rub off on you. We know that in a sense we become a part of what we read, and that what we call writing style is born from our unconscious attempt to imitate what we like.

We hope it has occurred to you that English extends beyond a single classroom; that your success or failure in your other classrooms is largely due to your ability to read, to understand, to speak, and to write. English is just as all-embracing in a business organiza-

tion. Whether we are at drafting board, desk, machine, or calling on customers, we are involved more or less in communication.

We say that English—especially to American boys and girls—is an easy language to learn. Making English behave may be a little troublesome. You can play safe by writing dull little sentences, and they, of course, are less frustrating to the reader than involved wrong sentences. But since the sentence you write or speak is what the reader or listener uses as a criterion in judging you, it is good sense to learn how to become its master.

We know from our experience at General Electric that too many of our younger employees say to themselves before spreading their wings for a flight with words: "But if I write that report the way I *feel* it should be written, my boss will think that I am a child." If an engineer, for example, is testing an insulating material and it chars and smells like burned string beans, we can think of no reason why he should not say so.

Our business world needs young people whose minds are packed with facts, but with the boldness of imagination to release them in a form that is easy and pleasant to take.

We have on our desk copies of the *General Electric Review* and the *Scientific American*—both written for thousands of top-flight engineers and scientists. The editors of both magazines know that factual reporting is necessary so that their readers, who are so brilliantly expert in many fields, will have confidence in the authority of their articles. But they know, too, that men and women, whatever their job or profession, are willing to begin and stay with an article only if it is well-written. Only you can guess how many books and articles you have thrown aside after tasting the first few paragraphs. Everyone who reads and listens is so very human.

Without interested readers, whether the magazine is *Scholastic* or *Scientific American*, its survival depends upon the skill and labor-of-love that editors and authors lavish upon it. Your survival, too, as the adult you are aiming to be, depends upon your ability, desire, and courage to put your best foot forward in a world that will judge you by your words as well as your actions.

Who is the next most important man or woman in your life? We aren't thinking of the next prom date, but an understanding person who is sitting at a desk studying a filled-in application blank. Whether he's a college admissions or an employment officer, he hopes he is so right before saying yes or *no*.

Can you live up to your expressed desires? Will you fit in? Have you enough preparation, enough intellectual background? Can your brain direct your hands in performing skills? Can you stand the pace of competition? Can you accept responsibility? Will you worry a workaday problem, like a dog with a bone, till you have conquered it—and then brace yourself for a tougher assignment?

If what you have said on the application blank shows a glimmer of hope, you are brought in for a personal interview. This can be rough going if you haven't habituated yourself to accurate and well-organized expression.

The interviewer across the desk from you has been charged by his college or company to weigh your worth; he has accepted the responsibility of determining the future of the organization he represents—any good organization is but the lengthened shadow of qualified men.

Your job interests. Your participation in school activities. Your subject preferences. Your hobbies. Your ambitions. These and many other topics are brought forward for you to discuss.

The minutes speed by. You summon up the skills of presentation you have practiced in English and other classes. It strikes you, as you talk, that in neither writing nor speaking can you conceal your inadequacies.

As you move up the success ladder, what you write and what you say will determine in part your rate of climb. It is neither too early nor too late to become practiced in the art of communication; certainly not too late to accumulate background through reading experiences. . . .

We pause and listen to the unceasing whine of a motor across the yard. In the distance three green-gray columns of smoke are rushing upward from three yellow-brick chimneys. We see them as symbols of mechanical might controlled by the will, the wit, and the intelligence of earnest men. And these men, adventurers and pioneers of industry, can move ahead with their plans, because their own thought processes have been built upon such logical disciplines as history and math —and English.

WHAT YOUR LETTERS REVEAL ABOUT YOU

J. Harold Janis

In spite of more modern means of communication, the letter retains its popularity. The reasons? It is personal, it is reasonably fast, it conforms to social custom, and it leaves a permanent record. Some important principles of letter writing are treated in this informal article.

A young insurance salesman I know wrote a letter recently to a prospective client asking for an appointment. Two weeks passed without a reply from the gentleman, who was head of an automobile agency. Then one day they met at a businessmen's lunch. When they were introduced the automobile man said, "I hope you'll forgive me for not answering your letter. I'll be glad to have you come around and see me any time."

"Fine," said the insurance representative, pleased at the friendly invitation. "I wondered why you didn't answer."

"If you want to know the truth," the automobile man explained, "your letter gave me the idea that you were a terrible stuffed shirt. Now that we've met, I realize you're a nice guy I'd be happy to talk to."

That's why the young insurance man became a student in one of my classes in business English. "I decided that if I was mailing out letters which made me sound like a horrible bore, I'd better see what could be done about it," he told me. "That kind of wrong impression could cost me my living."

This man discovered something that many people have learned in recent years—that the letters we write can give a false picture of us. They can make us appear selfish instead of generous, pompous rather than personable, flippant and fresh when we intend to be friendly. For the recipients, the picture our letters paint *is* our personality, for better or worse. With care we can make our letters reveal the more attractive rather than the worse side of our nature.

The letters we write can spell the difference between making and missing an important sale, between landing and losing a job, between a yes or no from the girl of our dreams. Many huge corporations hire experts to train their executives to put the company's best foot forward in their correspondence. They find that this pays off in cash and good will. In Washington, D.C., the Hoover Commission recently appointed a correspondence expert whose work has already saved the Government millions of dollars by cutting down wasted words in official letters.

Even in the personal notes we dash off every day, psychologists have dug

Reprinted from the *American Magazine*, June, 1955. Courtesy of *American Magazine*.

out startling demonstrations of how our words betray us without our realizing it.

What are some of these tricks that words can play on us if we're not careful? Here's an example from a letter received the other day by a neighbor of mine who asked two contractors for bids on a concrete driveway. One letter began like this:

"Dear Mr. Crandall:

"I am offering you a special price on this job because I am having a slack season just now, and my partner and I like to keep busy. I have some debts to pay and this work will be a big help to me. So I would appreciate your patronage."

This first paragraph showed that the writer was suffering from a bad case of "I-me" trouble. Not only the constant use of "I," "my," and "me," but the whole tone of the letter reveals that the writer was thinking of himself, not of the person he was writing to. "He sounds like a selfish kind of guy," was my neighbor's reaction.

This man had violated the first rule of good letter writing: *Take the "you" attitude.* In other words, think of your reader's problems and forget about your own if you want to interest him.

The second contractor wrote as follows:

"Dear Mr. Crandall:

"I can give you a good, solid driveway with a 6-inch bed of cinders and 3 inches of concrete. Properly graded and drained, this should last you 10 to 20 years without cracking."

This man got the job because he told his customer what he wanted to know—what he would get, how he would be served, and what good it would do him—not how much good it would do this contractor to get the work.

An effective letter like this one results when we put ourselves in the other fellow's place and think of what's in it for him.

A girl in one of my classes brought me a letter she had received from a girl-friend on vacation. "This shows how a letter can give you away," she said.

I read the opening sentence:

"Dear Ann:

"Please know my joy each time I receive one of your enchanting letters."

"What do you make of that?" I asked.

"Well," she said, "I always suspected this girl was insincere, even though she pretended to be a pal. Now I know she's a phony, writing like that."

I was inclined to agree. After studying thousands of letters in the past 20 years, I've observed that writers who use flowery, artificial language are almost always unsure of themselves, guilty of affectation, and not nearly as friendly as they pretend to be. The sincere person doesn't write of his joy in receiving one of your "enchanting letters." He says, "Your letter came yesterday and it was swell hearing from you."

This leads to the second rule for effective letter writing: *Be yourself.* The best letters are written as we would talk, in everyday language.

I've worked for a number of years as consultant to a large bank with many branch offices. My job is to help the bank make a good impression with the letters sent out by its officers. A couple of years ago, looking over copies of one day's correspondence, I found a letter that began like this:

"Yours of the 14th in hand, and we are pleased to advise that every endeavor will be made to conform with your wishes."

What did this letter tell me about the businessman who had written it? I pictured him sitting at an old-fashioned roll-top desk, one hand on an ample paunch and the other fingering a long, gray beard. Could any other kind of person have written or dictated such a stilted, stuffy sentence?

That was the mental image I got, but I was wrong. At our next letter-writing clinic I met the writer and found him to be one of the younger men in the group, alert and intelligent. He would never have worn spats or carried a gold-headed cane, yet his letter-writing style belonged to his grandfather's day. He had an idea that "business English" was a special language different from normal sidewalk English.

In a sense, I am a professor of business English who doesn't believe in "business English." In our supersonic, streamlined age, the old windy, artificial formulas which take up space and rob a letter of naturalness and personality are out of place. I believe in writing "talking English."

A new Government pamphlet published in Washington, D.C., campaigns for the same thing, which it calls "straightaway English." The authors point out that official jargon or "gobble-dygook" wastes time, tax money, and storage space in the National Archives, which bulge with 1,000,000,000 more letters every year. The booklet recommends that long, stuffed-shirt words and expressions such as "ameliorate," "compliance," and "enclosed please find" should be tossed in the waste-basket, and suggests that bureaucratic letter writers stick to the 4 S's of shortness, simplicity, strength, and sincerity.

The businessman who uses such phrases as, "Yours of the 14th in hand . . ." "Agreeable to your communication of July 23 . . ." "Receipt is acknowledged of . . ." gives the impression that he's a pompous old egotist who has no friendly feeling for the person he's writing to. If you want to tell someone that you received his letter, don't be like the schoolgirl who receives a letter with joy, or the fogy who is agreeable to your communication. Why not just say, "I received your letter . . ."?

It sounds easy, but words sometimes trap us into saying things we don't mean. Not long ago a New York bank changed the form of its checks and sent a letter to depositors ending with this sentence: "Continue to use old checks until exhausted." One of the bank's clients wrote back, tongue in cheek, "I've used one little old check, and I'm already exhausted."

I recently saw a memorandum from an executive in a large company which read, "If Joe Blick will see Art Smith and get the details, I'll talk to him later." Who was to be talked to, in this case, remained a mystery.

These examples lead to Rule 3 in letter writing: *Say clearly what you mean.* When this rule is broken, it's often the result of hurry. Before starting to write a letter, it is a good idea to think through what you want to say and the best way of saying it. As added insurance, every letter we send should be read over carefully before the envelope is sealed. When we use words that are confusing, in the wrong place, or with the wrong meaning, this tells the reader that we are careless and muddle-headed—qualities which inspire doubt rather than confidence.

The fourth rule to make us look good in our letters is this: *Be thrifty with words.*

The other day I saw a letter that began like this: "Mr. Bemis has offered a suggestion regarding a departure from our standard procedure with respect to remuneration for overtime employment." I didn't go any farther, because I had to stop and figure out what all those words meant. If the writer had said, "Mr. Bemis suggested a new way to pay for overtime," I'd have been interested at once.

"But how *should* I start a letter?" one of my students asked the other day. "That's where I waste most words." He had written a letter for his boss that began: "In reply to your letter calling attention to the fact that we sent you the wrong number of two-tone men's oxfords, we wish to apologize for our error."

I suggested he try to cut out every unessential word in the sentence. He came back with this result: "The error is ours and we're sorry." This version omitted unnecessary information— which the man to whom it was addressed knew anyhow. It was clear, and it used 7 words instead of 28. The way to begin a letter, then, is to dive right in and omit lengthy introductions.

Wordy letters reveal us as sloppy and wasteful. Some time ago, during a letter-writing clinic for an insurance company, I asked a group of executives to go over copies of all correspondence they'd turned out that day and chop out half the words. After doing so, they agreed that their letters were twice as readable in half the length.

Dictating to a secretary or a machine, in the modern manner, is one of the main reasons for rambling, wordy letters. In our clinics we've found that noting the main points of a letter on a scratch pad before dictating means saving hours of wasted time and miles of typewriter ribbon. Another word-waster we discovered is the standard large-size sheet of paper. Unnecessary words are used, both in business and personal correspondence, just because all that white space is there to be filled. One firm I know cut their executives' letter-writing time drastically by adding a small-size letterhead to their supply of stationery. Instead of a long-winded reply, a note saying "Thanks, I'll do it," was often enough.

As we all know, there are two ways to look at every situation—call them positive and negative, downbeat and upbeat, or simply gloomy and cheerful. Many letters we write reveal unwittingly our fears and doubts rather than the constructive ideas we intend to communicate.

Probably every family, like my own, has an "Aunt Clara" from whom we are always delighted to get a letter. One came the other day. Aunt Clara lives in a small town in Oklahoma, which always sounds like a wonderful place when she describes it. "It's so warm for April," she wrote, "that the trees are practically bursting into leaf, and old Mrs. Johnson is in the backyard swing next door thawing out her Arthur-itis, as she calls it, in the sunshine."

Clara's sister, Emily, lives in the same town and we got a letter from her last week, too. "You can't imagine how hot and dry and uncomfortable it is for early spring," she wrote. "This probably means another dreadful summer and a drought. I can already see the trees burning up. Poor Mrs. Johnson is very uncomfortable from arthritis, and hardly ever moves any more."

It's hard to believe that Clara and Emily are writing about the same place. But it's easy to see why everyone in the family loves to hear from Clara. She follows the fifth important rule for good letter writing: *Accent the positive.*

Very often this positive, pleasing effect can be achieved in a letter simply by changing the order in which we express our ideas. For example, a friend of mine who travels as a salesman used to worry about his family every time he left town. He showed me one of his wife's old letters, which began like this: "Dear Jim:

"The kids and I miss you terribly. We can't wait for you to get back, but I guess we'll manage to get along."

Her last letter was different:

"Dear Jim:

"We're getting along OK, even though we miss you and can't wait until you walk in the door."

"I compared the old letter with the new one," Jim told me, "and realized that they said practically the same thing. But one made me feel good and the other upset me." The difference was only that the cheerful-sounding letter put the happy thought first and subordinated the gloomier, negative idea.

Even in tragic situations, when we must write a note of condolence to someone who has lost a member of the family, it is still possible to find a positive note that will be comforting, instead of dwelling on death and bereavement. Such expressions as, "Our hearts ache for you in your grief," or, "We are sharing your sorrow with you," are usually sincere and may offer comfort to the bereft. But hopeful, forward-looking ideas can make such letters even more helpful.

Here is a note of condolence received in a Government research laboratory. It was written by a fellow-worker:

"Dear Julie:

"Martha and I are thinking of you today and we know that with God's help you are going ahead bravely, as you always do.

"Down at the lab yesterday we were talking about the project that you know was closest to Bob's heart. Everyone is determined to carry it forward with more energy than ever. You see, his work will always be an inspiration, and we'll never feel that he's far from our side.

                              "Affectionately,
                                  "George"

I like this letter because words such as "death," "loss," and "grief" are absent, and instead we find "going ahead," "energy," and "determination."

In business letters this upbeat accent is extremely important. A large manufacturer of building materials found not long ago that a new type of asbestos shingle was not selling as well as an older style, although it was superior. A young man handling orders for the company was writing the following letter to customers:

"Dear Mr. Willis:

"I am sorry to tell you that we no longer make the kind of shingle you inquired about. We have, however, a new style which may fit your needs."

This apologetic, negative approach was changed as follows:

"Dear Mr. Willis:

"I am happy to send you samples of our new roofing shingle, which now comes in a wider range of colors and textures than before. It is a great improvement on the old style, which it has replaced."

Both letters told the truth, but the second one took a positive approach which made the reader want to see the new shingles, instead of making him sorry about the discontinuance of the old style. Sales in the department began to rise immediately.

It is surprising how many letters disclose, unknown to the writer, a suspicious, distrustful, antagonistic attitude toward the person to whom the letter is addressed. Somehow things we would never say to an individual face to face often creep into correspondence. Just the other day my wife received a note from the adjustment department of a store. "As you claim that one of the cups you ordered arrived with a broken handle," it said, "we will have to replace it."

I'm sure the store didn't intend to antagonize a customer, and as they willingly made the adjustment, they evidently didn't doubt my wife's word about the breakage. Yet a sneaking accusation of dishonesty is implied in the words, "you claim."

You can see what a different impression is created by rephrasing the letter thus: "We are sorry that one of the cups you ordered arrived with a broken handle. Of course, we will replace it immediately."

And so the sixth rule we teach is: *Practice courtesy.*

This means generous use in correspondence of "please," "thank you," "I'm glad," "I appreciate." Words which rub the reader the wrong way— "We suspect," "You misunderstood," "We can hardly believe"—are eliminated from the persuasive letter writer's vocabulary.

Some years ago I was asked to help improve the correspondence of a number of agencies of the City of New York. Many letters from city offices were intended to soothe irate citizens, and yet they often had the opposite effect. I discovered a letter sent by one department which said: "If you will send us a sample of your product, we will determine its practical value, if any."

Here two little words—"if any"— revealed, no doubt unwittingly, the writer's suspicion.

Another letter ended thus: "Please let us know whether you intend to send us this information." Here was a challenging, discourteous suggestion that the receiver of the letter was withholding certain facts.

I lectured on the need for making letters express a courteous, helpful attitude. Finally one young man, after carrying on a long argument by mail with a particularly angry taxpayer, came up with the following opening:
"Dear Mrs. Brown:
"Believe it or not, this office is here to help you with your problem."

In her next letter Mrs. Brown con-
fessed that she had been more irritated by the tone of the letters she had been getting than by the problem she was trying to solve.

After the 6 rules of letter writing have been mastered, there is still an indefinable quality or tone in a letter which comes from the personality of the writer. It can't be taught, but it can be learned. Maybe the following letter, which I quote with the writer's permission, will show what I mean. It was written by William E. Robinson, recently elected president of the Coca-Cola Company, to an associate of mine at New York University.
"Dear Ed:
"You are a generous and thoughtful friend, as always, to take the trouble to write me about my new job at Coca-Cola.
"I deeply appreciate your good wishes, to which I hope you may add a prayer or two. There are bound to be some occasions when I will need both.
"My thanks—and only the best.
"Sincerely,
"Bill"

Notice, for one thing, that this letter is extremely informal. In the business and professional world today, dry, impersonal salutations, such as "Dear Sir," are rarely used. In writing to a stranger or someone we don't know well, we use the man's name: "Dear Mr. Randolph." Among personal or business friends, the first name or a nickname appears on most letters nowadays—the same name we'd use, in other words, if we met the man on the street.

Notice, also, the brevity of Mr. Robinson's letter. It wastes no one's time and says no more than is necessary, yet there is no feeling of haste or abruptness.

This letter illustrates another point: The more important a man's position, usually the less formal and stiff is his letter-writing style. It is often the beginner, still unsure of himself, who hides behind dusty old clichés in writing, while the boss at the top forgets his dignity and projects personality, relaxed charm, and vigor.

In personal correspondence even less formality survives today. No longer are old-fashioned, rubber-stamp phrases like this used in closing: "With all best wishes for the future, I remain your ever-devoted servant." Today a friendly letter is likely to end with a cheery "So long for now"—or whatever we'd say if face to face with the other person. In business writing, "Yours very truly" is a formal closing phrase still in use, while "Sincerely yours" is gradually being replaced by the single word, "Sincerely." "Best wishes," "Cordially," "Regards," or almost anything you honestly feel like saying will do as well.

After all, there are no laws about letter writing. It's a question of following generally accepted practice, which changes with the times, and of finding the best way to influence the reader the way we want him to be influenced.

Many of us often miss the chance to use letters to help us make friends and influence people. I have a colleague who keeps a diary. At the beginning of the year, when he buys a new one, he notes all his friends' birthdays and important anniversaries. He never forgets to send a note or card at the proper time. When he reads in the papers that someone he knows has been promoted, taken a new job, graduated, lost someone close to him, or gone to the hospital, he promptly sends appropriate congratulations, condolences, or words of cheer. As a result, this man has a wide reputation for being a warmhearted, thoughtful person.

Another faculty member writes a personal letter of congratulations to every student in his classes who earns an A grade. This simple, friendly gesture has helped make him one of the most popular teachers in the university.

Most of us overlook good letter-writing opportunities every day. The etiquette books tell us we must write thank-you notes for Christmas, birthday, and wedding gifts, and bread-and-butter letters when we visit friends. Unfortunately, these letters often sound as if they had been written as school assignments, instead of with warm, human feeling. Friends of mine got a note from a woman who wrote that an evening spent at their home was "one of the most delightful occasions I have ever enjoyed—one which I shall remember forever and ever." As this seemed to exaggerate the importance of the occasion, they couldn't help doubting the sincerity of the writer.

In contrast, a friend wrote my wife and me a note which contained only one sentence: "We had a lot of fun, but when we play *Scrabble* at our house next time you can't expect to be so lucky." That sounded like everyday, talking English, sincere and with a dash of humor.

I always make sure I have plenty of stationery and stamps in the house, so I can sit down and dash off a note whenever I happen to think about someone who's far away. Just saying "Hello" and "How are you?" is enough to tell a friend that I'm thinking of him, which is the important message.

The use of greeting cards for all kinds of personal notes is becoming increasingly popular. Many people now use cards—often adding a brief handwritten message—on occasions when only a personal letter was once considered acceptable. Recently a relative of mine got a polite note of condolence from an acquaintance and commented, "Look at so-and-so—too cheap to buy a card." A few years back she would probably have considered a card insulting.

Another sign of today's less conventional attitude is the fact that the type-writer is considered OK for informal personal letters. I'm pleased at this trend. After all, it's not our handwriting so much as the words we use which give pleasure. If the words are easier to read, so much the better.

Carbon copies which can be made on a typewriter are also useful. I knew a young Army officer, for example, who told me that when he first went overseas, he wore himself out writing to widely scattered relatives, with some of whom he had little in common except the family tie. "Then I began making three or four carbons of each letter," he explained. "Everybody got the news, and at the end I left space for a personal note to different individuals. I saved hours of time and no one back home felt left out."

Actually, it doesn't matter *how* a letter is written, so long as it gets written, and on time. During World War II a large department store in New York City was unable to buy enough typewriters to handle all its correspondence. Before and after the Christmas rush, college girls were hired to reply to inquiries and answer complaints in longhand. Even though their writing wasn't always easy to read, many customers thanked the store for the courtesy of quick replies.

Whenever possible, I answer a letter on the day I receive it. I've learned from experience that when I don't, the answer gets harder to write with every passing day, as the need to think up better excuses for the delay increases. The only letter that shouldn't be written quickly is the angry one. When your temper is boiling, it's better to write the letter tomorrow or the day after. For one thing, we all think better and express ourselves more clearly with the emotions under control. In addition, a violent and abusive letter seldom accomplishes anything.

Receiving such a letter, the editor of

a national magazine once sent the following reply:

"Dear Mr. Jones:

"I am returning to you your letter of January 14. If you read it after a lapse of several days, I'm sure you will be happier that it is in your wastebasket and not in my files."

Writing a letter can be an important act which changes the course of our lives. For example, applying for a job by letter is a test which most of us face from time to time. All the rules of good letter writing are needed in this case, but the most important is probably the first: Take the "you" attitude.

It is tempting, in this situation, for the writer to talk exclusively about himself, his aims, desires, and past experience, because, after all, he is selling himself to a prospective employer. I have seen many letters of application which began like this one:

"Dear Sir:

"I am just the man you described in your advertisement, and I am interested in a new job just now because I am not satisfied with my present position . . ."

This is a weak approach, because a prospective employer is never as much interested in an applicant's need for the job as he is in his own need for filling it. He wants, first of all, to know what the applicant can do for him. Many a good job has been landed with a letter which shows an intelligent understanding of the employer's business and his particular problems, and in addition indicates how the applicant can help solve those problems.

One of the best job-letter campaigns I know of was conducted many years ago, during the depression, by a young friend of mine. His problem was how to get a job as an accountant, when most business houses were laying off accountants instead of hiring them. He realized, however, that there must be some industries which were expanding, and by investigating he learned that one of these was radio broadcasting. He compiled a list of 100 radio stations and networks, and carefully prepared a form letter to be sent to all of them. His letter began:

"Dear Mr. _____:

"Your business is growing, so openings must exist from time to time on your staff. I would like to be considered for a place in your accounting department."

He went on to describe his qualifications and experience. The important thing about his campaign was that he had first figured out the proper targets for his letters, and then the kind of letter that would hit the bull's-eye. His opening sentence indicated an intelligent understanding of the opportunities in the field he was trying to enter, and was flattering to the recipient, besides. The 100 letters he mailed brought 47 replies, of which 36 were negative and 11 offered interviews. The 11 interviews brought 3 job offers, and my friend chose the one he liked best.

Here was proof that the right letter, sent at the right time to the right place, can bring exactly the results we want. Every letter we write can be just as effective, given thought and care in its writing. There is no reason why our letters should tell a reader that we are self-centered, pompous, old-fashioned, confused, or insincere, and they won't if we forget about outdated etiquette-book rules and unnatural "business English."

"I THINK I'LL WRITE TO THE MANUFACTURER"
Ruth Leigh Sclater

There was a time when the businessman looked upon consumer correspondence as a nuisance. Today he values letters from customers because they constitute a "pipeline" from the final judges of his merchandise and service. They also enable him to adjust complaints and improve his product before irreparable damage is done. This article performs a service to both readers and advertisers.

There are many reasons why you may sit down to write a letter to a big company.

Perhaps your new living-room carpet sheds an unusual amount of fluff. You're not sure that's normal. At dinner that night you mention it to your husband.

"Why not write to the manufacturer and find out?" he suggests. It sounds like a sensible thing to do, so next day you decide to send off a letter.

Or you're having trouble finding king-size sheets to fit your extra-long mattress. Somehow, the stores near you don't seem to carry the extra size you require. Next morning, while you're making the beds, an idea occurs to you: Why not write to a leading manufacturer and ask him where you can obtain them?

Again, you may be telling a neighbor about the remarkable satisfaction you've had from the vacuum cleaner you bought when you were married, 12 years ago. At this point you say enthusiastically, "I think I'll write to the manufacturer and let him know."

So for any of a variety of reasons, you write your letter to a big company. And as you address it and stamp it, you probably think, I wonder if anyone will ever bother to answer this?

Chances are someone will. If you've had any contact with business, through your own job experience before marriage or through your husband's connections, you are probably aware that all letters requiring a reply are carefully answered. In fact, the larger the company the more certain you can be that your letter will receive courteous attention.

But—and this is important—much of your satisfaction with the reply will depend on your letter and how you've written it. If you know how most large companies handle correspondence, you will have a clearer idea of the points to heed in writing to them.

Here are some pertinent suggestions, from an authoritative source, that may be helpful the next time you write a letter to a big company.

First, be absolutely certain that your name and address are on the face of

From *Good Housekeeping*, August, 1956. Reprinted by permission of *Good Housekeeping*.

the letter—not only on the envelope but also on the letter itself. The reason for this is all-important: In big companies, most general mail is opened in a mail room. Usually the envelopes are discarded, and the letters are distributed to various departments. By the time your letter reaches the desk of the person who will answer it and is ready for a dictated reply, several days may have elapsed. By then the envelope will have long since been destroyed. Imagine the regret of a business executive who desires, above all, to write you a helpful, friendly reply, when he finds, as he starts to dictate, that there is *no address on your letter to which he can address an answer.* So your letter is laid aside, unanswered, while you may be wondering why the big company to which you took the trouble to write fails to reply.

Incidentally, if you live in a small town or a remote area and you're having booklets or packages sent to you, it's important to mention the nearest big town or city. This helps the mailing department determine the postage zone.

Second, try, if possible, to write on medium- or standard-sized paper—the nearer to 8½" x 11" regulation business-letter size the better. There's a good reason for this: Smaller letters, especially tiny visiting-card-size notes or little flower-decorated informals, so suitable for social correspondence, are easily lost in an office. A tiny note among a pile of letters in a Manila folder can easily fall out—and often does!

If you can type your letter, that is a help, but typing is not essential. Business organizations pay as much attention to handwritten letters as to typewritten ones. Be sure, however, that your name is printed.

Third, you may believe that if you address your letter to the president of a big company it will receive special attention. This is not necessarily true. Today, most large, well-managed business firms are so highly organized that letters must "go through channels." Even if your letter is received and read by the president, chances are that it will be answered by the person or department responsible for the particular situation. Time may be saved, therefore, and the same result achieved, by writing directly to the company rather than to its chief executive. Moreover, you may be sure that if your letter is sufficiently important to receive top-level attention, it will.

Fourth, try, if possible, to state in the first paragraph of your letter (1) what you are writing about, (2) what you would like to know, and/or (3) what you wish done about your particular problem. Conciseness is a tremendous help to the busy person answering your letter. Often, in a busy office, "problem" letters may be laid aside for further investigation. The clearer and more explicit your note, the faster it can be handled and the more speedily a reply can be written.

Fifth, before sending money, stamps, or a money order to a manufacturer, be absolutely sure that the company you're ordering a purchase from sells its goods directly to the public. As you may know, many products are sold through stores, not directly by the manufacturer. And you'd be surprised how much time, trouble, and "red tape" is involved in handling unsolicited amounts of money sent with letters ordering goods incorrectly—eventually only to return the sums to the sender. It is always better to inquire before sending money.

Sixth, it is not necessary to send a stamped, self-addressed envelope unless you are specifically requested to do so. You can, if you wish, include a stamp for a reply, but self-addressed envelopes are often left unused. You see, business letterheads vary in size and dimensions, and the envelope you send may be much too small, or of the wrong proportions, to accommodate the company's paper. So company envelopes are usually used in the regular course of business correspondence.

Seventh, if you have a legitimate complaint about an article, instead of blowing off steam to your husband or neighbor, write directly to the manufacturer. State your complaint. Include in your letter the name of the store where you bought the item, the date and the price, the model and the serial number if it's an appliance, and any pertinent details that will help describe your dissatisfaction. These facts will save back-and-forth correspondence and will help the manufacturer to take quick action.

Eighth, remember that the big companies value the letters you write. Your experience, satisfactory or otherwise, can contribute toward the improvement of the company and of its goods.

Finally, be assured that your letters to big business organizations are welcome—whether they contain opinions, comments, experiences, or complaints!

HOW TO ORGANIZE AND WRITE EFFECTIVE TECHNICAL REPORTS

Ralph A. Richardson and C. A. Brown

Some of the most exacting writing in business is found in its internal reports and memorandums. Almost as hard as writing the reports is writing about them. This article was written by two staff members for General Motors' engineering personnel. It should be equally helpful to anyone who needs to put reports on paper. Mr. Brown is coauthor with Robert E. Tuttle, also of the General Motors Institute, of the textbook, *Writing Useful Reports*.

The very nature of the engineering profession dictates that those who practice it must be able to report their findings in a clear, concise, and accurate manner in order to insure the best utilization of the data being reported and to contribute significantly to the ever-expanding store of technical knowledge. There is a great deal of evidence that engineers do write and, as a matter of fact, with a considerable degree of proficiency. This is evidenced by the ever-increasing size of The Engineering Index and the many fine articles which appear in engineering periodicals. Moreover, the quality of the writings in the technical literature during the past 10 or 15 years has steadily improved. The engineering colleges and universities are to be commended for the outstanding work they have done over the past decade to effect this improvement.

Engineers too often think their part of the job is finished when they complete their tests, drawings, or designs. The part of the work that makes the job useful or successful is frequently an analysis of the results presented in a well-prepared report. One of the very important jobs of the engineer is, therefore, to produce technical writings that will be read, understood, and used by all groups, even though they are probably not familiar with the subject. This means that there must be a large element of sales and educational effort in any technical writing. Hours spent in writing may well prove to be an engineer's most productive time. Moreover, from a selfish standpoint, the engineer or scientist who can do an effective job of communicating his ideas to others—particularly to those in management—usually advances up the professional ladder somewhat faster than his colleagues who have not acquired this ability.

What constitutes a good technical

Reprinted by permission from *General Motors Engineering Journal*, September–October, 1955. Copyright 1955, General Motors Corporation, Ralph A. Richardson, General Motors Research Staff, C. A. Brown, General Motors Institute.

report? The following general comments may help to answer that question:

- The text should be neither ambiguous nor subject to misinterpretation by any reader, regardless of his technical background.
- The report should reflect sound, objective thinking.
- The content should be factual and easily read. Word choice should lean toward simple rather than complex words.
- A report demands and is strengthened by the use of the correct word. Knowledge of the language and its principles of usage will aid in the expression of the writer's thoughts.
- The neat and orderly report commands respect.

KINDS OF TECHNICAL REPORTS

Generally speaking, technical report writing falls into four categories: (a) letters, (b) memorandum reports, (c) progress reports, and (d) final reports.

LETTERS

It may seem strange that letters are considered a form of technical reporting. Often, however, they include important data or facts, and it is not uncommon to see a project engineer thumbing through his correspondence file for letters written to associates concerning a particular project or investigation which may help him in the preparation of a progress report or final report.

MEMORANDUM REPORTS

The memorandum report is usually written on a standard form for limited distribution within the organization. It is purposely kept as short and to the point as is practical to get pertinent information about a particular project on paper as quickly as possible and distributed to people in the organization who can use it effectively in connection with their own work.

PROGRESS REPORTS

The progress report generally is much longer and more formal in its style and format than the memorandum. Usually, a progress report is made when work on a project has reached the end of a particular phase or at regular intervals set by management. For example, a long-range project of possibly two or three years' duration should produce a progress report at the end of the preliminary investigation or literature-searching phase. At this point it would be decided whether or not to continue the project on the strength of the information uncovered. Progress reports many times are prepared to recommend steps in future planning or in some cases to indicate results that may be forthcoming. Such reports also keep top management informed regularly of the activities going on in the engineering department.

FINAL REPORTS

The final report, as its name implies, is the last to be written concerning a particular project or investigation. It is often quite long and covers in minute detail all the salient facts about the project. A great deal of care must be exercised in writing the final report as it becomes a permanent record, and the conclusions, recommendations, and data it contains may be used for many years as a reference for making decisions and in gathering material on new investigations. The final report should, therefore, be as complete as it is possible to make it.

Almost all organizations that employ engineers and other technical people use a form of report similar to one of these. Experience has shown that the engineer who performed the experiments should be responsible for writing the report, since he is the only one who knows all of the details.

ORGANIZING THE TECHNICAL REPORT

There are many ways of organizing and writing a technical report. The method used will depend upon the use to which the report will be put and the kind of subject matter it contains. In other words, the kinds of readers and what they need to get from the report will govern the organization and language. In addition, there are sometimes "ground rules" of the organization that must be observed.

No matter who the readers are they will want to know early in the report what it is about, the extent of the coverage, and the most significant information contained in the report. For this reason, reports that are predominantly informational are oftentimes preceded by a summary or abstract to provide the user with a quick understanding of the content. Incidentally, the validity of such report rests upon its completeness, accuracy, and ease of use. On the other hand, a report that gives the outcome of a study, an investigation, or research must provide a clear statement of the problem, an explanation of the method employed in solving the problem, and a clear statement of the results or conclusions.

One method of organization that is used in reporting a piece of research or information has evolved through years of experience and has proved to be a highly effective way of presenting technical material. The general organization of the material is as follows:

- Title
- Table of contents
- Opening
- Conclusions
- Recommendations
- Body of the report
- Reference list.

Although this sequence differs somewhat from the common practice of technical report writing in many organizations, it is recommended primarily because it is easier for the reader to grasp the problem and conclusions of the investigation without having to read through the entire manuscript, and leaves him free to peruse the details at his leisure. One of the first steps in an engineering investigation is to make a search of the literature in the field of the investigation to find out what others have done on the same or similar problems. It might be mentioned here that all engineers should be familiar with library services and how to use them efficiently. The next step is to select a suitable title for the work.

TITLE

The title should indicate the contents of the report to the prospective readers by being as descriptive as possible. Some authorities oppose this view, maintaining that very often the title becomes too long and involved; but it would seem that for technical reports, at least, the advantages of a descriptive title outweigh the disadvantages. Recent practice in many organizations is to give the report a short title composed of key words followed by a longer, more descriptive subtitle.

TABLE OF CONTENTS

A table of contents is included in most engineering reports to help the reader locate quickly and easily the main sections and subsections of the report and to give an idea of overall content. Usually, however, in the case of relatively short reports the contents page is omitted.

The table of contents is usually prepared from the author's outline used in writing the report, since it lists in detail all of the important points covered in the text. It might be well at this point to mention that a well-constructed outline is essential to good report writing. While it may seem that the preparation of an outline is a non-productive effort, experience has shown it insures that all points are discussed, that the chances of leaving something out are minimized, and that the writing is kept on target. Generally speaking, it is not necessary to outline the opening, conclusions, and recommendations unless these sections are long and complex. As a general rule, however, it is better practice to keep them as short as possible.

OPENING

The opening of an engineering report in some cases is called a foreword and in others the introduction. In either case, however, the opening should be a clear-cut statement of the problem or investigation undertaken and should be given careful thought. Many engineers make an entry in their logbook on the day the project is assigned, stating briefly what they are setting out to accomplish. Very often this log entry serves as the opening to their report. There is considerable merit in doing this because engineers, like other people, are human and sometimes have a tendency over a period of time to lose sight of the specific objectives of a particular project. Reference to the logbook and to the brief statement of the problem as expressed on the day it was assigned helps not only to keep the

objective in mind, but also proves helpful when starting to write the report.

CONCLUSIONS

The conclusions should follow directly after the opening of the report and, in general, should point out what the engineer found out about the problem stated in the opening. Although the conclusions are sometimes listed numerically, they need not be; however, each should be separate and distinct from the other so as not to confuse the reader about the points being emphasized. Each conclusion should be a specific, positive statement and should leave no doubt as to its true meaning.

RECOMMENDATIONS

An author's recommendations very often can be the most important part of a technical report, and their adoption or rejection depends to a large extent on the manner in which they are presented. Like the conclusions, they should be positive statements suggesting some specific thing to be done or course to be followed, and should include an estimate of the cost involved, if any. Few engineers like to be concerned with how much it costs to do things, but it is almost a sure bet that the first question asked after reading the recommendations in a report will be, "How much will this cost?" It is good report writing technique to anticipate this question by giving solid figures based on the best estimates that can be made. If this is done, the chances of the recommendations being accepted will be greatly enhanced. Moreover, this technique of anticipating questions should be considered not only with regard to costs, but with regard to every phase of the report. It is a practice that is highly recommended.

These three parts, the opening, conclusions, and recommendations, are the most difficult for the majority of technical men to write satisfactorily because they must summarize the work in simple language. They are written for the person who does not have enough time to familiarize himself with the many details of the subject—particularly for the executive who must make engineering decisions.

DISCUSSION

The body or discussion of an engineering report is generally the largest single section. In it are included details of the investigation such as:

- Text which supports all conclusions and recommendations
- The kind and accuracy of the instrumentation used
- Test setup and problems encountered in this phase of the work
- Detailed explanation of the test procedure
- Presentation of data taken along with an interpretation and analysis of these data.

Illustrations such as curves, photographs, charts, and tables should be included to enrich the discussion. (Details as to handling illustrative material are discussed under the heading *Illustrations* in this paper.)

Usually, the biggest problem in connection with the body or discussion section of the engineering report has to do with organization of the material being presented. Care should be taken to arrange the material in a logical manner so that a reader unfamiliar with the subject can readily grasp the meaning of what has been written. Thus, the first subheading in a typical report might be *Historical* or *Background Information*. A few opening remarks outlining the project and pointing out some of the thinking leading up to the work are very helpful in orienting the reader to the problems and objectives of the investigation. Following this, the information gathered should be presented as simply and as straightforwardly as possible, avoiding trite expressions and techniques which lower the literary and informational quality of the report.

While this paper is primarily concerned with the organization of material and the mechanics of technical report writing, it should be emphasized that the application of the rules of good grammar and composition is a prerequisite to quality report writing. This does not mean that every engineer is expected to be an expert writer, but does assume that he is well grounded in grammar, spelling, and the rules of good composition.

A generous use of subtitles throughout the discussion helps the reader to visualize more completely the overall picture or scope of the work, as well as to gain a more lasting impression of the material presented. Moreover, subtitles tend to break up long expanses of straight text which very often are dull and difficult to read. Subtitles also tend to dramatize the material and improve greatly the overall quality and readability of a technical report.

REFERENCE LIST

The reference list is an important part of the technical report and much care should be given to its preparation. This should consist of two lists: (a) the periodical list and (b) the book list. References are best listed alphabetically by author, each entry to include the title of the article or book, the volume and number in the case of periodicals, the publisher in the case of books, the date of publication, and finally page references. Only those works which the author has read and feels are pertinent to the subject of the report should be included in the reference list. Numerous titles of books and periodicals listed merely to impress the reader or to add bulk to the manuscript most often accomplish the opposite effect.

ILLUSTRATIONS

Illustrations are included in an engineering report to enrich the text as well as to make it easier to understand. Like the reference list, illustrative material should not be used just for the sake of having it or to increase the bulk of the report. Nor should it be used as a crutch for poorly written material. Rather, illustrations should be looked upon as aids in explaining points covered in the text. Good illustrations not only enhance the appearance of a report, but they also aid greatly in making more lasting impressions upon the reader than do words alone.

Illustrations include such things as photographs, drawings, curves, sketches, and tables of data. Very often the discussion section of a technical report is devoted almost entirely to the interpretation of illustrative material. Many authors, however, experience difficulty in deciding what and how many illustrations to use. A general rule to follow in this connection is to use illustrations only when they are necessary to support the thoughts, ideas, or points in the report. Many engineering reports are inadequate because of a lack of good quality illustrative material.

Illustrations should be large enough to convey the message clearly and quickly. Too often, size is sacrified for economy reasons. Authors sometimes select small photographs or print too many illustrations on a page. Pictures should be reproduced large enough so that all pertinent details are readily apparent. Sometimes, photographs are retouched to highlight or accent a particular area which helps to clarify points discussed in the text. Curves which graphically illustrate engineering data should be plotted neatly and reproduced page size, if possible, particularly if the author has prepared them with the idea they will be used for "picking off" values. Sketches and drawings, like photographs, always should be large enough to show clearly all necessary details.

SUMMARY

Success in engineering, as in all other organized undertakings, depends as much on the ability to present an idea convincingly as it does upon the ability to perform experiments and calculations. The most miraculous discovery in the laboratory is not a contribution to the store of knowledge until the results are recorded and transmitted to others. A written report is often the only record which is made of the results that have come out of years of thought and effort. It is used to judge the value of the engineer's work and serves as the foundation for all future action on the project. If the report is written clearly and precisely, it is accepted as the result of sound reasoning and careful observation. If the report is poorly written, the results presented in it are often dismissed as the work of a careless or incompetent worker. Most engineers can become good writers if they will put the same thought and effort into this phase of their work as they do in conducting their experiments.

HOW TO WRITE MEMOS
Shepherd Mead

"Are you trying to get ahead the hard way (e.g., by means of education, intelligence, ability, hard work)? Forget it!" So reads the blurb for the book from which the following selection was taken. In real life, author Shepherd Mead has no real aversion to education, intelligence, etc., laboring as he does in the Madison Avenue vineyards of the Benton and Bowles advertising agency. Still, he can be as irrational as the next man and a whole lot funnier when he writes about anything as important as The Wicket Situation.

You will soon learn that the heart, the very lifeblood of modern business is the interoffice memo. If you're a good man with a memo you have small cause to worry.

The memo, like the meeting, is concerned only incidentally with its apparent subject. The main object of the memo is to *impress the people who read it*.

NEVER COME STRAIGHT TO THE POINT

The neophyte can be spotted quickly. He comes right out and states his business. Since very few problems can't be covered in a paragraph or two, the reader is finished with it rapidly, and the whole point of the memo is lost.

A good man can expand the simplest subject into three or four closely written pages, during the course of which

he can inject sympathetic understanding, wit, and a few well-chosen anecdotes. Those who read it will see that he not only has a complete grasp of the subject, and of the entire industry, but that he is a capital fellow, and is somehow slightly above the whole thing.

HOW TO GET PEOPLE TO READ MEMOS

Memos are like seeds in the forest or the eggs of a salmon. The waste is staggering. One authority feels that if one in ten falls on target, or is at least partly read, the mission is accomplished. Another feels that one in twenty-five is a fair average. This is defeatist thinking! Make sure your memos are read. Address them to the highest officer who might be even remotely connected with the subject, especially the man who is in charge of those you are trying to impress. This name is usually referred to as "nominal sendee," or "reader guarantee." Address it:

To: Mr. Biggley
From: Pierrepont Finch   cc.

Under "cc.," or "carbon copy," list all those you're trying to impress.

This will make some of the carbon copy people read it on the chance that Biggley *might* read it and refer to it.

It is, of course, unnecessary to send out Biggley's copy.

THE SECONDARY TARGET

The secondary target is the person who really has to do something about the memo, if he can find the right paragraph. This fellow, probably in some menial job, will receive the ninth carbon, which is not readable, except in a general way. It is sufficient to call him up:

"Say, don't know whether my memo got there yet."

"Oh, yessir, it did, Mr. Finch. Little trouble reading it."

"Well, don't bother. I can tell you in a nutshell. J. B. called from the agency and wanted to make sure you ship out a case to Akron."

"Oh, yes. I will."

"Fine."

The subtleties, the sly humor, and the gentle wisdom of your five closely written pages will have been lost upon this dolt, but no matter. Your purpose has been achieved.

DON'T PIN PEOPLE DOWN

It is not considered cricket to pin people down to specific details in a memo. If you ask a colleague if he has "seen" your memo and he answers "yes," accept the statement. Those who ask what he thought of paragraph three will soon have few friends.

WHAT TO DO WITH OTHER PEOPLE'S MEMOS

There are two schools of thought on this. One holds that it's enough to place a bold red check on the upper right-hand corner. This shows your secretary you have "seen" it. She will then place it in a neat pile until you "have time to read it." This, of course, will never be necessary. Instruct her to throw away all memos six inches below the top of her pile.

The other procedure is to take freshly received memos, and, before reading, return to sender with a penciled note at the top. "Mighty clear exposition!" is always good, or "See you've really thought this through!" This way is more trouble, but it will make you friends.

If there is anything you really have to do about a memo, have no fear! The sender will phone you, as noted above.

SAMPLE MEMO

Excerpts from a sample memo are printed here, almost exactly as they appeared in Finch's personal file. No need to add that names—and an occasional fact—have been changed.

Study this carefully. It is a fine example of the memowright's art, coming as it does in the middle of Finch's early, or bold, period. But do not try to imitate it too slavishly. Remember that a memo is you, and one that may express another's personality will do you scant justice.

Memo
To: Mr. J. B. Biggley   Date:

The copy to J. B. Biggley, the "nominal sendee," was not sent, as explained above.

cc. Messrs. Axel

E. Biggley	D. Osterly
Cottery	Sprockett
Fribble	Taffle
Lightly	Womper

The above names are "impressees," or those the sender was trying to impress. They are always listed in alphabetical order—no use offending anyone! The "executor," or the one who was supposed to do something about the memo, was a lad named Bud Frump of the shipping department. His name was never actually included in the typed version, but was written in red pencil on the tenth carbon. See "Secondary Target," above.

From: Pierrepont Finch

Some authorities favor "Mr. Finch" in this position, but there is a certain disarming modesty and easy familiarity about plain "Pierrepont Finch." In fact, some of Finch's better-known memos were signed simply "Pont Finch."

SUBJECT: THE WICKET SITUATION

Never neglect a resounding title! This memo could have been titled "Put Plenty of Excelsior in Future Wicket Shipments," since that was the real, or secondary, purpose. A clod would have done so, but not Finch!

Few of us are aware of the alarming situation that confronts us with regard to our current wicket shipments.

This is good! It alerts the reader, puts him on his guard against real danger, and keeps him going through the meaty, or impressive, passages. The surefooted memowright knows the value of the word "alarming" in the first sentence. It is a particularly well-chosen word because it indicates that even though there is a real threat, you are on top of it.

I think first we should all be brought up to date on the background.

"Background," too, is good. All memos should have plenty of "background." It promises rich rewards for those who follow you through the ensuing paragraphs.

And because—though I hesitate to say it—the wicket background has become more or less inseparable from my own, I may have to sketch in a few personal details.

You are losing readers here, face it! But plunge on. This is the real treasure, or pay dirt, that you are bringing to your carefully chosen group of readers.

My intimate connection with the wicket situation dates back to its very inception.

At this point the memo becomes technical, and will be of small value to the lay, or non-wicket reader. Suffice it to say that two or three closely written pages follow. One who threads his way through this treasure-trove will discover that—lo!—Finch not only has a firm grasp on wickets, but on the entire industry as well. The branches are fairly groaning with such ripe fruit as this:

—Furthermore, my long research into the matter led me to the conclusion that—

And:

Though this is only my personal belief, it is one that few, at this stage, can dispute!

Perhaps the following anecdote will help to illustrate my point. Wander with me back through the years to the old Maple Street Plant.

For a page and a half one well-turned phrase follows another. The story, charming as it is, has little to do with the wicket situation. Its purpose is finer, higher, and broader. Rare indeed is the reader who does not emerge with the conviction that Finch is a capital fellow, stouthearted, clear-headed, brave, and reverent.

"Take your money," I said. "A Biggley boy I began and a Biggley boy I'll stay, damn you!"

After a few more scattered *bon mots*, Finch concludes thus:

There are a number of major steps that we can surely take in the future, but for the moment, aside from packing more excelsior in the wicket cases, we find ourselves in somewhat of a cul-de-sac. However, time will tell.

Small reason to remind the critical reader that this is true artistry, and in the Finch tradition. Finch has disposed of his real, or secondary, subject with a rapier thrust, piercing it concisely in one parenthetical phrase: "aside from packing more excelsior in the Wicket cases." A fine example to follow!

(Signed)
Ponty

Though actually all copies—except the one to Bud Frump—had "Ponty" written in longhand at the end, the impression conveyed was that the *others* were signed "P. F." and that *only your own* was signed "Ponty," personally, in a spirit of brotherly affection. Finch's secretary had long since become expert at writing "Ponty" so that it was indistinguishable from the real thing.

OPEN LETTER TO A NOVICE HOUSE ORGAN EDITOR

Audrey E. Heusser

Employee publications—there are now fully 7000 of them in the United States—provide a means of expression for management and for articulate workers as well. To justify their cost, however, they must attract and persuade readers. Mrs. Heusser, who is publications supervisor of the Olin Mathieson Chemical Corporation, New Haven, here describes some of the ways in which a house organ can justify its existence.

Dear Alice: You have asked me to write you about some of the problems that you are likely to face in your first job as a house organ editor. Let's not waste time talking about the mechanical problems of the graphics art trade. Concerning these you will find ample help in the books at your local library, the courses available in your nearby schools, and through membership in the industrial editors' association that serves your area.

What I'd like to write about, instead, is the place that the house publication holds in the industrial communication program. Before I do that, I want to remind you that an employee publication is one of the costs of doing business and, as such, must pay its way to justify its existence.

The quickest way to set yourself straight, once this financial fact is firmly fixed in your mind, is to consider for a minute what your house organ is not. It is not a newspaper in any commercial sense. It isn't a magazine in any newsstand sense. It isn't a periodical, as the Post Office uses the word: you'll never get a second-class mailing permit for it. In short, it isn't published to be purchased: the purchase was underwritten by your company before you set pen to paper.

But it is published to be *read* and, more than that, to be read and *believed*, so that the employee-reader is persuaded to a course of action that will help reduce the cost of doing business for the company-sponsor. And right here, let me make clear that such persuasion is possible only when the course of action *is* beneficial to both the company and the employee. It is not within the power of any editor to create this condition.

And this brings us to the very basis of all industrial publication success—it must be built upon the understanding that nothing is accomplished by the house organ except insofar as it has some impact upon the employee-reader. Few of us come to our jobs with a clear understanding of this fact.

If we had our training on commer-

Reprinted by permission from *Personnel Journal*, September, 1955.

cial newspapers, we find it hard to believe that what builds circulation is not always the thing with the greatest influence on the employee-reader. Or if we come from the magazine field, we usually think a flamboyant feature presentation will do as much for an industrial employee as though he paid the subscription price to get it.

If our training has been in some field other than journalism, it is some time before we understand that people don't necessarily read all that they should read, let alone believe it. Under normal conditions, it will be some time before the novice editor sees clearly that his job calls for attention to what the article says, how it says it, and what it does not say—right down to the final impression left upon the reader.

Let us take, for instance, the articles which you find in a newsstand magazine concerning traffic accidents. "The Terrible Traffic Toll," the headline says; and there is a series of excellent pictures showing superhighways crowded with automobiles, a gory body half hanging from a wrecked car, a weeping mother bending over the limp form of a small child.

You read the article and you don't skip a word. The magazine goes up a notch in your estimation. If you haven't renewed your subscription, you surely will. If you are a newsstand buyer, you'll probably pick up next month's issue on the strength of this one excellent article. The publication is a success by the best measurement its publisher can apply.

Yet, you go right out and drive your car just as fast as you ever drove it and you contribute your full share to the terrible traffic toll just as though the article had never been written. And the fact that this is true detracts in no way from the success of that publication.

HOUSE ORGAN ARTICLES DIFFER

But consider the house publication that presents an article on industrial accidents. The headline must be carefully written, so that the person who only scans will not get the erroneous impression that a factory is a dangerous place to work. Your most spectacular headline gets thrown out before you start. From the beginning, your job is more intricate than that of the commercial publication because you must make contact with the reader without scaring the reader's wife half to death. Nor may you use pictures of mangled bodies, however much they might increase your readership.

A good rule is that no employee will ever be pictured in an unsafe act. Showing the right way to do a thing leaves a more lasting impression. Yet, within these limits, the copy must be so skillfully written and presented that it will be read in its entirety. And— here's the rub—as a result of that reading, the employee should be persuaded to do his job more safely.

Perhaps safety is not a problem in your organization. But if it is, you can never escape your share in the safety record. Though no one will imagine that as the result of one article the safety record is going to improve, the improvement of that record is a continuous bread-and-butter job for the editor. Over a period of years, as the result of the house organ's treatment of safety, supplementing a sound plant-wide safety program, that record had better improve if the house organ hopes to justify its existence.

H. O. MUST GET RESULTS

For the house organ's success is measured by its ability to influence the employee's thinking. And, other things being equal, if it doesn't make him a more careful workman, then to that extent it's a failure. If you have no safety problem, you can apply this same formula to some other problem—customer relations, quality workmanship, good housekeeping, or high productivity.

In any case, let no house organ editor imagine that because his circulation is not charted like that of a newsstand magazine, there are no charts to tell how well he does his job. The charts are there—accident reports, employment turnover, absenteeism, productivity, employee relations—all these and others tell the story of the house organ's success or failure. Only a small share of the credit goes to the house organ, but that share means a lot.

It is with the recognition of these facts that you really begin to build a house organ. You see at last that somehow or other you have got to reach the reader, and your first job must be to find out what the reader is really like. Probably you will want to improve your relationship with your volunteer staff, or build one. The volunteer, you will see, is very likely a typical reader. Readers differ, and the more volunteers you have, the better, since these give you a better cross-section. And this concern for readers has another effect. Once the editor appreciates readers, he wants to please them.

EDITOR'S CONCERN FOR READERS

At one time, my office window looked out on a house where a retired employee lived. I have never forgotten the pleasure I got from watching that retiree when the house publication was delivered. In the summer, he'd sit on the porch reading it, and reading parts out loud to his wife sitting beside him.

Without knowing his name, or anything about him, it became terribly important that the publication should meet with his approval. He became for me the typical reader . . . and nothing that happened that summer did me more good than to be reminded once a week that I wasn't publishing that house organ for national awards, or personal approbation, or to impress some editor in a neighboring city, or even to please myself. It was being published for its readers—its employee-readers; and, even more, to influence them.

Much the same pleasure comes on distribution day from watching employees stream out of the gates with the house organ in their hands or rolled up and stuck in their back pockets. You see them peeking at it as they hurry for the bus, commenting on the cover, looking for familiar names, and suddenly it comes to you that this is what you were working for. I know that there are many conditions which make distribution within the plant difficult if not impossible, but when practicable, it makes a good and simple test of employee acceptance. Any individual employee may never become a reader, but you've accomplished something if he's willing to carry the publication home.

All this, of course, is leading you to the place where you become almost obsessed with the business of readers. A reader, you see at last, is a most unusual person. He has to be stalked and lured. There is no graphic arts trick known to the trade but it must be tested and perfected (or discarded) to win you readers. The commercial magazines must be studied for what makes people read. But, here as elsewhere, things like four-color art work, which win readers for some popular newsstand magazines, could easily repel the employee-reader. His first reaction might well be: "If they'd put what that cost in my pay envelope, they'd be doing something!"

BAIT TO CATCH READERS

Every editor will develop his own formula for catching a reader. But, in general, it will be found that these are the principal kinds of copy which successfully bait the trap: those which interest, inform, entertain, or appeal to the reader's ego.

Now, a great many other people are also trying to catch readers, and with this same bait. So you had better be a realist if you hope for any success. When it comes to being interesting and entertaining, your house organ is getting some really stiff competition. Everything that comes to the reader's attention, from the television commercial to the handbill at the door, is trying to snag a reader, and for the most part by being interesting and amusing.

As a consequence, some of the most brilliant writers in the country are giving the house organ editor a run for his money. As a realist, you might as well face the brutal fact: try though you will, you are never going to be so interesting and amusing that you can snatch a reader away from the competition. And this is not to say that you shouldn't be as interesting and amusing as you know how. If nothing else, it's good practice.

However, this shouldn't discourage you. The house organ editor has two other lures and with these, if you apply yourself, you can catch all the readers you need. First of all, as the company editor, you have information that the employee can get nowhere else. How successful this lure can be is demonstrated by countless company newspapers which carry nothing but information about the company and company-sponsored activities.

People who believe that you must print personals in order to get employees to read company news have a hard time explaining the success of these newspapers, because there isn't a personal in them anywhere. Yet, there is no question about their reader acceptance and the only possible explanation is that employees are eager for news about the place where they work and will read the publication that gives it to them.

RECOGNIZE WORKERS AS INDIVIDUALS

There is another way to catch the employee-reader—by giving him a sense of personal gratification. And lest you think that what I have said about a newspaper free from personals means that I have something against personals, let me tell you something I have observed in my years as a house organ editor: every day, some publication that carried no personals announces that it is going to extend its coverage to include them. But no publication ever says it's going to stop printing personals. The only way to do that is to stop printing altogether.

You see, the need of the industrial worker to be recognized as an individual is so real that the editor can, if he wishes, insure something better than 90 per cent readership by so simple a device as printing the names of 90 per cent of the employees in every issue. And this, of course, a great many editors are doing . . . to the despair of those who are concerned with the future of industrial journalism.

This leads us back to the beginning, right to the very heart of the whole problem. For the industrial journalist, it can never be enough to catch a reader. That reader has got to be influenced, persuaded, if you will, to the end that some useful company purpose is served. And printing the names of 90 per cent of the employees, though it may attract 90 per cent of the employees as readers, will not serve much, if any, useful company purpose.

BUT KEEP PURPOSE IN MIND

This is the obvious danger: that as an industrial editor you will become so enthralled with the business of catching readers that you forget that this is not your end purpose.

I give you this as the handwriting on the wall: the death warrant of your publication has been signed when your boss says: "Oh, sure, we have a house organ. The employees seem to like it. I don't know that it does us any good, but it certainly doesn't do us any harm." The house organ of which the management can say this, truthfully or no, is for sure doing some harm: it is wasting the company's money. Your employee-reader may not see the good that the house organ does, but the management should be able to see it in a very real and convincing form.

Never fool yourself that your publication cannot be made a dollars-and-cents, dividend-paying investment. First as last, you might as well understand that part of your job is to demonstrate the worth of the publication. You cannot hope to hide for long behind such words as "intangibles" and "good will" and "favorable reaction." What accidents cost—what it costs to train a new employee—what it costs to lose a customer—what waste and scrap and inefficiency cost—what public antagonism costs—these are not intangibles. The work of the house organ is to reduce some or all of these costs. It is, of course, the work of lots of others, too, and the failure of the house organ will affect the whole industrial relations program.

As an editor, you are going to have your own ideas of just how you intend to carry your share of the industrial relations load. You will probably want to extend your objective to include a share in the sales and community relations job, too. You may want to say, for instance, that your purpose is to show that your company is a good place to work; or that it is a human kind of corporation; or that it is a good corporate citizen; or that the people who work for your company are good people to work with. To the extent that you can convince your readers that these things are true—and if you don't think them true, for heaven's sake get another job!—you will have helped establish a favorable climate in which the other agents of industrial, public, and community relations can do their work.

H. O. IS FOR ALL EMPLOYEES

And when you think of employees, don't just think of production workers. Everyone who works for the company is an employee, and can be reached and influenced by the house publication. It is just as important for a graduate engineer to believe the people who work for your company are good people as it is for an elevator operator to believe it. A great deal of good may come out of the fact that a plant manager who raises orchids reads about a boiler tender at the far end of the plant who also raises them, or vice-versa.

There are even instances when it does good to print 125 items about 125 employees buying new cars . . . and what kind of cars. In the first place, it reminds management that parking facilities can be of primary importance. But, on top of that, what better proof do you want that a company is a good place to work than the news that substantial numbers of its employees are buying new cars, or new homes, or sending their kids to college?

But, here you see I am talking about personals that are something more than a list of names. These are personals that contain facts to substantiate a claim, even though the claim is never mentioned.

News, you probably tell your volunteer staff, can't be gathered in wholesale lots; it doesn't come that way. Well, readers can't be gathered in wholesale lots, either. One by one, employee-readers have to be reached, and persuaded. None of them is persuaded by any single thing he reads. Each has to be inched along so slowly that the point at which his opinion changes is never recognized.

MAKING A SALESMAN BETTER

Let's take, for instance, a young sales executive who believes that the company would be flat on its back if it weren't for the fact that he has tripled sales in his territory. So far as he is concerned, the production end of the job is a mechanical process . . . anybody can do it. But selling . . . that's something else again.

Yet, like most employees, he reads the company publication . . . not thoroughly, but at least he reads the part which gives him information or personal gratification. He gets some gratification from reading about the product he sells. He reads the cutlines under pictures and skims through the department news, looking for mention of his product.

Gradually he becomes familiar with the names of the people who work on his product. One day he notices that one of them is retiring. Another time he sees that one of them is getting married. Over many months, these people take on personalities. Then one day he reads that there are 250 people employed in the departments that make his product.

Being a person of vision, he finally sees that he is not alone. He is tied to the jobs of 250 other people. His relationship with the company has a new significance. His idea that the company depended only on him is gone. He is a better salesman.

Because he is a better salesman, those 250 people are a little more secure in their jobs. The company prospects are a little brighter. All because the house organ snagged a reader and influenced him.

Idealistic, you say. Of course. But this is one business where ideals have a way of becoming realities. It was some degree of idealism which led your company to sponsor a house publication . . . your company and over 6,000 others.

Leaders of industry, careful with their company's money, underwrite the house publication to the tune of several million dollars a year. And, oddly enough, it is the house organ with a clear-cut goal that is growing. Editors who want to grow need goals comparable to those of the people footing the bill.

BUILDING GOOD PRESS RELATIONS
General Motors Corporation

Public opinion, unlike advertising, cannot be bought. It has to be cultivated. One accepted method is the distribution of information about the company and its employees. If such information has genuine news value, editors will print it as a service to their readers. As one of the largest companies, General Motors is especially sensitive to its relations with the public. Here it tells its executives how to deal with the press.

Editors know that the most interesting stories in their papers are the ones about people. That's why they always welcome releases and pictures of home-town employes who are promoted, feted for long company service, or who receive awards for suggestions. Retirements are also news, and so are journeymen certificates given at the end of apprenticeship periods, and "old-timers" dinners. General Motors, in other words, is people and—*people make news.*

Here is a typical release that serves to strengthen local identification:

From:
(Name of Division)
      For Immediate Release

Promotion of John B. Smith, 31, of 1616 Main Street, to foreman in the parts warehouse at (Name of Division) General Motors, was announced this week.

Mr. Smith, who joined (Name of Division) in 1947, is a member of (church and clubs) and is active in (civic activities such as the Red Cross, Community Chest, etc.).

Mr. Smith served in the Navy during World War II, as a Machinist's Mate, 1st Class. His hobbies are fishing and all active sports, and he was a member of the plant's undefeated softball team last summer.

He and his wife Barbara, have two daughters, Irene, 8, and Joan, 4, and a son, John, Jr., 6.

A constant flow of news stories, such as this one, keeps the division and General Motors continually identified with individuals who *live next door* or *go to the same church* or *belong to the same organizations* as the local newspaper reader. Such stories contribute much toward making the plant, division and General Motors an *integral part* of the local community.

One of the most important aspects

Reprinted from *GM Lives Here*. Courtesy of General Motors.

of press relations is answering questions from newspapers, radio and television. It is an easy matter to develop good relations with reporters and editors—by answering promptly and reliably.

Reporters and radio commentators want as much information as they can get and they want it as quickly as possible. Most editors endeavor to tell both sides of a story involving controversy. They deal in facts, though, and only can use the facts that are at their disposal. They frequently are pressed to meet a deadline. If unable to reach someone in authority at the plant, they may disregard the plant's side of the story.

That's why it's important to *designate a responsible executive* to handle press, radio and television contacts.

Sometimes reporters and commentators cannot be given the information they seek for security or competitive reasons. If so, it's better to tell them such information is not available and give them the reasons why.

Good press relations can often nip in the bud a misunderstanding that, allowed to continue, might cost the division and General Motors a tremendous amount of good will. For instance:

Some time ago people in an eastern seaboard county were irritated over inability to get deliveries on a certain General Motors automobile. Their irritation was increased by the daily sight of a huge lot filled with the much-sought cars.

One day the editor of a local newspaper called a General Motors executive, told him rumors were spreading that the domestic automobile shortage was "a phony," that "automobile companies like General Motors are deliberately holding up delivery of new cars to intensify demand."

"I know you don't operate that way," he added. "So what's the explanation?"

The explanation was that the field-full of cars was designed for export. The steering wheels were on the wrong side for use in this country. Their movement was being held up by legal restrictions.

That paper and all the others in the country carried the story prominently. Good press relations ended the problem before it became serious.

YOUR EDITORIAL NEIGHBORS

In building good press relations it's important to become acquainted with members of the working press—managing editors, city editors, columnists, reporters, and photographers—those who gather and edit the day's news. In the case of radio—the station manager, program director, special events director, news editor, and commentators.

A good way to get better acquainted is to invite them for a day at the plant —have lunch, see new installations, see what's going on.

Some plants, for example, put on regular press luncheons or dinners two or three times a year. Top management attends and answers any questions the newsmen might have. But the fundamental purpose is just to get better acquainted—enjoy good fellowship.

Another plant, proud of its facilities for employe recreational activities, has for two years invited editors of all nearby community newspapers to an "Editors' Shoot." Trapshooting events are held at the range on plant grounds, with prizes and dinner as the climax.

The important things in developing good press relations are:

Knowing and understanding press and radio people in the area.

Preparing and furnishing news re-

leases, and pictures where possible, on newsworthy events.

Developing a reputation for prompt, adequate replies to requests for information.

Keeping up regular contacts with newsmen and radio and TV commentators.

Putting the press on the mailing list for educational materials, reprints of speeches, and other useful information.

TIPS ON TALKING BETTER

Dale Carnegie

What businessman has not had to talk around a conference table, or from a dais or rostrum? His effectiveness is of deep concern to him and just as important to his company. Dale Carnegie's methods have taught a great many businessmen to speak in public. At the time this article appeared, General Motors was offering the Dale Carnegie course to 80,000 salaried supervisors. Author of *How to Win Friends and Influence People*, Mr. Carnegie here answers fourteen questions asked by readers of a leading business publication.

1. THIS MAY SOUND SILLY, BUT LOTS OF OPERATING EXECUTIVES WONDER: WHY BOTHER TO LEARN TO SPEAK IN PUBLIC? WHAT'S IN IT FOR US?

Learning to speak in public can help you in these six ways:

1. I have been training adults to speak in public since 1912. If taught sensibly, public speaking is the best way ever yet devised to help a man develop poise, courage, and an abounding self-confidence. It works veritable miracles.

2. Your ability to stand before groups and express and sell your idea increases your ability for leadership.

3. In factory, shop, or general business management, the man who can express himself before his employees and his employers—the man who can put his ideas for improvement into spoken words, the man who can con- vince others that his ideas are sound— is the man who is going to get ahead.

4. If you develop the ability to speak effectively before groups, you will be more quickly recognized by executive management and more willingly fol- lowed by the men who work for you.

5. As you develop your ability to speak before business groups, you will also develop the ability to speak before civic groups in your community, and thereby increase your value and prestige in that community.

6. As you increase your value to the community, you become an inspiration to your children; and through this you teach them to be self-confident and courageous.

2. SHOULD I EVER TRY TO MEMORIZE A TALK?

Never, never memorize a talk word for word. If you do, you're almost sure to forget it. And if you do forget it,

Reprinted from *Factory Management and Maintenance*, August, 1952. Copyright by McGraw-Hill Publishing Company, Inc.

your audience will probably be glad. Nobody wants to listen to a canned speech.

Even if you don't forget your talk, it will probably *sound* memorized. You will probably have a far-away look in your eyes, and a far-away ring in your voice. You won't sound like a human being, trying to communicate with people.

Occasionally it will be necessary to use a direct quotation or cite exact figures in a talk. In such cases, it's always wise to have these written out, and to read them right off the card or sheet of paper.

If you were going to talk to only two listeners, you wouldn't dream of memorizing a talk. It would sound formal and silly and cold. It's just as silly to give a memorized talk to 200 or 2000 people as it is to two people.

3. HOW ABOUT SPEAKING FROM NOTES? DO YOU HAVE ANY SUGGESTIONS THAT MIGHT HELP US?

The kind of notes you use will naturally depend a lot on the kind of talk you plan to give, and on your knowledge of the subject.

Short, informal talks to small groups in the plant will rarely call for much more than a few quick reminders on the back of an envelope. Their biggest value probably will be to keep you from talking too long. For longer, more formal talks you'll want your notes to be a little longer, simply because you will probably have a larger number of key ideas to put across.

If you know your subject-matter thoroughly you may need no more than three or four key words or phrases—even for a long talk. And with a little practice, you'll find that you can often get along with no notes at all where you're really expert.

As a general rule, keep notes as brief as possible, while still covering every *main idea* you want to get into your talk.

I'm often asked about the physical appearance of notes. Anything that you can read will do, of course—from the traditional 3 x 5 inch cards on up in size.

Personally, I use 8½ x 11 inch paper for my notes (when I use any)—printed in black ink with letters nearly two inches high. When these notes are laid on a table, I can read them—if necessary—three feet away. I find this type of note far more efficient than small cards.

Another point: Never try to "hide" your notes. There's nothing to be ashamed of in using them. And your listeners won't even be aware of them—*unless you force them to.* If you play with notes, wave them around, or spend half your time peering down at them as if you couldn't read them, you're well on the way to ruining a potentially good talk.

4. HOW CAN I READ A SCRIPT WITHOUT SOUNDING AS THOUGH I'M READING?

There's just one answer: Practice! Familiarize yourself beforehand with what you're going to read. Read it aloud several times. Read it carefully, so that you will be thoroughly familiar with the meaning, and can get the "feeling" of the script.

It will help you more if you read to someone else and have your listener offer suggestions. You might underline in red pencil the words you wish to stress and indicate by vertical lines the pauses you want to make in your reading.

Admittedly, there are times when you simply *must* read something—a report, a paragraph, or even a full page excerpt from something. But if possible, avoid it. It's difficult to sound conversational and convincing while reading.

5. CAN YOU GIVE ME ANY RULES ABOUT TALKING SPEED AND VOLUME?

Forget about your speed! You've been getting along all your life without worrying about whether or not you talk at a "proper speed." Why start to worry about it now? If you know your subject, if you are excited about it, if you have an eager desire to tell your listeners about it—your normal speaking speed will be just right to put your talk over.

As for your speaking voice: Under most conditions your normal speaking voice, with slightly increased volume, will be sufficient. But if you should be scheduled to speak in a large room, and you're not familiar with the acoustics of the room, here are two things you might do:

1. Plan to arrive early enough so you can test conditions. Bring a friend with you and sit him in the back of the room. Take your place on the platform and start to speak. As you speak, your friend will tell you if your words are reaching the last row of seats.

2. When it isn't possible to arrive early enough to make the above test, perhaps you can seat your friend in the last row. Work out with him a simple signal whereby he can let you know if your voice is too weak.

It's possible that you may be able to do neither of the above. In that case, there's nothing wrong with stopping after your first few sentences and asking the audience "Can you people in the back of the room hear me?" After asking that question, I sometimes get a little chuckle from the audience by saying: "Well, if you can't hear me you *ain't* missed anything so far."

This question serves three purposes. First, it lets you know if you are being heard. Second, it gives you a moment's pause that helps to relax you on the platform. Third, it brings the audience into the act.

6. TO WHOM SHOULD I TALK? PICK OUT ONE PERSON IN THE AUDIENCE—OR WHAT?

Talk to the entire audience. When you first stand up to speak, directing your talk briefly to one person in the audience may give you the "feel" of conversation and make it easier for you to get over your nervousness. Once you have done this and are warmed to your audience and subject, you will automatically talk to the entire audience. You will get the feeling that you have in conversation at a dinner table. Perhaps there, too, you start talking to one person—but in a matter of a few moments, you will find yourself talking to everyone.

The above technique, however, is one that most speakers will use automatically once they start to speak on a subject that they have earned the right to speak about.

7. HOW FAR SHOULD I GO IN WORKING OUT EXACTLY WHAT I'M GOING TO SAY? SHOULD I WRITE OUT THE WHOLE TALK IN ADVANCE, AND SPEND TIME POLISHING THE LANGUAGE?

Go as far as you feel you need to in planning and organizing your *ideas*. Make notes which will serve as reminders to yourself.

But there are very few occasions when it's worth your while to waste time writing down the exact words you'll use in the talk. If you do write them out, your talk will *sound* written out. And that's exactly what you don't want.

It's far more important to be natural and easy and use conversational language, and to have sparkle and animation in your delivery.

Be sure that you talk about something you have earned the right to talk about. What's that? It's something you know as the result of study and experience. It's something you feel deeply about—that will well up out of you like a fountain when you get warmed up to speaking.

There will, of course, always be a few occasions when you *will* have to write out a talk in advance. Some technical societies demand it, for example. But even in such cases good speakers often depart from the prepared text. As a result they sound much less stiff and unnatural when presenting their ideas. This practice often drives newspaper reporters to distraction. But it gives your listeners the thing they really want—a chance to hear the *real* you, not a parrot reciting a prepared lesson!

8. WHAT ABOUT HUMOR, FUNNY STORIES AND THE LIKE?

Humor is one of the best ways of getting your audience into the palm of your hand. It's also one of the most dangerous techniques of speaking.

For every natural humorist, there are ten thousand people who linger under the false impression that they are humorists. They can't be funny, but insist on boring everyone by trying. So unless you're absolutely sure that the mantle of Mark Twain has descended on your shoulders, it's smart to avoid most temptations to be funny.

If you're in doubt about your ability to be humorous—just ask your wife!

Canned jokes, Pat and Mike stories, and radio comedian quips all have a sad tendency to fall flat when used by the average speaker. So, unless you *know* you have the talent to make them click, leave them out. And if you do have the talent, hold yourself in check. Remember that the jokes you tell should always be relevant to the point you're trying to make.

9. IN USING VISUAL AIDS (CHARTS, GRAPHS, PICTURES, ETC.) TO WHAT EXTENT CAN I RELY ON THEM TO TELL THEIR OWN STORY?

The answer to this question depends a great deal upon how familiar your audience will be with the points for which you use visual aids. If you were discussing the mechanism of a new machine in your shop with your employees, it would be necessary to explain at length. But if you were using a picture of a familiar piece of machinery to illustrate a point, you could skip over a detailed explanation. Again, use common sense.

As for charts and graphs, it is always wise to explain the purpose of the chart, what it proves or disproves and why it illustrates your point.

Here are a few simple rules for the use of exhibits:

1. Be sure your exhibit is large enough to be easily seen by everyone.

2. Be sure it actually illustrates your point.

3. If you must hold the exhibit in your hand, be sure that you hold it high enough to be seen by everyone. Don't hold it to one side and try to look at it yourself. You already know what it looks like, so hold it in front of your chest. The audience will see it in that position, and you will not be tempted to look around to one side to see it yourself.

4. Always talk to the audience—not to the exhibit.

5. When you have finished with it, *put it down!*

10. WHAT ARE SOME HINTS THAT WILL HELP ME MAKE THE BEST USE OF A MICROPHONE IF I HAVE TO USE ONE?

1. Be sure to find out in advance if there will be someone in charge of the microphone all during the time you are speaking. If there is, he will be able to increase the volume of your voice if you speak too low and decrease it if you speak too loudly. If there is a good, experienced man in charge of the microphone, you can forget all about volume. He will take charge of that.

2. When speaking into a microphone, stand with your feet planted firmly in one place. Do not move around. The microphone hasn't any legs. It can't follow you. Don't even turn your head too far to the right or left. Talk straight at the mike, or a few inches above it.

3. If possible, have a short rehearsal over the mike before the audience arrives.

4. Test out the mike. If it gives a mechanical reproduction—maybe you had better do away with it. If you are wondering whether or not you are being heard distinctly, stop and ask the audience for a show of hands. Asking for a show of hands pleases the audience. They like to be consulted. It breaks up the formality of a talk and will probably make you feel more at home.

All a good microphone does is bring the audience closer and make it more intimate. Pay no attention to it. In fact, you would be better off if you didn't even know it was there.

Recently I gave an address to the Missouri Farmers Association. They wanted to know if they could make a record of it. I said "Yes, but I am sorry you told me about it. I am going to try to forget it. If I am conscious that you are making a record of the talk, it may be slightly distracting. But, if I can forget it, it won't matter at all."

11. SOME PUBLIC SPEAKING TEACHERS EMPHASIZE PROPER BREATHING, "THROWING" THE VOICE, AND GRACEFUL GESTURES. HOW IMPORTANT ARE THESE THINGS, ACTUALLY?

Instead of worrying about your delivery, get busy and deal with the causes that produce it. A lot of harmful, misleading nonsense has been written about delivery of a speech. The truth is, when you face an audience, you should forget all about voice, breathing, gestures, posture, emphasis. Forget everything except what you are saying.

What listeners want, as Hamlet's mother said, is "more matter, with less art." Do what a cat does when she is trying to catch a mouse. She doesn't look around and say: "I wonder how my tail looks, and I wonder if I am standing right, and how is my facial expression? Am I breathing from my diaphragm?" No, indeed. That cat is so intent on catching a mouse for dinner that she couldn't stand wrong or look wrong if she tried. And neither can we in making talks if we are so vitally interested in our listeners and in what we are saying that we forget ourselves.

Let's not imagine that expressing our ideas and emotions before an audience is something that requires years of technical training such as we would have to devote to mastering music or painting. Anybody can make a splendid talk at home when he is angry. If somebody hauled off and knocked you down this instant, you would get up and make a superb talk. Your gestures, your posture, your facial expression would be perfect because they would be the result of an emotion deep within you.

Remember you don't have to learn to express your emotions. I have a little daughter six months old. She has never taken a lesson in how to express herself. However, if she is happy and wants to play, or if she is hungry and wants some milk, or if she is cold and wants a blanket wrapped around her, she can express her feelings as effectively as Sarah Bernhardt could in her most glorious days. We don't have to learn to express our feelings. We need to relax and forget ourselves and let our emotions express our feelings.

Our problem isn't to try to learn how to gesture and how to stand and how to speak with emphasis. Those are merely effects. Our problem is to deal with the causes that produce those effects.

Those causes are deep down inside us. They are our own mental and emotional attitude. If we get ourselves in the right mental and emotional condition and let ourselves go and forget we are making a speech, we will speak superbly. We won't have to make any effort to do it. We will do it as naturally as we breathe.

To illustrate, a rear admiral of the United States Navy once took my course. He had commanded a squadron of the United States Fleet during the First World War. He wasn't afraid to fight a naval battle, but he was so afraid to face an audience that he made weekly trips from his home in New Haven to New York City to attend the course. Several sessions went by, and he was still scared.

So one of our instructors, Elmer Nyberg, had an idea that he felt would get the admiral to forget himself and make a good talk. There was a chap with some left-wing ideas in this class. Professor Nyberg took him to one side and said: "Now don't let anybody know that I told you to do this, but tonight, just as a stunt, I want you to advocate the overthrow of the government by force. Do it just as a stunt. I want you to get the admiral so stirred up that he will forget himself and make a good talk."

That evening the speech hadn't gone very far when the rear admiral leaped up and shouted: "Stop! Stop! That's sedition!" Then the old sea dog gave this speaker a fiery lecture on how wrong he was.

Professor Nyberg turned to the naval officer and said: "Congratulations, Admiral! A magnificent speech!" The rear admiral snapped back: "I'm not making a speech; but I am telling that little whipper-snapper a thing or two." Then Professor Nyberg explained that it had all been a put-up job to make him forget himself.

This officer discovered just what all of us will discover when we get stirred up about a cause bigger than ourselves. We will discover that our fears of speaking will vanish, and that we don't have to worry about delivery.

Let me repeat: *Your delivery is merely the effect of a cause that preceded and produced it. So if you don't like your delivery, don't piddle around trying to change it. Get back to fundamentals and change the causes that produced it. Change your mental and emotional attitude.*

12. WHAT ARE SOME WAYS TO CONTROL "SPEAKERS' JITTERS"? HOW MUCH OF THIS "UPSET" IS ACTUALLY HELPFUL?

All speakers, no matter how well known or how familiar with public speaking, feel a slight nervousness as they start to talk. *Nervousness can be an asset. It is bottled-up energy.* Once a speaker gets into his talk, gets excited and animated, this nervousness releases itself in effective energy.

When I asked Gen. Alexander A. Vandergrift, former Commander of the U.S. Marines, whether a marine wasn't terrified when he first went into battle, he replied:

"Any man who says he isn't terrified under these conditions, is either weak-minded or a liar. But the thing to do in battle is to go right on. Keep busy and ignore your fears; and they will vanish." The same idea applies to talking to groups of people.

13. HOW CAN A MAN WHO KNOWS HE'S A POOR SPEAKER GET SOME EXPERIENCE, SO HE CAN IMPROVE BY PRACTICE?

The first thing to do to learn more about speaking in public is to take a public speaking course—a good, practical, common-sense course where each student will speak at least once a session.

Many academic courses in public speaking do not develop the ability to speak in public. Such courses often stress breathing, vocabulary, posture, graceful gestures, and even the right position of the tongue while speaking. If that is the correct way to teach speech—then I have been taking money under false pretenses ever since I taught my first class on Oct. 22, 1912. And I, who have been speaking before groups for 40 years, am all wrong. I don't know how I breathe or whether my epiglottis is functioning correctly —and I don't care.

I don't try to make graceful movements while gesturing. I would fail if I did. I spent the first 20 years of my life milking cows, plowing corn, and pitch-

ing hay—and my bodily movements are about as graceful as the movements of a Missouri mule. After all, who cares about my lack of graceful movements or my Missouri accent?

Remember that our listeners aren't interested in you or me. They're interested only in what we can *do* for them.

Continue to speak in public whenever you have the opportunity and have something to say. Welcome the chance to speak before your employees and employers. Seek speaking engagements in the community, for civic and charity groups.

As you gain in experience, you will continue to improve yourself as a speaker, as a citizen, and as an employee.

An excellent method to use to polish yourself as a speaker is to listen carefully to as many good speakers as possible. If you do that, you will learn some things you ought to do and some you ought not to do.

14. ANY OTHER SUGGESTIONS —THINGS WE'VE MISSED IN OUR QUESTIONS YOU THINK WE OUGHT TO WATCH FOR?

Here are a few points:

1. Don't try to be an arm-waving, loud-shouting, Senator Claghorn type of talker. Very few people can get away with such tactics. Moreover, today's audiences have little taste for fancy oratorical flights. Let your subject matter and the depth of your conviction about it determine the extent of your oratorical exertion.

2. Keep your head up, and look right at your audience. Even when you're reading something, you can develop the knack of seeming to be looking at your audience most of the time. Watch some good speakers giving ad-

dresses over your TV. Notice how they deliberately raise their eyes when they get near the end of a sentence, delivering the rest of the sentence looking straight out. Notice, too, that they choose a location for their notes that makes it unnecessary to bend their heads.

Many speakers give the impression that they're reading notes when actually they're not. Keep your head up, and you'll have no trouble.

Another advantage of doing so is that you'll be more alert to your audience. Telltale signs of inattention—fidgeting, sidetalk, newspaper reading, etc.—will warn you when you're failing to get your points across.

3. There's nothing like examples, illustrations, and quotations to help get ideas over, and to keep an audience interested. I believe a two-minute example can prove a point more effectively than an hour's preaching.

4. Above all else, do not talk too long. The hands of your watch will tell you precisely how long you have been speaking, but the hands of your listeners will tell you when you have talked too long. When your listeners twist and turn and look up at the ceiling or out of a window—or when they look at the hands of their wristwatches —then, brother, you have talked too long—even though it may not have been more than 20 seconds.

My final advice is this: *Always stop before your listeners want you to.*

YOU AND YOUR TELEPHONE
New York Telephone Company

If the telephone has given business a quick and personal way to communicate, it has also multiplied a natural hazard of distant communication: unintentional discourtesy. An expert on this problem is the New York Telephone Company which since 1912 has taught that "the voice with the smile wins." The service message that follows is designed to help the company's customers use one of the great tools of communication to their own best advantage.

"Oh yes, I know the company well. That's a good outfit to do business with—I've talked with them by telephone."

With people whose business starts and ends over the telephone *that* kind of recognition builds reputations.

When you talk on the telephone you become a public relations committee of one. Every time you pick up the telephone, you make a definite impression —good, bad, or indifferent—on the person at the other end of the line. Your voice, what you say and how you say it, is what reveals you to others. A pleasant personality is like a share of stock, and a cordial voice pays dividends.

The art of getting results by telephone—meriting good will, having people enjoy telephoning you—is largely a matter of dealing with others as you would have them deal with you. "Phone as you would be phoned to," is the way one successful salesman put it.

This booklet outlines methods of applying that principle.

"PHONE AS YOU WOULD BE PHONED TO"

The telephone provides communication by voice—the natural and quickest way of making your thoughts and personality known to others. You like to deal by telephone with people whose voices and telephone manners show them to be courteous, interested and alert.

Business people have become keenly aware of the value of good telephone habits. One company tells its employees, "The telephone, if properly used, will foster a spirit of friendliness within and toward our organization."

In a newspaper article which carried the headline "Pleasing Voice Now An Important Business Asset," correct telephone speech and cordial manner are rated *the foremost requirement* of employees who have telephone contacts with customers.

Charm schools now stress a pleasant speaking voice as one of the first requisites of natural poise.

It pays to have a good telephone personality. Whether you are an executive, secretary, switchboard attendant, salesman, clerk, or in some other position where you deal with people, success depends largely upon how you treat customers, make friends, create good will.

THE VOICE WITH A SMILE

If you were able to call yourself up, do you think you would be satisfied with what you hear?

If not, it's high time for you to try to improve your telephone personality.

If you train yourself to speak clearly and distinctly, you can make a good impression from that one feature alone.

You'll want to study your voice and speech.

Think about using the voice with a smile and putting it to work effectively every time you make or answer a call.

ARE YOUR CALLERS WELCOMED?

Do you want to hear how those voices at the office sound to others? Just call up your headquarters once in a while and listen with an attentive ear to the kind of welcome you get. If you were the head of the business, you'd find it helpful to rate the voices representing you. For instance, are they: Pleasing? or Curt? Helpful? or Indifferent?

If you are aware of the importance of a good telephone reputation, you'll be pleased and rewarded with the results. Your callers will too.

Let's look at some of the specific situations in telephoning.

HOW TO MEET YOUR CALLER

Never underestimate the power of a first impression. Remember you don't know who's calling. It may be one of the company's best clients, a prospective customer "shopping around," or a good friend. You'll want to make sure callers feel they are welcome—as you would if you met them face-to-face.

The welcome you offer is the promptness and pleasantness of your answer, the friendly attitude shown in your first greeting, even before you know who your caller is. This is good business. Time and again it actually determines the attitude of the caller and assures an agreeable tone to the interview.

People don't like to be kept waiting. Some of your callers may grow impatient with a delayed answer, and give their business to firms who will answer more promptly.

It's an interesting fact that a minute, while talking, flits by in no time at all, but those 60 seconds, while waiting, seem agonizingly long.

GET RIGHT TO THE POINT

When you answer, don't use such old-fashioned and time consuming words as "Hello" and "Yes?" The best way to answer is to identify yourself with your name, your company, department, or your telephone number—or combinations of these—depending upon what will be most helpful to the person calling:

"Mr. Brown," or "Brown" ("Mr." is optional).

"Duane Roberts and Company."

"Phillips Brothers, Mr. Johnson."

"Rug Department, Mr. O'Brien."

"MUrray Hill 4-9970."

Much can be accomplished simply by the tone of these few words of identification. The important welcome is conveyed by a tone of helpful cordial interest. A slightly rising inflection will imply "May I help you?" without actually saying the words.

The person calling responds by identifying himself. The conversation can then proceed with no time wasted on annoying questions like, "Who's this?" or "What company do you represent?"

Suppose you are answering someone else's telephone or a firm telephone. You'd want to say:

"Mr. Brown's office, Miss Smith."

"Phillips Brothers, Mr. Johnson."

SOME FACTS ABOUT TACT

When you answer another's telephone, it's often wise to find out who's calling—if the caller does not identify himself. The best way to do this, without appearing inquisitive and to make it clear that the information is for the other person, is to ask a question like one of these:

"May I tell him who's calling?"

Very often the person called may be talking on another extension or be busy with other pressing office business. At such times, steer clear of such remarks as: "Mr. Brown is busy right now." You'll earn a better response if you say:

"I'm sorry but Mr. Brown is talking on another extension. May I take a message for him, please?"

"Mr. Brown is at a meeting this morning. I'll have him call you as soon as possible."

This method indicates your willingness to serve. Incidentally, whenever you take a message for someone, be sure to write it down and leave it where the right person will see it.

Occasionally, when you answer your telephone, the caller may not give his name. If that's the way he wants it, don't make an issue of it. He'll call

again if it's important. Avoid abrupt questions like: "Who are you?"

Phrasing of a question can change it from one that may be resented to one that is willingly answered.

"May I ask who's calling, please?"

ATTENDING ANOTHER'S CALLS

If you are employed by a firm which has its telephones served by a private switchboard, remember that being transferred from one telephone to another is annoying to the person calling. No one likes to repeat the same message to several different people before reaching the one who can take care of him. If you can attend to a call yourself satisfactorily, always do so instead of transferring it. If this is not possible there are ways to handle it:

(1) You should offer to transfer the calling party to someone who can take care of him.

"I'm sorry, but I don't have that particular information. Our credit department is familiar with that problem. May I transfer you?"

(2) You may say that you'll refer the matter to the proper person. In some cases you will want to indicate that the proper person will call back. For instance:

"You want Mr. Brown's department. Shall I have him call you?"

When transferring calls be sure that the caller knows what you're doing. Signal the switchboard attendant *slowly* to get her attention. Explain the situation to her so she will not have to ask the person calling to repeat.

This saves time and assures the caller that he is getting courteous and efficient treatment.

"Will you please transfer this call to Mr. Brown in the credit department?" (Or use extension, if known.)

Wait for the attendant's reply to make sure she understands you.

EARNING YOUR WELCOME

Up until now you've been on the receiving end of a call. Now let's put you on the other end of the line. The situation is reversed, but the courtesy doesn't change. Your first job is to make a good impression to earn that welcoming answer.

Your self-introduction must be effective. You are the caller. You are in the position of wanting something or selling something. In either case, your success will be spurred by genuine, well-expressed courtesy.

If you're doing your job, you'll make every second count in your introduction.

Promptly give your own name and firm:

"This is Mr. Wood of Curtis and Sons."

If the one who answers the telephone is not the person you want, or does not identify himself, ask politely for that person.

"May I speak to Mr. Baker, please?"

If you're not interested in any particular person, simply state your wishes in a cordial way in the form of a request.

"The accounting department, please."

Incidentally, it's always helpful to speak politely to switchboard attendants, secretaries and others upon whom you depend for further assistance. They —like everyone else—respond to the voice with a smile.

BAD IMPRESSIONS

Perhaps you've had this experience —and annoyance. Your telephone rings. You answer, and a secretary's voice says, "Just a moment, please, Mr. Jones would like to talk to you." Then a wait. Finally, long lost Mr. Jones comes to the telephone.

Presumably Mr. Jones is busy and thinks he can save time by telling his secretary to get you on the telephone and then call him back. But he somehow forgets that he is the one who asks the favor of your time. Actually he requires you to waste your time, waiting for him.

Always being ready at the telephone, ready to greet the called person when he answers is the courteous way to telephone. It reflects favor on you and your company.

A busy executive said recently: "My time is precious. The time of the people with whom I usually talk is just as valuable. They don't like to have me keep them waiting and I share the sentiment when the situation is reversed. So the only sensible and fair thing is to be at my best, ready for the answer of the person I'm calling."

CONVERSATION ACCESSORIES

Few things sour a pleasant telephone conversation more than unnecessarily excusing yourself from your caller. Always have pencil and paper within arm's reach of your telephone. If you have to get some business records on file, first request permission from your caller and explain what you are going to do. Make it a point to justify your absence with:

"I'll check our files. Would you hold the line a moment, please?"

"Will you wait, please. I'll check our records."

When returning to the telephone, if there has been some delay in doing so, apologize for it and thank your caller for waiting. Add a few words of explanation if it seems necessary.

In some instances, it might require considerable time to get the information or to take required action. If so, offer to call back.

"I'm sorry but it may take some time

to get that information. I'll be glad to call you back in an hour."

ABSENCE WITHOUT LEAVE

When you expect to be away from your telephone, it's a good plan to leave word where you are going and how you can be reached—with the telephone number and extension—and when you will return. This is especially advisable if those who answer the telephone in your absence are not qualified to speak for you.

SORRY—WRONG NUMBER

Nobody likes wrong numbers. To operators they mean work to be done over again, work that could be devoted to handling another call. To the dial apparatus it means machinery that could be occupied with someone's "right" number. Everything possible is constantly being done by your telephone company to reduce the number of wrong connections.

Telephone users can help greatly by pronouncing telephone numbers distinctly, by dialing carefully and by obtaining telephone numbers from directories, private lists and letterheads, rather than trusting to memory. Keep your own personal list of telephone numbers.

When you are called by mistake, be quick to correct the person calling to avoid a prolonged waste of time on both ends of the line. A smart way to do this is to reply:

"I'm sorry, but this is not Phillips Brothers."

Tell the caller politely that he has the wrong number or extension.

If you sense you've reached the wrong number, verify it immediately. Don't say, "What's your number?" or "Who are you?"

If it's evident that some error has been made, express regret in some way, even if you were not responsible:

"I'm sorry. Please excuse it."

EASY DOES IT

When you have finished your visit, replace the telephone *gently*. Slamming it might cause a sharp crack in the ear of the person with whom you have been talking. All the personality pluses you have chalked up during a telephone conversation can be erased by such carelessness. Since you wouldn't slam the door after a face-to-face visit, be just as mindful in closing your "telephone door."

THERE'S A METHOD TO GOOD MANNERS

People like to be addressed by their names, together with titles when appropriate. In your conversations, sound the personal as well as the courteous note. Time-honored expressions of consideration, like "Thank you," "I'm sorry" and "I beg your pardon" are jewels when properly used in the art of making good impressions. So are such things as letting the other person finish what he has to say without interruption, avoiding argument or signs of impatience.

As to other details, such as the general character of your speech—the avoidance of slangy and careless expressions, and the use of good English—they are matters for each person to decide for himself. The most effective speech is correct speech, natural and unaffected. The best manners are those which are in good taste and prompted by a genuine consideration for others.

YOUR TELEPHONE NUMBER

Your telephone number is as vital as

your calling card. It should be featured as prominently as your address, on your business stationery, on billheads, promotional booklets, folders and in newspaper and other advertising.

Your telephone number is needed by the reader of your letter or advertising material, when he has the impulse to reach for the telephone.

For your own convenience you should keep a list of the telephone numbers you often call. A telephone numbers booklet, which provides a practical form for your telephone list, is yours for the asking at any New York Telephone Company business office.

A PARTNER—YOURS FOR SUCCESS

Your success by telephone takes thoughtful effort and intelligent observance of certain basic principles. It also takes a lot of common sense to develop a pleasant telephone attitude.

Keeping these factors in mind, make your telephone a "junior partner" in your business activities. It's a small investment, and the returns are big.

TIPS FROM ARMA'S READING COURSE

Ben B. Mason

If business executives read everything that came across their desks, they would have no time to do anything else. And yet there is a minimum they must read if they are to make informed and intelligent decisions. Many such executives see a solution to their problem in learning to read more efficiently. One company that conducted a speed reading course for supervisors found afterward that the training had actually doubled reading speed and increased comprehension by 15 percent. In the article below a personnel executive who participated in the program passes on to other executives some of the things he learned. "Arma" stands for the Arma division of the American Bosch Arma Corporation.

HOW YOU READ

Your eyes don't roll smoothly from one side of the printed page to another as you read. Instead they take a photograph of a group of words, then jerk ahead to the next group of words and take another photograph. The number of words your eye can photograph at once is called the *recognition span*. The time you spend on photographing the span is called *fixation*. The return of the eye from the end of the line to the start of the next is called *sweep*. When your eye is *sweeping*, all it sees is a blur. And since this effort is non-productive so far as reading is concerned, it should be done as rapidly as possible.

BREAK DOWN THESE BARRIERS

. . . *Eye defects.* Starting point for your reading improvement is a check of your eyes. You may need glasses. Unless defects are corrected, you may never increase your speed.

. . . *Narrow span.* By a conscious effort, you can extend your "eye photograph" so that you need make only three or four fixes per line.

. . . *Long fixation.* Holding the eyes in position too long for each photograph slows you down. You've got to keep forcing your eyes ahead.

. . . *Lack of concentration.* Don't daydream. Reading means work. Paying greater attention to what you're reading will speed you up.

. . . *Regressions.* Rereading phrases or sentences is one of the worst things you can do. In most cases, what you've missed isn't important. Ability to keep going ahead will depend largely on self-confidence.

. . . *Inward speech.* Saying the words to yourself—using your lips or any part of the vocal apparatus—can put brakes to your speed, particularly when you try to read fast.

. . . *Poor vocabulary.* A college education doesn't necessarily mean a good vocabulary. Try building yours by looking up in the dictionary words you're not sure of.

. . . *Weak thought organization.* Mental processes may be your block. As in decision-making, you've got to develop your ability to sort out the important from the trivial.

. . . *Lack of practice.* Over the years you and your eyes have developed a lot of bad reading habits. And these habits can be hard to break. But lots of practice reading the right way will overcome them. And experience shows that the new habits will stick.

FIND THE MAIN IDEA

Once you've mastered the mechanics of faster reading, the trick is to look for the main idea. Here's where you're most likely to find it:

. . . *In a business letter.* Start with head, then body, then signature.

. . . *In a newspaper article.* Read headlines and subheads, then first paragraph. Read on only if you want details.

. . . *In a technical journal* or business magazine. Read title, blurb and first paragraph. Skim the text for major theme, check subheads. Read last paragraph.

. . . *In a reference book or text.* Start with table of contents, introduction, and any preliminary notes. Read first and last chapters—reading first and last paragraphs of each and skimming rest of text. Treat other chapters the same way.

THE KEY TO RAPID READING

Norman Lewis

In the following article, an expert takes up the single most important way to increase reading speed. Mr. Lewis teaches at New York University. With Wilfred Funk he wrote *30 Days to a More Powerful Vocabulary*.

Actual reading, you recall, is done during the fractional seconds in which the eyes fixate, or remain at rest. The efficient reader absorbs a number of words at a single fixation: his unit of absorption is a complete phrase, a thought sequence. The inefficient reader absorbs single words, one at a time; or, if his reading is very poor, parts of words, individual syllables.

Thus, to cover a line of print such as is used in this book, a highly skilled reader might make three fixations. After coming to rest at the first point on a new line, his eyes need move only twice more before he is ready to make a return sweep to the beginning of the next line. After that first fixation, then, there are only two moments of blindness, only two fractional seconds in which his eyes are not reading. The unskilled reader, on the other hand, may have to move his eyes five or six or more times before he has read the whole line: there is a correspondingly greater number of moments of blindness, of nonreading. This extra time allotted by the poor reader to nonreading accounts in part for his slowness.

But only in part.

Suppose there are two boxes in front of you, both nailed to the top of a table. Box A contains a thousand marbles. Box B is empty. It is your job to transfer the marbles from one box to the other. How would you do it?

You could, if you liked, pick up the marbles one by one, dropping each into the second box before you picked up another from the first one. That would take a long time. The muscles in your arm and hand would become tired long before you finished. You would be doing your task in as inefficient a way as possible.

Or you could pick up the marbles two at a time. That would double your speed. But to do the job as quickly and as efficiently as possible, you would grab up handful after handful. The more you grabbed each time, the sooner you'd be through, and the less you would be likely to tire.

This analogy is admirably applicable to reading. If your eyes pick up only one or two words at a time, the process must perforce be a slow and painful one. However, if your eyes grab up "handfuls" of words, you can read like the wind. *The more words you absorb* in a single fixation, the faster you read. That is the second part of the reason why increased efficiency in eye movements can so radically speed up your reading.

There is a third, and very significant, factor.

Reading is not done exclusively by the eyes, of course; it is also done by the mind. If your eyes feed your mind one word at a time, you grasp the thought of a printed page choppily, disconnectedly; for thought comes in phrases, not in single words. There is practically no meaning at all in the single word "one." There is very little thought in the single word "bright." The word "morning," while it has a fuller significance by itself than either "one" or "bright," contains a good deal less meaning than the complete phrase, "one bright morning."

The word-by-word reader forces his mind to slow up because his eyes are continually feeding it words that are devoid, or nearly devoid, of meaning. His mind receives the impulse "one" —and must wait patiently for the second impulse, "bright"—and must wait still again for the third impulse,

"morning"—before it has something definite to work on.

The eyes of the efficient reader feed his mind, in a single impulse, a complete thought, "one bright morning." No dead spots. No waiting. No interruption to the process of thinking. Most important, no waste of time—for the idea, "one bright morning," can be absorbed by the eyes and registered in the mind more quickly than can the separate words that make up that thought.

In reading, the whole is more significant than the sum of its parts. The "whole" is an idea, a thought; the parts are individual words which, by themselves, one by one, are generally useless for comprehension.

The third factor, then, is that the reader who takes in more words in a single fixation understands quicker; and, since the final purpose of reading is to understand, the more instantaneously the thought of a printed line is grasped, and the more smoothly the mind and eyes co-operate, the more rapid the entire process becomes.

The key to rapid reading is the absorption by the eyes of large numbers of words at each fixation. . . .

BE A GOOD LISTENER YOURSELF
Alfred G. Larke

Listening is indispensable to understanding. It also has a therapeutic value for the person listened to. Thus listening is an integral part of communication and human relations, and one that deserves the close attention that businessmen are now paying to it. Mr. Larke is employer relations editor of *Dun's Review and Modern Industry.*

How to speak clearly and effectively is the subject of innumerable executive training courses, mail-order and other. Given a free choice, executives on the way up, at least, will elect a course in public speaking as their first preference. And, in recent years, instruction in reading has had increasing vogue. Everyone is learning to read faster and more efficiently.

Comparatively rare, however, is instruction for the individual in how to listen.

A poor speaker finds out the facts of his disability fast, when his audience falls asleep on him, or the man he is trying to persuade stays unsold. And, as the amount of paper-work in business increases, an executive may soon find himself snowed under if he cannot fill his "out" basket as fast as the office mailboy fills the "in."

But poor listening ability appears harder to detect in oneself. The other fellow establishes quality control on one's speaking, but only the listener and slow developments of time can check up on listening skill.

Because listening seems as natural as breathing, unless a man is deaf, it has been necessary to prove that listening abilities differ. Some work in this line has been done by Professor Ralph Nichols, professor of speech at the University of Minnesota, and by Dr. Paul Rankin at Ohio State University.

Methods Engineering Council, Pittsburgh, impressed by Dr. Nichols' observations on listening, incorporated a course in listening in a number of its executive training courses, and found that trainees who started off with instruction in listening got more out of the following sessions than those who did not have an opportunity for such advance instruction.

On the basis of tests at the end of the courses, according to Warren Ganong, director of training, those who had instruction in listening achieved marks 12 to 15 per cent better than those who did not have it.

Another check the Council uses is to read a short article to a group, then give them a series of twelve multiple-choice questions to answer which will

From April 1955 issue of *Dun's Review and Modern Industry.* Copyright 1955 by Dun & Bradstreet Publications Corporation.

indicate their receptive and reflective comprehension—how much they retain of what they have heard. At best, the testees are about 25 per cent effective at listening, according to Col. Donald E. Farr, vice-president of the organization.

Farr cites Dr. Rankin as establishing from a survey of "management men's" activities that about 70 per cent of their day is spent in communication, and 45 per cent of that 70 per cent in listening (speaking, 30 per cent; reading, 16 per cent; writing, 9 per cent).

No breakdown is given as between top administrators and middle- and lower-level executives and supervisors, nor among the various purposes for listening.

The obvious main reason for listening is to learn what the other man has to say. But there is at least one other good reason: to give the speaker or speakers the satisfaction of getting something off their chests that has been bothering them.

This second reason may sound like something that has been dug up since Freud, but as a matter of fact, the morale-building value of letting a man talk himself out has been recognized for at least 4,400 years.

Back about 2400 B.C., one of the pharaohs, Ptahhopet, expressed it neatly in his instructions to his viziers and other far-flung officials, in these words:

"An official who must listen to the pleas of clients should listen patiently and without rancor, *because a petitioner wants attention to what he says even more than the accomplishing of that for which he came.*"

The kind of listening the pharaoh asked for is a sort of human relations therapy. Its purpose is more to show respect for the speaker than to gain knowledge of what he has to say—though woe betide the listener who betrays such a purpose.

The whole practice of non-directive counselling is based on this kind of listening, and it is advised by personnel experts both for hiring and for exit interviews, as well as for discussions of grievances and, indeed, sometimes for collective-bargaining sessions.

In most cases where a top executive needs to listen well, however, chances are it is a much more simple purpose that is to be served—getting the most from what others have to say.

How many sales have been lost because the salesman talked too much? How many ideas have been lost because the man who might have received them and made use of them was concentrating on how to break into the conversation, instead of how to absorb its meat? Many men have talked themselves out of jobs, orders, loans, because they were so intent on telling their story they found no time to listen to the other man's. Or because, being agile mentally, they assumed they knew what the other man was going to say, said it for him—and missed what he really said.

Dr. Earl Planty, executive counsellor for Johnson & Johnson, New Brunswick, N.J., says, "By far the most effective method by which executives can tap ideas of subordinates is sympathetic listening in day-to-day informal contacts. . . . There is no full-blown system that will do the job in an easier manner. . . . Nothing can equal an executive's ability to hear."

Dr. Nichols has compiled a list of eight bad habits that work against good speaking:

1. Hop-skip-jump listening. Average thinking time (400 words per minute) exceeds average speed of talking (125 words). The busy executive therefore

falls into the habit of taking outside excursions in thought during another's conversation. When his attention rushes back, he finds the speaker has got ahead of him. Correction: Use the extra time thinking not of irrelevancies but of such related matters as, "What points are already made?" "What facts are not being brought out?"

2. Fact listening. Attempting to spot "just the facts" can be confusing. It's better to go after the main ideas and weigh facts against them.

3. Emotional deafness. Words and phrases like "Communist," "red tape," "taxes," excite the listener emotionally and tend to deafen him to what is actually said. Deep-seated opinion or prejudices will trip up good listening. In planning embarrassing questions or a smart retort, the listener can miss the true point.

4. Premature dismissal. Some men, feeling they know in advance that a subject will be boring or too difficult, close their minds, let them wander to something more interesting. Yet, the most uninteresting or difficult subject often offers worthwhile ideas to chew upon.

5. Pretended attention. Some think they can get away with pretended attention. They not only waste time but seldom fool the speaker.

6. Criticizing speaker's appearance. A lisp or rumpled clothing has little to do with the value of a talk. Save the criticism until it's over and you know what the speech was worth.

7. Yielding to distraction. When outside hubbub or inner turmoil competes with the speaker, it's easy not to listen. Good listeners fight distractions by doing what they can to reduce outside noise, keep minds on what's being said.

8. Pencil listening. One listens with the ears, not with a pencil, and note-taking seldom improves retention. The note-taker becomes so involved in writing he often misses the sense, like a proofreader looking for errors instead of for meaning.

Good listening habits result largely from a turn of mind. The more one accepts the philosophy that everyone has something worth listening to, the more one gets out of listening.

Exercises

"Why Study English?" by Dwight Van Avery

1. Write a 400-word summary of General Electric's answer to the question, "Why Study English?"
2. Taking your cue from this article, write a theme on "Why Study Mathematics?" "Why Study History?" or "Why Study Economics?"
3. The author says in effect that one's proficiency in language depends on one's attitude. Write a theme entitled, "My Attitude Toward Good English." Write what you really feel, not what you think the instructor wants you to say.
4. Write a theme on one of the following topics, all suggested by this article:
   a. English Beyond the Classroom
   b. My Biggest Mental Block
   c. Literate People Aren't Necessarily Snobs
   d. The First Time I Saw ——————— (Name a place or thing or event that excited you.)
   e. Is Correct Spelling Necessary?
5. What do you consider to be the most important point in this article? Discuss.

"What Your Letters Reveal About You," by J. Harold Janis

1. Choosing a single limited topic suggested by this article, write one of the series of *Better Letters* bulletins for The Hanover Bank (see pp. 113–115).
2. For a business publication like *Factory Management and Maintenance* (see pp. 79–86 and 93–94), write an article entitled "Six Ways to Write Better Letters." Write it as an interview with Mr. Janis.
3. Write a letter of condolence to a close relative or associate of a person of your acquaintance who has died recently.
4. Write a letter to your instructor in this course asking to be excused from the next class meeting. Request the assignment for the following meeting.
5. Write a letter to a department store in your town or nearby city ordering for yourself three different items of wearing apparel as actually advertised in your newspaper. Assume that you are enclosing a check or money order for the proper amount.
6. Assume that the Economics Club of your college has asked the Dean to buy a good-will advertisement on behalf of the school in the souvenir program of the annual banquet. It is against the policy of the college to place such advertisements. Write the reply for the Dean's signature in a way that will not offend.
7. Write to a well-known company asking for material for a college report.
8. Write a letter of appreciation to one of your professors who has sent you a congratulatory note upon your election as class president.
9. Assume that a friend has sent you a basket of grapefruit from Florida at Christmastime. Write an acknowledgment.

"I Think I'll Write to the Manufacturer," by Ruth Leigh Sclater

1. Write a single sentence expressing the idea of this article.
2. Write a paragraph telling why this article is good business for *Good Housekeeping* as well as good journalism.
3. Discuss the ways in which the author gets her readers' point of view.
4. Write a composition in which you support with internal evidence the idea that the author has an intimate knowledge of her subject.

5. Have you had any experience in writing to companies to make complaints, suggestions, or requests? If so, indicate the nature of your correspondence and give your impressions of the replies.

6. Write a letter to the manufacturer complaining about the performance of some article (radio, typewriter, washing machine, car, etc.) that you or your family own.

7. Write a letter of suggestion to the manufacturer of a nationally known product which you have used.

8. Write to the manufacturer of a nationally advertised product asking where in your neighborhood the product can be bought.

"How to Organize and Write Effective Technical Reports," by Ralph A. Richardson and C. A. Brown

1. Write a paragraph using as your topic sentence one of the five criteria of a good report listed early in this article.

2. Write a paragraph clearly differentiating the four kinds of technical reports.

3. Do you think the authors' suggestions about organizing the technical report are also applicable to your college reports? Explain.

4. The authors say that "the application of the rules of good grammar and composition is a prerequisite to quality report writing." Elaborate on this statement, getting any help you can from the article itself.

5. Compose a topical outline of this article, such as that which may have guided the authors.

6. Discuss this article from the point of view of the selection, arrangement, and development of ideas. In what other ways do the authors set a good example for their readers?

"How to Write a Memo," by Shepherd Mead

1. Discuss the elements of humor in this article.

2. In the vein of Shepherd Mead write a seriocomic theme on one of the following topics:

a. How to Get a College Degree Without Really Trying

b. How to Write a Theme

c. How to Impress Your Instructor

3. Write a *serious* memorandum on The Wicket Situation.

4. Discourse on the names invented by the author: Pierrepont (Ponty) Finch, J. B. Biggley, Cottery, Fribble, Lightly, etc.

"An Open Letter to Novice House Organ Editors," by Audrey E. Heusser

1. Discuss the main editorial difference between employee house organs and publications with paid circulations.

2. What is a "personal"? What point does the author make about personals in employee publications?

3. Discuss the author's view of "scare" stories. Do you see any relation between such stories and the use of the negative in business letters?

4. Assume you are the editor of a house organ published by the manufacturer of Rainbow sports cars. Write one of the following stories, supplying the details:

a. Jim Allen of the welding department has just returned from a two-weeks' trip with his wife and two children. He drove a Rainbow sedan.

b. George Traubel of the maintenance department is sending his son David to

Cornell next fall, where he will study engineering. George came to work for the company right after his marriage twenty-seven years ago. He also has two married daughters and a grandson.

c. A fire in the bookkeeping department, caused by a carelessly thrown lighted cigarette, was put out at once because of the quick thinking of Anna Merston. Anna came to work as a payroll clerk last October.

d. Mary Penton was awarded $25 for a suggestion that makes possible a reduction in the number of carbon copies needed for purchase requisitions from four to three. Mary is a file clerk in the purchasing department. She won $10 for another suggestion in May of last year.

5. In Section 9 you will find an employee house-organ article entitled, "The Sea Around Our Cables." What do you suppose Mrs. Heusser would think of it? Support your answer by specific references to both articles.

"Building Good Press Relations," General Motors Corporation

1. Following the General Motors pattern, write a news bulletin on one of the following subjects for release to local or home-town newspapers. Invent any necessary details.

a. A member of your family is going to be married.

b. You have returned to college for your sophomore year.

c. Someone you know has received a job promotion.

d. Your parents are leaving on the *Constitution* for a six-weeks' tour of Europe.

2. Suppose one of your professors has written a popular book in his specialty. Write a memorandum suggesting ways in which he might publicize the book.

3. Select a large men's or women's wear store in the vicinity of your home or school and write a letter to the proprietor, assumedly at his suggestion, proposing ways to get free newspaper publicity for the store.

4. Suppose a local branch bank was about to move temporarily into the main office a short distance away because the branch building was to be torn down and replaced by a new bank building. Considering the inconvenience and the possibilities of public misunderstanding, suggest some of the positive steps the bank might take with the coöperation of the local press.

"Tips on Talking Better," by Dale Carnegie

1. Following Dale Carnegie's suggestions, deliver a three-minute talk to your class on a subject decided in consultation with your teacher. Submit your notes to the instructor after the speech.

2. What do you think of Dale Carnegie's advice about memorizing a talk? Discuss briefly.

3. Write a theme on your first public speaking experience.

4. Dale Carnegie is of course directing his remarks to business people. Point out the ways in which the author has adapted his article to his readers.

5. Write a theme on the validity of Carnegie's argument that learning the techniques of delivery is unimportant. If you are taking public speaking, it is suggested that you first discuss this point with the instructor.

6. Prepare a chart (actual size) to accompany a talk on using the library effectively. You need not deliver the talk unless your instructor requests it.

7. Who was Senator Claghorn? If you do not know, see if you can find out.

8. What does Dale Carnegie say about public speaking that also applies to business writing? Discuss.

9. From your own experience, relate on paper a humorous story suitable for recital to your class.

"You and Your Telephone," New York Telephone Company

1. List five specific rules for telephone courtesy.
2. Write the copy for a small pamphlet designed to be put in the hands of the telephone operators of your college. Give specific directions for handling telephone calls of the kind you would expect your college to receive.
3. Write mainly in dialogue a report of a recent telephone conversation that caused you some annoyance because of bad telephone manners.
4. Out of your imagination write a theme on one of the following topics. Use any treatment you see fit.
   a. Jingle, Jangle—It's the Telephone
   b. A Picture of Modern Business Without the Telephone
   c. Don't Write—Telephone
   d. How to Make a Telephone Call
   e. A Dramatic Telephone Call

"Tips from Arma's Reading Course," by Ben B. Mason

1. Check your reading habits against the points made in this article. Write a report on your conclusions.
2. Do you believe your vocabulary is adequate for your reading needs? Write a theme supporting your answer.
3. Write a theme on your powers of concentration for reading. Where do you do your reading? Do noises and people distract you? Under what conditions do you read best? These are some of the questions you might try answering.
4. In a textbook you are now using, refer to the chapter immediately following the last chapter you have read. After skimming the contents, write a synopsis in the author's own words. Borrow from headings, topic sentences, summary paragraphs, etc. See how fast you can do this assignment. Note at the bottom of the theme the total time both reading and writing have taken you.

"The Key to Rapid Reading," by Norman Lewis

1. Repeat the theme sentence of this selection. Explain it in a paragraph.
2. Name and discuss briefly the three factors that explain why increased efficiency in eye movements can materially speed up reading.
3. Try reading the columns of this book with two or three eye fixations per line. Practice until your self-consciousness vanishes and you become fully aware of what you are reading. Write a paper describing your experience.
4. Write a theme on one of the following topics:
   a. I Am a Slow (or Fast) Reader
   b. Must College Students Read Too Much?
   c. Some Bad Reading Habits I Have Observed
   d. I Went to a Reading Clinic
5. In a paragraph comment on Mr. Lewis' use of the "marbles" illustration. Why is it effective?

"Be a Good Listener Yourself," by Alfred G. Larke

1. Define "listening" in the sense in which the author uses it.

2. Write an analysis of your own listening habits and tell what you can do to improve them.

3. Write a theme on one of the following topics, blending ideas in this article with your personal experiences:

    a. Learning by Listening

    b. In One Ear—and Out the Other

    c. The Closed Mind

    d. Note-Taking Versus Listening

4. What is nondirective counseling? With the help of library sources, write a report on nondirective counseling in business.

5. Make a study of the proportion of your time you spend in communicating, and write a report on your findings. Give separate percentages for listening, speaking, reading, and writing. Include a chart or graph with your report.

3

The Symbols of Communication

Whether a businessman is inventing a trademark, compiling a set of figures, or just dictating a letter, he is using symbols to communicate. Because these symbols—mainly words and figures—only stand for things and are not the things themselves, they challenge the user to select them with an awareness of what they will mean to the reader or listener. The problem of communication is further complicated by the strong hold of words upon the emotions and the common use of words and figures for their effect rather than for their accuracy.

As the following readings suggest, anyone who wishes to use the language of business proficiently needs to cultivate a large stock of words and to develop a sensitivity to the character of words and to their meanings and nuances. He needs also to sharpen his knowledge of human nature.

THE LANGUAGE OF BUSINESS
William H. Whyte, Jr.

"Not so long ago," writes Mr. Whyte, in introducing the article from which the following excerpt is taken, "the businessman used to take his language pretty much for granted. . . . But no longer. . . . In company after company, executives have been setting up 'writing clinics' to scour management copy, staging correspondence-improvement courses, holding school in conference and public-speaking techniques, and, at the very least, peppering subordinates with 'For-God's-sake-won't-you-people-learn-to-use-English-around-here' memos." All this, concedes Mr. Whyte, is clearly to the good. Whereupon he himself takes a look at two aspects of business English and throws in for extra measure "The Composite Business Speech." Mr. Whyte's article was part of his *Fortune* series on business communication, later published in book form under the title, *Is Anybody Listening?*

. . . Almost invariably, businesese is marked by the heavy use of the passive construction. Nobody ever *does* anything. Things *happen*—and the author of the action is only barely implied. Thus, one does not refer to something, reference is made to; similarly, while prices may rise, nobody *raises* them. To be sure, in businesese there is not quite the same anonymity as is found in federal prose, for "I" and "we" do appear often. Except when the news to be relayed is good, however, there is no mistaking that the "I" and "we" are merely a convenient fiction and that the real author isn't a person at all but that great mystic force known as the corporation.

Except for a few special expressions, its vocabulary is everywhere quite the same. Midwesterners are likely to dispute the latter point, but a reading of approximately 500,000 words of business prose indicates no striking differences—in the Midwest or anywhere else. Moreover, in sounding out a hundred executives on the subject, *Fortune* found that their views coincided remarkably, particularly so in the matter of pet peeves (principally: "please be advised," "in reference to yours of . . . ," "we wish to draw attention," "to acknowledge your letter"). The phrases of businesese are everywhere so uniform, in fact, that stenographers have a full set of shorthand symbols for them.

Because of this uniformity, defenders of businesese can argue that it doesn't make for misunderstanding. After all, everybody knows the symbols, and, furthermore, wouldn't a lot of people be offended by the terseness of more concise wording? There is something to this theory. Since businesese generally is twice as wordy as plain English, however, the theory is rather expensive to uphold. By the use of regular English the cost of the average letter—commonly estimated at 75 cents to $1—can be cut by about 20 cents. For a firm emitting a million letters a year, this could mean an annual saving of $200,000. Probably it would be even greater; for, by the calculations of correspondence specialist Richard Morris, roughly 15 per cent of the letters currently being written wouldn't be necessary at all if the preceding correspondence had been in regular English in the first place.

Where do the terms of businesese come from? Most, of course, are hand-me-downs from former generations of businessmen, but many are the fruit of cross-fertilization with other jargons. A businessman who castigates government bureaucrats, for example, is at the same time apt to be activating, expediting, implementing, effectuating, optimizing, minimizing, and maximizing—and at all levels and echelons within the framework of broad policy areas. Similarly, though he is amused by the long-hairs and the social scientists, he is beginning to speak knowingly of projective techniques, social dynamics, depth interviewing, and sometime soon, if he keeps up at this rate, he will probably appropriate that hallmark of the sound sociological paper, "insightful." Businesese, in fact, has very nearly become the great common meeting ground of the jargons.

Why do people who in private talk so pungently often write so pompously? There are many reasons: tradition, the demands of time, carelessness, the conservative influence of the secretary. Above all is the simple matter of status. Theorem: the less established the status

of a person, the more his dependence on jargon. Examine the man who has just graduated from pecking out his own letters to declaiming them to a secretary and you are likely to have a man hopelessly intoxicated with the rhythm of businesese. Conversely, if you come across a blunt yes or no in a letter, you don't need to glance further to grasp that the author feels pretty firm in his chair.

The application of euphemism, a favored device of businesese, further illustrates this status principle. Take the field of selling. At the top of the ladder you will find a great many people in it: *sales* managers, vice presidents for *sales*, etc. As you go down the ranks, however, it becomes difficult to find people in this line of work. Field underwriters, estate planners, merchandising apprentices, social engineers, distribution analysts, and representatives of one kind or another, yes. But *salesmen*? Rarely.

Not only does businesese confer status, it protects it as well, by its magnificent usefulness for buck passing and hedging. "All you have to remember," one executive says, "is the one basis which characterizes all such intra-communication: let the language be ambiguous enough that if the text be successfully carried out, all credit may be claimed; but if the text be unsuccessfully carried out, a technical alibi can be set up out of the text itself."

For this purpose there is a regular subglossary of businesese. Most notable terms: "in the process of," "at this time," "under consideration," "in the not-too-distant future," "company policy," and, when one is unable to explain something properly, "obviously." People who have to submit periodic reports to their superiors are particularly dependent on such terms—salesmen, for example, would have a hard time if they couldn't report of some prospects that they were "very impressed." ("I am allergic to that word," says one sales manager. "It results in so few orders.")

The full application of businesese to hedging occurs when more than two heads are put to work on a problem. As the members of top management sit around the table, a relatively simple policy statement is introduced for discussion. This is kicked around a bit, as the saying goes, for though it certainly is a fine statement, couldn't agree with it more, there are just a few little angles and suggestions that maybe ought to be noted. Thereupon each executive, much as a baseball captain grasps a bat in choosing up sides, adds his qualification, until finally the original statement has been at once pointed up, toned down, given more dignity, made more forceful, altered to anticipate possible objections, concretized, amended, and resolved. Now no longer a mere statement but a philosophy, or collection of philosophies, it is turned over to the Public Relations Department to give to the waiting public. There is nothing, as so many people say, quite like what you get when everybody on the team works together.

REVERSE GOBBLEDEGOOK

Besides written businesese, there is another and far more influential category of business English. Generally, it is found in the spoken language of business—in particular, that brand to be heard at the banquet table, the convention, and the conference table.

It might best be called *reverse gobbledegook*, for in almost every outward respect it is the opposite of written jargon. Where written jargon is multisyllabic, the other is filled with short terse words; its sentences are short and their construction so much more active than passive that exclamation marks occur almost as frequently as periods.

It is English that is on the beam, English with its feet on the ground; in short, *shirt-sleeve* English.

Thanks to reverse gobbledegook, the less you have to say, the more emphatically you can say it. All one has to do is use certain hard-hitting expressions, and refer as frequently as possible to the fact that these expressions are being used. A sure forewarning of its onrush, accordingly, is a prefatory announcement by the speaker that he is not going to beat around the bush, pull any punches, pussyfoot, use two-dollar words, or the like. The rest is inevitable; so standardized are the expressions of reverse gobbledegook that an audience would be stunned to attention were a single one of them altered by so much as a word. (One of these days a clever speaker is going to capitalize on this. "Gentlemen," he will say, "I offer a panacea.")

As a result, reverse gobbledegook can be self-defeating; that is, since its whole effect lies in the dynamic quality the words convey, their constant use tends to neutralize them. This can be overcome, however, by adding strengtheners—so that, in a very real sense of the word, it cannot be overemphasized that you sincerely, and unquestionably, meant what you said in the first place.

Like written businesese, reverse gobbledegook also confers status. For this purpose, it provides a sort of slang that, skillfully applied—particularly at the conference table—will impart to the user an appearance of savviness, cooniness, and general know-how. Want to mark yourself as a comer in the advertising field? Speak, then, of fun stories, sweet guys, the hard sell, straw men you set up to back into, and points you can hang your hat on.* For each field

* Other current advertising favorites: "let's pull all the stops out on this one"; "let's noodle this one"; "let's sneak the message across"; "we'll touch all bases on this

you will find a subglossary, and, common to all of them, such universal terms as "play it by ear," "the pitch," "the deal," and the many expressions built on the suffix "wise." ("Budgetwise, Al, the pitch shapes up like this . . .")

Another characteristic of reverse gobbledegook is its dependence on analogy and metaphor. During a single banquet you may find business problems equated with an airplane, a broad highway, a boat being rocked, a river, a riverbank, a stream, a bridge, a train, a three-legged stool, and, sometimes, three or four of these things at once in which case the passage is generally summed up with something like "It's as simple as that," or "That's all there is to the problem." (From a recent speech: "So business enterprise of America is trying to hone a sales force into the cutting edge of an economy and there is a virus running rampant in the flock. Security-mindedness is a log across the stream when it comes to developing the optimistic salesman outlook.")

Outstanding is the great American football analogy. No figure of speech is a tenth as seductive to the businessman. Just why this should be so—baseball, curiously, is much less used—is generally explained by its adaptability to all sorts of situations. Furthermore, the football analogy is *satisfying*. It is bounded by two goal lines and is thus

---

one"; "means absolutely nothing to the lay mind"; "we'll get plus value on this one"; "it was quite a hassle"; "let's not hassle over this."

Journalists laugh and laugh at this sort of thing. Just why, it is difficult to say, except possibly that being less inventive, they prefer to hang on to the old expressions rather than coin new ones. Terms now nearing the end of the run (including some of *Fortune's*): ambivalence, dichotomy, schizophrenic, "two hours and four martinis (beers, etc.) later"; "it's as difficult (easy, etc.) as it is complex (difficult, etc.)"; "their profits (feelings, etc.) are showing."

finite. There is always a solution. And that is what makes it so often treacherous.

For analogy and metaphor can be insidiously attractive substitutes for thought. They are not, of course, when fleetingly used, when, as H. W. Fowler puts it (in *Modern English Usage*), they "flash out for the length of a line or so and are gone," but this is rarely the case in reverse gobbledegook. The user starts innocuously enough; his policy is *like* a thingamajig in one respect. But only the stanchest mind can resist the analogy further. Before long he is entwined, and unconsciously operating on the premise that his policy *is* a thingamajig. The language, in short, has molded thinking, and the results can be a good bit more serious than a poor speech.

The mishaps of one consumer-goods corporation illustrate this hazard. Not so long ago, the men who owned the company were casting about for a Goal. Up to then it had been money. But now they had acquired a lot of it, they were getting on in years, and anyway it didn't sound good. And so, on this enlightened-goal problem, the Chief fell to pondering at the conference table. When you get right down to it, the company was just like a big football team. You don't win unless you have a good team, do you? You could say that again. Well, before he gets a good team, what does the coach have to do? Very simple. He has to go out and find good players. Just thinking out loud, mind you, but wasn't the big job then to get the right recruits?

Almost automatically, this was mimeographed as the company's rationale—"The Touchdown Play" it was called—and before long executives were spending almost as much time on the new trainees as they were on their regular jobs, and when they weren't doing this, they were scouring the colleges for more. Everything went swimmingly; the policy was soon the wonder of the merchandising world; the top executives were suffused with a sense of enlightenment—and the place was jammed with eager young men.

In only one respect did the analogy break down. A year later practically all of the competition came out with a new product embodying a notable technical advance. Our company didn't. It was still getting the team ready.

Now with almost every use of the cliché and stereotype mentioned so far, a better case could be made out for the use of simple, unhackneyed English. It is a mistake, however, to be too rigorously critical on this score. Since the symbols of language convey emotion as well as communicate facts and ideas, many a prefabricated phrase has become inextricably tied with certain emotional responses. This infuriates the semanticists—"intensional thinking" is their cuss word for it—but a good part of business has been built on it. The American sales meeting, certainly, would be quite impossible otherwise.

Furthermore business, like many another occupation, is governed by a ritual as rigid as the steps of ballet, and while the efficient executive makes fun of all this, he has the good sense to know when to put it to use himself.* The dinner for the retiring employee, for example; for years this has been prime fodder for short-story writers. But what if the toastmaster were to dispense with the timeworn expressions and thus tacitly concede what everyone knows to be nothing less than the truth: that old Charlie has been getting in everybody's hair for the last fifteen

* Since a large proportion of businessmen's speeches, as a *Fortune* investigation indicates, are written all or in part by public-relations people, the latter must share some of the responsibility for reverse gobbledegook.

years and it'll be wonderful to see him go. Everyone, Charlie's worst enemies included, would be shocked, morale would suffer, and the usefulness of the executive to the organization would be lessened.

So with the interoffice memo about the man being horizontally promoted to some branch office. Again the ceremonial is unvarying: pillar of strength . . . larger responsibilities . . . Ed's invaluable experience in this field makes him the logical . . . know the whole staff will join me in wishing Ed good luck in his new job . . . Nobody is fooled in the slightest, of course, but what could have been a disagreeable, and for Ed a shattering, experience is smoothed over by the blessed analgesic of businesese. There is *something* of a case for timeworn expressions. But it is a case that needs no further making. . . .

THE COMPOSITE
BUSINESS SPEECH

(This is not a parody. It is a loose compilation, based on a systematic count of the expressions and constructions most commonly used in current U.S. business speeches. Included are the sixty principal clichés of reverse gobbledegook.)

COOPERATION—AN OPPORTUNITY AND A CHALLENGE

An address
It is a pleasure and a privilege to be here with you today. These great annual meetings are always an inspiration to me, and doubly so today. After that glowing introduction by our toastmaster I must confess, however, that I'd like to turn the tables and tell a little story on Chuck. When I say it's about the nineteenth hole and a certain gentleman whose baritone was cracked, those of you who were at the Atlanta conference last year will know what I

mean. But I won't tell it. Chuck Forbes is too good a friend of mine and, seriously, I know full well we all realize what a tower of strength his yeoman service has been to the association in these trying times.

Yes, gentlemen, trying times. So you'll pardon me if I cast aside the glib reverberation of glittering generalities and the soothing syrup of sugar-coated platitudes and put it to you the only way I can: straight English.

We're losing the battle!

From every corner the people are being weaned from the doctrines of the Founding Fathers. They are being detoured from the high-speed highways of progress by the utopian highwaymen.

Now, the man in the street is a pretty savvy fellow. Don't sell him short. Joe Doakes may be fooled for a while, but in the end he wants no part of the mumbo jumbo the global saboteurs are trying to sell him. After all, he is an American.

But he has to be told.

And we're not telling him!

Now let me say that I do not wish to turn the clock back. None of us do. All forward-looking businessmen see themselves as partners in a team in which the worker is a full-fledged member. I regard our employees as our greatest business asset, and I am sure, mindful as I am of the towering potentials of purposeful energy in this group of clear-sighted leaders, that, in the final analysis, it is the rock foundation of your policies too.

But the team can't put the ball across for a first down just by wishing it. The guards and the tackles can't do

their job if the quarterback doesn't let them in on the play. And we, the quarterbacks, are muffing the ball.

How are we to go over for a touchdown? My friends, this is the $64 question. I don't know the answers. I am just a plain-spoken businessman. I am not a soothsayer. I have no secret crystal ball. But I do know one thing: before we round the curve into the homestretch we have a job to do. It will not be easy. I offer no panaceas or nostrums. Instead, I would like to suggest that the real key to our problem lies in the application of the three E's.

What are the three E's?

ENTERPRISE! ENDEAVOR! EFFORT!

Each and every one of us must appoint himself a salesman—yes, a missionary, if you will—and get out and do some real grassroots selling. And when we hit the dirt, let's not forget the customers—the greatest asset any business has.

Now, much has been done already. But let's not fool ourselves: the surface, as our chairman has so wisely said, has hardly been scratched. The program is still in its infancy. So let me give it to you straight from the shoulder. The full implementation, gentlemen, depends on us.

So let's get on the beam! In crackerbarrel fashion, let's get down to earth. In good plain talk the man in the street can understand, let's remind Joe Doakes that the best helping hand he will ever find is the one at the end of his own shirt sleeve.

We have the know-how.

With sights set high, let's go over the top!

BETTER LETTERS
The Hanover Bank

One company's interest in the language of business is demonstrated in the following bulletins, part of a continuing series issued to its correspondents by The Hanover Bank of New York.

WORDS WE COULD DO WITHOUT

A recent article in the New York Times told of the need for new words in the English language. After reading a million or more letters, we should like to name some of the words the English language could probably do without.*

abeyance
absolutely
advise
  (for *inform*)
aforesaid
alleged
beg
(you) claim
(to) contact
commence
communication
  (for *letter*)
deem
due
  (as in *due course*)
duly

* The possibility of exceptions to the aforesaid statement is duly recognized. Accordingly, the usages appended herewith are deemed to be merely suggestive, and readers are advised to kindly note same.

endeavor
engaged
  (as in *engaged in manufacturing*)
enthuse
esteemed
expedite
facilitate
favor
  (for *letter*)
finalize
(you) forgot
hereby
hereon
hereto
herewith
humble
institution
  (for *bank*)
kindly (for *please*)
lieu
locate
  (for *find*)
must
neglected
oblige
party
  (for *person*)
(as) per
(our) policy
presently
  (for *now*)

Reprinted from *Better Letters*. Courtesy of The Hanover Bank, New York.

proportions
  (as in *five-figure proportions*)
pursuant
relative (to)
(we) remain
said
  (as in *said account*)
same
  (for *it* or *them*)
subsequent
terminate
thereon
thereto
thereto
transpire
  (for *happen*)
unfortunate
verbal
  (for *oral*)
wish
  (as in *wish to state*)

WHICH WRITER ARE YOU?

Stodgy?
  "We are in receipt of yours of the 15th . . ."
  "You are hereby advised . . ."
  "We wish to call your attention to . . ."
  "Please return same and oblige."

Grouchy or overbearing?
  "You claim . . ."
  "You must have overlooked . . ."
  "We are not responsible . . ."
  "We must request . . ."

Long-winded?
  "We wish to take this opportunity to acknowledge receipt of your recent communication in the matter of the checks for your account which you were so kind as to favor us with recently and in reply wish to say that . . ."

Or pleasing and natural?
  "We are pleased to know . . ."

  "Thank you for writing us so promptly about . . ."
  "We have received your letter . . ."
  "Be sure to write us again if there is anything we can do."

THE ANATOMY OF AMBIGUITY

One of the most common and most insidious violations of clearness occurs when a statement can be taken in more than one way. Some of the causes of this fault are indicated below. In each instance compare the meaning of example (a) with that of example (b).

1. Wrong Word
   a. It is our opinion that you can deal with Blank & Co. *in confidence*. (Means "secretly.")
   b. It is our opinion that you can deal with Blank & Co. *with confidence*.

2. *Misplaced Word or Phrase*
   a. He returned the stock certificate he had received in error *by registered mail*.
   b. He returned *by registered mail* the stock certificate he had received in error.

3. *Confused Reference of Pronoun*
   a. Mr. Gates submitted the figures to his client, but *he* was not entirely satisfied with them. (Who's "he"?)
   b. Mr. Gates submitted the figures to his client, but *the client* was not entirely satisfied with them.

4. *Omitted Words*
   a. Please continue to use the old forms *until exhausted*.
   b. Please continue to use the old forms *until they are exhausted*.

ACKNOWLEDGING AN ERROR

You can't always prevent a mistake.

But you can help to alleviate the effects when a complaint is received. It's largely a matter of words and attitudes. Perhaps these suggestions will prove useful:

1. Be natural and cordial, not perfunctory. Compare "We wish to acknowledge receipt of your letter of March 6 advising us of our error in your February statement" with "We are sorry about the error in your February statement."

2. Don't show distrust of the reader by such phrases as "you claim," "the alleged loss," and "we suspect."

3. Don't dwell on the error by drawing out the apology. It's better to say, "Please accept our apologies," than to say, "Please accept our apologies for the inconvenience caused you by our unfortunate error."

4. Don't magnify the seriousness of the error by using such strong terms as "blunder," "complaint," "unfortunately," "delinquent," "failed," and "neglected." Compare "Unfortunately, we neglected to send you the corrected copy" with "We should have sent you the corrected copy."

5. Don't say, "This will never happen again." (It usually does!) If you're stuck for a closing sentence after you've already said you're sorry, you might try, "Thank you for calling this matter to our attention."

AREN'T YOU GLAD YOU DIDN'T WRITE THESE LETTERS?

1.

Gentlemen:

In response to your letter of March 26 which was in reply to our letter of March 24, which was in reply to yours of March 16, we are enclosing herewith the photostatic copy of our check No. 60432 dated February 26, 19—, payable to (Name) in the amount of $6,455.54. This check was enclosed with your letter of March 16.

We should be pleased to hear further from you.

Very truly yours,

2.

Gentlemen:

. . . In connection with the above, we wish to thank you for your information supplied in your above quoted communication, and in connection with this matter, we would appreciate your advising us the address of (Name) so that we may write them for further information regarding this matter.

Very truly yours,

3.

Gentlemen:

We are carrying you on our mailing list as follows: . . . Will you please return this notice with any corrections shown thereon which should be made. If the above information is correct, we would appreciate advice from you to that effect so that our records will be complete.

Yours truly,

P.S. In other words we would appreciate having your correct mailing address.

WORDS AND THEIR IMPORTANCE

S. I. Hayakawa

In recent decades, scientists have given increased attention to the relationship between words and human behavior. Businessmen have followed the studies for clues to their own communication problems. Dr. Hayakawa, the author of this condensation from his popular exposition of semantics, is Lecturer on Language Arts at San Francisco State College and editor of *ETC: A Review of General Semantics*.

Most of our knowledge, acquired from parents, friends, schools, newspapers, books, conversation, speeches, and radio, is received verbally. All of our knowledge of history, for example, comes to us only in words. The only proof we have that the Battle of Waterloo ever took place is that we have had reports to that effect.

By the time a child is a few years old he has accumulated a considerable amount of second- and third-hand information about morals, geography, history, nature, people, games—all of which information together constitutes his verbal world.

If the child grows to adulthood with a verbal world in his head which corresponds fairly closely to what he finds around him in his widening experience, he is in relatively small danger of being shocked or hurt, because his verbal world has told him what, more or less, to expect.

If, however, he grows up with a false map in his head—that is, with a head crammed with false knowledge and superstition—he will constantly be running into trouble, wasting his efforts, and acting like a fool. He will not be adjusted to the world as it is; he may, if the lack of adjustment is serious, end up in an insane asylum.

Some of the follies we commit because of false verbal maps in our heads are so commonplace that we do not even think of them as remarkable. There are those who protect themselves from accidents by carrying a rabbit's foot in the pocket. Some refuse to sleep on the thirteenth floor of hotels —this is so common that most big hotels, even in the capitals of our scientific culture, skip "13" in numbering their floors. Some plan their lives on the basis of astrological predictions. All such people are living in verbal worlds that bear little, if any, resemblance to the extensional world.

We all inherit a great deal of useless knowledge, and a great deal of misinformation and error, so that there is always a portion of what we have been told that must be discarded. But the cultural heritage of our civilization that is transmitted to us—our socially pooled knowledge, both scientific and humane—has been valued principally because we have believed that it gives us accurate maps of experience.

The educated are frequently quite as naïve about language as the uneducated, although the ways in which they exhibit their naïveté may be less easily discernible. Indeed, many are worse off than the uneducated, because while the uneducated often realize their own limitations, the educated are in a position to refuse to admit their ignorance and conceal their limitations from themselves by their skill at word-juggling. After all, education, as it is still understood in many circles, is principally a matter of learning facility in the manipulation of words.

All words have, according to the uses to which they are put, some ability to arouse an emotional response in their hearers. There are many words that exist more for their affective value than for their informative value; for example, we can refer to "that man" as "that gentleman," "that individual," "that person," "that gent," "that guy," "that hombre," "that bird," or "that bozo"—and while the person referred to may be the same in all these cases, each of these terms reveals a difference in our feelings toward him.

We also tend to think in opposites, to feel that what is not "good" must be "bad" and that what is not "bad" must be "good." This feeling is heightened when we are excited or angry. Children manifest this same tendency. When they are taught English history, for example, the first thing they want to know about every ruler is whether he was a "good king" or a "bad king." In popular literature and movie scenarios written for childish mentalities, there are always "heroes" on the one hand, to be cheered, and "villains" on the other, to be hissed.

Now, in terms of a single desire, there are only two values, roughly speaking: things that gratify or things that frustrate that desire. If we are starving, there are only two kinds of things in the world so far as we are concerned at the moment: edible things and inedible things. If we are in danger, there are the things that we fear and the things that may help and protect us. Life at such levels can be folded neatly down the middle, with all good on one side, all bad on the other, and everything is accounted for, because things that are irrelevant to our interests escape our notice altogether.

Except in quarrels and violent controversies, the language of everyday life shows what may be termed a multivalued orientation. We have scales of judgment. Instead of "good" and "bad," we have "very bad," "bad," "not bad," "fair," "good," "very good"; instead of "sane" and "insane," we have "quite sane," "sane enough," "mildly neurotic," "neurotic," "almost psychotic," "psychotic."

The greater the number of distinctions, the greater becomes the number of courses of action suggested to us. This means that we become increasingly capable of reacting appropriately to the many complex situations presented by life.

Even more multi-valued is the language of science. Instead of saying "hot" and "cold," we give the temperature in degrees on a fixed or agreed-upon scale: $-20°$F., $37°$C., and so on. Instead of saying "strong" and "weak," we give strength in horse-power or voltage; instead of "fast" and "slow," we give speed in miles per hour or feet per second. Instead of being limited to two possible answers or even to several, we have an infinite number when we use these numerical methods. The language of science, therefore, can be said to offer an infinite-valued orientation.

The infantile mind, equating words with things, regards unkind words as unkind acts. Attributing to harmless sets of noises a power of injuring, such a person is "insulted" when those noises are uttered at him. So-called "gentlemen" in semi-savage and infantile societies used to dignify signal reactions of this kind into "codes of honor." By "honor," they meant extreme readiness to pull out swords or pistols whenever they imagined that they had been "insulted."

The tendency to talk too much and too readily is an unhealthy sign. We should also be wary of "thinking too much." "Thinking too much" often means that somewhere in the back of our minds there is a "certainty"—an "incontrovertible fact," an "unalterable law," an "eternal principle"—some statement which we believe "says all" about something. Life, however, is constantly throwing into the face of our "incontrovertible certainties" facts that do not fit our preconceptions: "communists" who don't need a shave, "politicians" who aren't corrupt, "friends" who aren't faithful, "benevolent societies" that aren't benevolent, "insurance companies" that don't insure.

Refusing to give up our sense of "certainty" and yet unable to deny the facts that do not fit, we are forced to "think and think and think." And, as we have seen before, there are only two ways out of such dilemmas: first, to deny the facts altogether, and secondly, to reverse the principle altogether, so that we go from "All insurance companies are safe" to "No insurance companies are safe." Hence such infantile reactions as, "I'll never trust another woman!" "Don't ever say politics to me again!" "I'm through with newspapers for good!"

The mature mind, on the other hand, knows that words never say all about anything, and it is therefore adjusted to uncertainty. In driving a car, for example, we never know what is going to happen next; no matter how often we have gone over the same road, we never find exactly the same traffic conditions. Nevertheless, a competent driver travels over all kinds of roads and even at high speeds without either fear or nervousness. As driver, he is adjusted to uncertainty—the unexpected blowout or the sudden hazard—and he is not insecure.

Similarly the intellectually mature person does not "know all about" anything. And he is not insecure, because he knows that the only kind of security life offers is the dynamic security that comes from within: the security derived from infinite flexibility of mind —from an orientation that is infinite— valued.

ON APPEALING TO FAVORABLE OPINIONS

Edward J. Kilduff

This essay entertainingly describes how the power of word suggestion is used to advance personal and business interests. The author is Professor Emeritus of Business English, New York University, a founder of the American Business Writing Association, and author or coauthor of many books on word use and business correspondence.

Many superstitions persist even in what we like to think is an enlightened age. No small number of persons still believe, for example, that walking under a ladder may bring bad luck; that unless one knocks on wood when he boasts or says anything good about himself, some harm may befall him; that fortunate or unfortunate events occur in a series of three.

Many strange notions, not substantiated by facts, are likewise entertained by no small percentage of our American population. A few are: that one American soldier is equal to at least two German, French, or Japanese soldiers; that, if one eats lobster and ice-cream at the same meal, one will become deathly ill; that the U.S. Marine Corps has no superior as fighters; that ministers' sons turn out badly; that there is really no point in one's voting in a presidential election, for a single vote cannot possibly affect the outcome; and that college Greek-letter fraternities and such national societies as the Masons and the Knights of Columbus individually are in posses-sion of dread mysteries of no inconsiderable value.

Of a higher level are those widely-held favorable opinions that, although they usually have some basis in fact, are not wholly sound. Some of these opinions are: that French dressmakers [1] are unsurpassed; that English-made men's clothing and men's shoes are without exception better than American-made; that imported goods are superior to domestic goods; that hand-made articles are better than machine-made articles; that things were better in "the good old days."

The user of prepossessive words makes capital of just such favorable opinions already existing in the minds of the audience he is addressing. Singling out an opinion suitable to his purpose, he seeks to employ words that appeal to that opinion. For example:

[1] At the present writing, Mainbocher, Molyneux, and Schiaparelli are three of the most famous French dressmakers. Mainbocher (born Bocher) is a native-born American (Chicago, U.S.A.); Molyneux, a native-born Englishman; Schiaparelli, a native-born Italian.

The opinion is widely held that home cooking [2] has no superior. The advertising manager of a large bakery is cognizant of such fact. Accordingly, he capitalizes on it by advertising that the apple pies of his bakery are *homemade* apple pies. There the expression *homemade* is prepossessive, for it appeals to the favorable opinion already held by the readers about home cooking and emotionally persuades them that these apple pies (since they are advertised as *homemade*) must therefore be excellent.

A large candy manufacturer in advertising that his candies are *homemade* makes capital of the same favorable opinion. [How readers of these advertisements can reconcile such obviously self-contradictory concepts is difficult to understand.] Some large restaurants, hotels, etc. advertise *home cooking* or *home-style cooking*. And some, lest the patron still be skeptical, intensify the expression on the menu by prefixing *real* or *genuine*, as in, *real home-baked beans* or *genuine homemade pie*.

A high-class, men's retail shoe dealer advertises "These *imported English-made* shoes $35." There, the words *imported* and *English-made* are prepossessive. *Imported* appeals to the reader's preconceived opinion that imported articles are superior to domestic articles; *English-made* appeals to his preconceived opinion that English-made shoes are of superlative quality in respect to workmanship.

Many persons entertain a favorable opinion respecting things made or done by hand. Hence the use of the word *hand* in the following examples is likely to make a strong appeal to such persons: *hand-sewn* gloves, *hand-tooled*

leather bindings, *hand-embroidered* initials, all *hand-stitched, hand* laundry, *hand-dipped* chocolates.[3]

The campaign manager of a candidate seeking public office often strives to make it known that the candidate is a *home-loving* or *family man*. The manager proceeds on the generally sound theory that voters (especially the women voters) hold a favorable opinion of men who are described as "home-loving." If the voters can be made to think of the candidate as one such, they will believe that he is a respectable man and that, therefore, illogically enough, he will make an able, say, Senator.

With the religiously inclined groups of the electorate, it also helps if the candidate can be referred to as *a churchgoer* or as *a God-fearing man;* with other groups, if he is known as *a practical man, a man of humble origin, a man of the people, a two-fisted fighter, a man who* (although a college man) *worked his way through college.* [This last descriptive expression appeals to the preconceived opinion that such a means of obtaining an education is highly commendable and proves the candidate to be democratic. It also helps to reduce resentment toward a candidate who is a "college man."]

Although, in general, people assume that this year's new model of an automobile is better than last year's, a notion seems to prevail that with respect to certain things the older they are the better they are. Hence *old* is often used as a prepossessive word. Of course, in advertising whisky, *old* and *very old* are quite helpful even though they may be followed by the statement

[2] Except that done by young brides which, by almost universally accepted opinion, is uniformly bad.

[3] *Hand* is employed in some contexts as a prejudice word, as in: "From oven to you, untouched by the human *hand*," "Don't eat candy that other *hands* may have contaminated," and, "He was a *hand-picked* candidate."

"8 years"; for *old* and *very old* influence many readers to believe that the whisky must be good because of the fact of age alone. They fail to give consideration to the original quality of the whisky.

The idea of age conveyed by the expression *"Established in 1888"* is prepossessive in that it inclines the reader to believe that because the company so advertising is old it must therefore be good and, perhaps, better to deal with than a company established in, say, 1941.

Original is frequently prepossessive, as in, "Major Bowes' *original* amateur hour," and "The *original* and genuine Worcestershire sauce." In the instances cited, *original* appeals to a widely-held opinion that the first in order of existence is the best in quality—an obviously illogical generalization.

Genuine, which means *real, authentic, true*, is commonly prepossessive when used in such expressions as "*genuine* cultured pearls" and "*genuine* synthetic leather."

Only, in its adverbial meaning of *no more than* or *not more than*, has a prepossessive allure when used with the price of an article or service, as in "*only* $5," "*only* $50," "*only* $500." In these uses, the addition of *only* to the price seems to convey the impression that the price may be expected to be greater but is not. It also helps the prospective purchaser to justify to himself the purchase by minimizing the cost—i.e., by suggesting that, after all, the article or service costs "*only* $5," or "*only* $50," or "*only* $500," or "*only* 3c a day."

Whereas it is general practice to minimize the price of an article offered for sale, it is similarly general practice in appropriate instances to magnify (at least by descriptive words) the size of the article. For most persons desire something physically big for their money, and size is often more important in their eyes than quality. Hence, as noted in *The New Yorker*, a bottler of California ripe olives grades his olives by size as follows, in descending order: *Super-Supreme-Colossal* are the largest, *Super-Colossal* are next, *Colossal* next, and then *Jumbo*. His smallest size is labeled *Giant*.

VOCABULARY AND SUCCESS

Johnson O'Connor

The intriguing connection between a man's vocabulary and his chances for success in business is explored in this classic study by the founder (now director) of the Human Engineering Laboratory. Mr. O'Connor, a psychometrician by profession, was formerly associated with the General Electric Company, Stevens Institute of Technology, and the Massachusetts Institute of Technology.

What is success? And how is it gained? Whether one thinks of success as financial reward, or as assured social position, or as satisfaction in able work accomplished and recognized, or as a combination of the three and something more, many factors contribute. Most of them elude our understanding and remain intangibly beyond definition. A vital force drives some individuals over every obstacle. With others that great generalization, character, adds strength of a different sort. Neither may ever be restricted to a hard and fast formula; certainly, at the moment, neither can be measured. But other more concrete constituents of success have been isolated and studied in the laboratory. One of these is a large English vocabulary.

An extensive knowledge of the exact meanings of English words accompanies outstanding success in this country more often than any other single characteristic which the Human Engineering Laboratories have been able to isolate and measure.

What is meant by vocabulary? Just what the word signifies. Does the word *enervating* mean *soothing, exciting, distressing, invigorating,* or *weakening?* For most well-educated persons the choice is between *invigorating* and *weakening.* Fifty-two per cent of the college graduates whom we have measured choose *invigorating* as the synonym; only sixteen per cent choose *weakening,* the dictionary definition. Does *stilted* in the phrase, 'his stilted manner,' mean *irresolute, improper, cordial, stiffly formal,* or *vicious?* A majority of educated persons mark *stiffly formal,* but more than a third mark *irresolute.* Answers to the meaning of *scurrilous,* in the phrase, 'scurrilous rogue,' divide themselves more or less evenly between *hurrying, desperate, abusive, frantic,* and *diseased,* with *desperate* the most popular. For *peremptory,* a majority mark *decisive,* but many choose *persuasive, uncertain,* and *angry. Pleasant,* the fifth choice, is not as popular. *Linguist* and *glutton* are equally enticing as synonyms for

This article first appeared in The Atlantic Monthly February 1934 and is reprinted in the Johnson O'Connor English Vocabulary Builder, Volume I, 1948, copyrighted 1934 by the Atlantic Monthly Company, Boston, and in 1948 by Eleanor Manning O'Connor.

polyglot. For *refulgent,* in 'a refulgent smile,' *repellent* is most intriguing and *very bright* next, with *mischievous, flattering,* and *sour* all following closely in popularity. For *monograph* forty per cent choose *soliloquy* and less than twenty per cent *treatise* and *epitaph* each.

The word *vocabulary,* as used in this article, signifies a knowledge of the dictionary meaning of just such words as *enervating, stilted, scurrilous, peremptory, polyglot, refulgent,* and *monograph.* Not until one attempts to pick an exact synonym does one realize the difficulty. One may like the sound of a word and use it in a picturesque way without being accurate in its meaning.

I

To measure the vocabulary of an individual, the Laboratory uses a list of one hundred and fifty test words. Each is printed in italics in a short phrase and is followed by five choices, all of which fit the phrase but only one of which is a synonym of the test word. The instructions are: 'Underline that one of the five choices which is nearest in meaning to the word in italics.' The words to be defined were selected by Alexander Inglis of the Graduate School of Education, Harvard University. His intention was to include words which appear once or twice in 100,000 words of printed matter. It is a general reader's vocabulary from which technical terms have been excluded. The test words vary from some that are quite easy, such as

Thrilling experiences—dangerous, exciting, unusual, disgusting, profitable,

to others that are more difficult, such as

Glabrous heads—bald, over-sized, hairy, square, round,

which only twenty-one per cent of college graduates mark correctly. Since one fifth, or twenty per cent, should guess the correct answer, the meaning of *glabrous* is practically unknown. The test measures knowledge of words one recognizes, not necessarily of those one uses. The words one uses accurately are, no doubt, fewer than those one recognizes, but there is probably a relation between the two.

Three hundred high-school freshmen average 76 errors in the list of 150 words. Seven hundred college freshmen average 42 errors. One thousand college graduates from a wide variety of colleges—most of them, however, in the eastern part of the United States —average 27 errors, and vary from the one person in a thousand who achieves a perfect score to the one who knows less than 50 of the 150 items. The college professors whom we have measured average 8 errors; major executives average 7 errors. Major executives score higher in this English vocabulary test than any other selected group with which we have experimented.

By the term 'major executives' is meant all individuals who, for five years or longer, have held the position of president or vice president in a business organization. Such a definition includes both successful and unsuccessful executives, provided only that they have survived five years; it includes alike forceful personalities and figureheads; but it has the great advantage of excluding our personal judgment from the process of selection. Major executives as thus defined average in the top ten per cent of college graduates as a whole.

Although it is impossible to define success rigidly or scientifically, it seems to be true, nevertheless, that a large vocabulary is typical, not exclusively of executives, but of successful individuals. It happens that in the business world successful men and women are designated by this special appellation, 'executive.' The successful lawyer or doctor is marked by no such name. But if, to the best of one's ability, one selects successful persons in the professions, they also score high in vocabulary.

For one meaning of success the Century dictionary gives 'a high degree of worldly prosperity.' The measured English vocabulary of an executive correlates with his salary. This does not mean that every high-vocabulary person receives a large salary, but the relation between the two is close enough to show that a large vocabulary is one element, and seemingly an important one.

Furthermore, the executive level which a man or woman reaches is determined to some extent by vocabulary. In many manufacturing organizations the first step in the executive ladder is the leading hand, called sometimes the working foreman. This man is in charge of half a dozen or a dozen others. He works at the bench or at a machine as they do, but is the executive of the group. The next step is the foreman, who may be in charge of as many as a hundred or more individuals. He does no bench work, he is not a producer, but devotes full time to his executive duties, to the keeping of records and to the handling of the personnel. The next step in many large organizations is the department head or superintendent or manager, who ordinarily does not come in direct contact with the workers, but handles them through his foremen. The final step is the major executive or official, the vice president or president of the organization.

These four executive ranks represent four degrees of success, in one sense in which that word is used. One is *advanced* from leading hand to foreman, from foreman to manager, from manager to president. As far as we can determine by measurements, the leading hand and the official have much the same inherent aptitudes. They differ primarily in vocabulary. Typical non-college-graduate shop foremen average, as a group, about as high as college graduates. Department heads score higher, roughly fifteen errors, and major executives the highest of all, averaging only seven errors. Whether the word 'executive' refers only to the major group or is used in the broader sense to mean anyone in charge of other workers, it is still true that the executive scores higher than those under him and higher than other persons of similar age and education.

II

An interesting sidelight on the high vocabulary scores of executives is that they were unforeseen. When a scientist expects a result and finally achieves it there is always the feeling that, regardless of the care he has taken, personal bias may have entered. Six or eight years ago the Human Engineering Laboratories tested forty major executives of the Telephone Company who had offered themselves as victims to be experimented upon in a search for executive characteristics. At the same time the Laboratory was also revising the vocabulary test, not with the notion of using it with executives, but with the hope that it might prove of value in education. One day, with no thought of the consequences, I gave it to an executive, and from then on was asked for it regularly because of the interest it aroused. I paid little heed to the results until one day an executive refused to take the test. He had been obliged by lack of money to leave school at fourteen, and had earned his own living since. With no further formal education, he had worked his way to a major position. He had taken the aptitude tests without hesitation, but vocabulary seemed to him so directly the result of schooling that he knew in advance he would fail. His own words were that he had made his way without being found out and he was not willing to give himself away. But in scientific work one cannot test only those who think they will do well, and we finally persuaded him to try the vocabulary test. He made two errors where the average college graduate makes twenty-seven.

Was it luck? Or was it significant of something which we had not recognized? The Laboratory listed the vocabulary scores of one hundred executives and, parallel with them, the scores of one hundred miscellaneous college graduates. The difference between the two arrays was striking. Only nine per cent of the college graduates scored as high as the average major executive.

Why do large vocabularies characterize executives and possibly outstanding men and women in other fields? The final answer seems to be that words are the instruments by means of which men and women grasp the thoughts of others and with which they do much of their own thinking. They are the tools of thought.

Before accepting so far-reaching a conclusion several more obvious explanations must be examined and excluded. The first and most natural supposition is that successful persons acquire words with age and with the experiences of life. Success does not usually occur early. The successful group were necessarily older in both years and experience than the general run of college graduates with whom they were compared; and their large vocabularies might be the inevitable result of age.

To probe this point a study of the growth of vocabulary with age was undertaken. From twelve, the earliest age for which we have a large number of measurements, to twenty-two or twenty-three vocabulary expands steadily and at a uniform rate. Through this school period the score on the vocabulary test of one hundred and fifty items improves five words a year. From twenty-three to fifty vocabulary continues to increase, but changes no more in these twenty-five years than in two school years—not enough to explain the high scores of executives. Normally, vocabulary is acquired early in life, before most men have made appreciable progress toward a responsible position. The large vocabularies of successful individuals come before success rather than after. Age and the experiences of life may contribute new words, but certainly do not explain in full the high vocabulary scores of business executives.

The next thought is that effective schooling may be the source both of a wide vocabulary and of executive success. It is known, from the work which the American Telephone and Telegraph Company has undertaken, that there is a relationship between school success and business success later in life. Although not everyone who leads his class becomes a brilliant executive, and although not everyone who fails in school fails in life, in general school success preludes executive success. Schooling may be the vital factor of which the large vocabularies which we are measuring are but by-products.

To obtain evidence bearing on this point, we measured the vocabularies of twenty men who had left school at the age of fifteen and who had worked their way into major positions. They also averaged only seven errors. Their scores equaled those of the college-graduate executives. In the case of these twenty men it is their vocabularies which are important rather than their formal school education. Their large vocabularies are not the result of schooling and must, we therefore conclude, be significant for some other reason than as a by-product of an educational background.

Is, then, a college background of no importance? Has the non-college man the same chance of becoming an executive as has the college graduate? This fact seemed worth determining. Of the major executives in a large industrial organization, sixty per cent are college graduates, forty per cent non-college. At first glance, college would seem to have done little, for almost half are not college men. But, to be fair to education, there is another angle from which to view this result. Of the college graduates with this same company, more than three quarters are in executive positions, whereas, of the non-college men, well under a tenth are in similar positions. College graduates, in general, average measurably higher in vocabulary than do non-college persons. Furthermore, of the college group a significantly larger percentage are executives.

One would like to conclude without further preamble that the vocabularies of the college group are large because of directed effort and that these purposefully gained vocabularies have contributed to executive success. Non-college executives, then, are those rare individuals who pick up words so easily that their vocabularies are large without effort. But there is one further possibility which must be investigated.

Although the vocabulary test was designed to measure knowledge which must have come through books or by word of mouth, a high score may reveal an underlying aptitude for language. It may be this flair which is the contributing factor in both vocabulary and success later in life.

It should be possible to isolate and measure diathesis apart from knowledge. We have worked on this approach for a number of years, thus far unproductively. For the time being we must leave the conclusion of this part of the research in abeyance and admit that the vocabularies of successful executives may reveal an aptitude.

III

Vocabularies may always be consciously increased regardless of the presence or absence of any gift. A knowledge of the meaning of each word at one's command must have been obtained by word of mouth or through reading, by some educational process.

Furthermore, with groups of individuals of apparently similar aptitudes, the amount of vocabulary added in a given period varies with different educational techniques. At Stevens Institute of Technology the freshman class is divided alphabetically into four sections. Each of these studies freshman English under a different member of the faculty. Four years ago the entire class took the vocabulary test the first week of freshman year. The four sections averaged about the same in vocabulary, and there was no reason to suppose that, selected as they were, one would score higher than another or have more ability. Yet, when remeasured nine months later, two of the sections had improved more than average academic freshmen, one section had improved only half this amount, and the fourth had retrogressed slightly.

The improvement of one section may have been due to the fact that the instructor was interested in the vocabulary test and its implications. The important fact is that differences in vocabulary improvement were caused by differences in teaching techniques— in other words, that an improvement in vocabulary score can be produced by education.

Those boys and girls whom the

Laboratory has measured and urged to better their vocabularies, and then re-measured at the end of two or three years, have shown more than average improvement. Here again vocabulary is induced independent of aptitude. It is for this reason that the Human Engineering Laboratories, in helping a youngster to find himself and start in the right direction, use a vocabulary test in lieu of a general intelligence test.

We come now to the question of whether or not that increment of vocabulary directly due to educational stimulation contributes to success. The four sections of the freshman class at Stevens Institute of Technology to which reference has been made, which took freshman English with different members of the faculty and improved different amounts in vocabulary, were followed to see the effect of these new vocabularies on school work the next year. The four sections averaged nearly the same in school marks freshman year. Sophomore year the two sections which had enlarged their vocabularies the previous year showed general gain in all school subjects—not strikingly, not enough to prove the point once and for all time, but enough to suggest that a vocabulary acquired consciously reflects in general school improvement the next year.

It is always possible that the improvement in school work was due to inspired teaching, to added incentive, but if this were true it would seem as if the improvement in school work should appear immediately freshman year, whereas it did not appear until sophomore year after the vocabulary had been acquired. This seems to indicate that it is the additional words themselves which are the tools used the next year, that words are important in and for themselves.

IV

Granted that diction is important, and many would agree without elaborate proof of the point, how, from the standpoint of the school, can it best be given; and, from that of the individual, how best achieved? Is it a knowledge of Latin and Greek which lays a sound foundation for a real understanding of words? Or is it constant reading? Or the assiduous perusal of the dictionary? Probably all contribute; as yet we have found no straight and easy road.

In the search for a road to vocabulary we have unearthed several facts which throw light on the learning process. One of these, which, if rightly interpreted, may prove to be of far-reaching importance to education, is that vocabulary advances with an almost unbroken front. The words at the command of an individual are not a miscellany gathered from hither and yon. With a very few exceptions they are all of the words in the dictionary up to those of an order of difficulty at which his vocabulary stops abruptly, and almost no words beyond. In the revised form of the test which is now available for school use, the items are arranged in order of difficulty as determined by actual test results. The first fifteen or twenty words of the test are known to the average high-school freshman or sophomore. The next thirty to forty are on the border line of his knowledge. Some he recognizes, others are vaguely familiar, and others he has not yet encountered. The balance are so far beyond him that he marks correctly no more than the one in five which he guesses by pure chance.

For convenience of scoring, the words are divided into ten groups of constantly increasing difficulty. One who knows the words of Group II, second in difficulty, almost invariably marks correctly every word of Group I.

Another youngster who may know the words of, let us say, Group VI rarely fails on a single word in any of the first five easier groups. Similarly, one who fails on twelve of the fifteen words in any one group—that is, marks correctly only the one word in five which he guesses—almost never knows a word in any more difficult group. There are not, as we had expected, stray words in the difficult part which one who fails earlier in the test has stumbled upon and remembered. These unusual words, if previously encountered as they must have been in reading and conversation, are too far beyond the point he has reached to make any lasting impression.

The one exception to this rule is the foreign student who may know difficult words because of their similarity to his own language, but miss much easier ones. Thus the Southern European often marks correctly such difficult words as cephalic, garrulity, and piscatorial, because of knowledge of Italian and French, but fails to know much easier words of Old English origin, such as, for instance, knack, blotch, and cope.

In the region where learning is taking place, the commonest error is the confusion of a word with its exact opposite. Among seventh- and eighth-grade and first-year high-school pupils, nearly a third mark found guilty as the correct meaning of acquitted. Upright is the most popular misconception for the meaning of reclining; and, strange as it may seem, neat is the commonest misconception of untidy. The seventh-grade youngster berated for keeping an untidy room quite often evidently receives the impression that he is too orderly. The failing is not limited to the high-school group. For incontrovertible the correct answer indisputable is usually marked by college men, but of the remaining four choices unsound is by far most popular. In the phrase

'You allay my fears,'—where the five choices are justify, calm, arouse, increase, and confirm,—calm is usually answered by the educated group, but arouse is next most popular. In the phrase 'He retracts his criticism,' withdraws is the correct answer and repeats is the most common delusion. In 'He vented his wrath,' poured forth is correct and restrained is the commonest misapprehension.

One need but turn to words of which one is not quite certain to see how difficult it is to distinguish opposites. One evening at dinner with a delightful dean of education, we fell to discussing this question. He recognized cathode and anode instantly as electrical terms designating the two poles, but hesitated a moment before saying which was which. Port and starboard he admitted he had never straightened out and resorted to some such phrase as 'Jack left port.' Gee and haw were beyond him. He surmised that they meant up and down, but said frankly he did not know the words. When told that they were used in ploughing, he was instantly interested, but did not care at all which was which. He was taking the first step in the learning process, placing them in their correct environment. The fifty-two per cent of college graduates who choose invigorating as the meaning of enervating are on the verge of knowing the word. The dictum of modern education, never to teach what a thing is not, has perhaps come from a realization of this confusion of opposites. The confusion seems, however, to be a natural step in the learning process.

v

In the study of human beings the factors involved are so numerous and so intertwined with one another that the experimenter, in unraveling the strands, must pause periodically to make certain that he is progressing. What then has been discovered? An exact and extensive vocabulary is an important concomitant of success. So much is known. Furthermore, such a vocabulary can be acquired. It increases as long as an individual remains in school or college, but without conscious effort does not change materially thereafter.

There may be some subtle distinction between a natural vocabulary picked up at home, at meals, and in reading, and one gained by a study of the dictionary. The latter may not be as valuable as the former. But there is nothing to show that it is harmful and the balance of evidence at the moment suggests that such a consciously, even laboriously, achieved vocabulary is an active asset.

TRADEMARKS MIGHT BE SKRAMEDART

Jess Stein

An important word to any businessman is his trade name. Because a fortune may depend on it, the name is chosen only after considerable anguish, testing, and expense. Whether the end justifies the means is a question that the consumer must eventually answer. Mr. Stein is managing editor of the *American College Dictionary*.

In everyday life we use such words as *linoleum, cellophane, shredded wheat, dry ice, celluloid, kerosene, milk of magnesia,* and *aspirin*. They are indispensable for clear, convenient indication of certain products. Yet we rarely realize that all these words were once trademarks, the vigilantly guarded words owned privately and exclusively that are among the most valuable assets of business concerns.

The trademark is defined in the ACD as "the name, symbol, figure, letter, word, or mark adopted and used by a manufacturer or merchant in order to designate the goods he manufactures or sells, and to distinguish them from those manufactured or sold by others."

The use of trademarks is traceable to antiquity. In ancient Egypt each slave put his own mark on the bricks he made so that the slavemaster could determine whose work was faulty enough to warrant a lashing. And, as craft guilds developed in medieval times, trademarks were required as a means of placing responsibility for poor work, inferior material, or dishonest weight. In the beginning, then, trademarks were primarily a means of detecting fraud or incompetence.

Gradually, however, the trademark took on positive value. It became the proud symbol which a person or firm put on its product as an assurance to the buyer of dependable quality. Thus, for example, the great Italian printer Aldus Manutius identified his work with a dolphin around an anchor. Today we are constantly aided by common trademarks in spotting the products of certain companies. These trademarks may be symbols, such as the camel on a pack of cigarettes, the encircled bell of the telephone company, the flying red horse of a gasoline company, the three rings of a brewery. They may be a special monogram, such as the GE of General Electric or the A&P of the supermarket chain. Or, they may be words—words that are stretched, shrunk, abbreviated, blended, compounded, misspelled, reversed, or otherwise shaped into trademarks.

Suffixes—usually of no direct significance, but somehow imparting a familiar and reliable ring—are often

Reprinted by permission of Harper & Brothers from *Inside the ACD*, February, 1955.

added to a meaningful root. Some of the more frequent suffixes are –o (as in Perfecto, Excello, Jello); –ine (as in Murine, Oculine, Absorbine, Ovaltine, Vaseline, Listerine); –ola (Victrola, Mazola, Shinola, Pianola, Motorola); –ox (Clorox, Hydrox); –et (Chiclet, Sucret, Co-et); –ette (Cellarette, Tonette); –ite (Masonite, Alemite, Oakite, Samsonite); and –ex (Kleenex, Cutex, Pyrex, Simplex, Tintex, Larvex).

Sometimes a trademark is developed by taking part of a longer word, such as Rem from remedy, Rel from relief, or Coke from its parent trademark Coca-Cola. Often the initials of a firm or the first few letters are run together to form a trademark, such as Alcoa (Aluminum Company of America), Socony (Standard Oil Company of New York), Duco (DuPont Company), Nabisco (National Biscuit Company), and Ebasco (Electric Bond and Share Company).

Compounds and blends are frequently forms of trademarks. Some familiar examples are Oldsmobile (R. E. Olds—automobile), Exercycle (exercise—bicycle), Band-aid (bandage—first aid), Organo (organ—piano), Frigidaire (frigid—air), Odorono (Odor? Oh, no!), Dri-Brite, Eversharp, Wearever, and Linotype (line of type).

Another method of creating trademarks consists of misspelling a word, preferably in a gross enough misspelling to make it memorable. Thus we get Uneeda (You need a biscuit, etc.), E. Z. Walker (Easy walker shoes), Enna Jettick (Energetic shoes), Ken-L-Ration (Kennel ration dog food), Renuzit (Renews it cleaning fluid), My-T-Fine (Mighty fine desserts), Biltrite (Built-right heels), Pick-Ka-Nick (Picnic jugs), and a host of others.

A few other processes are reversals, such as Klim (for milk), Peredixo (for Peroxide), Serutan (for nature's), and Fiberglas (for glass fiber); alliteration, such as Ground Grippers (shoes),

Super Suds (soap flakes), Big Ben (clocks), Killer Diller (insecticide), and Tuff Stuff (insecticide); or completely arbitrary combinations of letters, such as Kodak, Tek, Saran, and Probak.

Although many trademarks have little or no direct significance so far as the product is concerned (Camel cigarettes, Arrow shirts, Swan soap, General tires, Sunbeam shavers, etc.), many trademarks are intended to suggest something about the products to which they are applied. Typically suggestive trademarks are Palmolive (soap), Magnavox (radios), Ditto (duplicating machine), Frigidaire (refrigerators), Chux (disposable diapers), Velveeta (cheese), Thermos (hot-cold vacuum bottles), and Lucite (transparent plastic).

When a trademark becomes the common descriptive name of an article or substance on which the patent has expired, the owner of the trademark may lose his exclusive right to use it. Thus, such trademarks as aspirin, linoleum, cellophane, celluloid, etc., passed into the common domain and may now be used by any manufacturer or merchant. To the original owner of the trademark this means a costly, often disastrous loss of a priceless asset. For this reason, trademark owners proceed with constant guidance by their attorneys in the formation, use, and defense of their marks. The casual, improper use of a trademark in a magazine article or book will bring a prompt letter of protest, for the law requires an active defense of the trademark against misuse. The Coca-Cola Company, for example, is engaged in a steady fight to protect its trademarks Coca-Cola and Coke—it is said that the company has had one lawsuit a week for the last 35 years—although it was not able to prevent the use of "cola" by a number of competing companies because "cola" was judged to be a generic word for that type of drink.

Although many trademark attorneys recognize the fact that a dictionary must record generic uses regardless of the legal consequence to the trademark owner, most of them take the position that a trademark is a private property that may only be used according to specified rules (capitalize it; mark it as a trademark; recognize no generic use). As a result, the lexicographer must move between the Scylla of actual usage and the Charybdis of threatened lawsuits, and not even a disclaimer of the kind that appears on the copyright page of the ACD seems enough to satisfy some trademark attorneys.

THE SAMPLE WITH THE BUILT-IN BIAS
Darrell Huff

Figures, as much as words, are the symbols of communication. Sometimes, perhaps, businessmen rely on them too much and read into them what they do not mean. Darrell Huff learned to spot a phony statistic as a student at the University of Iowa. But his sharp eye and equally sharp sense of humor are native.

"The average Yaleman, Class of '24," *Time* magazine noted once, commenting on something in the New York *Sun*, "makes $25,111 a year."

Well, good for him!

But wait a minute. What does this impressive figure mean? Is it, as it appears to be, evidence that if you send your boy to Yale you won't have to work in your old age and neither will he?

Two things about the figure stand out at first suspicious glance. It is surprisingly precise. It is quite improbably salubrious.

There is small likelihood that the average income of any far-flung group is ever going to be known down to the dollar. It is not particularly probable that you know your own income for last year so precisely as that unless it was all derived from salary. And $25,000 incomes are not often all salary; people in that bracket are likely to have well-scattered investments.

Furthermore, this lovely average is undoubtedly calculated from the amounts the Yale men *said* they earned. Even if they had the honor system in New Haven in '24, we cannot be sure that it works so well after a quarter of a century that all these reports are honest ones. Some people when asked their incomes exaggerate out of vanity or optimism. Others minimize, especially, it is to be feared, on income-tax returns; and having done this may hesitate to contradict themselves on any other paper. Who knows what the revenuers may see? It is possible that these two tendencies, to boast and to understate, cancel each other out, but it is unlikely. One tendency may be far stronger than the other, and we do not know which one.

We have begun then to account for a figure that common sense tells us can hardly represent the truth. Now let us put our finger on the likely source of the biggest error, a source that can produce $25,111 as the "average income" of some men whose actual average may well be nearer half that amount.

This is the sampling procedure, which is the heart of the greater part of the statistics you meet on all sorts of subjects. Its basis is simple enough, although its refinements in practice have led into all sorts of by-ways, some less than respectable. If you have a barrel of beans, some red and some white, there is only one way to find out exactly how many of each color you have: Count 'em. However, you can find out approximately how many are red in much easier fashion by pulling out a handful of beans and counting just those, figuring that the proportion will be the same all through the barrel. If your sample is large enough and selected properly, it will represent the whole well enough for most purposes. If it is not, it may be far less accurate than an intelligent guess and have nothing to recommend it but a spurious air of scientific precision. It is sad truth that conclusions from such samples, biased or too small or both, lie behind much of what we read or think we know.

The report on the Yale men comes from a sample. We can be pretty sure of that because reason tells us that no one can get hold of all the living members of that class of '24. There are bound to be many whose addresses are unknown twenty-five years later.

And, of those whose addresses are known, many will not reply to a questionnaire, particularly a rather personal one. With some kinds of mail questionnaire, a five or ten per cent response is quite high. This one should have done better than that, but nothing like one hundred per cent.

So we find that the income figure is based on a sample composed of all class members whose addresses are known and who replied to the questionnaire. Is this a representative sample? That is, can this group be assumed to be equal in income to the unrepresented group, those who cannot be reached or who do not reply?

Who are the little lost sheep down in the Yale rolls as "address unknown"?

Are they the big income earners—the Wall Street men, the corporation directors, the manufacturing and utility executives? No; the addresses of the rich will not be hard to come by. Many of the most prosperous members of the class can be found through *Who's Who in America* and other reference volumes even if they have neglected to keep in touch with the alumni office. It is a good guess that the lost names are those of the men who, twenty-five years or so after becoming Yale bachelors of arts, have not fulfilled any shining promise. They are clerks, mechanics, tramps, unemployed alcoholics, barely surviving writers and artists . . . people of whom it would take half a dozen or more to add up to an income of $25,111. These men do not so often register at class reunions, if only because they cannot afford the trip.

Who are those who chucked the questionnaire into the nearest wastebasket? We cannot be so sure about these, but it is at least a fair guess that many of them are just not making enough money to brag about. They are a little like the fellow who found a note clipped to his first pay check suggesting that he consider the amount of his salary confidential and not material for the interchange of office confidences. "Don't worry," he told the boss. "I'm just as ashamed of it as you are."

It becomes pretty clear that the sample has omitted two groups most likely to depress the average. The $25,111 figure is beginning to explain itself. If it is a true figure for anything it is one merely for that special group of the class of '24 whose addresses are known and who are willing to stand up and tell how much they earn. Even that requires an assumption that the gentlemen are telling the truth.

Such an assumption is not to be made lightly. Experience from one breed of sampling study, that called market research, suggests that it can hardly ever be made at all. A house-to-house survey purporting to study magazine readership was once made in which a key question was: What magazines does your household read? When the results were tabulated and analyzed it appeared that a great many people loved *Harper's* and not very many read *True Story*. Now there were publishers' figures around at the time that showed very clearly that *True Story* had more millions of circulation than *Harper's* had hundreds of thousands. Perhaps we asked the wrong kind of people, the designers of the survey said to themselves. But no, the questions had been asked in all sorts of neighborhoods all around the country. The only reasonable conclusion then was that a good many of the respondents, as people are called when they answer such questions, had not told the truth. About all the survey had uncovered was snobbery.

In the end it was found that if you wanted to know what certain people read it was no use asking them. You could learn a good deal more by going to their houses and saying you wanted to buy old magazines and what could be had? Then all you had to do was count the *Yale Reviews* and the *Love Romances*. Even that dubious device, of course, does not tell you what people read, only what they have been exposed to.

Similarly, the next time you learn from your reading that the average American (you hear a good deal about him these days, most of it faintly improbable) brushes his teeth 1.02 times a day—a figure I have just made up, but it may be as good as anyone else's —ask yourself a question. How can anyone have found out such a thing? Is a woman who has read in countless advertisements that non-brushers are social offenders going to confess to a stranger that she does not brush her teeth regularly? The statistic may have meaning to one who wants to know only what people say about toothbrushing but it does not tell a great deal about the frequency with which bristle is applied to incisor.

A river cannot, we are told, rise above its source. Well, it can seem to if there is a pumping station concealed somewhere about. It is equally true that the result of a sampling study is no better than the sample it is based on. By the time the data have been filtered through layers of statistical manipulation and reduced to a decimal-pointed average, the result begins to take on an aura of conviction that a closer look at the sampling would deny. . . .

Exercises

"The Language of Business," by William H. Whyte, Jr.

1. See if you can find "gobbledegook" in the dictionary. Write a paragraph on its origin and meaning.
2. Define and explain "businesese."
3. Define and explain "reverse gobbledegook."
4. Assume that you have just received your allowance check from home. Write a letter of acknowledgment in businesese. Write the same letter in your natural style.
5. Do you detect any evidences of reverse gobbledegook on the campus? Write a theme on the language of the college student.
6. Write a theme entitled, "Why Do Businessmen Write That Way?"
7. All of the following terms are used in this article: ambiguous, castigates, tacitly, cliché, the company's rationale, "intensional thinking," semanticists, analogy, metaphor. Define the terms and explain or illustrate each in an original sentence or short paragraph.
8. In your own words, how does language "confer status"? How does it mold thinking?
9. List what you consider to be 30 of the 60 principal clichés Mr. Whyte says he has used in "The Composite Business Speech" (pp. 111–112).
10. Write in a plain style what you think the speaker is trying to say in the parody on pages 111–112.
11. Do you remember the last banquet you attended? Write a report on the speeches, putting the emphasis wherever you wish.
12. Write a theme entitled, "Why Do Businessmen Speak That Way?" You may take illustrative phrases from this article.

"Better Letters," The Hanover Bank

1. Explain the objections to the words listed in "Words We Could Do Without." What do you make of the footnote?
2. Incorporate the ideas of "Which Writer Are You?" in another bulletin in essay style.
3. Write a theme on the subject of ambiguity (see "The Anatomy of Ambiguity"), supplying examples from other sources.
4. Assume that you are working for the State Department Store. Mr. Joseph Blank of 55 Maple Street, your city, has written that you sent him only two of the three pairs of black nylon socks that he ordered, even though he sent a check for $3.75 to cover the cost of the three pairs. Your records show that only two pairs were sent. You are therefore going to send the third pair through your regular parcel delivery. Write a letter to Mr. Blank taking advantage of the suggestions in "Acknowledging an Error."
5. Write a criticism of the letters in "Aren't You Glad You Didn't Write These Letters?"

"Words and Their Importance," by S. I. Hayakawa

1. Put the sense of this article in a couple of paragraphs.
2. What does the author mean by "false verbal maps"? Give illustrations of your own invention.
3. Write a theme on superstitions.

4. Write a theme on emotion in words. Relate your ideas to the language of business. (See also "On Appealing to Favorable Opinions," which follows.)

5. Write a theme about "thinking in opposites." Look for examples in current advertising.

6. What does the author have in mind when he cautions against "thinking too much"? Explain in the light of your own experience.

7. Explain the meaning of "multi-valued orientation." Give an example from business.

8. What can business learn from this article? Write a paper of about 400 words.

9. Spend a few hours in the library finding out what you can about semantics. Write a report on your findings.

"On Appealing to Favorable Opinions," by Edward J. Kilduff

1. Explain the relation between the terms "connotation" and "prepossessive words." Give illustrations.

2. Write a theme, also under the title "On Appealing to Favorable Opinions," using only examples that you can find in current news or advertising.

4. Develop a list of synonyms for one of the following words. Then write a theme in which you discuss the relative suggestive values of the synonyms for advertising purposes.

a. home
b. automobile
c. boarding house

"Vocabulary and Success," by Johnson O'Connor

1. Write a 500-word abstract of this article.

2. This article raises the question, "What is success?" Write a theme in which you answer the question in your own way.

3. Write a theme on the subject of words as "the tools of thought."

4. Do you have to go to college to acquire a big vocabulary? Discuss.

5. How do you account for the common error of confusing a word with its opposite? Use your own examples. Do you see any relation between this tendency and that of "thinking in opposites" mentioned by Dr. Hayakawa (p. 117)? Discuss.

6. Do you think you have a good vocabulary for your speaking and writing needs? An adequate vocabulary? An inadequate vocabulary? Discuss.

7. Write a theme in which you suggest some ways to enlarge one's vocabulary.

8. From this article (or from anywhere in this book) select several words you understand but do not use in your own speech or writing. Use these words as examples in a paper in which you explain the lag in transferring words from one's passive vocabulary to one's active vocabulary.

9. Do you think one should avoid using words that people may not understand? Write a paper on this subject.

10. Write a theme on one of the following subjects:

a. What Good Is a Big Vocabulary?
b. A Man Whose Vocabulary I Admire
c. Vocabulary Tests
d. When Words Fail Me

"Trademarks Might Be Skramedart," by Jess Stein

1. Invent a descriptive trade name for one of the following products and justify your choice in a paragraph:
   a. Refrigerator
   b. Foam-rubber under-rug cushion
   c. Menthol cigarettes
   d. Portable typewriter
   e. Frozen grapefruit juice
2. Examine the trade names you find in the advertisements in a single issue of a magazine like *Good Housekeeping* or *Ladies Home Journal*. Write a report on your findings.
3. Write a theme under one of the following titles:
   a. Trademarks I Don't Like
   b. I Heard You the First Time (a complaint about the annoying repetition of trade names on radio and television)
   c. Is There a Trend in Recent Trademarks?

"The Sample with the Built-In Bias," by Darrell Huff

1. State the author's point in a single paragraph.
2. Go back to the article, "What Do College Grades Predict?" (Sec. 1). How well do Dr. Husband's figures weather the kind of analysis suggested by Mr. Huff? Explain your position by references to both articles.
3. Find a newspaper or magazine article containing statistics based on sampling. Discuss the validity of the conclusions.
4. Suppose your composition teacher were to take a poll among your fellow students on the question, "What grade did you receive in English in your senior year at high school?" Discuss some of the factors that would influence the answers.
5. Study closely the language used by Mr. Huff. Give your opinion of it as informal English. Support your answer with examples from the text.

4

Mass Communication and Distribution

As America's population grew, so too did the markets for its goods. Transportation kept pace, and eventually the absence of a "carriage trade" was remedied by the automobile, which put the luxury of mobility at the doorsteps of millions. Developments in physical transportation were paralleled by developments in the transportation of ideas. Newspaper and magazine circulations increased, wires carried messages as fast as sound, and radio and television reached eager audiences right in their homes. Business promptly converted these media to their own needs, using them to open vast new markets for all the tempting products man and nature could devise. The marketing "revolution" is thus the result of progress in both communication and distribution. Some of the forces that characterize the revolution are treated in the selections that follow.

WE HAD NO CARRIAGE TRADE

Carl Crow

What was America like before the age of mass production and distribution? In a model of popular social history, Carl Crow shows how the needs of the common man started America on the road to industrial greatness. Mr. Crow spent many years in the Orient as a writer, editor, and advertising man before returning to America to become special assistant to the Director of War Information at the beginning of World War II.

There were only about three million of us—three million Americans who, after September 3, 1783, were free to earn money in any honest way that opportunity afforded and equally free to spend our money in any way we liked. It was on that historic but almost forgotten date that England signed a generous treaty with us formally and legally recognizing the independence of the thirteen rebellious colonies. The British army, which had remained in New York after the surrender of Cornwallis, sailed home before the end of the year. All the vexations of old restrictions on trade, manufacturing and navigation were ended. John Adams, who was one of the American negotiators, was not at all certain that freedom to do our own manufacturing would bring us any prosperity, and he managed to get the right to dry codfish on the Atlantic coast of what remained of British North America. While the treaty was under negotiation the codfish had been adopted as the symbol of the prosperity of Boston.

Here was a new market ready for us to develop—a market destined to become the greatest in the world—but at the time of our new freedom one of the poorest. Some Americans owned a great deal of land, but it was undeveloped and untenanted and brought in no revenue. There was no wealthy landlord class as in England and Europe. Naturally there were no important manufacturers, for manufacturing had been prohibited by British laws or severely restricted. There were no royal or noble families—no carriage trade important enough to be taken into account in any market survey. A few wealthy shipowning families lived in great houses in New England seaports, but they continued to buy goods from England just as they had done in the past.

There was, in fact, only one large class of customers either for merchant or manufacturer—the farmers. More than ninety out of every hundred people lived on poorly cultivated farms, grew their own food, spun and wove the cloth from which they made their own clothing. It was by catering to the needs of this class of poor and unpromising customers that American manufacturing and merchandising has developed and prospered. The fact that the early manufacturers and merchants had to cultivate the trade of this one class of homespun customers gave them a point of view which has never been changed and which has made our industrial development different from that of any other country.

Let us try to picture this American customer of 1783 living on his small farm, usually surrounded by the forest. It was because of the richness of the virgin soil rather than his skill or industry that crops were successfully produced. His farming methods were little better than those of the Indians and, like the Indians, he found it easier and much more interesting to shoot game in the forest or to fish in the streams than to grow crops and breed livestock at home. The armed revolt against British authority would have been impossible but for the fact that every farmer owned a squirrel rifle and was expert in its use. He was, of course, without any of the modern tools and so could cultivate what appears today to be pitifully small farms. There are innumerable records in New England of farms of between twenty and thirty acres, half of which were pasture, one quarter woodland and the other quarter cultivated. No wonder corn and wheat and practically all farm produce were relatively much more expensive then than they are today. The farmer was lucky if he raised enough beans, peas, corn or other grain to last from one season to the other. He usually raised a few pigs, which meant nothing more than that he held the ownership in the pigs his sow had farrowed. The rangy beasts roamed the woods in search of fallen acorns and in the winter ate the bark

off trees. All were scavengers of the vilest sort and pork produced under similar conditions today would not be passed by any health department. A hog weighing as much as two hundred pounds was remarkable.

The other livestock, cows and sheep, were better cared for, were allowed the hospitality of the barn and hay loft. If there were any children in the family there was a period of distress beginning with the time when the cow went dry and ending when she came fresh again. The sheep were of poor breed and the wool they produced would be used today only in carpet manufacture. This wool and equally coarse linen provided the clothing of the family, hand-carded, hand-spun, hand-woven and hand-tailored. Cotton cloth which was imported was too expensive to be worn by any but the very wealthy. Horses were not numerous. The heavy, slow-moving oxen were more useful in pulling the clumsy plow or in moving loads through areas that were practically roadless. There were no wagons—only a few carts with wooden wheels.

The standard-sized frame house appears to have consisted of a single room eighteen by twenty-four feet, a size mentioned frequently throughout colonial records and for several generations after independence. That size provided a large room by modern standards, but it was quite frequently the only room, with a low, windowless attic where some of the children slept. Here the whole family—often as many as nine or ten—lived throughout the year. Here was the place of giving birth and the place of death. It was also the place where all the household manufacturing was carried on—a crowded place, hot in summer and cold in winter and at almost all seasons permeated with odors ranging from unpleasant to foul. The puncheon floor consisted of roughly squared logs laid on the ground.

The most conspicuous as well as the most important object in the room was the great open fireplace on which all the food was cooked. (It was not until fifty years later that the first American pie was baked in that Yankee invention, a cook stove.) Some, but not all, of the huge fireplaces were equipped with Dutch ovens, a bricked-in aperture which could be closed by a door. A bright fire of well-seasoned pine would be built in the oven itself and fed until the proper heat had been obtained. The oven was then swept out and with the door closed retained enough heat for baking.

A fire once kindled in the fireplace was never allowed to go out but was kept burning from month to month and year to year like the flame over an altar in a Buddhist temple. But there was no religious significance to this procedure. If the fire was inadvertently allowed to go out, live coals had to be borrowed from a neighbor or a new spark kindled with flint and steel and tinder. Children soon became expert at banking fires with ashes.

The Dutch oven did not play as large a part in early American cookery as has been supposed. Its operation took quite a little time as well as skill. The housewife had too much to do to bother with elaborate meals, and she had nothing but the coarsest of ingredients. Much more commonly used were the pots of varying sizes which were suspended over the open fire. Corn meal mush was a staple. Beans, peas, fresh vegetables, game and salt pork all went into the pot. Potatoes were sometimes roasted in the hot ashes, but potatoes were not common and were looked on as something of a delicacy. A kind of corn bread was produced by tilting the filled baking pan toward the open fire. The housewife, who had many duties to attend, did not cook three meals a day nor did she necessarily cook a fresh meal every day. The cooking pots were large enough to hold provisions for several days, or a week, and in most cases the contents of one pot were devoured before the next was put on the fire. In many households the whole culinary process was based on the theory that any foodstuff boiled in a pot was edible. The food on which the average American farmer lived would cause a riot in any modern penitentiary. Throughout colonial biographies one occasionally finds some prominent citizen characterized by his fellows as "amiable." This characteristic was notably uncommon and, it would be reasonable to suppose, was applied only to those with stomachs so valiant as to withstand the indigestible Colonial food. It was not until a generation after the invention of the cook stove (1830) that amiability as a characteristic of men in public life was taken for granted and the adjective was dropped from biographical sketches.

There was always a spinning wheel in the room and sometimes a loom. Clothing of the poorest and coarsest sort was much more expensive than it is today. The development of machine-made textiles had just begun, and cloth of all kinds cost three to five times the present prices. No farmer could hope to earn enough money to buy clothing for his family and they were all dressed in homespun or skins or not at all. If there were any candles in the house, they were home made. Tallow dips took hours to make, sperm candles were too expensive for any but the rich or for use in the meeting house. Therefore the only artificial illuminant in many homes was provided by the flame of the open fire. This could always be augmented by splinters of pitch pine stuck in cracks in the hearth where they burned brighter than any candle.

The housewife freed the wool of its

grease by soaking it in urine. She carded, spun and wove the cloth, dyed it and fashioned it into clothing. In the summertime she did the gardening. She also made soap, but there is no evidence that the institution of Monday wash day had been established. Life was not simple but extremely complex, for the farmer and his wife had to be masters of a dozen trades.

It was a rare house that possessed chairs enough for everyone. It was taken for granted that children should sit on stools or benches, just as it was taken for granted that they should eat off their parents' plates. A communal drinking cup was the rule rather than the exception. Few families possessed any chinaware or glass. Wooden trenchers were commonly used. These were blocks of wood about a foot square, hollowed out in the middle. There was such a dearth of ordinary humble articles that it was not uncommon for a man to mention a pewter bowl, a pair of scissors or linen sheets in his will. The wool curing process, like all other home manufacturing, was carried on in the communal room and the covered vat provided a seat for one of the children. Another odorous receptacle in the room was the salt pork barrel. Hams and bacon hanging beside the mantel piece added their contribution to the odors.

As soon as children began to grow up and become curious about the facts of life, the married couple had to add a bedroom to this communal chamber or install a four-poster bed. Since the latter cost less, a great many of them were made. It was only when concealed behind the curtains of this bed that the fathers and mothers enjoyed any degree of privacy. An heirloom four-poster does not, as many believe, always indicate the opulence of some revered ancestor, but often the reverse. Many of these beds were not four-posters at

all but just cubicles built inside the room, the sides covered with rough boards.

It is fortunate for the marriageable young ladies of the period that no such soul-scorching phrases as *halitosis*, *body odor*, and *tattletale gray* had been introduced into the sedate English language. With dentifrices and bathtubs completely absent, there can be no doubt that the daintiest New England maiden was, by present standards, always decidedly spicy in odor.

It was many years after the end of the Revolution before that English symbol of aristocracy, the bathtub, was accepted as something that could be fitted into the democratic way of life. During this period the greatest contribution to personal cleanliness was the "wash room," a cubicle between the main building and the out buildings. Here there was, in well appointed houses, a pail of water with a gourd dipper, a wash basin, a bowl of homemade soft soap and a towel. Those who were finicky enough to want to wash their hands before they ate were provided with the opportunity to do so. That was the early predecessor of the powder room and the guest towels of today. It was not until 1850 that a bathroom was installed in the White House.

From checking over the possessions and the needs of this typical family of consumers of 1783, it is obvious that a merchant or manufacturer would require the trade of a great many of them if he expected to make a fortune, for individually they bought very little. Still less cash changed hands, for there was very little money of any kind in circulation and its place was taken by an intricate system of exchange and barter. Grain was taken to the mill where the farmer helped grind it and paid the miller a toll of one-fourth to one-third of the meal or flour. Salt, about the only foodstuff that was not produced on the farm, had to be bought for use in curing pork and for the cattle; it was very expensive, costing from ten to twenty times the prices which have prevailed during the past half century. Children liked molasses on their corn bread but that didn't necessarily mean that they had to be humored. Coffee was as scarce as champagne is today, nor was tea as common as it generally was supposed. No available statistics of the importations of tea indicate any large per capita consumption.

The articles of furniture were usually homemade and, like the pots and pans on the hearthstone, were supposed to last a lifetime. As a matter of fact, they usually lasted through several generations. Although every housewife could spin, some could not weave or did not own a loom. In such cases the yarn was woven on terms similar to those of the miller. The weaver kept part of the yarn. Buttons had to be bought but they were used over and over again, and no one but the comparatively well-to-do town people bothered about buttons matching. Needles and sewing thread had to be bought, also the pots and kettles. The farmer made most of his tools for his farm work but in his capacity as carpenter and Jack-of-all-trades he had to buy hammers, saws, chisels and other hardware.

Shoes were a problem—a seasonal problem, for they were not essential in warm weather. The farmer often met this problem halfway by tanning his own hides, and the odor of tanning vat in the living quarters competed with great success over those of the dye pot, the salt pork barrel, the manure pile and the privy, if there was one. An itinerant shoemaker would cut and peg and sew this rough leather into shoes. Each pair of shoes was made to order, but that does not mean that they were fitted

after the manner of expensive custom-made shoes of today. The shoes had to be large enough to get your feet into but not so large that you would step out of them when walking. It was not until the turn of the century that anyone thought of shaping shoes differently for the left and the right foot and another twenty years passed before any but the most fastidious dressers insisted on this distinction. The word cordwainer is now listed in the dictionaries as archaic. It was in common use in 1783, and everyone knew that a cordwainer was a kind of shoemaker who made moccasins. A great many people wore moccasins, which were easier to make.

Not only did the typical American customer need very little, but he did not make enough money on his farm to pay for what he needed. Cash revenue from farming operations could not be depended on. There were not many city dwellers, but even these usually kept a cow, raised chickens and pigs and maintained a kitchen garden and a few fruit trees. The sale of such farm products as eggs, fruit and fresh vegetables to city dwellers did not become a source of revenue until the towns grew much larger and more congested.

In order to get money to pay the taxes and buy the few necessities, the farmer usually had one or more additional occupations. He was not a good farmer but his abilities could not be judged on that accomplishment alone. His wife was a poor cook but she was in addition a worker in wool and flax, a dyer, soapmaker, candlemaker, etc. The husband was something of a carpenter, blacksmith, tanner, trapper and curer of furs—something of a Jack-of-all-trades, one or more of which could be depended on to bring in some ready cash. One of the common occupations was making nails.

Pelts of wild animals provided some revenue as they still do in many parts of the country. The trapping of beaver was so profitable that it was soon played out in many parts of the country. A more dependable source of forest revenue came from what was known as "pot ashes," later simplified to the one word potash. The method of manufacture was very simple. The manufacturers went into the forest, cut down the timber and, after it was seasoned for a few months, burned the logs and collected the ashes. These were leached into lye by the filtering of water, the lye boiled in a pot until it became a solid or semi-solid mass. This was a product of considerable value which could be profitably shipped long distances. That was not true of tan bark and charcoal, two other forest commodities so bulky that they could only be sold in the neighborhood of production. Many young men with plans to set up homes for themselves spent one or two winters in the forests making potash in order to earn enough cash to build a home for their brides. Many others about the turn of the century employed the same method to earn enough money to start some small factory or business enterprise.

It was on the scant trade of these early customers that the industries of the country were founded, and on the constantly increasing trade of their descendants that these industries have grown and prospered. The sons and grandsons of the few wealthy men in the new United States were not, with few exceptions, pioneers in manufacturing or merchandising. Perhaps some of the snobbish English contempt for the "tradesmen" deterred them, or perhaps their imaginations were not stirred by the prospect of great fortunes to be made from petty transactions. They invested their inherited money in real estate, banks, shipping and insurance, followed occupations that bore the insignia of wealth.

Leadership in the industries which were later to become so great was assumed by the sons and grandsons of the poor farmers who raised big families in crowded and foul-smelling houses. When they started to manufacture goods for sale to their new and rapidly growing country they did not think of John Hancock, George Washington, Robert Morris and the few other wealthy men of the country. There were few of them and they lived in remotely scattered areas. The customers they had in mind were of the same class and generation as themselves, descendants of men who worked their farms inefficiently and made nails and potash in order to earn a little cash.

Because the carriage trade was not important enough to cater to, because the only large group of customers consisted of men and women who were poor or only moderately prosperous, American manufacturing and merchandising started at the bottom. Success was only to be found by catering to the needs of the common man. This meant the mass production of goods to be sold in quantity at the cheapest possible price. The best artisans in England or Europe had their attention fixed on the wealthy trade—the prince or rich landlord whose patronage alone would keep them in business and possibly make them wealthy. The American artisans who later became manufacturers had to think of securing the trade of a hundred or a thousand customers in order to enjoy the same sense of security. As the years passed and their undertakings grew, the number of steady customers they required grew to hundreds of thousands, millions and finally, or presently, to tens of millions.

It wasn't until we had a head start in manufacturing that other nations woke up to the fact that the carriage trade was one of vanishing importance.

HENRY FORD AND THE MODEL T

Roger Burlingame

In this account of Henry Ford's determination to build the Model T, the author describes a turning point in the philosophy of factory production. Ford held on perhaps too long to the idea that the public was interested only in utility, but his influence on the course of industry is not to be questioned. Roger Burlingame is the author of many books dealing with facets of the American scene, including *The American Conscience*.

Mass production is peculiarly and almost uniquely American in its origins. The main reasons for this are, first: the American belief, in spite of many demonstrations to the contrary, that all men are created equal; and, second: the unparalleled need to supply a constantly migrating and constantly increasing agrarian population with goods produced under an acute labor shortage.

In European and Asiatic societies, tradition prescribed that the best things went to a privileged few. Clocks, watches, fine fabrics, shoes, and, later, sewing machines and bicycles were perquisites of an upper class and filtered slowly, if at all, down to the masses. With abundance of labor many goods could be produced in limited quantities more or less by hand. In the United States, where everyone considered himself "as good as the next man," and where land fever and the pull of the frontier robbed the static centers of skilled workmen, machines had to be designed to multiply the productiveness of a few men and to keep the democracy supplied with what the "inalienable rights" demanded.

Through all of later American history, as social democracy became more and more complete, industry has been continuously occupied in turning luxuries into necessities. Early Connecticut clockmakers made it possible for timepieces—regarded abroad as property of the well-to-do—to become part of the furnishings of the humblest frontier cabins. Machine production plus installment-selling brought reapers, harvesters, and threshers to farmers penniless but for their land. Factory-made shoes and clothing raised the living standard of American "masses" above that of other peoples, and, finally, such astonishing luxuries as electric refrigerators, oil burners, radio, and television gained markets that to foreigners are truly fabulous.

It is largely to quantity production through semi-automatic machinery that Americans owe the rapid development of their country. With the coming of the twentieth century the enormous territory had been surprisingly integrated, considering the sparseness of its population in the frontier period; yet much of the land was still unexploited, almost unexplored. Cities and towns followed one another in long, straight lines along rivers and railroads: to these communities the rural population had flocked, leaving hundreds of ghost villages, lonely farms, or large barren stretches that were virtually wilderness. The railroads had killed the improvement of highways, and wagon roads had lapsed into conditions that, a half century later, are impossible to visualize.

By 1900, however, many Americans had had glimpses of other horizons. An entirely new taste of individual freedom —freedom to escape, to explore, to discover the allures of nature—had come in the nineties with the bicycle. Supposing that the bicycle was a social fixture, several eager promoters had started good-roads movements. Imported techniques of roadbuilding— notably McAdam's—were tried and proved successful. Finally, in the first year of the new century, road conditions and the possibilities of new frontiers in the interior were brought sensationally to public attention in the exploit of Roy Chapin, who drove a one-cylinder, curved-dash Oldsmobile buggy from Detroit to New York. "He was forced," Mr. Arthur Pound tells us, "to leave the muddy highways, and drive along the towpath of the Erie Canal, contesting with mule trains for the right-of-way."

Such things as this undoubtedly sank into the subconscious minds of Americans everywhere and prepared the way for the revolution. It is probable, for instance, that the great army of boys who followed automotive development with acute interest saw visions of their own futures, driving horselessly into far country. A child taught to believe that he might well one day become president was still easier to convince that he might one day drive and even own a car. On the surface, however, Roy Chapin's feat was regarded as a daring sporting effort—not quite so reckless as going over Niagara Falls in a barrel, but in that general category.

Even six years later, when 142,000 motor vehicles were registered in the United States, private ownership of a car was a mark of distinction or, perhaps, evidence of extravagant frivolity: indeed, as we have seen, business trends seemed to be toward increasing its luxurious characteristics. Keith Sward, writing of the early 1900's in *The Legend of Henry Ford*, says:

In this day the rich themselves thought of the automobile as a luxury reserved for the few. . . . It was understood at the same time that the plain people of the country were to function as the tenders and repairers of the motor car. Guided by such a conviction, the Detroit *Saturday Night* said in 1909 that the best chauffeurs were to be recruited from the ranks of former coachmen. Such drivers, observed the *Saturday Night*, were dutiful members of the "servant class" who could be counted on to know "exactly what is expected of them by their masters."

Whatever may have been Henry Ford's motives during his company's experimental period, we may be sure that such statements as this must have exasperated him. Above all else, this man suspected and despised the rich and shied away from anything that smacked of luxury. It would have been wholly out of character for him to favor the production of expensive cars except for technical purposes. It must, therefore, have been a satisfaction to him that there was a sharp decline of sales when his $2,500 Model K was introduced and a quick up-curve when the cheaper Model N went on the market. It was obvious by 1907, though no suggestion of a "universal car" had yet engaged the public fancy, that the name of Ford was popularly associated with low-priced automobiles.

We may put our finger precisely on 1907 as the year in which revolution came. It seems, looking back on it, as if fate played then into Ford's hands— as if it were a wind of destiny that shook the stock market in March, brought the most hopeful securities to the ground, and sowed the seeds of October panic. The rich were hard hit. Low-priced cars were more than ever sought after. In the course of the year Ford production jumped to about eighty-five hundred, five times that of the previous year; and the great bulk of it consisted of the latest experimental light cars—Models N, R, and S, all selling for less than $1,000.

Watching these things, keeping careful track of costs, thinking of the future in terms of expansion beyond all dreams of the time in this first adolescence of the industry, Henry Ford evolved his great concept. It was in the light of this vision that he felt too confined in the Piquette-Beaubien plant, to which the company had moved when Strelow's Mack Avenue shop would no longer hold it. He planned for the purchase of the sixty-acre Highland Park race track, where he talked of building "the largest automobile factory in the world."

Various employees of the Ford Motor Company have claimed credit for the revolutionary idea. It has been said that it was not one man's brainstorm, but the result of the focusing of many minds. It is undoubtedly true that others contributed details of design and, especially, production methods.

But no one can examine the records or analyze the reminiscences of Ford workers of the period without knowing beyond question not only that Henry Ford's was the master mind but that the whole of the broad project originated with him. Indeed, we find evidence of discontented and sometimes angry rumblings throughout the time when the plan was taking shape and, indeed, of the disgusted exit of two of the most important production men in the plant. And with Ford's contemplation of the new gigantic installations at Highland Park—to be financed entirely by the plowing back of profits—the waves of unrest spread out to the stockholders. So the project had far from unanimous support.

The project was Model T.

The way for the realization of Model T was now open. If the idea had occurred to Henry Ford before—as it probably had—there were difficulties to be overcome. He had not had full control. Malcomson, with whom he had shared equally the majority stockholding, was opposed to concentrating on a low-priced car. But here too the gods were conniving. Malcomson had sold out to Ford. Speculating in other directions, he had needed cash and, as the stock for which he had originally paid $12,000 was now worth $175,000, he was content. Albert Strelow and three minor stockholders had followed Malcomson's exit. Ford bought all of these shares. Those who like to play the game known as "the if's of history" enjoy speculating on the millions these men might have made had they remained aboard. Yet if they had stuck, perhaps there would have been no Model T. Poor Strelow put the $25,000 he received into a gold mine, which almost immediately turned out to be barren, and he was later reported standing in line for a lowly job with the company he had once partly owned.

By 1907, then, 58½ shares of stock in the Ford Motor Company had been acquired by Henry Ford, giving him full power in the management of the company. In these fateful years some valuable technical assets had also arrived. To make crankshafts for Model N, Ford had hired a great, brawny, uncouth ox of a man named Walter Flanders, who, nevertheless, was original, ingenious, and highly versed in mass-production techniques. Also, working creatively in the company since 1904, another giant, physically and mentally, was a Dane named Charles Sorensen or "Cast-iron Charlie." This man, whose later contributions to the moving assembly were perhaps without equal anywhere, was an old friend of Henry's going back to the days of the Edison company. A third was the brilliant mechanic, P. Edward ("Pete") Martin.

These men and others picked by the chief's almost infallible instinct must, by the methods of economy and speed they installed—rearranging machinery, devising jigs and fixtures for accurate machine-tool work, dividing labor, and insisting on interchangeability—have led Ford over the months into his large, over-all view of the most adaptable product for full mass production. He was constantly moving through all the departments, watching every man and every machine. Like Frederick Taylor, the great inventor of scientific management, Ford had a passion for simplifying operations, for economy of time and materials, for eliminating little waste motions from each worker's performance.

It is remarkable how close all this came to the carefully worked-out plans of Taylor, because Ford had certainly not read Taylor's treatises. It must be assumed that the efficiency patterns came into the Ford plant with the factory men he hired, but in the use of them Ford exercised a critical judgment and creative force that everyone acknowledged. His power lay in an instant recognition of what was right and what was wrong in any new method. The reminiscences of the workers taken, after Ford's death, on tape recordings testify to the master's almost constant pressure, walking over miles of factory floor, stopping at every work center to watch or speak, to say no, to nod approval, to berate—perhaps fire on the spot—an inflexible perverse, or skeptical worker. A man in these times who hinted, even by the expression of his face, that he thought one of the master's schemes impossible was doomed. "Mr. Ford" [Charles Sorensen recalls] "never caught me saying that an idea he had couldn't be done. If I had the least idea that it couldn't be done, I wouldn't announce myself on it to him. . . . I always felt the thing would prove itself."

Walter Flanders thought the Model T project was impossible. He did not think the Model T itself was impossible. He was willing to try that. But he thought the *project* would be fatal to the company. He thought Ford was crazy to pursue it and said so. He then walked out before Ford had a chance to invite his departure.

It was not Ford's determination to produce Model T—a simple, sturdy, utilitarian, low-priced job—that worried Flanders. It was his determination *to produce nothing but*. It was a profound obsession in the industry that no manufacturer could survive concentrating on a single model—that he must offer a choice and make annual changes. Today we may sympathize with this view. The industrialists of 1907 were merely thinking twenty years ahead of their time. Mass production of this highly complex machine had to be established first—not only technically but economically as well. We know

now that a Model T project had to be injected into American society before the universal market and the universal desire could become facts. The *flexible* mass production that engineers are dreaming of in the 1950's will probably follow more flexible tastes of the future. But *inflexible* mass production had to precede it: neither the techniques nor the popular demand of the years immediately following 1907 would have permitted anything else. That was the fact: but of all the eager folk who were then engaged in pushing the horse off the American road, only Henry Ford knew it.

Against the advice, then, of those who should have known better—yet who, curiously enough, provided many of the technical needs of the scheme— Henry Ford announced that thereafter there would be only one Ford. "I will build a motor car" [he stated] "for the great multitude. It will be large enough for the family but small enough for the individual to run and care for. It will be constructed of the best materials, by the best men to be hired, after the simplest designs that modern engineering can devise. But it will be so low in price that no man making a good salary will be unable to own one—and enjoy with his family the blessing of hours of pleasure in God's great open spaces."

Advertising men have done a great deal of talking about "psychology" and much solemn experimenting with it. Yet it would be hard to find in all their copy anything as appealing in its time as this simple, almost biblically worded statement. What American before 1910 could be indifferent to the vision of transporting his family, of a Sunday or holiday, into "God's great open spaces"? What head of a family would not be inflated by the prospect of running and caring for this family machine? What "equal" citizen would

admit to making anything less than a "good salary"?

In his autobiography Ford recalls that his rivals were delighted by this announcement and by the news that he had bought the sixty acres at Highland Park for his production. The question, he says, asked so many thousand times since, was already being asked in 1908 and 1909: "How soon will Ford blow up?" "It is asked" [he adds] "only because of the failure to grasp that a principle rather than an individual is at work, and the principle is so simple that it seems mysterious."

The principle was to decide on your design, freeze it, and, from then on, spend all your time, effort, and money on making the machinery to produce it —concentrating so completely on production that, as volume goes up, it is certain to get cheaper per unit produced. Changing your design every year means retooling your factory every year; it means not continuing one process long enough to study ways of making it more economical; it means constantly changing your orders for materials; it means that the customers have to learn new tricks; it means that salesmen have to keep changing their story; it means expensive advertising.

The "great multitude," Ford thought, was not interested in fashions or experiments; it did not care about pretty lines or colors in a car: it wanted something useful to drive to town or country, something that would meet any road conditions, something that took no thought to drive, no expense to maintain, no special skill to repair. And the multitude, Ford believed, *would want these things forever* and nothing else. This was the theory and philosophy of mass production carried to its extreme.

Workers still living remember Ford in his elation, the almost fanatical excitement of his drive as this concept came to full flower in his mind. He would look at the design for a cylinder block or differential or steering unit and say: "There! We won't change that until we've built a hundred thousand cars!" At the beginning he wanted to simplify the manufacture until skilled workers were eliminated—until, as one pattern-maker remembers, "he just took a man off the street and broke him in like a piece of machinery doing a certain job." This was not an effort to get cheap labor. It was simply that, for the tremendous production that he envisioned, there was not enough skilled labor in the world; also, production could never become fast enough until the worker's motions were almost automatic and without thought. . . .

THE MARKETING REVOLUTION

Charles F. Phillips

Improvements in the distribution of goods have always lagged behind improvements in their production. Nevertheless, the last fifty years have produced changes in marketing procedures that affect everyone from the buyer of industrial steel to the consumer of frozen chicken pies. Dr. Phillips, who highlights the changes, is president of Bates College and author of many books and articles on marketing.

. . . What do I mean when I say that a Marketing Revolution has taken place in this country and in the United States? Just this: Such great changes in marketing procedures, methods, and policies have taken place in our economy during the past fifty years that we can describe them in nothing less than the term "revolutionary."

You can see this revolution in any direction you wish to look. To take just two illustrations, glance at what has happened to the number of people employed in the performance of marketing functions. Census figures make it clear that at least one out of every four people employed in my country performs marketing functions. These figures also indicate that the number of people employed by marketing activities is growing far more rapidly than the number engaged in production. For example, during the last fifty years alone, the number in marketing has increased nine times, as against a threefold increase for production.

As our second illustration, look at the key executive positions occupied today by marketing men. In 1920, but 18% of a representative group of American corporations had given the title of vice-president or president to its key marketing executive. By 1938, this percentage had increased to 56%. While a current comparable figure is not available, it is obvious that this percentage today would be even greater than it was eighteen years ago.

CHANGING MARKETING POLICIES AND PRACTICES

With marketing executives occupying key executive positions, it is not surprising that recent years have seen a substantial increase in the amount of executive attention given to marketing policies. Fifty years ago little attention was given to them. At that time executives didn't worry too much about concentrating on selected channels of distribution; rather, they sold to anyone who stood ready to buy from them. They didn't burn the midnight oil worrying about their after-sale service policies; rather, if their product broke

From an address before the Marketing for Management Seminar, Toronto Chapter of the American Marketing Association, University of Toronto, Canada, January 6, 1956.

down, they would decide in each individual case whether or not they should trouble themselves to repair it. Or again, many executives of 50 years ago would feel quite out of place were they to sit in on a present-day discussion of price policies. To them, price was a matter of finding a unit cost figure and adding something for profit. And still again, fifty years ago can you imagine your company letting you have time off to come to a seminar, such as we are having here today?

Why are we willing to devote so much executive time and company money to marketing policy formation? On the fiftieth anniversary of his wedding to Mrs. Ford, the great automobile manufacturer, Henry Ford, was asked how he explained his long and successful married life. He replied that a successful married life was produced in exactly the same way as a successful automobile; that is, you merely begin with one model and stick to it. Well, this may be the key to a successful married life, but most of us have discovered long ago that this is not the key to a successful business. Our competitors won't let us follow such an easy policy. Instead, we must continue to adjust our policies to changing conditions. It may be dignified for a company to have traditional policies and practices—but we also need to remember that there is nothing more dignified than a corpse!

As a result of all the thinking marketing men have given to their policies, major changes in company outlook and practices have resulted. In fact, so many have been the changes that I shall not even attempt to list all of them, let alone discuss them. For example, we could spend hours discussing the revolution which has taken place in the retail field alone—shopping centers, self-election and self-service, the development of mass retailing.

Or we might, and profitably, devote an hour to the impact of fashion on marketing. But let me just emphasize four of these changes which I believe to be especially important to you.

1. Increased recognition of the customer point of view. Much of the seller's philosophy concerning the customer of fifty years ago is expressed in the story of the grocery store operator who called to his son in the basement of the store to say "Son, sand the sugar, water the vinegar, and get upstairs for evening prayer."

Today that philosophy of "the customer be damned" has largely disappeared. I say "largely" because occasionally I still come across a seller who practices it. I met one of them a couple of summers ago in the course of a trip to the West Coast. He wanted to determine exactly where I should sit in his restaurant, despite my desire to sit elsewhere. When we reached an impasse in the final decision, I exercised my consumer-king rights and enjoyed dinner in another restaurant. But that experience was exceptional. . . .

In other words, today's marketing plans must be based on service to the customer. It is our obligation to discover what he wants, how and where he wants it, and under what conditions. Recognition of this fact represents a revolutionary change in the marketing world.

2. More emphasis on marketing research. In part, the greater recognition which is given to marketing research today as compared with even twenty years ago is a direct result of trying to find out what the customer wants and under what circumstances. But customer research—as exemplified by so-called consumer surveys—is but a small part of today's marketing research activities. We also use it to forecast sales, set quotas, measure salesmen's performances, set standards for wholesalers and

retailers, test package design, study advertising effectiveness, establish prices, and in a host of other areas. While the total amount still spent on marketing research is small as compared with technical research, and while our research techniques are still rather crude, the increased emphasis on this tool as a more scientific approach to marketing problems is a step in the right direction—and it marks a revolutionary change in the thinking of those engaged in marketing activities.

3. Recognition that merchandising or product planning or development, as it is referred to by many, is an essential function of marketing. Here again, the change has been revolutionary. Fifty years ago a man got an idea of a product for which he *thought* there might be a market. He hired a couple of workers and began to turn it out in his basement. If the market proved to be there, he succeeded—at least until someone else came along with a better product; if the market was not there, he failed, and went back to his old job of selling for someone else.

Today's large manufacturers have too much invested to let someone else take their markets away from them with better products. They have learned that to avoid this result they must concentrate on improving their products. This improvement may take the form, for example, of a better quality of product, more attractive packaging, eliminating products with which users have found fault, or adding new products to supplement existing lines. Representatives of the manufacturer must be in close touch with consumers, retailers, and wholesalers to determine their reactions to the merchandise produced. Competitors' products must be studied continuously, and contests may be held to obtain suggestions for additional uses of products and to learn methods by

which they may be improved. All in all, the manufacturer's merchandising job is one of seeking constantly to improve his present products, of creating new products to supplement his existing line, and of timing the introduction of new items to obtain the most favorable response.

4. Greater reliance upon advertising as a selling tool. I will not bore you with statistics as to the revolutionary growth of advertising in recent years. It has become a major selling tool for producers' goods as well as for consumers' goods. In fact, today it serves several purposes:

(1) It aids in the introduction of new products to the market through familiarizing potential consumers with their uses and middlemen with their availability;

(2) It assists in the expansion of a market;

(3) It helps to obtain desirable dealer outlets through making it easier for dealers to sell;

(4) It prepares the way for the salesman through acquainting prospects with the name of the company and the merits of a product;

(5) It informs potential customers of new developments and new applications of existing products, as in the case of major plant equipment;

(6) It affords the seller—where catalogs are used—with representation even when the salesman is not present. All these uses, of course, should result in increased sales and profits.

So great is the reliance upon advertising today that I would warn you that some users have expected far too much from it. They have assumed that an expensive advertising campaign might make up for a poorly selected channel of distribution; or that it could help sell a product which was of unsatisfactory construction, overpriced, or not even desired by many customers. A few have anticipated a great increase in sales as the result of advertising for a short period.

Those who have the foregoing expectations are guilty of wishful thinking. Advertising is but one factor in a successful selling program. It gives best results when used continuously for a product which customers want, which is well priced, designed, and constructed, and which is sold through adequate trade channels. On its own part, advertising will not contribute its share to the sales program of the manufacturer, wholesaler, or retailer unless it is carefully planned in advance, proper appeals are selected and presented, the right types of media are used, and its cost is not excessive. . . .

WHERE ARE THE ADS OF YESTERYEAR?

Robert L. Heilbroner

Of course one has to be over eighteen to believe that anything used to be better than it is right now. Robert Heilbroner, whose memory takes him back a few years, has the notion that advertisements used to be better, but he does not tell how importantly nostalgia figures in his rating scale. A free-lance writer specializing in business subjects, Mr. Heilbroner won a wide audience with his informal survey of economics, *The Worldly Philosophers*.

Let me begin by stating that I am a devotee of advertising. Its social significance, or its cultural insignificance, doesn't faze me a bit. I am not one of those who deplore the Human Wastage of the profession, nor do I view with alarm its gentle prevarications. The caricature of admen as hucksters amuses me, but doesn't raise my blood pressure a single notch. I just get a tremendous kick out of watching the advertising brain knock itself out in a bid for my patronage.

Nevertheless, I have a bone to pick with the trade. I don't think advertising packs the wallop it used to. Maybe the trouble is in me: maybe I'm older and more jaded and no longer the susceptible quarry I undoubtedly once was. But I think there's more to it than that. I have a feeling that advertising doesn't come at you the way it once did—that it doesn't take you by the lapels, back you into a corner, and leave you stupefied, glazed, and as pantingly acquisitive as it did in the good old days.

There was a time, I am convinced, when a copywriter who couldn't sell an icebox to an Eskimo wouldn't have been worth his $17.50 a week.

That was back in the days when people still thought cultured pearls were only worn by uncultured people. So some hero composed this masterpiece for the Técla Pearl firm, and in exactly thirty-five words and five figures wrote what I consider to be an absolute rockcrusher of an ad:

A $10,000
Mistake

A client for whom we had copied a necklace of Oriental Pearls, seeing both necklaces before her, said: *Well, the resemblance is remarkable, but this is mine!*

Then she picked up ours!

TECLA

389 Fifth Avenue, New York
10 Rue de la Paix, Paris

The man who wrote that could have signed up Carrie Nation as a Woman of Distinction.

Or take this one. It sold the most dreary and intangible of goods: learning piano by mail. It did it in a closely-packed page of print from which not one cliché of the English language was omitted. But the effect? Well, read it and judge for yourself:

They Laughed When I Sat Down At the Piano But When I Started to Play!—

Arthur had just played "The Rosary."

The room rang with applause. I decided that this would be a dramatic moment for me to make my debut. To the amazement of all my friends, I strode confidently over to the piano and sat down.

"Jack is up to his old tricks," somebody chuckled. The crowd laughed. They were certain that I couldn't play a note.

"Can he really play?" I heard a girl whisper to Arthur.

"Heavens, no," Arthur exclaimed. "He never played a note in all his life. . . ."

I decided to make the most of the situation. With mock dignity I drew out a silk handkerchief and lightly dusted off the piano keys. Then I rose and gave the revolving piano stool a quarter of a turn as I had seen an imitator of Paderewski do in a vaudeville sketch.

"What do you think of his execution?" called a voice from the rear.

"We're in favor of it!" came back the answer and the crowd rocked with laughter.

Then I started to play.

Instantly a tense silence fell on the guests. The laughter died on their lips as if by magic. I played through the first few bars of Beethoven's immortal "Moonlight Sonata." I heard gasps of amazement. My friends sat breathless —spellbound.

I played on, and as I played, I forgot the people around me. I forgot the hour, the place, the breathless listeners. The little world I lived in seemed to fade—seemed to grow dim—unreal. Only the music was real. Only the music and visions it brought me. Visions as beautiful and as changing as the wind blown clouds and drifting moonlight that long ago inspired the master composer.

That, to me, is advertising. I am the guy at whom they laughed, and the prospect of Arthur slinking out of the room (I'll bet he never played "The Rosary" again) is my personal triumph. The starry-eyed girls, the breathlessly hushed guests—why, it's *me* they're clapping!

Yes, those were the days when an advertising man was a poet. A commercial poet, of course, for it was sheer larceny what his verses did to you.

You picked up a magazine, you saw the picture of a tender young woman, her fingers raised to her parted lips, you noted her tear-touched happiness, and then you read with her this unbeatable note:

for marrying me in the first place . . .

for bringing up our children—while I mostly sat back and gave advice.

for the 2,008 pairs of socks you've darned.

for finding my umbrella and my rubbers Heaven knows how often!

for tying innumerable dress ties.

for being the family chauffeur, years on end.

for never getting sore at my always getting sore at your bridge playing.

for planning a thousand meals a year— and having them taken for granted.

for a constant tenderness I rarely notice but am sure I couldn't live without.

for wanting a *good* watch ever so long . . . and letting your slow-moving husband think he'd hit on it all by himself.

for just being you . . . *Darling, here's your Hamilton with all my love!*

I'll give you a moment while you blow your nose. Please note that Hamilton is mentioned but once, at the very end. But who could stop reading sooner? Some sixty-odd people wrote to the company just thanking them for running the ad at all.

Do you want to know what all these ads had? One thing. A love for prose— pure, rich, beaded prose. They didn't sell cigarettes in those days with the purchasable hauteur of a society matron; they sold 'em with "Not a Cough in a Carload"—at least until the Federal Trade Commission made them stop. They didn't sell cars with dyna, hydra, torque, and flyte; they sold them with a picture of Walter P. Chrysler leaning purposefully on a fender and saying to you, "Look at All Three!" (The Plymouth dealers were mobbed.) When they sold handkerchiefs they didn't give you this stuff about Father's Day; Weber and Heilbroner ran an ad which simply said, "We traveled 2,000 miles to save you 65 cents." When B. Altman's wanted to get rid of some corsages they did it with this superlative full-page spread:

We believe there are at least 500 men in New York who love their wives—and want to give them flowers for Easter. So we've provided 500 old-fashioned bouquets. . . . ready now and packed in beautiful boxes. They're just inside the Fifth Avenue entrance . . . all at one price, and that one price very easy to afford.

Who could resist?

They sold a memory course with the unforgettable picture of one middle-aged man advancing to meet another and saying, "I remember you. You're Addison Sims of Seattle." They sold an etiquette book with a picture of a bewildered girl, ill at ease in a swanky restaurant amid the shiny napery and the French menus: "Again She Orders —'A Chicken Salad, Please!'" And they punched that one home with this subhead: "*Are you conscious of your crudities? . . .* Would you use your fork for your fruit salad or a spoon? Would you cut your roll with a knife or break it with your fingers? Would you take olives with a fork?" (Two million people were sufficiently conscious of their crudities to buy the book.)

Social taboos? They mowed them down with ads like this one for Odorono:

Within the Curve of a Woman's Arm

A frank discussion of a subject too often avoided.

A woman's arm! Poets have sung of its grace; artists have painted its beauty.

It should be the daintiest, sweetest thing in the world.

And yet, unfortunately, it isn't always.

And a hundred others—slogans hammered from the gold. Ask The Man Who Owns One; B. O.; The Skin You Love to Touch; You Press the Button —We Do the Rest; Even Her Best Friend Wouldn't Tell Her. They did their Trojan bit for Packard, Lifebuoy, Woodbury, Kodak, and Listerine respectively.

That for me was advertising at its peak. It beguiled, it tickled, it intrigued, it sold. That was the prose that made America sit up and take nourishment from Campbell's Soup, that made its sinks sparkle with Sapolio, that launched a thousand million ships of Ivory Soap, that stacked Dr. Eliot's shelf from here to the moon, that awakened America first with a whisper and then with a shout, that made it reach for Luckies instead of sweets.

Are those days gone forever? Sometimes I fear so. I emerge from the Christmas issue of a magazine which had weighed on my lap like a telephone book and I feel bothered and bewildered, but definitely not bewitched. I read the insides of match-book covers and the outsides of delivery trucks, the one-inch ads that furtively hawk the Secrets of Life, the two-inchers that tell you how to build your own kennel, the six-inchers that extol cantilevering devices for all the parts of the human body that need cantilevering, and when I'm all done, damned if I can remember who's selling what.

Worse than that, I feel I am being positively unsold by ads which seize on the macabre and the bizarre in an effort to arrest my roving eye. I resent being sold a necktie by the scabrous device of peeking under a man's beard to see one. My thirst for bitters is not whetted by sadistic little cartoons of what happens to people who don't use them. My liking for shirts is offset by a deep-seated distrust of a Cyclops.

And then so much advertising is such a bore. I am tired unto the death of beautiful girls drinking beer. I am weary beyond belief of cars, all two city blocks long, and all souped up to travel at dangerous speeds. I am immune— utterly immune—to the meaningless superlative and unconvinced by the inconclusive comparative (They're Milder . . .). Isn't anyone ever going to sell me a cigarette again, instead of telling me that it's less irritating (which implies that it's still somewhat irritating)? How long must I listen to business men telling business men to believe in the business system? Down how many alimentary canals must I wander with Dr. Schnurrbart of the Wiener Schnitzel Institute?

Is the end product of the advertising imagination no more inspiring than the gimmick? Are my children to believe that the alphabet runs ABCLSMFT?

I'm not quite reduced to a state of

despair. Good prose has been pretty near clubbed to death, but it's still breathing. There was a Lever Brothers ad comparing margarine to you-know-what that was so persuasive it actually got me to trot around to the store and try their product. There are the jaunty penguins smoking Kools and the mouth-watering Guinness ads; the clever ones for *Holiday;* the brocade of Gimbels' prose ("Big bargain-y Gimbels' sprawls right out at the hub of the universe"); the wanderlust-creating travel-to-England ads; the brilliant brevity of Modess (Because . . .); the Bache & Company financial ads ("Don't be a two percenter"); the continuing good humor of the Burma-Shave jingles.

Good advertising is getting scarce, but it's still around. So stand back, you copywriters, and give prose a little air. Give us back those wonderful meat-axe ads. Away with the precious, the pallid, and the paltry. As a parting shot, to remind you of the incomparable power of the properly chosen word, let me recommend to you this, perhaps the greatest of all advertisements. It appeared in a little box in the London *Times* of 1900. A few lines of type, no pictures, no women, no coupons, no gimmicks, no rhymes, no tinsel. It pulled answers from all over England:

Men wanted for Hazardous Journey. Small wages, bitter cold, long months of complete darkness, constant danger, safe return doubtful. Honor and recognition in case of success. —*Sir Ernest Shackleton.*

THEY'RE SELLING YOUR UNCONSCIOUS
Lydia Strong

Something older advertisers were unaware of is motivational (or *motivation*) research, the science that explains why cereals have crunch and beer is best imbibed with one's coat off. Although unkind words have been said about the probing into the consumers' unconscious (as in Vance Packard's *The Hidden Persuaders*), a more charitable view is taken in this free-lance article by the contributing editor of *The Management Review*.

Remember the old chestnut about the store that advertised: "We stand behind every bed we sell?"

The advertiser is not just standing behind the bed today; he's wired it for sound. Your dreams, your desires, and the rumblings of your subconscious, formerly sacred to you and your analyst, have been charted by advertising psychologists, eager to learn how you buy and why you buy, and therefore how they can sell you many, many more products.

Why do you smoke cigarettes, and is your favorite brand male or female? How do you really feel toward your breakfast cereal? What kinds of occasion make you think of beer? What does your new car tell about your personality?

Don't try to answer these questions. The true answers, say the motivational researchers, lie buried deep in your subconscious mind. And the psychologists mining that area certainly have struck pay dirt. Motivational research is the hottest trend on Madison Avenue.

The fatter the advertising budget, the greater the probability that Freud helped write the copy. Firms pay huge fees to psychological consultants for what *Business Week* has called bluntly "an effort to pry off the top of the consumer's head" and to "find out what makes him tick."

Social Research, Inc., an M.R. agency in Chicago, made a study of attitudes toward cigarette smoking for *Chicago Tribune* advertisers. Psychiatric techniques were used to break through the "impersonal and objective attitudes" of the men and women tested. They were shown pictures of people smoking and asked to make up stories about them. They played the parts of total strangers and talked as they thought these people would talk about situations involving cigarettes. Such tests are standard psychiatric procedure for pinpointing the emotional problems of individuals; here they were used, perhaps for the first time, to solve the merchandising problems of cigarette manufacturers.

One finding was that, although in

Reprinted from the *Saturday Review*, November 13, 1954, by arrangement with the publisher.

blindfold tests most smokers could not tell brands apart, they nonetheless felt definite preferences based on unconsciously determined brand reputations. Cigarettes were felt to be masculine or feminine, strong or mild, ordinary or "classy." Camels and Luckies were considered masculine and "for ordinary people," while Chesterfields were both masculine and feminine and not tied to any special class. King-size and cork-tip cigarettes were considered most feminine and "classy."

Smokers seemed to want to strike a balance between the strongest cigarette (felt as evil) and the mildest (considered too prissy). Therefore few smokers would admit their brand was the strongest.

The seemingly casual gesture of lighting up was found to cover a tough struggle. Most smokers considered their habit morally and physically wrong; filthy and dangerous. Yet they felt compelled to smoke to prove their strength, sophistication, and sociability, to gain poise, to relieve tension, and experience pleasure. Hence the psychologists recommended that cigarette advertising should combine a promise of pleasure with a note of reassurance. Pall Mall's "Let your throat enjoy smooth smoking" and Camels' "Agree with more people than any other cigarette" seem to follow this advice.

Characteristics of smokers and non-smokers will be probed in a psychological project announced by the Tobacco Industry Research Council. Perhaps the industry hopes to prove that many of its customers are neurotic individuals subject to psychosomatic strains. This could mean they are more likely than non-smoking types to develop cancer, even if they never light a cigarette.

Attempts to probe the consumer are not new. Since 1903, when Walter Dill Scott wrote his historic treatise on "The Psychology of Advertising," a thriving industry has grown up in this field. But most of the research was confined to nose-counting surveys which showed, for example, that 79 per cent of native-born white housewives in six-room houses in East Cupcake, Illinois, wanted washing machines for Christmas, while 68.7 per cent of their sisters in Split Level, Oregon, preferred home harmonica lessons. These statistics were produced by asking the ladies what they wanted, a technique definitely old hat, though still used. Motivational research, based on the Freudian concept that action is determined by the subconscious, attempts to learn not what the consumer says he wants but what he really wants, and why he wants it.

The difference is shown in a story told by Dr. W. G. Eliasberg, a psychiatrist with industrial clients. A nail-polish manufacturer wanted to bring out red nail polish, then unknown. He had a market researcher do a "nose count" survey on the acceptability of such a product. The result was an overwhelming "No!" Red nails were rejected with disgust, called "degrading" by almost every woman polled. But the manufacturer trusted his hunch and brought out the product, with results that are highly visible today. Had he consulted a psychoanalyst, says Eliasberg, he would have learned that the very strength of the women's protest proved the strength of their desire.

Motivational research investigates conscious, preconscious, and unconscious feelings. Conscious material is readily available. The preconscious is half-forgotten, but can be recalled. But unconscious motivations are concealed from the conscious mind because they seem undignified, sinful, silly, or otherwise unacceptable.

Dr. Ernest Dichter, Viennese-born psychologist who has pioneered in this field, conducted an investigation for

MandM candy. The company had assumed that their coated chocolate candies were bought mainly for their flavor. Dichter conducted a series of interviews in which he persuaded his subjects to relive and to report, step by step, occasions when they had eaten candy. He learned that, for many, candy was associated with doing a job they didn't want to do, using the sweet as a stimulus and a reward. MandM switched slogans in two test areas from "smooth, rich, creamy coated chocolate —everybody likes 'em" to "Make that tough job easier—you deserve MandM Candy." Sales ratios doubled in these areas.

In a subsistence economy hidden buying motives might not matter. A family with money only for bread and beans must by and large stick to bread and beans. But in the United States millions have more than satisfied survival needs. We have extra money with which to indulge our fancies, and depth psychology plays a large part in the battle for these "discretionary dollars."

Auto styling illustrates the change. Henry Ford's Tin Lizzie that got you there and brought you back sold well as long as other automobiles remained out of reach. But now that most families can own a car Fords must be as conspicuous and attractive as others if they are to sell.

Autos no longer represent just a means of transportation, a study by Social Research showed. They constitute definite symbols of social status, and each car has its own reputation. The purchaser buys the best car he can afford which expresses his approach to living.

Buyers of Ford, Mercury, Olds, or Lincoln, especially the two-tones and bright colors, may be expressing a trend toward modernism and individuality, the researchers say. Those who prefer to appear responsible, serious,

and dignified lean toward Packard, Dodge, DeSoto, and Plymouth four-door sedans, dark, with a minimum of gadgets. A Cadillac may be purchased to tell the world that its owner can afford the best.

Buick headlined a recent ad: "It makes you feel like the man you are." Phrases like "a car that fairly breathes success," "command," "luxurious obedience," and "immediate mastery" were sprinkled lavishly through the copy.

A second, less publicized reason for depth research is the growing incredulity of consumers. Less than three persons out of ten believe most of the advertising they see, read, and hear, the Boston College School of Business Administration has reported. With resistance so strong at the conscious level, small wonder that advertisers try to sink a pipeline to the subconscious.

What techniques are used by the advertising analyst? Anything from a depth interview in which the respondent rambles on for hours to a hardware store where customers serve as unwitting guinea-pigs. All methods have the same purpose: to secure reactions deeper and less guarded than the subject would express in a straightforward interview.

Dr. Dichter, at his Institute for Research in Mass Motivations, has organized a "psycho-panel" of several hundred families classified not only by income but by character. Dichter knows whether each member of each family is secure or insecure, resigned or ambitious, an escapist or a realist. Should a promoter of, let's say, correspondence courses want to learn primarily how to appeal to ambitious persons, persons of that type alone can be surveyed.

The depth interview is the most widely used M.R. technique. It lasts one to three hours and may seemingly cover a great many topics, gradually narrowing down to the actual topic under study. A psychologist interviewing a housewife about her preferences in buying bread might start out: "Do you remember what you did Monday?" She answers: "I went downtown—but I don't usually go downtown Mondays —it was just that . . ." As she continues, with the interviewer murmuring "Mhm" and "I see" at appropriate intervals, she reveals through words, gestures, and tone of voice how she really feels about housework. When this topic runs dry the interviewer may ask about shopping and meal planning. Again, the actual foods bought and served tell more of her attitude toward nutrition than she could tell if asked directly. The next question might be: "How about your mother? What kind of cook was she?" If this evokes wistful memories of Mom's superb, lavish cooking and homebaked white bread it's possible, though by no means certain, that the housewife would like to buy such bread for her family. If the question calls forth a horrified "Mother's meals were so fattening!" this woman probably prefers a high-protein, low-starch loaf. The interviewer may go on to ask about family food habits, thus learning whose tastes are most consulted in the choice of bread.

Two hundred depth interviews with selected subjects will give a bread-baking corporation a good idea of who its best customers are and how to reach them; also whether to say "Just like mother's" or "Only five calories per slice."

James M. Vicary, a New York City consultant to top-ranking ad agencies, leans heavily on word-association tests. A word is given and the subject responds as quickly as possible with another word or string of words. These associations help Vicary to determine possible reactions to a new brand-name or to words used in advertising, and also they indicate how people feel about a product.

Vicary advised a brewer to avoid the word "lagered" because though some consumers knew it meant "aged before use" others thought it meant tired, drunk, lazy, or dizzy. Words like complaint, cooperate, and voluntary, he has warned, produce "a deep emotional disturbance with a sizable group." A study on "Chicago" for the Commonwealth Edison Company showed that to the average non-Chicagoan the name has more connotation of farming than of industry. The power company, which was trying to bring more industries into the city, responded with an advertisement stressing the partnership of agriculture and industry in Chicago.

Procter and Gamble, after similar tests, dropped the word "concentrated" from soap advertising when they learned that 40 per cent of housewives thought it meant "blessed by the Pope."

Picture tests are used widely. In such a test, borrowed directly from the psychological clinic, the subject may imagine himself as part of a pictured situation and may speak for one person in that situation, or he may tell a story inspired by the picture. Either way, he reveals his own feelings.

Weiss and Geller, ad agency for the Toni Company, conducted picture tests with little girls before planning their campaign for Tonette, a home permanent kit for children.

They showed each of their small subjects a series of pictures with straight-haired and curly-haired girls. For each picture they asked her to tell a story. Overwhelmingly, straight-haired girls were pitied because they were considered not only unattractive, but unwanted and unloved.

They asked the children to draw the figure of a person. One after another they drew figures with long, wavy hair.

Inspired by these findings, the agency's copywriters wrote a TV commercial with the wistful tagline: "All little girls dream of natural curls." It sold a good many Tonette kits.

Sentence completion tests as well as depth interviews were used by the Charles R. Rumrill company of Rochester, N.Y., in preparing copy for the Union Trust Company. They reported that the average potential customer subconsciously sees the bank as a parent, but at the same time feels afraid. He is haunted by fear that if he applies for a loan he may be turned down or treated discourteously, or his personal life may be investigated.

They used non-professional models and heart-to-heart copy to convince their readers that the bank was really concerned about their problems and wanted to do business with them. An ad headed "How I hated to open that door" told first hand of the cordial reception given a borrower.

A Chicago firm, the Ad Detector Research Corporation, straps consumers into a lie detector and flashes advertising copy before their eyes. The subjects talk about the copy while the lie detector measures what it does to their pulse, breathing, and blood pressure.

Alfred Politz, a researcher whose clients include DuPont, Chrysler, and Coca-Cola, has bought a large hardware store, location undisclosed, where he will try out on consumers the effects of differing sales approaches, displays and advertising policies. One of his objectives is to develop advertising copy that will sell products regardless of what the salesclerk says.

Politz has also devised a billboard which will spy on its spectators by taking pictures of them at three-second intervals. This can give a count of the persons attracted by a test poster, and an impression of their reactions to it.

Not every question is answered by actual test. Social scientists are presumed to have expert knowledge of human reactions and motivations. On the crucial question: "What kind of TV salesperson is most effective?" Weiss and Geller assembled a team of eight eminent scientists (Gardner Murphy of the Menninger Foundation was one) and subjected them to thirteen and a half hours of straight TV while a stenotypist recorded their comments.

Often, when planning a campaign, a firm will consult experts on conscious and unconscious drives related to the specific product.

What are these basic drives which turn out to be helpful to the advertiser? Sex and sex-connected feelings probably head the list. A campaign for Luxite Lingerie played up narcissism or self-adoration. The campaign was based on a picture of a woman looking at herself in a mirror, with the slogan: "See yourself in Luxite."

A closely allied theme, exhibitionism, sparked the William Weintraub agency's successful series, "I dreamed I went walking (or stopped traffic—or was a lady editor) in my Maidenform Bra." In each ad the model appears partly undressed in public. The fact that this is only a dream makes it respectable and therefore all the more enjoyable.

Perfumes, soaps, creams, deodorants, and the other products guaranteed to make you smell better inside and out are routinely sold through sex promises.

But sex is not the only salesman. Other drives exert equal if not greater influence on buying. Many come under the general heading of security.

Relief of tension caused by frustration or hostility is one such drive. In a project for Wrigley, Weiss and Geller developed through depth interviews the hypothesis that people chew gum to relieve boredom and tension, and to work off hostility. A test area was selected, a mining region where living standards and literacy were low, frustrations high. The job was to convince consumers that they could relieve anxieties which they didn't even want to admit they had, by chewing gum. A series of comic strips was prepared, in which children and adults faced by everyday problems overcame their difficulties by chewing Wrigley's Spearmint Gum. The advertising used less space than previous ads, and all other promotion activities in the territory were suspended for the test period. Yet sales boomed.

Even so simple a product as breakfast food can appease hostility, according to E. L. Bernays, veteran publicist whose agency now offers M.R. services. The most successful breakfast cereals crunch, thus satisfying an aggressive desire to overcome obstacles, he points out.

The longing for social ease and equality is another drive tied to security. A series of depth interviews on beer drinking showed that people enjoy beer most when it makes some social event more relaxed and friendly. Discomfort was expressed over ads showing distinguished people drinking beer in rich surroundings. When they drank beer, the subjects said, they did not want to be reminded of people and situations that made them feel intensely discontented.

The conclusion, now followed by most beer advertisers, was that the ads should show family and friends in informal gatherings, should steer clear of rich people, "men of distinction," artists and intellectuals.

This hostility toward persons with pretensions of expertness or superior status is reflected also in consumer reaction to TV commercials. In a test by NBC a chef was shown pulling pastry out of the oven, and explaining how simple it was to make pastry with this mix. A second commercial showed a little girl, proud of the pastry she had made with the same product. The tot outpulled the chef, 4 to 1.

According to the Weiss and Geller social-science panel, the most effective TV personalities are those which appear human and fallible—not too glib, not too expert, and just a bit vulnerable. This, they said, is one of the secrets of Arthur Godfrey's success. Women particularly resist other women who "know too much" and who remind them of nagging mothers telling them just what to do.

Many of us feel secretly more vulnerable than we could bear to admit. The desire for reassurance of virility was exploited by Dr. Dichter in a study for the Tea Council of the U.S.A. In this country, he said, tea carries a stigma of effeminacy. This unfortunate impression had been reinforced by Tea Council ads in pale colors, with such slogans as "Tired? Nervous? Try tea." On his advice the colors were switched to bright red, and the slogan to a dynamic "Make it hefty, hot and hearty, take tea and see." Tea sales rose 13 per cent in two years, even before zooming coffee prices forced millions more to "take tea and see."

Results of this sort have convinced many advertising executives that M.R. is here to stay.

C. B. Larrabee, publisher of *Printers' Ink*, calls it the next great leap in market research, and a survey of leading advertisers has shown more than half of the big ones using M.R.

Even the admen come under the X-ray. *Sponsor* magazine reported after extensive depth interviews that the choice of magazines, newspapers, and other advertising media is strongly influenced by irrational, unconscious drives. Among these influences are background (the adman clings to the media he knows best); job security (he's afraid to take a chance); personal bias; and the desire to make a big splash and impress prospective clients.

A few flies still buzz in the ointment. Not all the depth research findings turn out to be useful. A Foote, Cone and Belding executive complained: "We had a facial soap . . . killed germs better than most other soaps. We wanted to know how we could best advertise it to teen-agers. . . . Well, we got a lot of talk about when a young girl uses soap it is to wash off the feeling of guilt that comes from newly awakened sexual desire. Where the heck do you go with that?"

Another firm employed a researcher to help determine attitudes of nonflying citizens. His major finding was that men who don't fly have a deep fear of plane crashes, but an even more devastating fear of sexual relationships with strange women. The information did not help sell plane tickets.

Nevertheless, the M.R. trend keeps growing. Will it develop to the point where we consumers have no further secrets and no defenses? Will we move in trance state, wallets wide open, toward the store?

Don't worry too much over this possibility.

Some thirty years ago Dr. J. B. Watson's theory of behaviorism was supposed to revolutionize advertising and selling. According to this doctrine all behavior, including buying, could be conditioned to take place in response to set stimuli. A dog is trained to jump through a hoop. In the same way, behaviorists reasoned, consumers could be conditioned to buy soap flakes. The craze swept the ad agencies, but the expected conquest of the consumer did not quite come off. We read the ads and we bought the soap flakes, but we simply refused to stay conditioned. Maybe too many people were trying to condition us at the same time.

Like microbes and other tough, low organisms, consumers are adept at developing new defenses against almost any form of attack. Perhaps we'll devise a sub-conscious to use as a kind of psychological storm cellar. Perhaps we'll resort to that Cinderella of psychology, the conscious mind. Either way, chances are that we'll survive.

"AND NOW A WORD FROM OUR SPONSOR"
Broadcasting • Telecasting

Considered by its critics to be the lowest form of business communication, the radio and television commercial nevertheless has its sponsors, its history, and even its listeners. This article by the editors of a leading trade publication in the field of commercial broadcasting records the development of the commercial with an affection shared by many and deepened by the passage of time.

At 5 P.M. on Aug. 28, 1922, an announcer stepped to the microphone of WEAF New York and said:

"This afternoon the radio audience is to be addressed by Mr. [H. M.] Blackwell of the Queensborough Corp., who through arrangements made by the Griffin Radio Service Inc. will say a few words concerning Nathaniel Hawthorne and the desirability of fostering the helpful community spirit and the healthful, unconfined life that were Hawthorne's ideals."

Mr. Blackwell then came forward and talked for 10 minutes about the happy, healthful, unconfined advantages of Hawthorne Court, a group of "high-grade dwellings" in Jackson Heights, New York, where people "can enjoy all the latest conveniences and contrivances demanded by the housewife and yet have all of the outdoor life that the city dweller yearns for but has deludedly supposed could only be obtained through purchase of a house in the country."

In the spirit of Nathaniel Hawthorne,

then 58 years dead, Mr. Blackwell exhorted the "city martyrs" to heed the "cry of the heart," a voice which he described as clamoring for "more living room, more chance to unfold, more opportunity to get near Mother Earth, to play, to romp, to plant and to dig.

"Let me enjoin upon you"—Mr. Blackwell now was warming to his task of really selling the Hawthorne Court apartments—"as you value your health and your hopes and your home happiness, get away from the solid masses of brick, where the meagre opening admitting a slant of sunlight is mockingly called a light shaft, and where people grow up starved for a run over a patch of grass and the sight of a tree."

Thus radio listeners in New York heard what is generally accepted as the first radio commercial. It is testimony to the innate appeal of the medium that the first was not also the last.

By way of contrast, a few months ago Campbell Soup Co. filled the western airwaves with a series of commercials, carried on an ABC regional network, that consisted in their entirety of phrases like: "Campbell soups are mm-mmm good."

These chronologically extreme examples are neither the long nor the short of the commercial, but side by side they point up the distance that the broadcast sales message has come. En route, it has taken many forms—dramatic episodes, jingles, program integration, subtle wit and shrill exhortation, to name a few—and when it got into television it became a complex thing whose production, once involving one man and a few dollars, enlisted scores of people, cost thousands of dollars.

Actually the Hawthorne Court apartments, of which Mr. Blackwell thought so highly and talked so long, were not the first products sold by radio.

Some seven years before that, in 1915, a young fellow named Arthur B. Church, whose name later became synonymous with KMBC Kansas City, helped build himself a business in radio parts and supplies by "advertising" them over his ham station 9WU in Lamoni, Iowa. And in 1919 Dr. Frank Conrad, on his experimental 8XK (later KDKA Pittsburgh), boosted the business of a friendly music store by giving it on-the-air credit in return for free records with which to program his station.

THE PRE-EMPTION

Sponsorships increased gradually after Queensborough Corp. paid WEAF $100 for its 10 minutes. On WEAF, A&P figured big—and, incidentally, was one of the first victims of the institution that later became known as The Pre-emption: On the night of Nov. 15, 1926, when NBC's inaugural program was presented, listeners to WEAF heard this announcement:

"Thanks are due the Great Atlantic & Pacific Tea Co. which regularly engages these facilities, between the hours of 9 and 10 P.M. on Monday evenings, for they have consented to withdraw tonight's program by the A&P Gypsies so that we may broadcast the special opening program of the National Broadcasting Co. . . ."

NBC's special opening program was presented without sponsorship, but the next night WEAF and a lineup of 13 stations carried a sponsored program of music from 8 to the odd closing time of 8:33, with opening and closing commercials as follows:

"These facilities are now engaged by the makers of Scott's Emulsion of Pure Norwegian Cod Liver Oil for the broadcasting of another Vikings program."

And:

"The Vikings come to you through the courtesy of Scott & Browne, the makers of Scott's Emulsion of Pure Norwegian Cod Liver Oil."

The closing announcement also invited listeners to let the sponsor know what they thought about his program. "Each of you who write," the announcer said, obviously wanting to find out how many were listening, "will receive a copy of the Viking Hand Atlas of the World."

The Vikings program was followed that night by a series of other sponsored programs utilizing assorted station lineups. Among the programs were the Jolly Buckeye Bakers, sponsored by Buckeye Malt Syrup; Eveready Hour, sponsored by National Carbon Co., and an account of the auction bridge games sponsored by U.S. Playing Card Co. Almost uniformly their commercials followed the "These facilities are now engaged by . . ." pattern.

The evidence of the Queensborough commercial to the contrary, commercials at the outset clearly were expected to be kept to a bare mention of sponsor and product. As far back as about 1923, when Browning, King & Co., New York—one of the first broadcast advertisers—applied to AT&T for time on WEAF, a set of rules had been laid down by that station:

(1) Entertainment on sponsored programs had to be up to the standard set by the station for its sustaining programs; (2) the commercial must be kept, so far as reasonably possible, to the mention of the sponsor and product; (3) direct selling and price mentions were forbidden; (4) if the sponsor failed to conform to these rules, the station could cancel his advertising.

The commercials went a little further, however, in the first sponsored broadcast on CBS. That was an hour and five minute program—nothing seemed to come out even in those days —immediately following the CBS inaugural show on Sept. 18, 1927. The program consisted of music, jokes (?), and patter, with announcements by Maj. J. Andrew White, then president of CBS, and Harry C. Browne, who used the title of "judge," told Negro dialect stories, and helped out with the commercials.

After a few preliminaries, the opening commercial worked into this:

Judge: ". . . Well, then, I'm representing the Emerson Drug Co. of Baltimore, Md. I know you recollect that little blue bottle of Bromo Seltzer—well, that's one of the things we make. Am I permitted to say all this?

Major White: "You say it first and then ask me if you are permitted. Pretty wise old fox. Go on."

Judge: "No, I guess I told enough. Everybody knows Bromo Seltzer so well, we are already acquainted anyhow . . ."

A little later in the program came the chainbreak announcement:

"For those who are listening in and who may have tuned in late, this is the *Effervescent Hour* in charge of Judge Browne, representing the Emerson Drug Co. . . . The Columbia chain station to which you are listening will now identify itself . . ."

A few jokes and musical numbers later, time came for another sales message:

Judge: ". . . It seems to me, suh, that the folks out there who are listening may not know as well as we do the virtues of that dainty, delightful, appealing, exquisitely refreshing—"

Major: "Yes?"

Judge (laughs): ". . . fragrant, delectable, soda fountain drink, Ginger Mint Julep."

Major: "You are entitled to tell them what it is, sah."

Judge: "Tell them what Ginger Mint Julep is? There aren't words sufficient for expression, suh."

Major: "You were going along pretty well a moment ago."

Judge: "Why, I hadn't got started, Major. The only way you can ever know how good a Ginger Mint Julep is, is to try it."

Major: "And how do I rate that distinction?"

Judge: "It is my pleasure, suh, to extend to you this little hospitality, if you will accept the drink.

"Now, here it is, and if it doesn't remind you of putting your face into a fragrant bed of mint and sipping the nectar fit for the gods, suh—well, I know it will mean more than that to you. And while you are enjoying its cooling flavor, I shall endeavor to indicate the contrast by having a hot number played by the Ginger Mint Julepers. This number is known as 'Let Her Fizz.' "

End of commercial, suh. For the closing, Major White said:

"That brings to a close the visit of

Judge Browne and his friends from Baltimore, appearing very frankly in the interest of the Emerson Drug Co., which makes Bromo Seltzer and Aperio and Ginger Mint Julep, and we leave you with the refrain of the appropriate song of this old established concern—'There Is No Love Like the First Love.' "

Apparently the commercials, or the program, or both, brought a pleasing reaction. The following week Judge Browne told his listeners that "we are gratefully conscious and appreciative of the many kindly comments made across the counters of soda fountains throughout America about Ginger Mint Julep and its delightful bouquet."

And right there Judge Browne and Emerson Drug got into what was to become a familiar broadcast habit: they announced a contest. "So," said Judge Browne, "the Emerson Drug Co. announces to the soda fountain dispensers a reward for mailing to them the best comments of those whom they serve . . ." Pretty good rewards, too: $500 each month for the 10 best comments; $250 for the next 10; $150 for the third 10; and $100 for the fourth 10.

For the most part, the early commercials were practically carbon copies of the sponsors' print ads. For example, American Tobacco Co.—which later came up with such unforgettables as the chant of the tobacco auctioneer and "Sold American!", "LS/MFT," "Be Happy, Go Lucky" and the Hit Parades of both radio and tv—in the early days put its print copy on the air virtually without change. This was about 1928, and the habit among major advertisers continued for several years.

Not until 1934, in fact, did an agency hire a copywriter to handle radio commercials exclusively. The agency was Young & Rubicam. The copywriter was Joseph A. Moran, now vice president of Y&R. In Mr. Moran's words, "when

radio commercials were first written, they were written by the left hand of a right-handed copywriter."

But changes came, and the late 1920s and early 1930s brought a number of new developments—among them informality in handling the sales message, the dramatized commercial, the integrated commercial, the heresy of kidding the product.

Among the earliest dramatized commercials was one for Fels-Naptha soap which was heard about 1929. It was a long-winded story of a girl who won a handsome mansion by proving she was a good housekeeper. Her proof? She used Fels-Naptha, of course.

The integrated commercial was born, according to the best available vital statistics, in the mid-30s—about 1934–35—with Fred Allen, Ed Wynn, Jack Benny, Burns & Allen, and Phil Baker among the foremost practitioners of this new art form. Many of these performers also found in this technique an unpassable opportunity to kid the commercial, which they did with considerable sales effectiveness. It was an approach that was developed into a way of life by Arthur Godfrey and other latter-day salesmen.

The early '30s saw the networks shake off one set of shackles which they had imposed on themselves from the beginning (but which many stations had disregarded in their own commercial operations). This was the ban on quoting prices on the air.

In July 1932 NBC withdrew its price-mention prohibition insofar as daytime hours were concerned (except on Sundays). Roy Witmer, NBC sales vice president at the time, explained that NBC felt prices would be interesting to housewives. First advertiser to take advantage of the new policy was A&P, then one of NBC's biggest accounts, which listed the prices of certain commodities on two morning programs.

Two months later both CBS and NBC lifted the ban—for nighttime as well as day. A&P again was first in line, carrying price mentions on the *A&P Gypsies* on NBC on Sept. 12, 1932. CBS' new policy became effective three days later, on Sept. 15. Both networks imposed limits on the number of price mentions permissible within 15-minute periods.

A mid-30s development that worked itself into a future was the transcribed spot announcement. Cecil Widdifield of Schwimmer & Scott Adv. has been credited with pointing out the commercial possibilities of the 20-second intervals between programs—and with selling the idea of the transcribed spot. Comedian George Givot ("The Greek Ambassador") was one of the first—if not the first—to be featured in a series of transcribed commercial announcements.

Pretty soon, transcribed commercials were being heard all over the U.S. In the 1940's a related phenomenon, the transcribed jingle, had become the rage —and to many, the bane—of radio. A storm developed, in which some stations banned all jingles. In 1944, WQXR New York imposed such a ban (and it still stands; a fortnight ago, Barney's clothing chain went to the expense, in order to get its commercial on WQXR, of having its "Calling All Men to Barney's" jingle arranged and recorded as an instrumental number to be played on WQXR without words).

Also in 1944, WWJ Detroit announced it was banning not only jingles but all transcribed announcements, effective the following Feb. 1. Harry Bannister, then manager of WWJ (now NBC station relations vice president), explained that the move was made to enable the station "to carry out its mandate of operating in the public interest. We believe that transcribed announcements have impaired the entertainment value of radio . . ."

Agencies were concerned by the move; meetings were held at which alternatives to the WWJ ban were proposed and considered. But WWJ held fast, at least for the time being. WWJ representatives explain that the ban remained in force throughout the rest of World War II and on to about 1948, when it was dropped.

Singing commercials meanwhile were the subject of considerable research. Pulse Inc. reported on the basis of a study made in 1947 that, whatever their artistic value, they must have selling power: in each of five separate product categories, Pulse found, brands identified with singing commercials were remembered best.

The singing commercial that touched off the jingles wildfire was "Pepsi-Cola Hits the Spot," which hit radio about October 1939. But this was not the first.

Earl Gammons, former Washington vice president for CBS, now a consultant, has been credited with offering the first singing commercial on Christmas Eve, 1926. The station was WCCO Minneapolis, where he was then commercial manager. The product was Wheaties. And the commercial, sung by a male quartet, went so:

"Have you tried Wheaties?

"They're whole wheat with all of the bran.

"Won't you try Wheaties?

"For wheat is the best food of man."

From then till now there have been more jingles than man can count, much less sing. One of the hardiest, dating from the early 1930's is Jello's choral "J-E-L-L-O." Others among a vast lot of especially noted ones are "Duz does everything"; Adler elevator shoes' "You can be taller than she is"; Chesterfield cigarettes' "Sound off—for Chesterfield!"; Gillette's chimes and "Look sharp—be sharp!"; Luckies' "Be Happy, Go Lucky"; Arrid's "Don't be half-safe"; Halo shampoo's "Halo Shampoo Halo"; Pepsodent's "You'll Wonder Where the Yellow Went."

But the ring-tailed wow that led the parade was Pepsi-Cola's. This was a product of the team of Allen Kent and Ginger Johnson (Herbert Austen Croom-Johnson), who had met at NBC and, about 1935, turned out a series of Mother Goose parodies that they sold to a bread sponsor.

Edgar Kobak, who now is a business consultant and station owner and then was with the Lord & Thomas agency but preparing to return to the old Blue Network, was one of a small group who, in 1939, encouraged Kent-Johnson to apply their talents to the writing of a jingle that would sell a 12-ounce bottle of cola for five cents. The result, using a frisky adaptation of the English hunting song, "John Peel," is reprinted here for the benefit of the very young, the older deaf, and the extremely short-memoried:

"Pepsi-Cola hits the spot.
"Twelve full ounces, that's a lot.
"Twice as much for a nickel too.
"Pepsi-Cola is the drink for you!
"Nickel, nickel, nickel, nickel.
"Trickle, trickle, trickle, trickle.
"Nickel, nickel, nickel, nickel . . ."
Pepsi-Cola not only liked the song but acquired the copyright as well, which it still holds.

Another unforgettable one, often credited with turning a tide of public resentment that was by then running against the singing commercial, was a ditty that BBDO brought out about 1944 featuring "Chiquita Banana" and making the point that refrigerators and bananas are not compatible. "Chiquita" won critical as well as public acclaim—and, given new lyrics containing dietary

advice, received acclaim also from the radio head of the U.S. Dept. of Agriculture, from the head of Famine Emergency Committee, and from other officials for its work in combatting the postwar famine in the world.

Meanwhile, the commercial had been introduced to tv.

The first authorized tv commercials appeared July 1, 1941, and were on WNBT (now WRCA-TV) New York, the only television station that was then ready for business with both a commercial license and a rate card. There were five.

(1) Bulova Watch Co. opened and closed WNBT's transmissions that day with a visual adaptation of its long-familiar radio time signal—and promptly signed up for daily tv time signals for 13 weeks.

(2) Sun Oil Co. sponsored a television version of Lowell Thomas' radio newscast over the Blue Network. For the cameras, announcer Hugh James read the commercials from a desk piled high with cans of Sun oil.

(3) Lever Bros. put on a special version of *Uncle Jim's Question Bee*, one of its radio shows. "Aunt Jennie," star of another Lever radio series, did the commercials. Among other things, she opened a can of Spry and displayed its contents to viewers, and later cut and served a Spry-made cake to the cast and contestants.

(4) Procter & Gamble sponsored an adaptation of its *Truth or Consequences* radio series, in behalf of Ivory soap. In addition to the familiar "red hands" story for the viewers, contestants were given large cakes of Ivory whose labels were clearly visible to the home audiences.

(5) The Missouri Pacific Lines put on a half-hour travel film.

In the 15 years since then, tv commercials have in many ways followed the evolutionary pattern of commercials in radio, developing through trial and error, constant experimentation—and, by comparison with radio, almost staggering expense. Despite the comparative complexity of television, however, several parallels might be drawn between the development of the sales message in the two media. It is to be doubted, however, that television has yet produced the equal of a singing commercial that is said to have been carried on a Canadian radio station:

"Dignity, peace, and more for your dollar

"At Coopersmith's Funeral Parlor."

Exercises

"We Had No Carriage Trade," by Carl Crow

1. Express in a single sentence the essence of this article. Then use the sentence as the beginning of a single paragraph of about 200 words in which you develop the idea.
2. In what way has our industrial development been different from that of any other country? Write a paragraph in explanation.
3. Write a paper on some aspects of Colonial life that you believe are not generally known.
4. Write a theme entitled, "The Colonial Farmer—Jack-of-All-Trades."
5. Write a theme on the "carriage trade" in America today.
6. Write a theme on the "common" American today, contrasting him with his forebears.
7. To what factors do you ascribe the interest generated by this selection? Discuss.

"Henry Ford and the Model T," by Roger Burlingame

1. Discuss Henry Ford's contribution to mass production.
2. In the light of Ford's early success in freezing the design of his car, how do you explain the later failure of the same principle? Write a theme setting forth your views.
3. Do you think a simple announcement in the style Henry Ford used to herald his mass-produced car would be equally effective today in selling a new motor car? Discuss your views with reference to modern car advertising.
4. From the library obtain some figures on current car production and ownership, and write a report on your findings. Look for the significance behind the figures.
5. The author mentions a man named McAdam. Find out what you can about him and write a report on his contributions to road building in this country.
6. After library investigation, write a report on early cross-country car racing, such as that by Roy Chapin, and its influence on the spread of car ownership.
7. Write a theme under one of the following titles:
a. Is Bicycle Transportation Obsolete?
b. The Sports Car as a Hobby
c. Modern Car Design
d. Travel by Throughway
e. No Parking
f. Solving the Big-City Traffic Problem

"The Marketing Revolution," by Charles F. Phillips

1. How do you account for the fact that, in the past fifty years, the increase in the number of people engaged in distribution has been three times that in the number of people engaged in production? Write a paper setting forth your views.
2. Write a report, based on personal observation and experience, on modern-day customer service.
3. Write a paper on the effects of the marketing revolution on the sale of grocery products. A visit to your local supermarket should give you some ideas.

4. Discuss by reference to specific current advertisements the application of the six purposes of advertising named in this speech.

5. Find a single sales characteristic (e.g., consumer convenience, new package, use of premiums) common to a number of new products or to improvements in old products. Then write a theme on the subject.

6. In a paragraph define the term "marketing research."

7. Dr. Phillips describes marketing research as scientific. Explain why.

8. Write a spoof on consumer surveys under the title, "A Recent Survey Shows." (See also "The Sample with the Built-In Bias" in Sec. 3.)

"Where Are the Ads of Yesteryear?" by Robert L. Heilbroner

1. Judging from the examples quoted in this article, do you agree that the advertisements of yesterday were superior to those of today? Support your position.

2. From current advertising, select (a) the advertisement you like best, or (b) the advertisement you like least, or (c) the advertisement that best typifies modern advertising techniques, and write a theme supporting your choice. Clip the advertisement to your paper.

3. Find a current advertisement for ladies' watches and compare its copy approach with that of the Hamilton watch advertisement quoted in this article. Which do you think is more effective?

4. Write in a paragraph a critique of the Odorono advertisement in this article, with special reference to the choice of words.

5. Write a theme on one of the following topics:
a. Humorous advertising
b. Lingerie advertising
c. Beer adverising
d. Book advertising
e. Automobile advertising
f. Cigarette advertising

6. Have you ever found the claims of service made by an overenthusiaastic copywriter at variance with the kind of service you really received? Following this line of thought, write a theme entitled, "See Your Friendly Dealer."

7. Who was Sir Ernest Shackleton? After a little probing, write a theme on the subject.

"They're Selling Your Unconscious," by Lydia Strong

1. In a single paragraph, define and explain "motivational research."

2. What emotional factors do you think enter into the purchase of a car? Discuss.

3. The author mentions "the growing incredulity of readers" of advertising. Discuss this factor with reference to specific current advertisements.

4. Explain in a paragraph what you consider to be the psychology behind the Cadillac advertisement that stresses its "modest cost," "marvelous economy of operation," "remarkable dependability," and "great resale value."

5. Discuss the use of the sex appeal in current advertising.

6. Find several advertisements that promise or imply relief from anxieties. Discuss the appeals in a theme headed, "The Copywriter's Couch," drawing a humorous analogy between the advertising writer and the psychoanalyst.

7. Do you see any way in which motivation research could become a threat to personal security? Discuss.

"And Now a Word from Our Sponsor," Broadcasting • *Telecasting*

1. Write a 300–400-word history of advertising commercials based on the material in this article.

2. Write a critical report on the present state of television commercials.

3. Write a critical report on the radio or television commercials of a single advertiser. Quote liberally from the commercials.

4. Write a paper on the subject of good taste in television advertising.

5. Discuss radio and television commercials as a sales force.

6. Write a serious theme on "Are Television Commercials Necessary?"

7. Propose a set of rules for television commercials—the rules to be enforced by the television stations.

8. Write a review of a single performance of a sponsored television program from the point of view of an advertising trade publication. Indicate whether you think the program is good advertising for the sponsor.

9. From the point of view of an advertising trade publication, write a review of a sponsored television series.

5

Management and Human Relations

In spite of the introduction of fantastic new machines, the big test of management is not how it handles the machines, but how it handles people. A company must maintain good relations with many groups of people. These include the stockholders, the customers and prospective customers, the residents of the factory community, the public at large, and of course the company's workers. The last group is often the most difficult to deal with, not because it consists of difficult people, but because natural differences in point of view tend to keep management and workers apart. In the past several decades the social scientists have taken a hand in narrowing the gap. The result has been a new emphasis on the role of communication in management— an emphasis apparent in these selections.

COMMUNICATION IN INDUSTRY

United States Steel Corporation

The relation of communication to management is the subject of this presentation intended for the guidance of United States Steel executives. It gives a balanced picture of the role information plays in building good relations both inside and outside the plant.

Communication in industry is the exchange of information among the personnel of an organization and between the organization and the public, particularly those segments of the public with which the industry works, lives, or maintains business relations.

One aspect of communication is the devices or means which may be utilized to promote the effective exchange of information necessary to the conduct of business—the transportation system for ideas and information. In the complex business organization of today with its manifold interrelationships, maintenance of efficient operation requires devices for rapid transmittal of all kinds of information to all levels of the organization—the work schedule of the wage earner, the new order, the latest price quoted, the current business trend, the latest government decree, or how employees react to a new policy initiated the previous week.

Closely related is the question of what information should be transmitted. There has been a tremendous increase in the amount of information made available to employees and the public in recent years. Facts once classed as confidential business data are now broadcast through scores of channels; information once considered sacred is now collected by governmental agencies, analyzed by research agencies, interpreted by labor executives and union research staffs; and inside facts which twenty years ago some corporate managements held very close are now available to the average newspaper reader.

This increase in volume of information that may be transmitted makes it desirable that management make full and proper use of the natural communication instruments and opportunities present in the every day association of people at work in order to keep them fully informed.

WHY IS A COMMUNICATION PROGRAM NEEDED?

In the days before assembly lines and multioperation plants, every employee

From *Communication in United States Steel*. Reprinted by Courtesy of the United States Steel Corporation.

181

knew what orders were received, who the big customers were, whether materials were in stock, and how much was produced. He knew whether the business was prospering and, of course, could see when new men were added, when slack work forced layoffs. He knew when he did a good job and whether the shop produced merchandise of quality sufficient to maintain its reputation among competitors. He knew whether prices met competition and whether his wages were in line with those paid by other employers for similar work.

As businesses grow larger, the gap between employee and employer widens. Personal contacts diminish or disappear. The employer* has little or no knowledge of the employee and his personal problems and the employee has little knowledge of products, markets, competitors' activities, and other problems related to the conduct of the business—facts which were familiar to employer and employee alike in the small shop. Production lines and specialization have lessened the field of information readily available to the average employee. In view of these factors and the rising educational level of the work force, management is often hard put to provide employees with satisfaction of accomplishment essential to best effort. Yet, all recognize the value of such programs.

Also, lack of knowledge regarding the necessity of or reason for an action or decision has become a source of misunderstanding. This is true at all organizational levels from the vice president who is not informed of an important action which involves him, to the sweeper in the mill whose routine is changed with the order, "Do it this way now."

Everyone desires to feel he is in on things, a part of the organization, just as he has a strong abhorrence to surprise and change. To everyone at some time in his business life comes the question, "Why didn't I know about that before it happened?" Who in the steel industry hasn't wondered about the origin, efficacy, and accuracy of the Stove Pipe Committee—that organization with no charter, no constitution and bylaws, no regularly elected officers, and no dues-paying members? Where, how, why does it get information before the management team? Why are its rumors given credence?

A chronic complaint from foremen is that information that should emanate from them to their subordinates is too often received by way of the Stove Pipe Committee or, more embarrassing, from the grievance committeemen whose union headquarters keeps them better informed than the company keeps its management members. Why does that happen?

Some executives admit that despite their good intentions they are prone to forget to pass on all the information they should; others say they are just too busy to do a consistently good job. It is equally true that management's procedures have not adequately taken into account the communication problem inherent in every organization in which there is more than a single supervisory employee.

Management needs insight into the nagging, concrete problems at the work level. Unless management makes a special effort it will not hear all it should. Failure to listen can be a serious deterrent to upward communication, causing subordinates' hesitancy or reluctance to express any opinion. A similar obstacle is a superior's unapproachability. Key points are a willingness to discuss a situation frankly and sympathetically, and willingness to be influenced in making a decision.

Without this willingness attitude, management policies are impractical, and may be ignored.

A third type of communication problem is the development and maintenance of constructive relations with the public, particularly in the communities in which the company's employees work and live. Schools, churches, civic organizations, and the man on the street need to know the truth about free enterprise. How are the true facts to be made known? This question is fast pre-empting the attention of businessmen who realize that the answer must be obtained soon if our present economic system is to continue.

HOW A COMMUNICATION PROGRAM CAN HELP

Communication can discharge a most important role in the development and maintenance of morale. Availability of sufficient background information often makes the difference between monotonous, routine performance and that extra effort which brings premium results. In modern organizations the normal work contacts need assistance to do the job. Thus, a communication program can build and maintain sound working relationships by getting facts back and forth among employees about the work that is to be, and has been, done.

Also, there is the problem of the grapevine. Management must recognize that subordinates will listen to the informal communication of the grapevine with its inaccuracies and half-truths, if adequate information is not officially provided. A fraction of the time spent trying to find out how and where the grapevine gets its information, if spent on getting timely and accurate material to those most concerned, would enhance many times the foremen's pres-

tige and morale. Getting the truth fully and accurately and on time to management and employee is a major purpose of communication.

Closely related to disseminating appropriate information is the matter of finding out what is on the employees' minds. Unless special devices are provided, management will take for granted many times that it is in touch with employee thinking only to learn through costly error that it was mistaken. A communication system can help provide each management member the information required for sound decision and audit of his practices. Only by securing reaction of those affected by company practice and policy is it possible to evaluate past effort and make improvement in future plans.

Also, communication is important in forming opinion of the community and the public with whom the organization lives and does business. The starting point is, of course, with the employee. Every employee is an opinion molder at work, at home, in his community, and in the state and nation when he casts his vote. Beyond the employee himself, there are ways of creating community and public opinion regarding the company and its activities which require directed management effort if a good job is to be done. The public in general is interested in employment outlook for the plant in its community, what is being done regarding safety and health or other matters of common interest, and similarly the company has a vital stake in convincing the community that its organization is interested in community progress and that it is a desirable place to work.

Management, then, has an important stake in developing an effective program for communication internally among the management and work force and, in addition, in getting the business side of the story before the thinking public. To meet these problems there have been developed, over the past decade or two, devices to assist management in getting information transmitted promptly and accurately to appropriate personnel throughout the organization and to the community. These media * are as essential in helping management do a good job as the telephone, typewriter, or public address system.

* Editor's note: See Exercise 7, page 210, for the names of some of the media referred to here.

SCIENTIFIC MANAGEMENT
Frederick W. Taylor

The idea of scientific management is hardly more than seventy years old. It was formulated by Frederick W. Taylor who was at the time a foreman at the Midvale Steel Works. Because some practitioners of scientific management tended to look upon workers merely as machines, a wave of unrest followed its introduction. In 1912 a Congressional committee was authorized to investigate the so-called Taylor System and similar philosophies of shop management. In the testimony that follows, Taylor himself describes the idea of scientific management.

To give you one illustration of the application of scientific management to a rather high class of work, gentlemen, bricklaying, so far as I know, is one of the oldest of the trades, and it is a truly extraordinary fact that bricks are now laid just about as they were 2,000 years before Christ. In England they are laid almost exactly as they were then; in England the scaffold is still built with timbers lashed together—in many cases with the bark still on it—just as we see that the scaffolds were made in old stone-cut pictures of bricklaying before the Christian era. In this country we have gone beyond the lashed scaffold, and yet in most respects it is almost literally true that bricks are still laid as they were 4,000 years ago. Virtually the same trowel, virtually the same brick, virtually the same mortar, and, from the way in which they were laid, according to one of my friends, who is a brick work contractor and a student of the subject, who took the trouble to take down some bricks laid 4,000 years ago to study the way in which the mortar was spread, etc., it appears that they even spread the mortar in the same way then as we do now. If, then, there is any trade in which one would say that the principles of scientific management would produce but small results, that the development of the science would do little good, it would be in a trade which thousands and thousands of men through successive generations had worked and had apparently reached, as far as methods and principles were concerned, the highest limit of efficiency 4,000 years ago. In bricklaying this would seem to be true since practically no progress has been made in this art since that time. Therefore, viewed broadly, one would say that there was a smaller probability that the principles of scientific management could accomplish notable results in this trade than in almost any other. Mr. Frank Gilbreth is a man who in

From *Hearings Before Social Committee of the House of Representatives to Investigate the Taylor and Other Systems of Shop Management Under the Authority of H. Res. 90,* Vol. III, January 25 and 26, 1912.

his youth worked as a bricklayer; he was an educated man and is now a very successful contractor. He said to me, some years ago, "Now, Taylor, I am a contractor, putting up all sorts of buildings, and if there is one thing I know it is bricklaying; I can go out right now, and I am not afraid to back myself, to beat any man I know of laying bricks for ten minutes, both as to speed and accuracy; you may think I am blowing, but that is one way I got up in the world. I cannot stand it now for more than ten minutes; I'm soft; my hands are tender, I haven't been handling bricks for years, but for ten minutes I will back myself against anyone. I want to ask you about this scientific management; do you think it can be applied to bricklaying? Do you believe that these things you have been shouting about (at that time it was called the 'task system'), do you believe these principles can be applied to bricklaying?" "Certainly," I said, "some day some fellow will make the same kind of study about bricklaying that we have made of other things, and he will get the same results." "Well," he said, "if you really think so, I will just tell you who is going to do it, his name is Frank Gilbreth."

I think it was about three years later that he came to me and said: "Now, I'm going to show you something about bricklaying. I have spent three years making a motion and time study of bricklaying, and not I alone did it; my wife has also spent almost the same amount of her time studying the problems of bricklaying, and I think she has made her full share of the progress which has been made in the science of bricklaying." Then he said, "I will show you just how we went to work at it. Let us assume that I am now standing on the scaffold in the position that the bricklayer occupies when he is ready to begin work. The wall is here on my

left, the bricks are there in a pile on the scaffold to my right, and the mortar is here on the mortar-board alongside of the bricks. Now, I take my stand as a bricklayer and am ready to start to lay bricks, and I said to myself, 'What is the first movement that I make when I start to lay bricks?' I take a step to the right with the right foot. Well, is that movement necessary? It took me a year and a half to cut out that motion— that step to the right—and I will tell you later how I cut it out. Now, what motion do I make next? I stoop down to the floor to the pile of bricks and disentangle a brick from the pile and pick it up off the pile. 'My God,' I said, 'that is nothing short of barbarous.' Think of it! Here I am a man weighing over 250 pounds, and every time I stoop down to pick up a brick I lower 250 pounds of weight down two feet so as to pick up a brick weighing 4 pounds, and then raise my 250 pounds of weight up again, and all of this to lift up a brick weighing 4 pounds. Think of this waste of effort. It is monstrous. It took me—it may seem to you a pretty long while—but it took a year and a half of thought and work to cut out that motion; when I finally cut it out, however, it was done in such a simple way that anyone in looking at the method which I adopted would say, 'There is no invention in that, any fool could do that; why did you take a year and a half to do a little thing like that?' Well, all I did was to put a table on the scaffold right alongside of me here on my right side and put the bricks and mortar on it, so as to keep them at all times at the right height, thus making it unnecessary to stoop down in picking them up. This table was placed in the middle of the scaffold with the bricklayer on one side of it, and with a walkway on the other side along which the bricks were brought by wheelbarrow or by hod to be placed on the table without interfering with the bricklayer or even getting in his way." Then Mr. Gilbreth made his whole scaffold adjustable, and a laborer was detailed to keep all of the scaffolds at all times at such a height that as the wall goes up the bricks, the mortar, and the men will occupy that position in which the work can be done with the least effort.

Mr. Gilbreth has studied out the best position for each of the bricklayer's feet and for every type of bricklaying the exact position for the feet is fixed so that the man can do his work without unnecessary movements. As a result of further study both on the part of Mr. and Mrs. Gilbreth, after the bricks are unloaded from the cars and before bringing them to the bricklayer they are carefully sorted by a laborer and placed with their best edges up on a simple wooden frame, constructed so as to enable him to take hold of each brick in the quickest time and in the most advantageous position. In this way the bricklayer avoids either having to turn the brick over or end for end to examine it before laying it, and he saves also the time taken in deciding which is the best edge and end to place on the outside of the wall. In most cases, also, he saves the time taken in disentangling the brick from a disorderly pile on the scaffold. This "pack of bricks," as Mr. Gilbreth calls his loaded wooden frames, is placed by the helper in its proper position on the adjustable scaffold close to the mortar box.

We have all been used to seeing bricklayers tap each brick after it is placed on its bed of mortar several times with the end of the handle of the trowel so as to secure the right thickness for the joint. Mr. Gilbreth found that by tempering the mortar just right the bricks could be readily bedded to the proper depth by a downward pressure of the hand which lays them. He insisted that the mortar mixers should give special attention to tempering the mortar and so save the time consumed in tapping the brick.

In addition to this he taught his bricklayers to make simple motions with both hands at the same time, where before they completed a motion with the right hand before they followed it later with one made by the left hand. For example, Mr. Gilbreth taught his bricklayers to pick up a brick in the left hand at the same time that he takes a trowel of mortar with the right hand. This work with two hands at the same time is, of course, made possible by substituting a deep mortar box for the old mortar-board, on which the mortar used to spread out so thin that a step or two had to be taken to reach it, and then placing the mortar box and the brick pile close together and at the proper height on his new scaffold.

Now, what was the practical outcome of all this study? To sum it up he finally succeeded in teaching his bricklayers, when working under the new method, to lay bricks with five motions per brick, while with the old method they used 18 motions per brick. And, in fact, in one exceedingly simple type of bricklaying he reduced the motions of his bricklayers from 18 to 2 motions per brick. But in the ordinary bricklaying he reduced the motions from 18 to 5. When he first came to me, after he had made this long and elaborate study of the motions of bricklayers, he had accomplished nothing in a practical way through this study, and he said, "You know, Fred, I have been showing all my friends these new methods of laying bricks and they say to me, 'Well, Frank, this is a beautiful thing to talk about, but what in the devil do you think it amounts to? You know perfectly well the unions have forbidden their members to lay more than so many bricks per day; you know they won't allow this thing to be carried out.'" But Gilbreth said, "Now, my dear boy, that doesn't make an iota of difference to me. I'm just going to see that the bricklayers do the right thing. I belong to the bricklayers' union in Boston, and the next job that I get in Boston this thing goes through. I'm not going to do it in any underhand way. Everyone knows that I have always paid higher wages than the union scale in Boston. I've got a lot of friends at the head of the unions in Boston, and I'm not afraid of having any trouble."

He got his job near Boston, and he went to the leaders of the union and told them just what you can tell any set of sensible men. He said to them, "I want to tell you fellows some things that you ought to know. Most of my contracts around here used to be brick jobs; now, most of my work is in re-inforced concrete or some other type of construction, but I am first and last a bricklayer; that is what I am interested in, and if you have any sense you will just keep your hands off and let me show you bricklayers how to compete with the reinforced concrete men. I will handle the bricklayers myself. All I want of you leaders is to keep your hands off and I will show you how bricklayers can compete with reinforced concrete or any other type of construction that comes along."

Well, the leaders of the union thought that sounded all right, and then he went to the workmen and said to them, "No fellow can work for me for less than $6.50 a day—the union rate was $5 a day—but every man who gets on this job has got to lay bricks my way; I will put a teacher on the job to show you all my way of laying bricks and I will give every man plenty of time to learn, but after a bricklayer has had a sufficient trial at this thing, if he won't do my way or cannot do my way, he must get off the job." Any number of bricklayers were found to be only too glad to try the job, and I think he said that before the first story of the building was up he had the whole gang trained to work in the new way, and all getting their $6.50 a day when before they only received $5 per day; I believe those are the correct figures; I am not absolutely sure about that, but at least he paid them a very liberal premium above the average bricklayer's pay.

It is one of the principles of scientific management to ask men to do things in the right way, to learn something new, to change their ways in accordance with the science, and in return to receive an increase of from 30 to 100 per cent in pay, which varies according to the nature of the business in which they are engaged.

After Mr. Gilbreth had trained his complete force of bricklayers so that they were all working the new instead of the old way, a very great and im-mediate increase in the output per man occurred. So that during the latter part of the construction of this building the bricklayers—and I wish it distinctly understood that all of these men were union bricklayers; Mr. Gilbreth him-self has for years insisted on having what is known as the closed shop on his work—who were engaged in building a 12-inch wall with drawn joints on both sides—which you gentlemen who under-stand bricklaying will recognize as a difficult wall to build; a 12-inch wall with drawn joints on both sides—these bricklayers averaged 350 bricks per man per hour, whereas the most rapid union rate up to that time had been 120 bricks per man per hour. And you will recog-nize, gentlemen, that this is due prin-cipally to the very great simplification of the work brought about through Mr. Gilbreth's three years of analysis and study of the art of bricklaying, which enabled him to reduce the number of motions made by the workman in laying a brick from 18 per brick to 5 per brick.

The immense gain which has been made through this study will be realized when it is understood that in one city in England the union bricklayers on this type of work have limited their output to 275 bricks per day per man, when on municipal work, and 375 bricks per day per man when on private work.

HUMAN RELATIONS

Time

Business managers today find their work not so much an exact science as a social one, and they see in good relations with their employees a sure road to high production. The change that has taken place in recent decades and the factors responsible for the change are ably chronicled in this survey.

"If it were desired to reduce a man to nothing," wrote Fyodor Dostoevsky in *The House of the Dead*, ". . . it would be necessary only to give his work a character of uselessness." In the 20th century, such a character of uselessness was, in fact, imposed on much of the work done in American factories and offices. It was not a sudden occurrence; it was the result of a long historical process, sped by typical American haste and thoughtlessness.

The Industrial Revolution, which replaced the tools of the independent workmen with machines owned by lenders of capital, had transformed handicraftsmen who were their own bosses into hired hands subject to the orders of managers. Gradually, men felt themselves swallowed by a vast, impersonal machine, which rubbed away their self-respect and, in a way, their identities. In anger against this betrayal of the human spirit by the Industrial Revolution, millions of workers listened to the false promises of Marx's counterrevolution which, as Russia has proved, offered only greater loss of self-respect and, in the end, slavery.

Now a second Industrial Revolution, quieter but more profound, is sweeping through U.S. industry. Its name: Human Relations in Industry. Its purpose: to give the American worker a sense of usefulness and importance (and thus improve his work). Its goal (stated in one sentence): to make life more fun by making work more meaningful.

THE SHOVELERS AND THE SPINNERS

The seeds of this change were sown by two great pioneers whose names are scarcely known—Frederick Winslow Taylor, a onetime day laborer, and Elton Mayo, an Australian immigrant turned Harvard sociologist. Their work did not seem related, but it was. Taylor, who died in 1915, was the father of scientific management; he increased industrial production by rationalizing it. Mayo, who died in 1949, was the father of industrial human relations; he increased production by humanizing it.

While working at the Midvale (Pa.) Steel Works in the 1880s, young Taylor made a discovery: it was the workers, not the bosses, who determined the production rate. The workers could go only so fast because, having learned their jobs by rule of thumb, they wasted steps, motion and time. Using a stop-watch, Taylor found that he could determine the most efficient speed for every operation by breaking it into its component parts.

Later, for Bethlehem Steel, he studied employees shoveling ore, coal, ets. He found that because they used different sized shovels, output varied widely. Taylor tried the workers with a shovel holding 34 lbs. of ore, then shifted to a shorter shovel holding 30 lbs. For every reduction in the load, each man's daily tonnage rose—until a 21-lb. load was reached. Below that, output fell. Taylor set 21½ lbs. as the ideal shovel load. Result: the yard force was cut by two-thirds, yet daily loadings rose from 25 tons per man to 45.

Taylor's pioneering in time and motion studies helped bring the mass-production era which enabled workers to raise not only their output but their wages as well. Taylor's own ruling motive, as Justice Brandeis observed at a memorial for Taylor, was to help his fellow men. Yet he also created a monster. By gearing human operations to the precision of machines, Taylor's system caused management to think of workers as little more than machines that had to eat. Since the only measure of efficiency was the utmost utilization of time, men were subjected to the intolerable nervous strain of the "speed-up," where assemblies moved always a little faster than men's natural work pace.

A point came where greater "efficiency" no longer yielded greater output. Example: at a Pennsylvania textile plant where the labor turnover in one of the spinning departments was 41 times higher than elsewhere in the plant, efficiency experts in 1923 set up various wage incentives, yet production remained low and spinners kept quitting. When Elton Mayo was called in, he discovered the men were poor producers for a reason which had not occurred to anyone: they were unhappy. The machines had been set up so as to deprive the men of virtually all human contact with one another; lonely, they fell into melancholy and hypochondria. Mayo prescribed four daily rest periods when the workers could relax, brought in a nurse to whom they could complain. The change wrought by these two relatively minor steps was startling. Turnover immediately diminished; production for the first time reached the established quotas.

Four years later, something even more startling happened. At its Hawthorne Works near Chicago, Western Electric tried to determine the effects of lighting on the worker and his output. As a test, it moved a group of girls into a special room with variable lighting, another group into a room where lighting remained as before. To its amazement, production shot up in both rooms. When the lighting was reduced in the first room, production continued to rise. But it also kept rising in the second room. Not until Mayo was called in to make tests of his own did the company discover what had happened. The simple answer: both groups were producing more because they had been singled out for special attention. The excitement of the experiments made them feel that they were no longer mere cogs.

Mayo's Hawthorne experiments were widely hailed as a landmark in social science. Actually, they revealed nothing which could not have been learned from any factory hand: every human being likes to feel that his work is important, that the boss is interested in him, and appreciates what he does. In a sense, the importance attached to Mayo's findings is a measure of the indifference to people into which management had fallen in its singleminded pursuit of Taylor's efficiency. Because of this indifference, the deep-rooted mutual interests of workers and management, as partners in production, were lost in shallow attitudes of suspicion and hostility. The folklore of each nourished a class warfare disturbingly like that which Marx had predicted.

THE MYTHS OF LABOR AND CAPITAL

In the accepted myths of hardheaded, hardfisted management, tenderness was weakness; workers could not be "coddled" lest they loaf; the only drives to which they responded were greed (more money) or fear (of dismissal). To praise them was simply to invite increasing demands. Workers, for their part, nursed long memories of hired spies who betrayed their unions and of uniformed thugs (e.g., the "coal & iron police") who smashed them. In labor's mythology, management was a silk-hatted capitalist who automatically opposed anything good for the workingman; by reflex, the worker opposed anything management favored.

For Mayo's new science to make headway in this charged atmosphere, there had to be a great change in basic attitudes. The change began with the U.S. Supreme Court's 1937 decision upholding the Wagner Act; it made management realize it had to learn to live with unions. The change was sped by World War II, which not only brought the patriotic necessity for the U.S. industrial machine to achieve maximum output, but flooded the labor force with millions of housewives and other new recruits relatively free of the old suspicions and hostilities.

Management began to learn that the once-feared unions themselves held potentials of higher production. In Pittsburgh, the United Steel Workers challenged one management to name its most productive department. Then the union boosted production there by 210% in a month. In the Toronto plant of Lever Bros., union and management, working together, trimmed the payroll from 693 to 512, the wage bill by 17%, yet achieved greater output in a 40-hour week than in 48 before.

Moreover, housewives coming into war plants were amazed to discover that they could far exceed the normal output of old hands. At a big Cleveland war plant, one housewife found that she could easily produce 800 grenade pins daily, v. the plant quota of 500. When fellow workers warned her to slow down, she discovered another thing: old hands deliberately limited their output from fear that Taylor's time-and-motion-study disciples would cut their pay rates by raising production quotas. More and more managers realized that maximum output could be realized only by finding ways to remove these old fears.

In dozens of plants, surveys of employees exploded the prize cliché of management's folklore—that workers wanted only more money. Actually, higher pay rated far down the list of workers' desires. For example, 100 shop workers who were polled by Psychologist S. N. F. Chant on twelve alternatives rated "high pay" as sixth. The Twentieth Century Fund found that wage disputes, the ostensible cause of 80% of all industrial conflicts, are only secondary causes: "Some of the industries most plagued by strikes . . . are among those where the highest wages are being paid." After ten years of polling workers, Elmo Roper concluded that their four chief desires are 1) security ("the right to work continuously at reasonably good wages"), 2) a chance to advance, 3) treatment as human beings, 4) dignity.

Yet the alarming fact, as agreed by all investigators, was that modern industry largely frustrates these desires. Detroit Edison, in a poll of its 11,000 employees, found that 43% did not believe that the company was "really interested" in their ideas. After a study of the auto industry, Author Peter Drucker, management consultant, concluded that the average worker regards his status as frozen, with little hope of advancement, and hopes to keep his sons from doing the same work.

There was equal agreement on the causes of such widespread discontent and emotional frustration. Businesses had grown to such a size that the average worker lost all sense of personal contact with his employers. The constant increase in mechanization took away his sense of personal pride and self-identification with the final product; frequently he did not even know the use of the part he made. The robot nature of many tasks thwarted the craving for prestige; the hope of advancement was lost in the growing tendency to choose management material not from men up from the bench, but from young, college-trained technicians.

THE NEW MANAGERS

These discoveries came to a head at a time when U.S. management was best equipped to do something about them: management itself had undergone a revolution. Death and taxes had all but eclipsed the great owner-management dynasties epitomized by Carnegie, Ford and Rockefeller. In their place had come the professional managers, the engineer-trained technicians, e.g., Du Pont's Crawford Greenewalt, General Elecric's Philip Reed, General Motors' C. E. Wilson, Standard Oil's (N.J.)

Frank Abrams. They took over industrial societies grown so huge that the average owner (i.e., stockholder) seldom exercised more than theoretical control. Profits were still the test of efficiency, and a fair return to the stockholder a prime duty of management. But the tremendous diffusion of ownership enabled the professional manager to give first concern to the economic health of the whole corporate body, in which the welfare of workers was as vital as that of stockholders. Since increased welfare promised greater efficiency, the new managers welcomed experiments.

In Marion, Va., the Harwood Manufacturing Co., which had 600 employees, mostly women, making pajamas, discovered that whenever it changed the work, only one-third of the workers ever got back to their old output rate. Many others quit, and most union grievances followed such changes. The company tried an experiment: one group was simply told of the change, another was told of the necessity for it and permitted to work out for itself the necessary revisions in quotas and rates. Result: its production quickly passed the old average of 60 hourly units per worker, and reached more than 80. The first group barely exceeded 50 units, and 17% of its members shortly quit. It also filed a complaint with the union that the new rate was "unjust," although investigations proved it generous. Yet when the survivors of this group were trained in the new way, they went up to a score of 73 within eight days.

At Detroit's Bundy Tubing Co., which had a history of ill will against the speed-up and fear of cuts in output rates, every attempt to boost production by special incentives had failed. The company offered the union a novel proposal: set a certain standard for labor costs, and let workers and management share all the savings when increased output drove costs below that figure. Not only did production beat all records, but the workers themselves began prodding slackers and berating absentees.

These lessons have borne fruit. In most big U.S. corporations, the new field of human relations is regarded as important, and equally as promising, as industrial research. Ford Motor Co. is spending millions to explore the untapped potentials of man. General Motors, the world's biggest industrial corporation, is drawing useful lessons from its World War II experiences.

At one G.M. aircraft parts plant, the manager almost turned down the offer of a visit by a combat-scarred B-17 and crew; he feared it would disrupt production. Instead, output shot up, not because the workers were thrilled by the bomber, but because the maintenance crew told them for the first time what the parts they made were used for. Another G.M. plant, which had to train workers to make carbines, had each new employee shoot the actual carbine, take it apart to see the significance of the part he would make. Despite their lack of skill their output was high.

Other companies are tackling the problem of size and resulting loss of individual identity. Robert Wood Johnson, whose family's famed Johnson & Johnson had grown up as a huge plant at New Brunswick, N.J., decentralized much of it into small, new, ultramodern factories, each making a single product line and small enough so that the president can usually call every worker by name. Not only has Johnson & Johnson been free of strikes, but the CIO Textile Workers union is the first to praise its enlightened methods.

Many plants are encouraging their workers at self-government through broadening their corporate responsibilities. Parker Pen replaced the hated time-clock with an honor system, found

that tardiness virtually vanished. The Commerce Trust Co. of Kansas City met the time loss from the morning "coffee rush" by providing free coffee.

A new concept of the role of employers and employees in the corporation is being formed. Some examples: Pittsburgh's Wiegand Co. lends money, interest free, to employees who need it to buy homes, etc.; Allegheny Ludlum Steel holds "open houses" to let families see what their breadwinner does, and production goes up on visiting days; Weirton Steel now tags almost everything moving through the plant to let workers know what it will make.

THE NEW PHILOSOPHY

Actually, far from being an occult science, human relations is nothing more than good will—and applied common sense. Much of it depends on simple things, such as making a plant more comfortable, and a friendlier place to work. Virtually every big company now sponsors plant bowling, baseball, dances, etc.; Westinghouse abets employee operettas, orchestras, picnics, even shows movies in its plants during lunch hours.

Yet that does not mean that every employer has seen the practical value of the new concept, or has accepted it. Some bitter-enders still regard any concession to the workers as a threat to their own authority. Others sometimes do more than good by doling out favors with an air of paternalism. Said one Kansas City industrialist: "We give our employees a Christmas party and that keeps 'em happy until we throw 'em a summer picnic." Still others have made the mistake of trying to create good human relations by mere words.

But by and large, the intent of this swiftly growing trend is not only genuine, but represents a movement toward an entirely new philosophy of management.

Nowhere has this new philosophy been better expressed than by General Foods' Chairman Clarence Francis at a postwar convention of the National Association of Manufacturers. Said Francis: "You can buy a man's time, you can buy a man's physical presence at a given place; you can even buy a measured number of skilled muscular motions per hour or day. But you cannot buy enthusiasm; you cannot buy initiative; you cannot buy loyalty; you cannot buy the devotion of hearts, minds and souls. You have to earn these things . . . It is ironic that Americans—the most advanced people technically, mechanically and indusrially—should have waited until a comparatively recent period to inquire into the most promising single source of productivity: namely, the human will to work. It is hopeful, on the other hand, that the search is now under way."

In that search, at mid-century, lies the finest hope and promise of the Capitalist Revolution.

WHAT PRICE HUMAN RELATIONS?
Malcolm P. McNair

Agreeing that business probably showed too little understanding of human relations in the past, but fearful that the pendulum has now swung too far in the other direction, Dr. McNair here gives the reasons for his anxiety. The author is Lincoln Filene Professor of Retailing at Harvard University and a director of several large retailing organizations.

In 1956 the Inland Steel Company appointed a vice president of human relations. The Inland Steel Company, of course, is big business; but little business is not being neglected, for I note that the McGraw-Hill Book Company, Inc., is publishing a book on *Human Relations in Small Industry*. The Harvard Business School has had a chair of Human Relations since 1950; by now the number of courses in Human Relations in schools and colleges throughout the country has multiplied substantially. Even more marked is the rapid growth of executive development programs, some in schools, some in industry, but almost all of them placing emphasis on human relations.

Doctoral theses increasingly carry such titles as "A Case Study of the Human Aspects of Introducing a New Product into Production," "An Intensive Study of Supervisory Training in Human Relations and Foreman Behavior at Work," "A Case Study of the Administration of Change in the Large Modern Office," and "Emergence of Leadership in Manufacturing Work Groups." And recently the *Harvard Business Review* has reprinted a dozen articles on human relations, under the title "How Successful Executives Handle People, 12 Studies on Communications and Management Skills," which include such intriguing subjects as "Making Human Relations Work," "Barriers and Gateways to Communication," and "The Fateful Process of Mr. A Talking to Mr. B."

It is obvious that human relations is very much the fashion in business thinking today. And fashions in business thinking are not a novelty; there have been many others. I can well recall that when I first joined the Harvard Business School faculty, the reigning vogue in business thinking was scientific management. Only a few years later, however, the grandiose claims of scientific management were sharply debunked. What was of solid worth remained—but a considerable amount of froth had been blown off the top.

Must we go through the same process—with all its waste and possible

From *Harvard Business Review*, March–April 1957. Reprinted by permission.

damage along the way—to get to what is worthwhile in human relations?

*   *   *

My quarrel is not with the solid substance of much that is comprehended by the phrase "human relations," but rather with the "cult" or "fad" aspects of human relations, which are assuming so much prominence.

There can be no doubt that people are of absorbing interest to other people. To verify this fact you have only to look at what makes headlines in the newspapers. There is a fascination for most of us in speculating about people and their behavior. So it is not surprising that human relations has assumed so much prominence as a fashionable mode of thinking. But, as with any kind of fashion, it can be carried to the point where people accept it without questioning—and certainly this can be dangerous when we are dealing with such an important segment of man's activity.

Therefore, just because the tide has gone so far, I must make my points in the most emphatic manner possible. Though I feel I have not distorted the picture, I do not care whether businessmen accept my interpretation in full, or even in large part, *so long as they get stirred up to do some critical thinking of their own.*

*   *   *

Before going any further let me try to indicate the things in this area of human relations which are really basic and with which there is no conceivable quarrel. In the first place, there can be no dispute with research in the social sciences, including the behaviorial sciences. Obviously such research is highly important to business management and to business education. Business management and education must seek to understand the behavior of

people as workers, the behavior of people as members of organizations, and, of course, the behavior of people as consumers. In all these areas we need more and better understanding of human behavior.

Neither is there any dispute in regard to the things that are important for a man's conduct in relation to his fellow men. The foundation is good Christian ethics, respect for the dignity of the individual human being, and integrity of character. On these we should stand fast. Personally I have always liked this paraphrase of what Theodore Roosevelt once said in a commencement address: "On the Ten Commandments and the Sermon on the Mount, uncompromising rigidity; on all else, the widest tolerance." [1] But between acceptance of high moral principles and the exigencies of day-to-day conduct of affairs there can be, with the best intentions, a very wide gap. This is the gap which by better understanding of human motivation we should try to fill.

Also there can be little dispute about the observations on the behavior of people at work which Professor Fritz J. Roethlisberger, the leader of the human relations group at Harvard, summed up half a dozen years ago:

People at work are not so different from people in other aspects of life. They are not entirely creatures of logic. They have feelings. They like to feel important and to have their work recognized as important. Although they are interested in the size of their pay envelopes, this is not a matter of their first concern. Sometimes they are more interested in having their pay reflect accurately the relative social importance to them of the different jobs they do. Sometimes even still more important to

[1] From the Introduction to *Theodore Roosevelt's America*, edited by Farida Wiley (New York, Devin-Adair Company, 1955), p. xxi.

them than maintenance of socially accepted wage differentials is the way
their superiors treat them.

They like to work in an atmosphere
of approval. They like to be praised
rather than blamed. They do not like
to have to admit their mistakes—at
least, not publicly. They like to know
what is expected of them and where
they stand in relation to their boss's expectations. They like to have some
warning of the changes that may affect
them.

They like to feel independent in
their relations to their supervisors. They
like to be able to express their feelings
to them without being misunderstood.
They like to be listened to and have
their feelings and points of view taken
into account. They like to be consulted
about and participate in the actions
that will personally affect them. In
short, employees, like most people,
want to be treated as belonging to and
being an integral part of some group." [2]

In other words, "People behave like
people." They have feelings. They don't
always behave logically. The concept of
the economic man can be a dangerous
abstraction. Every individual wants to
feel important, to have self-esteem, to
have "face." Everybody likes to feel that
he is "wanted." He likes to have a
"sense of belonging." Group influences
and group loyalties are important. The
desire for psychological "security" is
strong. People don't always reveal their
feelings in words.

That all these human attitudes have
important consequences for management is likewise not open to dispute.
It is well accepted in management
thinking today that leadership has to
be earned, it cannot be conferred; that
authority comes from below, not from
above; that in any business unit there

will be "social" groups which will cut
across organization lines; that good
communication involves both the willingness to listen and the ability to "get
through" but not by shouting.

Dean Stanley F. Teele of the Harvard
Business School recently made the
statement, "As we have learned more
and more about a business organization
as a social unit, we have become increasingly certain that the executive's
skill with people—or the lack of it—is
the determining element in his long-
range success or failure." [3] Here we are
down to the nub of the matter. What
is this skill? Can it be taught? Are there
dangers in the teaching of it? Is skill an
appropriate concept?

Perhaps I can give a clue to the line
of thought which I am developing when
I say that I am essentially disturbed at
the combination of *skill* with *human
relations*. For me, "human relations
skill" has a cold-blooded connotation
of proficiency, technical expertness, calculated effect.

                    *   *   *

There is no gainsaying the fact that
a need long existed in many businesses
for a much greater awareness of human
relations and that, in some, perhaps in
a considerable number, the need still
exists. The very avidity with which
people prone to fashionable thinking
in business have seized on the fad of
human relations itself suggests the presence of a considerable guilt complex in
the minds of businessmen in regard to
their dealings with people. So it is not
my intent to argue that there is no need
for spreading greater awareness of the
human relations point of view among
many businessmen. Nevertheless it is

[2] From a speech entitled "The Human
Equation in Employee Productivity" before
the Personnel Group of the National Retail
Dry Goods Association, 1950.

[3] From a speech entitled "The Harvard
Business School and the Search for Ultimate Values" at the presentation to the
HARVARD BUSINESS REVIEW of a citation
from The Layman's Movement for a Christian World, New York, October 25, 1955.

my opinion that some very real dangers threaten.

The world's work has to be done, and people have to take responsibility for their own work and their own lives. Too much emphasis on human relations encourages people to feel sorry for themselves, makes it easier for them to slough off responsibility, to find excuses for failure, to act like children. When somebody falls down on a job, or does not behave in accordance with accepted codes, we look into his psychological background for factors that may be used as excuses. In these respects the cult of human relations is but part and parcel of the sloppy sentimentalism characterizing the world today.

Undue preoccupation with human relations saps individual responsibility, leads us not to think about the job any more and about getting it done but only about people and their relations. I contend that discipline has its uses in any organization for accomplishing tasks. And this is especially true of self-discipline. Will power, self-control, and personal responsibility are more than ever important in a world that is in danger of wallowing in self-pity and infantilism.

Most great advances are made by individuals. Devoting too much effort in business to trying to keep everybody happy results in conformity, in failure to build individuals. It has become the fashion to decry friction, but friction has its uses; without friction there are no sparks, without friction it is possible to go too far in the direction of sweetness and light, harmony, and the avoidance of all irritation. The present-day emphasis on "bringing everybody along" can easily lead to a deadly level of mediocrity.

We can accept the first part of a statement by Peter Drucker: "The success and ultimately the survival of every business, large or small, depends in the last analysis on its ability to develop people. . . . This ability . . . is not measured by any of our conventional yardsticks of economic success; yet it is the final measurement." Drucker, however, goes on to add a further thought, which opens more opportunity for debate. He says, "Increasingly from here on this ability to develop people will have to be systematized by management as a major conscious activity and responsibility." In this concept there is the familiar danger of turning over to a program or a course or an educational director a responsibility that is a peculiarly personal one.

The responsibility for developing people belongs to every executive as an individual. No man is a good executive who is not a good teacher; and if Drucker's recommendation that executive development be "systematized by management as a major conscious activity" is interpreted as meaning that someone trained in the new mode of thinking should be appointed as director of executive development, then the probable outcome will be simply another company program in human relations. While this may be good for some of the executives, no long-run contribution to the development of good people will be made unless the good individuals personally take the responsibility for developing other individuals.

Please do not misunderstand me. I am not talking about oldfashioned rugged individualism or the law of the jungle, and I am not holding up as ideals the robber barons of the nineteenth century, or even some of the vigorous industrialists of the early twentieth century. But I ask you to consider whether some of today's business leaders, well known to all of us—Clarence Randall, Gardiner Symonds, Neil McElroy, Tex Colbert, Earl Puckett, Fred Lazarus, and so on—are not primarily products of a school of friction and competitive striving. We need more men like them, not fewer. It may be appropriate here to cite the recent observations of Dean Teele on "inner serenity" and "divine discontent":

Any realistic approach to the nature of top business management, and therefore to the problems of selection and development for top business management, makes abundantly clear that the balance between these two [attributes] is perhaps the most important determinant of success in top business management. Let me elaborate.

Psychiatrists, psychologists, and religious advisers join with ordinary lay observers in noting how often human efficiency is greatly reduced by sharp inner conflicts—conflicts which usually center around value judgments. That is to say, conflicts as to basic personal purposes and objectives, as to the values to be sought in life, are far more often the barriers to effective performance than intellectual incapacity or lack of necessary knowledge. The goal then from this point of view is the development of that inner serenity which comes from having struggled with and then resolved the basic questions of purpose and values.

On the other hand, in business as in the world generally, discontent is an element of the greatest importance. Dissatisfaction with oneself, with one's performance, is an essential for improvement. So important to the progress of the world is discontent on the part of the relatively few who feel it, that we have come to characterize it as divine discontent. Here . . . the need is for both inner serenity and divine discontent—a need for both in a balance between the two appropriate for the particular individuals.[4]

To keep that important balance of

[4] "The Fourth Dimension in Management," an address to the American Management Association, New York, May 25, 1956.

inner serenity and divine discontent in our future business leaders, we need to focus educational and training programs more sharply on the development of individuals than is the fashion today. What is important for the development of the individual? Obviously, many things; but one prime essential is the ability to think, and the nurturing of this ability must be a principal objective of all our educational effort.

In the field of business education this ability to think, to deal with situations, to go to the heart of things, to formulate problems and issues, is not an innate quality. It has to be cultivated, and it requires long and rigorous and often tedious practice in digging out significant facts, in weighing evidence, foreseeing contingencies, developing alternatives, finding the right questions to ask. In all business education, whether at the college or graduate level or at the stage of so-called executive development, we must not omit the insistence on close analysis, on careful reasoning and deduction, on cultivation of the power to differentiate and discriminate.

There is a very real danger that undue preoccupation with human relations can easily give a wrong slant to the whole process of education for business leadership. For one thing, it tends to give a false concept of the executive job. Dealing with people is eminently important in the day's work of the business executive, but so are the processes of analysis, judgment, and decision making. It takes skill and persistence to dig out facts; it takes judgment and understanding to get at the real issues; it takes perspective and imagination to see the feasible alternatives; it takes logic and intuition to arrive at conclusions; it takes the habit of decision and a sense of timing to develop a plan of action.

On the letterhead of the general

policy letters that are sent periodically to the managing directors of all 80-odd stores in the Allied Stores Corporation there is this slogan:

To LOOK is one thing.
To SEE what you look at is another.
To UNDERSTAND what you see is a third.
To LEARN from what you understand is still something else.
But to ACT on what you learn is all that really matters, isn't it?

An executive's ability to see, to understand, to learn, and to act comprises much more than skill in human relations.

*   *   *

Awareness of human relations as one aspect of the executive's job is of course essential. But, in my view, *awareness of human relations* and the *conscious effort to practice human relations on other people* are two different things, and I think this is crucial.

As soon as a man consciously undertakes to practice human relations, one of several bad consequences is almost inevitable. Consciously trying to practice human relations is like consciously trying to be a gentleman. If you have to think about it, insincerity creeps in and personal integrity moves out. With some this leads by a short step to the somewhat cynical point of view which students in Administrative Practices courses have described by coining the verb "ad prac," meaning "to manipulate people for one's own ends."

A less deliberate but perhaps even more dangerous consequence may be the development of a yen for managing other people's lives, always, of course, with the most excellent intentions. In the same direction the conscious practice of human relations leads to amateur psychiatry and to the unwarranted invasions of the privacy of individuals.

Hence I am disturbed about the consequences to business management of human relations blown up into pseudoscience—with a special vocabulary and with special practitioners and experts. In fact, to my mind there is something almost sinister about the very term "human relations practitioner," though I am sure that all sincere devotees of human relations would vigorously disclaim any such imputation.

*   *   *

For me much of the freshness and the insight which characterized a great deal of the earlier work in this field—exemplified by the quotation from Professor Roethlisberger which I cited in my introductory statement—has been lost as the effort has progressed to blow human relations up into a science—something to be explored and practiced for its own sake.

I realize that many people in the human relations field—Professor Roethlisberger in particular—are also disturbed about this trend, and about its unintended repercussions. But it was almost inevitable that other people would run away with such a fruitful concept, and set it up as an idol with appropriate rituals of worship (usually called "techniques"). Once you throw yourself into trying to "listen," to "gain intuitive familiarity," to "think in terms of mutually independent relationship," and so on, you can easily forget that there is more to business—and life—than running around plying human relations "skill" to plumb the hidden thoughts of everybody with whom you come in contact, including yourself.

This is the same mistake that some consumer motivation researchers make, as Alfred Politz has pointed out—trying to find out the attitudes, opinions, and preferences in the consumer's mind *without regard* to whether these factors are what determine how he will act in a given buying situation.[5] In his words, the "truth" that such researchers seek —and he always puts the word in quotes—is not only of a lower order than the scientifically established facts of how consumers react in real life, but it is also of less use to managers in making marketing decisions.

The whole thing gets a little ridiculous when, as pointed out in another article in this issue, foremen are assumed to have progressed when they have gained in "consideration" at the expense of something called "initiating structure"—yet such was the apparent objective of one company's training program.[6]

From the standpoint of developing really good human relations in a business context, to say nothing of the job of getting the world's work done, the kind of training just described seems to me in grave danger of bogging down in semantics and trivialities and dubious introspection. I am totally unable to associate the *conscious practice of human relations skill* (in the sense of making people happy in spite of themselves or getting them to do something they don't think they want to do) with

[5] "Science and Truth in Marketing Research," HBR January–February 1957, p. 117.
[6] Kenneth R. Andrews, "Is Management Training Effective? II. Measurement, Objectives, and Policy," HBR March–April 1957, p. 63.

the *dignity of an individual person created in God's image.*

Apparently this "skill" of the "human relations practitioner" consists to a considerable degree of what is called "listening." The basic importance of the ability to listen is not to be gainsaid; neither is it to be denied that people do not always reveal their inward feelings in words. But in the effort to blow human relations up into a science and develop a technique of communication, some of the enthusiasts have worked up such standard conversational gambits as "This is what I think I hear you saying," or "As I listen, this is what I think you mean."

No doubt there are times when a silent reaction of this kind is appropriate, but if the human relations practitioner makes such phrases part of his conversational repertoire, there are times when these cute remarks may gain him a punch in the nose. Sometimes people damn well mean what they are saying and will rightly regard anything less than a man-to-man recognition of that fact as derogatory to their dignity.

That a group of foremen who were given a course emphasizing human relations thereafter turned out to be distinctly poorer practitioners than they had been before taking the course, as in the above case, would not, to my mind, be simply an accident. I think it a result that might well be expected nine times out of ten. In other words, the overemphasis on human relations, with all its apparatus of courses, special vocabulary, and so on, tends to create the very problems that human relations deals with. It is a vicious circle. You encourage people to pick at the scabs of their psychic wounds.

In evaluating the place of human relations in business, a recent incident is in point:

At a luncheon gathering Miss Else Herzberg, the highly successful educational director of a large chain of stores in Great Britain, Marks and Spencer, Ltd., described at some length the personnel management policies of that concern and the high state of employee morale that existed. Throughout her description I was listening for some reference to human relations. I did not hear it, and when she had finished I said, "But, Miss Herzberg, you haven't said anything about human relations." Immediately she flashed back, "We live it; we don't have to talk about it."

In point also is a recent remark of Earl Puckett, chairman of the board of Allied Stores Corporation, when in discussing a particular management problem he said, "Of course you treat people like people."

And so, although I concede that there is still too little awareness of human relations problems in many business organizations, I think that the present vogue for human relations and for executive development programs which strongly emphasize human relations holds some real dangers because it weakens the sense of responsibility, because it promotes conformity, because it too greatly subordinates the development of individuals, and because it conveys a one-sided concept of the executive job. . . .

NOW REPORT CARDS FOR BOSSES

Ernest Dale and Alice Smith

One phase of human relations in action is described in this report on executive rating systems. Dr. Dale is Associate Professor at the Graduate School of Business and Public Administration at Cornell and an Associate Fellow of Jonathan Edwards College, Yale. Miss Smith is a freelance writer and editor.

If a business executive hesitates to crack down on his offspring for poor report cards these days, it may be because he is inhibited by the knowledge that his own report card—not twenty or thirty years ago, but just the other day—was something less than perfect.

Chances are better than even, in fact, that the executive who works for a big company today is scored on a formal report card. And if his children go to a progressive school where more stress is laid on originality, self-expression and adjustment to the group than on the three R's, it is more than likely both generations are marked on many of the same things.

Here, for example, are portions of two report cards, one for 4-year-olds at nursery school, the other used by one of the largest corporations in the country for grading its executives.

REPORT CARD A

Very Satisfactory
Satisfactory   Unsatisfactory
Dependability
Stability
Imagination
Originality
Self-expression
Health and vitality
Ability to plan and control
Cooperation

REPORT CARD B

Satisfactory
Improving   Needs Improvement
Can be depended upon
Contributes to the good work of others
Accepts and uses criticism
Thinks critically
Shows initiative
Plans work well
Physical resistance
Self-expression
Creative ability

In case you were unable to tell the difference, Report Card A is for the business executives, Report Card B for the 4-year-olds.

Executive report cards—generally called "appraisals" or "evaluations"—are comparatively new in American business and industry. Only during the last

Reprinted from *The New York Times Magazine*, March 31, 1957, by permission of the authors and the publisher.

ten years have they been at all common, and the majority of the rating plans were probably introduced after 1950. Now the roster of those that grade their executives periodically includes such firms as General Electric, Standard Oil of New Jersey, General Foods, Chrysler, Koppers Company, Detroit Edison, Monsanto Chemical Company, Westinghouse and dozens of others. More are joining the movement every year.

Companies generally began to feel the need for regular appraisals of their executives just after World War II, when large-scale expansion opened new fields for management talent. As the new opportunities arose, the obvious course was to promote the best men. But it soon became apparent that nobody really knew who the best men were, or had any sure way of finding out.

One company, for example, accepted a candidate proposed by an outside consultant for a high-level post, then discovered it had already been employing him in a lesser capacity for some years. "It was months," the consultant reported, "before the V. P. in charge of personnel could hold up his head around the office again."

Such confusion is mainly the result of bigness. In a large corporation there may be literally thousands of executives of varying degrees of importance, and top management finds it impossible to have more than a nodding acquaintance with most of them.

Then, too, specialization goes along with size, which means that what the majority of these executives do may affect profits only indirectly. So there is no easy dollars-and-cents way of identifying the capable.

Regular report cards appeared to offer a way out. If each man's boss set down an evaluation of him periodically, there would be written records to go on when promotions and bonuses were to be passed out—or so many experts reasoned.

The idea, of course, was not new. Periodic merit rating of rank-and-file employes had been used by many companies for some time, and a considerable number had extended the systems to cover foremen as well. More than a century ago, the English reformer, Robert Owen, devised a rough-and-ready merit-rating plan for his model factories. Over each machine he hung a four-sided slab of wood, each side a different color. If the white side were turned outward, it meant that the operator's conduct had been "excellent" the day before; yellow stood for "good," blue for "indifferent"; black let everyone know the unfortunate worker was in temporary disgrace.

Today's personnel men, schooled in psychology and dedicated to the principle that all reprimands must be given in private, would shudder at the thought of stigmatizing an employee by hanging a sign over his head. They also recognize that appraisals of other human beings require considerable insight, and often find it necessary to train company supervisors before turning them loose on the score cards.

However, it is comparatively easy to decide just what a "good" production worker or a "good" clerk is, and draw up a report form accordingly. The executive's job is much less concrete, and the factors that separate the brilliant "doers" from the plausible phonies are often tantalizingly elusive.

Most companies, it appears from a study of the appraisal blanks, are concerned mainly with personality and character traits. They are looking for men who are extroverted, flexible in their outlook, vigorous, and presentable in appearance. Above all, they stress ability to get along with other people— subordinates, equals and bosses. So strong is the emphasis on personality, that "job knowledge" and even "job performance" may have only a minor place in the over-all rating.

Usually a company will try to define the ideal executive in terms of about ten traits. Sometimes only three grades are listed for each trait: good, fair or poor. On other blanks there are five classifications: outstanding, above average, average, below average and poor. Or descriptive phrases rather than grades may be used. A large chemical company, for example, offers the following choices for the single trait, "cooperation":

1. Concedes nothing. Obstructive, antagonistic.

2. Poor mixer. Tries to run with the ball. Occasionally indulges in obstructive argument.

3. Generally adapts self to persons and situations. Responsive to leadership and reasonably tactful.

4. Willing and eager to please. Works in complete harmony with group. Adaptable and courteous.

5. Adapts self very well without sacrificing standards. Goes out of his way to promote common end.

The rater is instructed to check the group of phrases that best describes the man he is rating, but to cross out any words that do not apply to him, and to underline phrases in other blocks that may clarify the appraisal.

On some of the earlier blanks, traits were given numerical weighting in accordance with their supposed importance. A top score in "cooperation" might mean 20 points, an equally good mark in "accuracy" only 10 to 15. Some companies even supposed they could add the scores and get an accurate idea of how one executive stacked up against another. A man with a score of 200 would automatically be considered twice as capable as one with only 100 points, and slightly better than the man with 195.

A little experience, however, has convinced most companies that it is impractical to try to measure a man's character and personality on a strictly numerical scale. There is also something of a trend now to place less emphasis on traits and more on actual behavior on the job.

Trait-rating has, in fact, a number of serious shortcomings. There is seldom any scientific basis for deciding that certain traits are essential for good performance on a given job. Such traits are, for the most part, selected by "common sense" reasoning, and experience often controverts the best logic exercised in a vacuum. It seems only common sense, for example, to assume that a top executive needs a full helping of tact and skill in public relations. Yet Charles E. Wilson guided the vast General Motors organization to outstanding success despite his admitted susceptibility to foot-in-mouth disease. Henry Ford Sr. got along pretty well without too much sense of humor. And Abraham Lincoln would never have been given a passing mark in appearance if his contemporaries had thought to grade him. Indeed, many of the hallowed figures of history would have registered poorly on one company's appraisal blank; it states that a top score in personality means that the executive is not only "poised, confident and courteous," but "radiant" as well.

Dr. Milton Blum, who has served as a consultant on the subject of executive appraisals, would not even go along with the theory that high intelligence is necessarily an advantage in an executive job. It takes somewhat more than average brain power to be a successful executive, he believes, but after a certain point a high I.Q. is just so much excess baggage.

"There are no executive traits per se," he states flatly. "The traits that make a man successful in one company may actually hinder him in another."

Nor is Dr. Blum alone among psychologists in his opinion. For instance, J. A. C. Brown, in his book, "The Social Psychology of Industry," points out that a number of studies have failed to isolate any specific "leadership traits."

Perhaps the most serious criticism, however, comes from Dr. Walter Mahler, head of a consulting firm that specializes in the development of appraisal systems. "Most trait-rating forms," he says, "ignore what the man is actually being paid for—results."

Some of the newer blanks, however, do recognize that results are, after all, what count. One such fairly usual plan requires a boss to list the duties of the job in order of their importance, and comment on the way the incumbent is handling each, giving facts and figures wherever possible. Other forms ask specific questions about the ratee, such as: "Does he meet production or service requirements of the job? Are his assignments accomplished on time? Does he do more than would normally be expected? Does he keep within his budget? Has he furthered cost control?"

One big advantage of the more job-oriented forms is that they make it easier for the boss to discuss the score with the man he has rated—as he is nearly always supposed to do since one of the purposes of the appraisals is to encourage improvement. Most bosses find it embarrassing to tell a man to his face that he lacks personality or a sense of humor. Moreover, the man who is informed that he hasn't enough "vision" or "leadership" is likely to feel pretty baffled about the whole thing. But if he is asked why he hasn't been meeting schedules, he may take a realistic look at his own conduct and begin to wonder whether his own shortcomings may not have something to do with it.

"I have actually had a man volunteer that the real reason for his lack of results was his own insufficient engineering training," Dr. Mahler says. "Once he'd admitted that, he was glad to accept a transfer to a job where his lack of knowledge wouldn't be a problem."

Attempts have also been made to develop purely factual ratings—that is, "ships on schedule 95 per cent of the time," or "developed new products that produced $——— profit." However, in the case of people with staff jobs (personnel men, accountants and the like) there may be no meaningful figures available, since the amount of work done is not necessarily a measure of the value contributed.

In an effort to get around the difficulty of breaking down executive success into its components, some firms have dispensed with both performance items and traits, and ask general questions that allow the rater to answer in his own words. Popular queries of this type are: "What are the man's strongest points? What are his weaknesses? What should be done to help him improve? How far can he be expected to go?" Often questions such as these are appended to the trait and performance ratings also.

Here, again, some troubles develop. For very few department and division heads can write an informative report on a man's performance and character. Further, even apparently simple questions mean different things to different people. American Cyanamid Company discovered that, to raters who had credited subordinates with "ability to go far," distance was entirely relative.

"Take a department head," says L. B. Olsen, a psychologist who worked on the Cyanamid studies. "He may think he's come pretty far, and that any man who will eventually be ready for a job like his should be credited with unlimited capacity for advancement. To another man the same question may mean, 'Will he some day be able to handle the president's job?' "

To bring a variety of viewpoints to bear, some companies using essay-type ratings have the boss bring in other executives on his own level. The group then "talks out" the rating, while one of the number takes notes.

Still another type of report card—at present used by only a few companies—gives what is known as "forced choice." Where this technique is employed, the rater is confronted with twenty or thirty blocks of statements, and checks the statement in each that is most applicable to the man he is rating, and the one that is least applicable. For example:

BLOCK I

Always does things on time
Does not get along well with others
Keeps his department very neat
Has an excellent personal appearance
Needs more training

BLOCK II

Is very well suited to his job
Has no trouble making decisions
Well-liked by those who work for him
Does not readily accept criticism
A good candidate for promotion

It can be seen that all the statements in any one block might well apply to a single person; conversely, none of them might apply. Nevertheless, the rater is compelled to check a "most" and a "least."

Some of the items that appear uncomplimentary may not count one way or the other. Some that appear complimentary may actually reduce the score, since, in view of the choice allowed,

checking them amounts to damning the man with faint praise. Hence, proponents of this system claim, there are built-in safeguards against partiality.

Under all other systems so far developed, the possibility that the boss may twist the ratings for his own purposes is a real one—though in some companies a partial check exists in that the boss' boss may sit in on the rating, or review it, and perhaps the next higher boss as well.

The biggest danger, the experts agree, is not that bosses will attempt to cut down possible rivals by giving them poor scores. If the appraiser errs deliberately, he is much more likely to do so out of simple kindheartedness, the desire to be a good fellow, or to preserve the relative standing of his own group.

A boss may remember that he will be rated, too, on his "ability to develop subordinates." One young executive, depressed at getting no more than "average" in any category, was astonished to have the boss' secretary compliment him on his showing. "Good grief, I didn't get more than 'average' in anything," he said.

"Oh, but that's good," said the young lady serenely. "Mr. Jones always marks everyone down on the first rating; generally they get almost all 'poors.' Then he brings them up gradually to show how well he's training them."

The various executive-appraisal plans described here all have fairly obvious inadequacies. Nevertheless, a few company presidents have swallowed them whole, and proceeded to reward and punish entirely on the basis of the results. One Texas tycoon had the air-conditioning units pulled out of the company Cadillacs used by executives who had made poor scores. The executives still rode in state, but they sweltered for several months until they brought their ratings up to par.

Most companies, however, are using what they have only for lack of something better, and are constantly on the lookout for new and improved formulas. "Every once in a while our president asks me if our appraisal system is 'up to date,'" one personnel director remarked. "That generally means he's seen some other company's appraisal blank and is wondering whether it isn't better than ours."

If any psychologist—professional or amateur—could devise a system that would be acceptable to everybody—that is, demonstrably fool- and prejudice-proof, and non-time-consuming—he could probably make a fortune in royalties. Vast sums are spent on executive training these days, and the big companies who pay the tuition would like to be sure they are working with the best material available.

Exercises

"Communication in Industry," United States Steel Corporation

1. Explain in a paragraph what in your opinion is the purpose of the United States Steel Corporation in publishing and distributing to its management staff the information in this article.
2. Put the ideas of this article into a theme of about 400 words.
3. Define in a sentence the term "Stove Pipe Committee."
4. Do you know an instance of particularly good (or bad) relations between a company and a community? Write a paper describing the relations.
5. Write a theme on "The Grapevine," drawing from your own experience.
6. Taking for your subject your college or some company you have been associated with, write a report describing the kinds of information it transmits to its various audiences.
7. After adequate investigation, write a report on the part played by one of the following media in promoting understanding between employer and employees: employee handbooks, plant visits and "open house," bulletin boards, suggestion systems, house organs (see "Open Letter to a Novice House Organ Editor" in Sec. 2), financial reports.
8. Discuss the problems of communication between teacher and pupil, and tell how these problems are customarily solved.
9. What can each student of your college do to maintain effective communication between the college and the community? Why is such communication important? Write a paper embodying your ideas.

"Scientific Management," by Frederick W. Taylor

1. Write a 300-word summary of the testimony printed here.
2. Write a paragraph explaining the meaning of scientific management in the light of the Gilbreth example.
3. See what you can discover in the library about Frank Gilbreth. Write a paper on your findings.
4. Observe some manual operation like washing dishes, changing a tire, making the beds, cleaning the house, or inserting circulars in an envelope, and describe the performance in detail. Tell, also, in the light of what you have learned from Mr. Taylor's statement, how the operation might be improved.
5. Discuss Mr. Gilbreth's use of the "you" attitude in getting union leaders and workers to agree to his method of laying bricks.
6. Write a paragraph on Frederick W. Taylor's powers of expression as revealed by his testimony.
7. Have you ever visited a construction job or a factory and observed the workers in action? If you have, write a theme describing what you saw, especially from the standpoint of the efficiency of workers and management.

"Human Relations," Time

1. Condense this story of human relations in industry to 400 words.
2. Write a theme on the quotation from Dostoevsky at the beginning of this article. Supply your own examples.
3. Discuss the significance of human relations to business majors preparing for executive careers. You may draw ideas from any of the articles in this section.
4. Taking your cue from the lesson learned in the Hawthorne experiments,

write a theme entitled, "On Being Appreciated," with special reference to your personal experiences.

5. According to this article, the idea that men work only for money is a myth. Is it also a myth that college students work only for grades? What do they work for? Write a theme expressing your views on the subject.

6. Explain in a paragraph what is meant by the statement that Taylor "increased production by rationalizing it." Refer to Taylor's testimony (see the preceding article) for an example.

7. Explain in a paragraph how communication can be credited with the increased production at the Harwood Manufacturing Company.

8. Discuss some corporate human relations techniques that have personally come to your attention. Draw on your own work experience or that of your family and friends.

"What Price Human Relations?" by Malcolm P. McNair

1. Sum up Professor McNair's quarrel with the "human relations" school.

2. Professor McNair says, "Too much emphasis on human relations encourages people to feel sorry for themselves." Do you think so? What is "too much emphasis"? Write a theme stating your views. It is suggested that you support your statements by references to the material in the other articles in this section.

3. Write a theme in which you discuss the statement, "No man is a good executive who is not a good teacher."

4. In what ways might the practice of human relations lead to undesirable business conformity? Other articles in this section may give you some ideas.

5. Write a theme on dissatisfaction as an essential element in the improvement of oneself and in the progress of the world.

6. What is the difference between the awareness of human relations and the conscious effort to practice human relations on other people? Do you agree with the validity of the author's distinction? Explain, giving an example or two if you can.

7. Do you see any relation between the practice of human relations in management, as seen by Mr. McNair, and the idea of motivation research in selling (see Sec. 4, "They're Selling Your Unconscious")? Explain.

8. Why do you suppose the author sees the practice of human relations as inconsistent with "the dignity of an individual person created in God's image"? Is he overstating the case? Explain your views.

"Now Report Cards for Bosses," by Ernest Dale and Alice Smith

1. Using Report Card A at the beginning of this article as a guide, write an analysis of yourself as a potential business executive. Back up your generalizations with specific details and instances.

2. According to this article, business puts so much emphasis on personality that job knowledge and even job performance may have only a minor place in the over-all rating. To what extent do your educational plans stress job knowledge? To what extent have you thought of personality development as an avenue to business success? Discuss.

3. Two questions on one of the rating forms cited by the authors read, "Are his assignments accomplished on time?" "Does he do more than would normally be expected?" Examine these and related work habits of both yourself and some of your schoolmates. Describe the habits and indicate the correlation, if any, between them and scholastic success.

4. Suppose you were asked to rate the performance of your teachers. Discuss the qualities you would look for and indicate their relative importance. Include a rating chart.

5. Write a 300-word summary of this article.

6. Write a serious theme on one of the following subjects:

a. The Nonconformer in Business

b. The Ideal Business Personality

c. How Smart Should an Employee Be?

7. Write a frivolous character sketch of one of the following business or collegiate types:

a. The Good Mixer

b. The Obstructionist

c. The Eager Beaver

6

Economic Man—A Diversity of Views

If the economic activities of man have not always received the attention they deserved, the drama, comforts, and frustrations of daily living have nevertheless been with him for a long time. And whether he has sailed the perilous seas with precious cargoes or bargained for a cost-of-living bonus, his gains have been subject to such forces as population growth, international rumblings, government edicts, scientific progress, and the weather.

Adam Smith and his progeny have tried to interpret these influences and chart their effects. Other contributions to economic understanding have been made by historians, statesmen, and unhappy speculators. All these categories are represented in the examples of business writing that have been collected here.

ALEXANDRIAN COMMERCIALISM

Miriam Beard

Business has often been called "the civilizer." As the epithet implies, its history is as old as the cities of the world. Among the ancient strongholds of civilization, Rome and Alexandria were preëminent. How far Alexandria had advanced toward the establishment of a modern economic society is described in this colorful passage from the work of a writer who has done much to put the businessman in historical perspective.

The city of Alexandria in Egypt, halfway port between East and West, was the greatest manufacturing and trading city of the second century of the Christian Era. She was supreme in commerce, as Rome in finance. In the elegant shops of her Main Street, or *Mesion Pedion*, were assembled the finest wares of the world. Twenty meters broad and lined with pillared arcades for five kilometers, paved with hardest basalt, it was the Fifth Avenue of antiquity.

Some of the luxuries represented there had been brought across the Indian Ocean by seven-sailed vessels and over the desert by camel caravan. To pay for these Eastern goods, the products of the West, wine of Italy, tin of Wales, and amber of Sweden, were gathered in the harbor of Alexandria, watched over by the renowned lighthouse, the marvelous Pharos. The intricacy of this traffic may be illustrated by the exchange of pearls and coral. Pearls were as necessary for the ears of Roman ladies as coral for the rosaries of Buddhist churchmen. To satisfy the former, pearls were shipped from the Persian Gulf, polished in Alexandrian shops, sent by a three weeks' voyage to Puteoli in Italy and thence carried to the shops of the Margaritarii, or pearl-dealers' corporation, in the Roman Forum. The coral, in return, had to be obtained by barter from the shields of barbaric Gallic warriors, and followed the same route back to Alexandria, whence it was dispatched to Ceylon and on to far Tibet.

The energetic merchants of the city were extending trade even beyond the limits of the Roman Empire. Greek sailors, merchants like that Hippalos who discovered the secret of the monsoons in the second century, were as active as Roman soldiers in pushing back boundaries. They coasted to the Ganges and even Canton, seeking the secrets of the silk and pepper routes and braving all sorts of perils to find the Gold Country, China. The role of the business man in binding together and expanding empire has been over-

From *A History of the Business Man* by Miriam Beard. Copyright 1938 by Miriam Beard Vagts. Reprinted by permission of The Macmillan Company.

shadowed in written history by the deeds of military heroes. But what would the Empire built by Roman soldiers have been without the Greek, Syrian and Jewish traders? What were Rome without Alexandria?

The Alexandrian business men were spreaders of civilization, intermediaries between hemispheres. They planted colonies in India, reproducing the shops, banks, warehouses and temples of their homeland; these were connected by regular post with Alexandria, thus ensuring the circulation of the chatty papyrus letters which are unearthed today in Egyptian towns. In the course of this traffic, Alexandrians and other Greeks brought to India the Jewish calendar, Roman law, Babylonian astronomy, Greek music and theater and weights and measures. Talented slaves were carried in both directions. India, as Pliny cried, was "brought nearer by lust for gain." She passed on to the West her medicine, legends and textile designs. "Effeminate philosophy and pepper" came together from the East, as Persius declared, and the trader was the agent for this momentous interchange.

If, therefore, it comes about that Christian and Buddhist saints, in two remote island corners of the world, Ireland and Japan, wear haloes round their heads, it is doubtless due to the spread of the symbol of the sun-ray crown, belonging to the Alexandrian Apollo, in that age of close-knit cultural and commercial connections.

But the trader was responsible for more than the mere spread of symbols and notions over the surface of the earth. He was an accumulator and concentrator of knowledge, as well. Alexandria was a focal point of caravan and sea routes, as Miletus had been hundreds of years before. It was the melting-pot of many races, and the result was a cosmopolitanism of culture,

a synthesis of thought, which would only have been possible in a place of such far-sweeping contacts.

A veritable department-store of information was Alexandria. The facts gathered by explorer-traders were collected into treatises like the world geography of Ptolemy. Cosmogonies, universal histories, general works in broad fields of science, fruitful mergings of philosophies and creeds were characteristic of Alexandria's wholesale mind. Business practice was being perfected at the same time through the councils of many men; Rhodian maritime law, Phoenician bookkeeping, Egyptian skill in documentation, Babylonian banking methods, brought by Jewish pupils, were all merged to form a general business practice which was much more complex than that of previous ages.

In this industrial city, where technology was esteemed, training-schools were maintained and science came into its own. The most advanced mechanical contrivances were perfected: washing-machines, gear-wheels, the famous first steam-engine—the steam-driven car of Hiero, which used to roll along the city streets in an annual religious procession. The water-clock was also the inevitable necessity in a town where time was being counted with more care, because it was more valuable than in rural regions. In the medical faculty of the Alexandrian university, dissection was practiced and an anaesthetic developed. Thus Alexandria was groping toward a rationalized, even a mechanized, society. If the city had been free from Roman exactions and interference, she might have gone much further.

Like Paris in the nineteenth century, Alexandria in the second was an arbiter of fashionable taste for the world, as well as the center of luxury trades. She set the styles and sold the goods. Her great garment center, managed largely by Jews, produced embroidered robes of Chinese silk, African cottons and Indian gauzes. She formed the mode in personal adornments, interior decoration, gardening and cookery. She sold the cookbooks, the pepper and spices, the trained cook-slaves, and the richly inlaid dining-tables. She also offered perfumes, incense, medicines from India, ginger, lip-salve, camphor of Sumatra, yak-milk, the melted fat of crocodiles, snow-leopard skins of Tibet, couches adorned with rock-crystal and Malayan tortoiseshell, vases of carnelian, Indian steel swords sheathed in African ivory, and tigers, fed on human flesh, for the circuses of popular and benevolent senators.

The city was a leading labor market as well, where black and white flesh of all kinds, from Spanish dancing-girls to Nubian porters, was available. Ingenious in salesmanship, Alexandria dressed little live children as cupids, and set the fashion of having them at parties to amuse the guests; it then offered babies in wholesale lots. Quaintly enough, the fad of Alexandrian elegants affected the Christian culture which was formed in that city; Christians continued the custom of representing these babies, now turned into cherubs, on their caskets. And so eventually the poor little slaves received their apotheosis in mediaeval religious paintings; often, in the Middle Ages, merchants in ordering pictures of saintly scenes had themselves portrayed kneeling in the foreground, while, from the clouds, the emancipated babies looked down upon the business men. . . .

OF THE DIVISION OF LABOR
Adam Smith

In the year of America's Declaration of Independence a Scottish professor of logic published the first systematic formulation of classical English economics. There is some significance in this concurrence, for Adam Smith had a democratic concept of wealth. To him wealth did not mean, as it did to his contemporaries, gold or kingly treasure; it was, rather, all of the goods people consume. His prime interest was in discovering the mechanism by which individuals working for their own benefit nevertheless contributed to the good of the whole society. The following passage, containing the famous reference to the making of pins, comes at the very beginning of Adam Smith's treatise.

The greatest improvement in the productive powers of labour, and the greater part of the skill, dexterity, and judgment with which it is any where directed, or applied, seem to have been the effects of the division of labour.

The effects of the division of labour, in the general business of society, will be more easily understood, by considering in what manner it operates in some particular manufactures. It is commonly supposed to be carried furthest in some very trifling ones; not perhaps that it really is carried further in them than in others of more importance: but in those trifling manufactures which are destined to supply the small wants of but a small number of people, the whole number of workmen must necessarily be small; and those employed in every different branch of the work can often be collected into the same workhouse, and placed at once under the view of the spectator. In those great manufactures, on the contrary, which

are destined to supply the great wants of the great body of the people, every different branch of the work employs so great a number of workmen, that it is impossible to collect them all into the same workhouse. We can seldom see more, at one time, than those employed in one single branch. Though in such manufactures, therefore, the work may really be divided into a much greater number of parts, than in those of a more trifling nature, the division is not near so obvious, and has accordingly been much less observed.

To take an example, therefore, from a very trifling manufacture; but one in which the division of labour has been very often taken notice of, the trade of the pin-maker; a workman not educated to this business (which the division of labour has rendered a distinct trade), nor acquainted with the use of the machinery employed in it (to the invention of which the same division of labour has probably given occasion), could scarce,

From *The Wealth of Nations* by Adam Smith.

perhaps, with his utmost industry, make one pin in a day, and certainly could not make twenty. But in the way in which this business is now carried on, not only the whole work is a peculiar trade, but it is divided into a number of branches, of which the greater part are likewise peculiar trades. One man draws out the wire, another straights it, a third cuts it, a fourth points it, a fifth grinds it at the top for receiving the head; to make the head requires two or three distinct operations; to put it on, is a peculiar business, to whiten the pins is another; it is even a trade by itself to put them into the paper; and the important business of making a pin is, in this manner, divided into about eighteen distinct operations, which, in some manufactories, are all performed by distinct hands, though in others the same man will sometimes perform two or three of them. I have seen a small manufactory of this kind where ten men only were employed, and where some of them consequently performed two or three distinct operations. But though they were very poor, and therefore but indifferently accommodated with the necessary machinery, they could, when they exerted themselves, make among them about twelve pounds of pins in a day. There are in a pound upwards of four thousand pins of a middling size. Those ten persons, therefore, could make among them upwards of forty-eight thousand pins in a day. Each person, therefore, making a tenth part of forty-eight thousand pins, might be considered as making four thousand eight hundred pins in a day. But if they had all wrought separately and independently, and without any of them having been educated to this peculiar business, they certainly could not each of them have made twenty, perhaps not one pin in a day; that is, certainly, not the two hundred and fortieth, perhaps not the four thousand eight hundredth part of what they are at present capable of performing, in consequence of a proper division and combination of their different operations.

In every other art and manufacture, the effects of the division of labour are similar to what they are in this very trifling one; though, in many of them, the labour can neither be so much subdivided, nor reduced to so great a simplicity of operation. The division of labour, however, so far as it can be introduced, occasions, in every art, a proportionable increase of the productive powers of labour. The separation of different trades and employments from one another, seems to have taken place, in consequence of this advantage. This separation too is generally carried furthest in those countries which enjoy the highest degree of industry and improvement; what is the work of one man in a rude state of society, being generally that of several in an improved one. In every improved society, the farmer is generally nothing but a farmer; the manufacturer, nothing but a manufacturer. The labour too which is necessary to produce any one complete manufacture, is almost always divided among a great number of hands. How many different trades are employed in each branch of the linen and woollen manufactures, from the growers of the flax and the wool, to the bleachers and smoothers of the linen, or to the dyers and dressers of the cloth! The nature of agriculture, indeed, does not admit of so many subdivisions of labour, nor of so complete a separation of one business from another, as manufactures. It is impossible to separate so entirely, the business of the grazier from that of the corn-farmer, as the trade of the carpenter is commonly separated from that of the smith. The spinner is almost always a distinct person from the weaver; but the ploughman, the harrower, the sower of the seed, and the reaper of the corn, are often the same. The occasions for those different sorts of labour returning with the different seasons of the year, it is impossible that one man should be constantly employed in any one of them. This impossibility of making so complete and entire a separation of all the different branches of labour employed in agriculture, is perhaps the reason why the improvement of the productive powers of labour in this art, does not always keep pace with their improvement in manufactures. The most opulent nations, indeed, generally excel all their neighbours in agriculture as well as in manufactures; but they are commonly more distinguished by their superiority in the latter than in the former. Their lands are in general better cultivated, and having more labour and expence bestowed upon them, produce more in proportion to the extent and natural fertility of the ground. But this superiority of produce is seldom much more than in proportion to the superiority of labour and expence. In agriculture, the labour of the rich country is not always much more productive than that of the poor; or, at least, it is never so much more productive, as it commonly is in manufactures. The corn of the rich country, therefore, will not always, in the same degree of goodness, come cheaper to market than that of the poor. The corn of Poland, in the same degree of goodness, is as cheap as that of France, notwithstanding the superior opulence and improvement of the latter country. The corn of France is, in the corn provinces, fully as good, and in most years nearly about the same price with the corn of England, though, in opulence and improvement, France is perhaps inferior to England. The corn-lands of England, however, are better cultivated than those of France, and the corn-lands of France are said to be much better cultivated than those of

Poland. But though the poor country, notwithstanding the inferiority of its cultivation, can, in some measure, rival the rich in the cheapness and goodness of its corn, it can pretend to no such competition in its manufactures; at least if those manufactures suit the soil, climate, and situation of the rich country. The silks of France are better and cheaper than those of England, because the silk manufacture, at least under the present high duties upon the importation of raw silk, does not so well suit the climate of England as that of France. But the hard-ware and the coarse woollens of England are beyond all comparison superior to those of France, and much cheaper too in the same degree of goodness. In Poland there are said to be scare any manufactures of any kind, a few of those coarser household manufactures excepted, without which no country can well subsist.

This great increase of the quantity of work, which, in consequence of the division of labour, the same number of people are capable of performing, is owing to three different circumstances; first, to the increase of dexterity in every particular workman; secondly, to the saving of the time which is commonly lost in passing from one species of work to another; and lastly, to the invention of a great number of machines which facilitate and abridge labour, and enable one man to do the work of many.

First, the improvement of the dexterity of the workman necessarily increases the quantity of the work he can perform; and the division of labour, by reducing every man's business to some one simple operation, and by making this operation the sole employment of his life, necessarily increases very much the dexterity of the workman. A common smith, who, though accustomed to handle the hammer, has never been used to make nails, if upon some particular occasion he is obliged to attempt it, will scarce, I am assured, be able to make above two or three hundred nails in a day, and those too very bad ones. A smith who has been accustomed to make nails, but whose sole or principal business has not been that of a nailer, can seldom with his utmost diligence make more than eight hundred or a thousand nails in a day. I have seen several boys under twenty years of age who had never exercised any other trade but that of making nails, and who, when they exerted themselves, could make, each of them, upwards of two thousand three hundred nails in a day. The making of a nail, however, is by no means one of the simplest operations. The same person blows the bellows, stirs or mends the fire as there is occasion, heats the iron, and forges every part of the nail: In forging the head too he is obliged to change his tools. The different operations into which the making of a pin, or of a metal button, is subdivided, are all of them much more simple, and the dexterity of the person, of whose life it has been the sole business to perform them, is usually much greater. The rapidity with which some of the operations of those manufactures are performed, exceeds what the human hand could, by those who had never seen them, be supposed capable of acquiring.

Secondly, the advantage which is gained by saving the time commonly lost in passing from one sort of work to another, is much greater than we should at first view be apt to imagine it. It is impossible to pass very quickly from one kind of work to another, that is carried on in a different place, and with quite different tools. A country weaver, who cultivates a small farm, must lose a good deal of time in passing from his loom to the field, and from the field to his loom. When the two trades can be carried on in the same workhouse, the loss of time is no doubt much less. It is even in this case, however, very considerable. A man commonly saunters a little in turning his hand from one sort of employment to another. When he first begins the new work he is seldom very keen and hearty; his mind, as they say, does not go to it, and for some time he rather trifles than applies to good purpose. The habit of sauntering and of indolent careless application, which is naturally, or rather necessarily acquired by every country workman who is obliged to change his work and his tools every half hour, and to apply his hand in twenty different ways almost every day of his life; renders him almost always slothful and lazy, and incapable of any vigorous application even on the most pressing occasions. Independent, therefore, of his deficiency in point of dexterity, this cause alone must always reduce considerably the quantity of work which he is capable of performing.

Thirdly, and lastly, every body must be sensible how much labour is facilitated and abridged by the application of proper machinery. It is unnecessary to give any example. I shall only observe, therefore, that the invention of all those machines by which labour is so much facilitated and abridged, seems to have been originally owing to the division of labour. Men are much more likely to discover easier and readier methods of attaining any object, when the whole attention of their minds is directed towards that single object, than when it is dissipated among a great variety of things. But in consequence of the division of labour, the whole of every man's attention comes naturally to be directed towards some one very simple object. It is naturally to be expected, therefore, that some one or other of those who are employed in each particular branch of labour should soon find out easier and readier methods of performing their own particular work, wherever the nature of it admits of such improvement. A great part of the machines made use of in those manufactures in which labour is most subdivided, were originally the inventions of common workmen, who, being each of them employed in some very simple operation, naturally turned their thoughts towards finding out easier and readier methods of performing it. Whoever has been much accustomed to visit such manufactures, must frequently have been shewn very pretty machines, which were the inventions of such workmen, in order to facilitate and quicken their own particular part of the work.

In the first fire-engines, a boy was constantly employed to open and shut alternately the communication between the boiler and the cylinder, according as the piston either ascended or descended. One of those boys, who loved to play with his companions, observed that, by tying a string from the handle of the valve which opened this communication to another part of the machine, the valve would open and shut without his assistance, and leave him at liberty to divert himself with his playfellows. One of the greatest improvements that has been made upon this machine, since it was first invented, was in this manner the discovery of a boy who wanted to save his own labour. . . .

REPORT ON MANUFACTURES

Alexander Hamilton

As the first Secretary of the Treasury, Alexander Hamilton had the opportunity to shape the country's economic policies. A firm believer in the freedom of enterprise from government intervention, he nevertheless saw government support of manufactures as the only way eventually to free the United States from its dependence on other countries and from the danger of that dependence to national prosperity, freedom, and security. His *Report on Manufactures* failed to win favorable action at the time, but it remains an impressive contribution to the literature of political economy. To the student who has read the preceding selection from Adam Smith's *Wealth of Nations*, Hamilton's borrowing from Smith will be obvious.

. . . To affirm that the labor of the manufacturer is unproductive, because he consumes as much of the produce of land as he adds value to the raw material which he manufactures, is not better founded than it would be to affirm that the labor of the farmer, which furnishes materials to the manufacturer, is unproductive, because he consumes an equal value of manufactured articles. Each furnishes a certain portion of the produce of his labor to the other, and each destroys a corresponding portion of the produce of the labor of the other. In the meantime, the maintenance of two citizens, instead of one, is going on; the State has two members instead of one; and they, together, consume twice the value of what is produced from the land.

If, instead of a farmer and artificer, there were a farmer only, he would be under the necessity of devoting a part of his labor to the fabrication of clothing and other articles, which he would procure of the artificer, in the case of there being such a person; and of course he would be able to devote less labor to the cultivation of his farm, and would draw from it a proportionately less product. The whole quantity of production, in this state of things, in provisions, raw materials, and manufactures, would certainly not exceed in value the amount of what would be produced in provisions and raw materials only, if there were an artificer as well as a farmer.

Again, if there were both an artificer and a farmer, the latter would be left at liberty to pursue exclusively the cultivation of his farm. A greater quantity of provisions and raw materials would, of course, be produced, equal, at least, as has been already observed, to the whole amount of the provisions, raw

From Alexander Hamilton's *Report on Manufactures*, written in his capacity of Secretary of the Treasury and communicated to the House of Representatives December 5, 1791.

materials, and manufactures, which would exist on a contrary supposition. The artificer, at the same time, would be going on in the production of manufactured commodities, to an amount sufficient, not only to repay the farmer, in those commodities, for the provisions and materials which were procured from him, but to furnish the artificer himself with a supply of similar commodities for his own use. Thus, then, there would be two quantities or values in existence, instead of one; and the revenue and consumption would be double, in one case, what it would be in the other.

If in place of both of these suppositions, there were supposed to be two farmers and no artificer, each of whom applied a part of his labor to the culture of land and another part to the fabrication of manufacturers; in this case, the portion of the labor of both, bestowed upon land, would produce the same quantity of provisions and raw materials only, as would be produced by the entire sum of the labor of one, applied in the same manner; and the portion of the labor of both, bestowed upon manufactures, would produce the same quantity of manufactures only, as would be produced by the entire sum of the labor of one, applied in the same manner. Hence, the produce of the labor of the two farmers would not be greater than the produce of the labor of the farmer and artificer; and hence it results, that the labor of the artificer is as positively productive as that of the farmer, and as positively augments the revenue of the society.

The labor of the artificer replaces to the farmer that portion of his labor with which he provides the materials of exchange with the artificer, and which he would otherwise have been compelled to apply to manufactures; and while the artificer thus enables the farmer to enlarge his stock of agricul-

tural industry, a portion of which he purchases for his own use, he also supplies himself with the manufactured articles of which he stands in need. He does still more. Besides this equivalent, which he gives for the portion of agricultural labor consumed by him, and this supply of manufactured commodities for his own consumption, he furnishes still a surplus, which compensates for the use of the capital advanced, either by himself or some other person, for carrying on the business. This is the ordinary profit of the stock employed in the manufactory, and is, in every sense, as effective an addition to the income of the society as the rent of land.

The produce of the labor of the artificer, consequently, may be regarded as composed of three parts: one, by which the provisions for his subsistence and the materials for his work are purchased of the farmer; one, by which he supplies himself with manufactured necessaries; and a third, which constitutes the profit on the stock employed. The two last portions seem to have been overlooked in the system which represents manufacturing industry as barren and unproductive.

In the course of the preceding illustrations, the products of equal quantities of the labor of the farmer and artificer have been treated as if equal to each other. But this is not to be understood as intending to assert any such precise equality. It is merely a manner of expression, adopted for the sake of simplicity and perspicuity. Whether the value of the produce of the labor of the farmer be somewhat more or less than that of the artificer, is not material to the main scope of the argument, which, hitherto, has only aimed at showing that the one, as well as the other, occasions a positive augmentation of the total produce and revenue of the society.

It is now proper to proceed a step further, and to enumerate the principal circumstances from which it may be inferred that manufacturing establishments not only occasion a positive augmentation of the produce and revenue of the society, but that they contribute essentially to rendering them greater than they could possibly be without such establishments. These circumstances are:

1. The division of labor.
2. An extension of the use of machinery.
3. Additional employment to classes of the community not ordinarily engaged in the business.
4. The promoting of emigration from foreign countries.
5. The furnishing greater scope for the diversity of talents and dispositions, which discriminate men from each other.
6. The affording a more ample and various field for enterprise.
7. The creating, in some instances, a new, and securing, in all, a more certain and steady demand for the surplus produce of the soil.

Each of these circumstances has a considerable influence upon the total mass of industrious effort in a community; together, they add to it a degree of energy and effect which is not easily conceived. Some comments upon each of them, in the order in which they have been stated, may serve to explain their importance.

1. AS TO THE DIVISION OF LABOR

It has justly been observed, that there is scarcely any thing of greater moment in the economy of a nation than the proper division of labor. The separation of occupations causes each to be carried to a much greater perfection than it could possibly acquire if they were

blended. This arises principally from three circumstances:

1st. The greater skill and dexterity naturally resulting from a constant and undivided application to a single object. It is evident that these properties must increase in proportion to the separation and simplification of objects, and the steadiness of the attention devoted to each; and must be less in proportion to the complication of objects, and the number among which the attention is distracted.

2d. The economy of time, by avoiding the loss of it, incident to a frequent transition from one operation to another of a different nature. This depends on various circumstances: the transition itself, the orderly disposition of the implements, machines, and materials employed in the operation to be relinquished, the preparatory steps to the commencement of a new one, the interruption of the impulse which the mind of the workman acquires from being engaged in a particular operation, the distractions, hesitations, and reluctances which attend the passage from one kind of business to another.

3d. An extension of the use of machinery. A man occupied on a single object will have it more in his power, and will be more naturally led to exert his imagination, in devising methods to facilitate and abridge labor, than if he were perplexed by a variety of independent and dissimilar operations. Besides this the fabrication of machines, in numerous instances, becoming itself a distinct trade, the artist who follows it has all the advantages which have been enumerated, for improvement in his particular art; and, in both ways, the invention and application of machinery are extended.

And from these causes united, the mere separation of the occupation of the cultivator from that of the artificer, has the effect of augmenting the productive powers of labor, and with them, the total mass of the produce or revenue of a country. In this single view of the subject, therefore, the utility of artificers or manufacturers, towards producing an increase of productive industry, is apparent.

2. AS TO AN EXTENSION OF THE USE OF MACHINERY, A POINT WHICH, THOUGH PARTLY ANTICIPATED, REQUIRES TO BE PLACED IN ONE OR TWO ADDITIONAL LIGHTS

The employment of machinery forms an item of great importance in the general mass of national industry. It is an artificial force brought in aid of the natural force of man; and, to all the purposes of labor, is an increase of hands, an accession of strength, unencumbered too by the expense of maintaining the laborer. May it not, therefore, be fairly inferred, that those occupations which give greatest scope to the use of this auxiliary, contribute most to the general stock of industrious effort, and, in consequence, to the general product of industry?

It shall be taken for granted, and the truth of the position referred to observation, that manufacturing pursuits are susceptible, in a greater degree, of the application of machinery, than those of agriculture. If so, all the difference is lost to a community which, instead of manufacturing for itself, procures the fabrics requisite to its supply from other countries. The substitution of foreign for domestic manufactures is a transfer to foreign nations of the advantages accruing from the employment of machinery, in the modes in which it is capable of being employed with most utility and to the greatest extent.

The cotton-mill, invented in Eng-land, within the last twenty years, is a signal illustration of the general proposition which has been just advanced. In consequence of it, all the different processes for spinning cotton are performed by means of machines, which are put in motion by water, and attended chiefly by women and children—and by a smaller number of persons, in the whole, than are requisite in the ordinary mode of spinning. And it is an advantage of great moment, that the operations of this mill continue with convenience during the night as well as through the day. The prodigious effect of such a machine is easily conceived. To this invention is to be attributed, essentially, the immense progress which has been so suddenly made in Great Britain, in the various fabrics of cotton.

3. AS TO THE ADDITIONAL EMPLOYMENT OF CLASSES OF THE COMMUNITY NOT ORIGINALLY ENGAGED IN THE PARTICULAR BUSINESS

This is not among the least valuable of the means by which manufacturing institutions contribute to augment the general stock of industry and production. In places where those institutions prevail, besides the persons regularly engaged in them, they afford occasional and extra employment to industrious individuals and families, who are willing to devote the leisure resulting from the intermissions of their ordinary pursuits to collateral labors, as a resource for multiplying their acquisitions or their enjoyments. The husbandman himself experiences a new source of profit and support from the increased industry of his wife and daughters, invited and stimulated by the demands of the neighboring manufactories.

Besides this advantage of occasional employment to classes having different occupations, there is another, of a nature allied to it, and of a similar tendency. This is the employment of persons who would otherwise be idle, and in many cases a burthen on the community, either from the bias of temper, habit, infirmity of body, or some other cause, indisposing or disqualifying them for the toils of the country. It is worthy of particular remark that, in general, women and children are rendered more useful, and the latter more early useful, by manufacturing establishments, than they would otherwise be. Of the number of persons employed in the cotton manufactories of Great Britain, it is computed that four sevenths nearly are women and children, of whom the greatest proportion are children, and many of them of a tender age.

And thus it appears to be one of the attributes of manufactures, and one of no small consequence, to give occasion to the exertion of a greater quantity of industry, even by the same number of persons, where they happen to prevail, than would exist if there were no such establishments.

4. AS TO THE PROMOTING OF EMIGRATION FROM FOREIGN COUNTRIES

Men reluctantly quit one course of occupation and livelihood for another, unless invited to it by very apparent and proximate advantages. Many who would go from one country to another, if they had a prospect of continuing with more benefit the callings to which they have been educated, will often not be tempted to change their situation by the hope of doing better in some other way. Manufacturers who, listening to the powerful invitations of a better price for their fabrics or their labor, of greater cheapness of provisions and raw materials, of an exemption from the chief part of the taxes, burthens, and restraints which they endure in the Old World, of greater personal independence and consequence, under the operation of a more equal government, and of what is far more precious than mere religious toleration, a perfect equality of religious privileges, would probably flock from Europe to the United States, to pursue their own trades or professions, if they were once made sensible of the advantages they would enjoy, and were inspired with an assurance of encouragement and employment, will with difficulty, be induced to transplant themselves, with a view to becoming cultivators of land.

If it be true, then, that it is the interest of the United States to open every possible avenue to emigration from abroad, it affords weighty argument for the encouragement of manufactures; which, for the reasons just assigned, will have the strongest tendency to multiply the inducements to it.

Here is perceived an important resource, not only for extending the population, and with it the useful and productive labor of the country, but likewise for the prosecution of manufactures, without deducting from the number of hands which might otherwise be drawn to tillage, and even for the indemnification of agriculture for such as might happen to be diverted from it. Many, whom manufacturing views would induce to emigrate, would, afterwards, yield to the temptations which the particular situation of this country holds out to agricultural pursuits. And while agriculture would, in other respects, derive many signal and unmingled advantages from the growth of manufactures, it is a problem whether it would gain or lose, as to the article of the number of persons employed in carrying it on.

5. AS TO THE FURNISHING GREATER SCOPE FOR THE DIVERSITY OF TALENTS AND DISPOSITIONS, WHICH DISCRIMINATE MEN FROM EACH OTHER

This is a much more powerful means of augmenting the fund of national industry, than may at first sight appear. It is a just observation, that minds of the strongest and most active powers for their proper objects, fall below mediocrity, and labor without effect, if confined to uncongenial pursuits. And it is thence to be inferred, that the results of human exertion may be immensely increased by diversifying its objects. When all the different kinds of industry obtain in a community, each individual can find his proper element, and can call into activity the whole vigor of his nature. And the community is benefited by the services of its respective members, in the manner in which each can serve it with most effect.

If there be any thing in a remark often to be met with, namely, that there is, in the genius of the people of this country, a peculiar aptitude for mechanic improvements, it would operate as a forcible reason for giving opportunities to the exercise of that species of talent, by the propagation of manufactures. .

6. AS TO THE AFFORDING A MORE AMPLE AND VARIOUS FIELD FOR ENTERPRISE

This also is of greater consequence in the general scale of national exertion than might, perhaps, on a superficial view be supposed, and has effects not altogether dissimilar from those of the circumstance last noticed. To cherish and stimulate the activity of the human mind, by multiplying the objects of enterprise, is not among the least considerable of the expedients by which the wealth of a nation may be promoted. Even things in themselves not positively advantageous sometimes become so, by their tendency to provoke exertion. Every new scene which is opened to the busy nature of man to rouse and exert itself, is the addition of a new energy to the general stock of effort.

The spirit of enterprise, useful and prolific as it is, must necessarily be contracted or expanded, in proportion to the simplicity or variety of the occupations and productions which are to be found in a society. It must be less in a nation of mere cultivators, than in a nation of cultivators and merchants; less in a nation of cultivators and merchants, than in a nation of cultivators, artificers, and merchants.

7. AS TO THE CREATING, IN SOME INSTANCES, A NEW, AND SECURING, IN ALL, A MORE CERTAIN AND STEADY DEMAND FOR THE SURPLUS PRODUCE OF THE SOIL

This is among the most important of the circumstances which have been indicated. It is a principal means by which the establishment of manufactures contributes to an augmentation of the produce or revenue of a country, and has an immediate and direct relation to the prosperity of agriculture.

It is evident that the exertions of the husbandman will be steady or fluctuating, vigorous or feeble, in proportion to the steadiness or fluctuation, adequateness or inadequateness, of the markets on which he must depend for the vent of the surplus which may be produced by his labor; and that such surplus, in the ordinary course of things, will be greater or less in the same proportion.

For the purpose of this vent, a domestic market is greatly to be preferred to a foreign one; because it is, in the nature of things, far more to be relied upon.

It is a primary object of the policy of nations, to be able to supply themselves with subsistence from their own soils; and manufacturing nations, as far as circumstances permit, endeavor to procure from the same source the raw materials necessary for their own fabrics. This disposition, urged by the spirit of monopoly, is sometimes even carried to an injudicious extreme. It seems not always to be recollected, that nations who have neither mines nor manufactures can only obtain the manufactured articles of which they stand in need, by an exchange of the products of their soils; and that if those who can best furnish them with such articles are unwilling to give a due course to this exchange, they must, of necessity, make every possible effort to manufacture for themselves; the effect of which is, that the manufacturing nations abridge the natural advantages of their situation, through an unwillingness to permit the agricultural countries to enjoy the advantages of theirs, and sacrifice the interests of a mutually beneficial intercourse to the vain project of selling every thing and buying nothing.

But it is also a consequence of the policy which has been noted, that the foreign demand for the products of agricultural countries is, in a great degree, rather casual and occasional, than certain or constant. To what extent injurious interruptions of the demand for some of the staple commodities of the United States may have been experienced from that cause, must be referred to the judgment of those who are engaged in carrying on the commerce of the country; but it may be safely affirmed, that such interruptions are, at times, very inconveniently felt, and that cases not unfrequently occur, in which markets are so confined and restricted as to render the demand very unequal to the supply.

Independently, likewise, of the artificial impediments which are created by the policy in question, there are natural causes tending to render the external demand for the surplus of agricultural nations a precarious reliance. The differences of seasons in the countries which are the consumers, make immense differences in the produce of their own soils, in different years; and consequently in the degrees of their necessity for foreign supply. Plentiful harvests with them, especially if similar ones occur at the same time in the countries which are the furnishers, occasion, of course, a glut in the markets of the latter.

Considering how fast and how much the progress of new settlements in the United States must increase the surplus produce of the soil, and weighing seriously the tendency of the system which prevails among most of the commercial nations of Europe, whatever dependence may be placed on the force of natural circumstances to counteract the effects of an artificial policy, there appear strong reasons to regard the foreign demand for that surplus as too uncertain a reliance, and to desire a substitute for it in an extensive domestic market.

To secure such a market there is no other expedient than to promote manufacturing establishments. Manufacturers, who constitute the most numerous class, after the cultivators of land, are for that reason the principal consumers of the surplus of their labor.

This idea of an extensive domestic market for the surplus produce of the soil, is of the first consequence. It is, of all things, that which most effectually conduces to a flourishing state of agriculture. If the effect of manufactories should be to detach a portion of the hands which would otherwise be engaged in tillage, it might possibly cause a smaller quantity of lands to be under cultivation; but, by their tendency to procure a more certain demand for the surplus produce of the soil, they would, at the same time, cause the lands which were in cultivation to be better improved and more productive. And while by their influence, the condition of each individual farmer would be meliorated, the total mass of agricultural production would probably be increased. For this must evidently depend as much upon the degree of improvement, if not more, than upon the number of acres under culture.

It merits particular observation, that the multiplication of manufactories not only furnishes a market for those articles which have been accustomed to be produced in abundance in a country, but it likewise creates a demand for such as were either unknown or produced in inconsiderable quantities. The bowels as well as the surface of the earth are ransacked for articles which were before neglected. Animals, plants, and minerals acquire a utility and a value which were before unexplored.

The foregoing considerations seem sufficient to establish, as general propositions, that it is the interest of nations to diversify the industrious pursuits of the individuals who compose them; that the establishment of manufactures is calculated not only to increase the general stock of useful and productive labor, but even to improve the state of agriculture in particular—certainly to advance the interests of those who are engaged in it. . . .

THE MERCHANT OF PRATO
Iris Origo

Francesco di Marco Datini was a fourteenth century Italian merchant who maintained a stout correspondence. From 150,000 of his letters and hundreds of other documents which are still preserved, Iris Origo has brilliantly reconstructed the Renaissance merchant's life. This passage deals with his worries over the characteristic dangers of the time: shipwreck and piracy. The Marchesa Origo is a Fellow of the Royal Society of Literature in England. She resides in Rome.

In the last ten years of the fourteenth century Francesco di Marco achieved all that he had set out to do. He finished his fine house in Prato, bought land, and built himself a villa; he became a member of the cloth guild of Prato and of the silk guild of Florence; his *fondachi* at home and abroad were firmly established; he was a rich and respected man. And he never knew a peaceful hour. Day after day, night after night, he brooded over the perils that might overtake his ships and his merchandise.

I dreamed last night [he wrote to his wife] of a house which had fallen to pieces, and all my household were therein. . . . And the meaning of this dream gives me much to ponder on, for there are no tidings of a galley that left Venice more than two months ago, bound for Catalonia; and I had insured her for 300 florins, as I did the other ships for Domenico di Cambio, which perished the next day. . . . I am so vexed with many matters, it is a wonder I am not out of my mind—for the more I seek, the less I find. And God wot what will befall. . . .

In the fourteenth century it was not customary for trading-companies to own ships of their own; they either sent their goods on a ship chartered from a ship-owner for a specified period, or—in the case of smaller consignments—paid for carriage on a vessel which also carried other cargo. When a merchant or one of his underlings travelled himself with his goods, the consigner often merely made an entry in the ship's log, but generally the goods of Datini's companies were sent, as had become the custom, unaccompanied, with a bill of lading and sometimes also a separate letter of advice, stating their amount and value, and giving instructions for their disposal. The contract of charter generally specified that half the price of the shipment was to be paid before departure, and the balance within a specified time of delivery. This was consistent with Pegolotti's advice: "Let merchants be warned not to pay the dues, in whole or in part, to the ship's master, not to lend him any money." But he added: "Let the merchant avoid this *if he can* . . . but let him act according to the need he has of the vessel." This advice certainly suggests that the need of trading-ships was greater than the supply, and that sometimes merchants in a hurry had to give way to inordinate demands, in order to be able to ship their wares at all.

Contracts of charter generally contained clauses stating whether the ship's master assumed full responsibility for the goods they carried, in which case the goods were said to be sent "*salvi in terra*" (delivery guaranteed), or disclaimed this responsibility, when the merchandise was said to be sent "*ad risicum et fortunam Dei, maris et gentium*" ("Subject to the hand of God and to hazards of the sea and of [hostile] people").

Regular convoys of trading-ships, escorted by war galleys, were sent out several times a year to the chief ports of the Mediterranean and the Black Sea from Genoa and Venice (supervised and sometimes subsidized by the governments of these cities), and a prudent merchant like Francesco would spread his merchandise over several ships, so that, in case of shipwreck or piracy, something at least might be saved. But it would appear that sometimes these convoys merely facilitated the pirates' task, for in 1393 Francesco wrote to his wife that he expected some of their ships to be captured, because "there are many ships at sea and only one trade route, by which some sail in one direction, and others sail back. . . . We have divers galleys at sea" [he added] "and we know naught for certain yet. . . . We have much merchandise therein and it is all insured, but we are not like to escape save with

great loss. May God be praised for all!"

It was Datini's rule, as this letter shows, to insure all his merchandise, even though some of his correspondents thought this expense unnecessary. "We would not insure these five galleys for even a groat," wrote Bindo Piaciti from Venice in 1401; "meseems we would cast away the money spent on this, for the passage is safe." But when Datini's own partner in Genoa once failed to insure some goods bound for Barcelona, he drew upon himself a sharp reproof, even though the ship had already safely arrived. "Touching your saying now, the ship has reached Barcelona safely, you are no prophet—and if some evil had come to her, it would have been the worse for you. . . . For you have our orders never to send any merchandise of ours lacking insurance, and let this be said to you once for all."

It appears, however, that insurance monies were not always easy to collect, for on one occasion, when Datini had goods worth 3,000 florins on a galley sailing from Venice to Catalonia, he wrote to his wife that, if it went down, he would lose at least 500 florins. "For when they insure, it is sweet to them to take the monies; but when disaster comes, it is otherwise and each man draws his rump back, and strives not to pay."

The successive stages by which the insurance contract reached its modern form have given rise to some controversy as to what trading-cities first made use of them, but certainly by the fourteenth century unmistakable insurance contracts—involving under-writers who were not the same persons as the ship-owners—were in use both in Genoa and in Tuscany. Datini's companies not only caused their own goods to be insured, but did some under-writing—in particular, the Pisan company, which kept a record of some of the policies it had issued in a note-book dated 1384, which has been preserved. On its cover is written: "This is the book of Francesco of Prato & Co., partners abiding in Pisa, and we shall write in it all insurances we make on behalf of others. May God grant us profit, and protect us from dangers." The goods insured included wool from Catalonia and Minorca to Porto Pisano, cloth from Porto Pisano to Tunis and Palermo and Naples, silk and fustian from Porto Pisano to Barcelona, and malmsey (in a Genoese ship from Cadiz) to Sluys and Southampton. The premiums varied from 3½ per cent to 5 per cent, except for the malmsey, for which the premium was 8 per cent. Each of these records ends with the note: "Arrived safely."

Another policy, dated 1385 and drawn up in the form then customary in both Florence and Pisa, enumerates the risks for which the insurers assumed liability: "from act of God, of the sea, of jettison, of confiscation, of princes or cities or any other person, of reprisal, mishap or any other impediment." Usually a time-limit was set for a ship's arrival—after which, if no news was forthcoming, the insurers had to pay full indemnity. When a ship was lost, the insurers' approval was required for any attempt of the owner to recover his goods: there is, for instance, a letter from Teramo and Tommaso Cattaneo, Genoese insurers, authorizing Andrea di Bonanno to recover, if he could, 22 sacks of wool, insured for 200 florins, from a ship captured by pirates off the coast of Elba.

"A TIME OF UNEXAMPLED PROSPERITY"
Washington Irving

Having himself been stung by the bee of speculation in the Panic of 1837, Washington Irving was well qualified to write of one of the great land scandals of history, the Mississippi Bubble. The piece that follows forms an introduction to his account of that fraud. Although closely associated with the whimsical and romantic, as in *The Legend of Sleepy Hollow*, Irving was born into a mercantile family, trained in bookkeeping, and educated for the profession of law.

In the course of a voyage from England, I once fell in with a convoy of merchant ships, bound for the West Indies. The weather was uncommonly bland; and the ships vied with each other in spreading sail to catch a light, favoring breeze, until their hulls were almost hidden beneath a cloud of canvas. The breeze went down with the sun, and his last yellow rays shone upon a thousand sails, idly flapping against the masts.

I exulted in the beauty of the scene, and augured a prosperous voyage; but the veteran master of the ship shook his head, and pronounced this halcyon calm a "weather-breeder." And so it proved. A storm burst forth in the night; the sea roared and raged; and when the day broke I beheld the late gallant convoy scattered in every direction; some dismasted, others scudding under bare poles, and many firing signals of distress.

I have since been occasionally reminded of this scene, by those calm, sunny seasons in the commercial world, which are known by the name of "times of unexampled prosperity." They are the sure weather-breeders of traffic. Every now and then the world is visited by one of these delusive seasons, when "the credit system," as it is called, expands to full luxuriance; everybody trusts everybody; a bad debt is a thing unheard of; the broad way to certain and sudden wealth lies plain and open; and men are tempted to dash forward boldly, from the facility of borrowing.

Promissory notes, interchanged between scheming individuals, are liberally discounted at the banks, which become so many mints to coin words into cash; and as the supply of words is inexhaustible, it may readily be supposed what a vast amount of promissory capital is soon in circulation. Every one now talks in thousands; nothing is heard but gigantic operations in trade; great purchases and sales of real property, and immense sums made at every transfer. All, to be sure, as yet exists in promise; but the believer in promises calculates the aggregate as solid capital, and falls back in amazement at the

Reprinted from *Wolfert's Roost and Other Papers* by Washington Irving.

amount of public wealth, the "un-exampled state of public prosperity!"

Now is the time for speculative and dreaming or designing men. They relate their dreams and projects to the igno-rant and credulous, dazzle them with golden visions, and set them maddening after shadows. The example of one stimulates another; speculation rises on speculation; bubble rises on bubble; every one helps with his breath to swell the windy superstructure, and admires and wonders at the magnitude of the inflation he has contributed to produce.

Speculation is the romance of trade, and casts contempt upon all its sober realities. It renders the stock-jobber a magician, and the exchange a region of enchantment. It elevates the merchant into a kind of knight-errant, or rather a commercial Quixote. The slow but sure gains of snug percentage become despicable in his eyes: no "operation" is thought worthy of attention that does not double or treble the investment. No business is worth following that does not promise an immediate fortune. As he sits musing over his ledger, with pen behind his ear, he is like La Mancha's hero in his study, dreaming over his books of chivalry. His dusty counting house fades before his eyes, or changes into a Spanish mine; he gropes after diamonds, or dives after pearls. The subterranean garden of Aladdin is nothing to the realms of wealth that break upon his imagination.

Could this delusion always last, the life of a merchant would indeed be a golden dream; but it is as short as it is brilliant. Let but a doubt enter, and the "season of unexampled prosperity" is at an end. The coinage of words is suddenly curtailed; the promissory capital begins to vanish into smoke; a panic succeeds, and the whole super-structure, built upon credit, and reared by speculation, crumbles to the ground, leaving scarce a wreck behind:

"It is such stuff as dreams are made of."

When a man of business, therefore, hears on every side rumors of fortunes suddenly acquired; when he finds banks liberal, and brokers busy; when he sees adventurers flush of paper capital, and full of scheme and enterprise; when he perceives a greater disposition to buy than to sell; when trade overflows its accustomed channels, and deluges the country; when he hears of new regions of commercial adventure; of distant marts and distant mines, swallowing merchandise and disgorging gold; when he finds joint stock companies of all kinds forming; railroads, canals, and locomotive engines, springing up on every side; when idlers suddenly become men of business, and dash into the game of commerce as they would into the hazards of the faro-table; when he be-holds the streets glittering with new equipages, palaces conjured up by the magic of speculation, tradesmen flushed with sudden success, and vying with each other in ostentatious expense; in a word, when he hears the whole com-munity joining in the theme of "un-exampled prosperity," let him look upon the whole as a "weather-breeder," and prepare for the impending storm.

The foregoing remarks are intended merely as a prelude to a narrative I am about to lay before the public, of one of the most memorable instances of the infatuation of gain to be found in the whole history of commerce. I allude to the famous Mississippi bubble. It is a matter that has passed into a proverb, and become a phrase in every one's mouth, yet of which not one merchant in ten has probably a distinct idea. I have therefore thought that an authen-tic account of it would be interesting and salutary, at the present moment, when we are suffering under the effects of a severe access of the credit system, and just recovering from one of its ruinous delusions.

CRASH!

Frederick Lewis Allen

In the present world of Wall Street, time is measured from Black Tuesday, October 29, 1929, the day the bottom fell out of the market. The following description of the debacle, written with the memory fresh in mind, is a poignant footnote to the beginning of the Great Depression. Frederick Lewis Allen was for many years editor of *Harper's Magazine*.

In September the market reached its ultimate glittering peak.

It was six months, now, since Herbert Hoover had driven down Pennsylvania Avenue in the rain to take the oath of office as President of the United States. He had appointed the Wickersham Commission to investigate law enforcement in general and prohibition in particular. At the President's instance Congress had passed the Agricultural Marketing Act; and Alexander Legge had assumed, among his duties as chairman of the new Federal Farm Board, the task of "preventing and controlling surpluses in any agricultural commodity." The Kellogg-Briand Treaty had been proclaimed in effect, and Ramsay MacDonald was preparing to sail for the United States to discuss a new treaty for the reduction of naval armaments. The long wrangle over the Harding oil scandals was at last producing definite results: Colonel Stewart, buried under a mountain of Rockefeller proxies, had left the chairmanship of the Standard Oil Company of Indiana, and Harry F. Sinclair was sitting in jail. Colonel Lindbergh, true to his rôle as the national superhero, had married Miss Anne Morrow. Commander Byrd, the man who put heroism into quantity production, was waiting in the Antarctic darkness of "Little America" for his chance to fly to the South Pole. Non-stop flyers were zooming about over the American countryside, and emulation of the heroes of the air had reached its climax of absurdity in the exploit of a twenty-two-year-old boy who had climbed into the cabin of the *Yellow Bird* and had been carried as a stowaway by Assolant and Lefèvre from Old Orchard, Maine, to the Spanish coast. And on the sands of a thousand American beaches, girls pulled down the shoulder-straps of their bathing suits to acquire fashionably tanned backs, and wondered whether it would be all right to leave their stockings off when they drove to town, and whether it was true, as the journals of fashion declared, that every evening dress must soon reach all the way to the ground.

This was the season when Tilden won his seventh and last American amateur tennis championship. It was Bobby Jones's penultimate year as monarch of amateur golfers—his seventh successive year as winner of either the amateur or the open championship of the United States. Babe Ruth was still hammering out home runs as successfully as in 1920, but he too was getting older: a sporting cycle was drawing to its close. Dempsey had lost his crown to Tunney, Tunney had hung it on the wall to go and foregather with the *literati*, and there was no one to follow them as a magnet for two-million-dollar crowds.

Everybody was reading *All Quiet on the Western Front* and singing the songs which Rudy Vallee crooned over the radio. The literary journals were making a great fuss over humanism. But even sun-tan and Ramsay MacDonald's proposed good-will voyage and humanism and *All Quiet* were dull subjects for talk compared with the Big Bull Market. Had not Goldman, Sachs & Company just expressed its confidence in the present level of prices by sponsoring the Blue Ridge Corporation, an investment trust which offered to exchange its stock for those of the leading "blue chips" at the current figures—324 for Allied Chemical and Dye, 293 for American Telephone, 179 for Consolidated Gas, 395 for General Electric, and so on down the list?

Stop for a moment to glance at a few of the prices recorded on the overworked ticker on September 3, 1929, the day when the Dow-Jones averages reached their high point for the year and compare them with the opening prices of March 3, 1928, when, as you may recall, it had seemed as if the bull market had already climbed to a perilous altitude. Here they are, side by side —first the figures for March, 1928; then the figures for September, 1929; and finally the latter figures translated into

	Opening Price March 3 1928	High Price Sept. 3 1929	Adjusted High Price Sept. 3 1929
American Can	77	181⅞	181⅞
American Telephone & Telegraph	179½	304	335⅝
Anaconda Copper	54½	131½	162
General Electric	128¾	396¼	396¼
General Motors	139¾	72¾	181⅞
Montgomery Ward	132¾	137⅞	466½
New York Central	160½	256⅜	256⅜
Radio	94½	101	505
Union Carbide & Carbon	145	137⅞	413⅝
United States Steel	138⅛	261¾	279⅛
Westinghouse E. & M.	91⅝	289⅞	313
Woolworth	180¾	100⅜	251
Electric Bond & Share	89¾	186¾	203⅝

Note—The prices of General Electric, Radio, Union Carbide, and Woolworth are here adjusted to take account of split-ups occurring subsequent to March 3, 1928. The prices of American Telephone, Anaconda, Montgomery Ward, United States Steel, Westinghouse, and Electric Bond & Share are adjusted to take account of intervening issues of rights; they represent the value per share on September 3, 1929, of a holding acquired on March 3, 1928, the adjustment being based on the assumption that rights offered in the interval were exercised.

1928 terms—or in other words revised to make allowance for intervening split-ups and issues of rights. (Only thus can you properly judge the extent of the advance during those eighteen confident months.)

One thing more: as you look at the high prices recorded on September 3, 1929, remember that on that day few people imagined that the peak had actually been reached. The enormous majority fully expected the Big Bull Market to go on and on.

For the blood of the pioneers still ran in American veins; and if there was no longer something lost behind the ranges, still the habit of seeing visions persisted. What if bright hopes had been wrecked by the sordid disappointments of 1919, the collapse of Wilsonian idealism, the spread of political cynicism, the slow decay of religious certainty, and the debunking of love? In the Big Bull Market there was compensation. Still the American could spin wonderful dreams—of a romantic day when he would sell his Westinghouse common at a fabulous price and live in a great house and have a fleet of shining cars and loll at ease on the sands of Palm Beach. And when he looked toward the future of his country, he could vision an America set free—not from graft, nor from crime, nor from war, nor from control by Wall Street, nor from irreligion, nor from lust, for the utopias of an earlier day left him for the most part skeptical or indifferent; he visioned an America set free from poverty and toil. He saw a magical order built on the new science and the new prosperity: roads swarming with millions upon millions of automobiles, airplanes darkening the skies, lines of high-tension wire carrying from hilltop to hilltop the power to give life to a thousand labor-saving machines, skyscrapers thrusting above one-time villages, vast cities rising in great geometrical masses of stone and concrete, and roaring with perfectly mechanized traffic—and smartly dressed men and women spending, spending, spending with the money they had won by being far-sighted enough to foresee, way back in 1929, what was going to happen.

Early in September the stock market broke. It quickly recovered, however; indeed, on September 19th the averages as compiled by the New York Times reached an even higher level than that of September 3rd. Once more it slipped, farther and faster, until by October 4th the prices of a good many stocks had coasted to what seemed first-class bargain levels. Steel, for example, after having touched 261¾ a few weeks earlier, had dropped as low as 204; American Can, at the closing on October 4th, was nearly twenty points below its high for the year; General Electric was over fifty points below its high; Radio had gone down from 114¾ to 82½.

A bad break, to be sure, but there had been other bad breaks, and the speculators who escaped unscathed proceeded to take advantage of the lesson they had learned in June and December of 1928 and March and May of 1929: when there was a break it was a good time to buy. In the face of all this tremendous liquidation, brokers' loans as compiled by the Federal Reserve Bank of New York mounted to a new high record on October 2nd, reaching $6,804,000,000—a sure sign that margin buyers were not deserting the market but coming into it in numbers at least undiminished. (Part of the increase in the loan figure was probably due to the piling up of unsold securities in dealers' hands, as the spawning of investment trusts and the issue of new common stock by every manner of business concern continued unabated.) History, it seemed, was about to repeat itself, and those who picked up Anaconda at 109¾ or American Telephone at 281 would count themselves wise investors. And sure enough, prices once more began to climb. They had already turned upward before that Sunday in early October when Ramsay MacDonald sat on a log with Herbert Hoover at the Rapidan camp and talked over the prospects for naval limitation and peace.

Something was wrong, however. The decline began once more. The wiseacres of Wall Street, looking about for causes, fixed upon the collapse of the Hatry financial group in England (which had led to much forced selling among foreign investors and speculators), and upon the bold refusal of the Massachusetts Department of Public Utilities to allow the Edison Company of Boston to split up its stock. They pointed, too, to the fact that the steel industry was undoubtedly slipping, and to the accumulation of "undigested" securities. But there was little real alarm until the week of October 21st. The consensus of opinion, in the meantime, was merely that the equinoctial storm of September had not quite blown over. The market was readjusting itself into a "more secure technical position." . . .

The expected recovery in the stock market did not come. It seemed to be beginning on Tuesday, October 22nd, but the gains made during the day were largely lost during the last hour. And on Wednesday, the 23rd, there was a perfect Niagara of liquidation. The volume of trading was over six million shares, the tape was 104 minutes late when the three-o'clock gong ended trading for the day, and the New York Times averages for fifty leading railroad and industrial stocks lost 18.24 points—a loss which made the most abrupt declines in previous breaks look small. Everybody realized that an unprecedented number of margin calls must be on their way to insecurely margined traders, and that the situation at last was getting serious. But perhaps the turn would come tomorrow. Already the break had carried prices down a good deal farther than the previous breaks of the past two years. Surely it could not go on much longer.

The next day was Thursday, October 24th.

On that momentous day stocks opened moderately steady in price, but in enormous volume. Kennecott appeared on the tape in a block of 20,000 shares, General Motors in another of the same amount. Almost at once the ticker tape began to lag behind the trading on the floor. The pressure of selling orders was disconcertingly heavy. Prices were going down. . . . Presently they were going down with some rapidity. . . . Before the first hour of trading was over, it was already apparent that they were going down with an altogether unprecedented and amazing violence. In brokers' offices all over the country, tape-watchers looked at one another in astonishment and perplexity. Where on earth was this torrent of selling orders coming from?

The exact answer to this question will probably never be known. But it seems probable that the principal cause of the break in prices during that first hour on October 24th was not fear. Nor was it short selling. It was forced selling. It was the dumping on the market of hundreds of thousands of shares of stock held in the name of miserable traders whose margins were exhausted or about to be exhausted. The gigantic edifice of prices was honeycombed with speculative credit and was now breaking under its own weight.

Fear, however, did not long delay its coming. As the price structure crumbled there was a sudden stampede to get out from under. By eleven o'clock traders on the floor of the Stock Exchange were in a wild scramble to "sell at the market." Long before the lagging ticker could tell what was happening, word had gone out by telephone and telegraph that the bottom was dropping out of things, and the selling orders redoubled in volume. The leading stocks were going down two, three, and even five points between sales. Down, down, down. . . . Where were the bargain-hunters who were supposed to come to the rescue at times like this? Where were the investment trusts, which were expected to provide a cushion for the market by making new purchases at low prices? Where were the big operators who had declared that they were still bullish? Where were the powerful bankers who were supposed to be able at any moment to support prices? There seemed to be no support whatever. Down, down, down. The roar of voices which rose from the floor of the Exchange had become a roar of panic.

United States Steel had opened at 205½. It crashed through 200 and presently was at 193½. General Electric, which only a few weeks before had been selling above 400, had opened this morning at 315—now it had slid to 283. Things were even worse with Radio: opening at 68¾, it had gone dismally down through the sixties and the fifties and forties to the abysmal price of 44½. And as for Montgomery Ward, vehicle of the hopes of thousands who saw the chain store as the harbinger of the new economic era, it had dropped headlong from 83 to 50. In the space of two short hours, dozens of stocks lost ground which it had required many months of the bull market to gain.

Even this sudden decline in values might not have been utterly terrifying if people could have known precisely what was happening at any moment. It is the unknown which causes real panic.

Suppose a man walked into a broker's branch office between twelve and one o'clock on October 24th to see how things were faring. First he glanced at the big board, covering one wall of the room, on which the day's prices for the leading stocks were supposed to be recorded. The LOW and LAST figures written there took his breath away, but soon he was aware that they were unreliable: even with the wildest scrambling, the boys who slapped into place the cards which recorded the last prices shown on the ticker could not keep up with the changes: they were too numerous and abrupt. He turned to the shining screen across which ran an uninterrupted procession of figures from the ticker. Ordinarily the practiced tape-watcher could tell from a moment's glance at the screen how things were faring, even though the Exchange now omitted all but the final digit of each quotation. A glance at the Board, if not his own memory, supplied the missing digits. But today, when he saw a run of symbols and figures like

R   WX
  6.5½5.4.   9.8⅞¾½¼.8.7½.7.

he could not be sure whether the price of "6" shown for Radio meant 66 or 56 or 46; whether Westinghouse was sliding from 189 to 187 or from 179 to 177. And presently he heard that the ticker was an hour and a half late; at one o'clock it was recording the prices of half-past eleven! All this that he saw was ancient history. What was happening on the floor now?

At ten-minute intervals the bond ticker over in the corner would hammer off a list of selected prices direct from the floor, and a brokers' clerk would grab the uncoiling sheet of paper and shear it off with a pair of scissors and read the figures aloud in a mumbling expressionless monotone to the white-faced men who occupied every seat on the floor and stood packed at the rear of the room. The prices which he read out were *ten or a dozen or more points below those recorded on the ticker.* What about the stocks not included in that select list? There was no way of finding out. The telephone lines were clogged as inquiries and orders from all over the country converged upon the Stock Exchange. Once in a while a voice would come barking out of the broker's rear office where a frantic clerk was struggling for a telephone connection: "Steel at ninety-six!" Small comfort, however, to know what Steel was doing; the men outside were desperately involved in many another stock than Steel; they were almost completely in the dark, and their imaginations had free play. If they put in an order to buy or to sell, it was impossible to find out what became of it. The Exchange's whole system for the recording of current prices and for communicating orders was hopelessly unable to cope with the emergency, and the sequel was an epidemic of fright.

In that broker's office, as in hundreds of other offices from one end of the land to the other, one saw men looking defeat in the face. One of them was slowly walking up and down, mechanically tearing a piece of paper into tiny and still tinier fragments. Another was grinning shamefacedly, as a small boy giggles at a funeral. Another was abjectly beseeching a clerk for the latest news of American & Foreign Power. And still another was sitting motionless, as if stunned, his eyes fixed blindly upon the moving figures on the screen, those innocent-looking figures that meant the smash-up of the hopes of years. . . .

GL.   AWW.
   8.7.5.2.1.90.89.7.6.   3.2½.2.
JMP.
   6.5.3.2½.

A few minutes after noon, some of the more alert members of a crowd which had collected on the street outside the Stock Exchange, expecting they knew not what, recognized Charles E. Mitchell, ertswhile defender of the bull market, slipping quietly into the offices of J. P. Morgan & Company on the opposite corner. It was scarcely more than nine years since the House of Morgan had been pitted with the shrapnel-fire of the Wall Street explosion; now its occupants faced a different sort of calamity equally near at hand. Mr. Mitchell was followed shortly by Albert H. Wiggin, head of the Chase National Bank; William Potter, head of the Guaranty Trust Company; and Seward Prosser, head of the Bankers Trust Company. They had come to confer with Thomas W. Lamont of the Morgan firm. In the space of a few minutes these five men, with George F. Baker, Jr., of the First National Bank, agreed in behalf of their respective institutions to put up forty millions apiece to shore up the stock market. The object of the two-hundred-and-forty-million-dollar pool thus formed, as explained subsequently by Mr. Lamont, was not to hold prices at any given level, but simply to make such purchases as were necessary to keep trading on an orderly basis. Their first action, they decided, would be to try to steady the prices for the leading securities which served as bell wethers for the list as a whole. It was a dangerous plan, for with hysteria spreading there was no telling what sort of débâcle might be impending. But this was no time for any action but the boldest.

The bankers separated. Mr. Lamont faced a gathering of reporters in the Morgan offices. His face was grave, but his words were soothing. His first sentence alone was one of the most remarkable understatements of all time. "There has been a little distress selling on the Stock Exchange," said he, "and we have held a meeting of the heads of several financial institutions to discuss the situation. We have found that there are no houses in difficulty and reports from brokers indicate that margins are being maintained satisfactorily." He went on to explain that what had happened was due to a "technical condition of the market" rather than to any fundamental cause.

As the news that the bankers were meeting circulated on the floor of the Exchange, prices began to steady. Soon a brisk rally set in. Steel jumped back to the level at which it had opened that morning. But the bankers had more to offer the dying bull market than a Morgan partner's best bedside manner.

At about half-past one o'clock Richard Whitney, vice-president of the Exchange, who usually acted as floor broker for the Morgan interests, went into the "Steel crowd" and put in a bid of 205—the price of the last previous sale—for 10,000 shares of Steel. He bought only 200 shares and left the remainder of the order with the specialist. Mr. Whitney then went to various other points on the floor, and offered the price of the last previous sale for 10,000 shares of each of fifteen or twenty other stocks, reporting what was sold to him at that price and leaving the remainder of the order with the specialist. In short, within the space of a few minutes Mr. Whitney offered to purchase something in the neighborhood of twenty or thirty million dollars' worth of stock. Purchases of this magnitude are not undertaken by Tom, Dick, and Harry; it was clear that Mr. Whitney represented the bankers' pool.

The desperate remedy worked. The semblance of confidence returned. Prices held steady for a while; and though many of them slid off once more in the final hour, the net results for the day might well have been worse.

Steel actually closed two points higher than on Wednesday, and the net losses of most of the other leading securities amounted to less than ten points apiece for the whole day's trading.

All the same, it had been a frightful day. At seven o'clock that night the tickers in a thousand brokers' offices were still chattering; not till after 7:08 did they finally record the last sale made on the floor at three o'clock. The volume of trading had set a new record —12,894,650 shares. ("The time may come when we shall see a five-million-share day," the wise men of the Street had been saying twenty months before!) Incredible rumors had spread wildly during the early afternoon—that eleven speculators had committed suicide, that the Buffalo and Chicago exchanges had been closed, that troops were guarding the New York Stock Exchange against an angry mob. The country had known the bitter taste of panic. And although the bankers' pool had prevented for the moment an utter collapse, there was no gainsaying the fact that the economic structure had cracked wide open.

Things looked somewhat better on Friday and Saturday. Trading was still on an enormous scale, but prices for the most part held. At the very moment when the bankers' pool was cautiously disposing of as much as possible of the stock which it had accumulated on Thursday and was thus preparing for future emergencies, traders who had sold out higher up were coming back into the market again with new purchases, in the hope that the bottom had been reached. (Hadn't they often been told that "the time to buy is when things look blackest"?) The newspapers carried a very pretty series of reassuring statements from the occupants of the seats of the mighty; Herbert Hoover himself, in a White House statement, pointed out that "the fundamental business of the country, that is, production and distribution of commodities, is on a sound and prosperous basis." But toward the close of Saturday's session prices began to slip again. And on Monday the rout was under way once more.

The losses registered on Monday were terrific—17½ points for Steel, 47½ for General Electric, 36 for Allied Chemical, 34½ for Westinghouse, and so on down a long and dismal list. All Saturday afternoon and Saturday night and Sunday the brokers had been struggling to post their records and go over their customers' accounts and send out calls for further margin, and another avalanche of forced selling resulted. The prices at which Mr. Whitney's purchases had steadied the leading stocks on Thursday were so readily broken through that it was immediately clear that the bankers' pool had made a strategic retreat. As a matter of fact, the brokers who represented the pool were having their hands full plugging up the "air-holes" in the list—in other words, buying stocks which were offered for sale without any bids at all in sight. Nothing more than this could have been accomplished, even if it could have been wisely attempted. Even six great banks could hardly stem the flow of liquidation from the entire United States. They could only guide it a little, check it momentarily here and there.

Once more the ticker dropped ridiculously far behind, the lights in the brokers' offices and the banks burned till dawn, and the telegraph companies distributed thousands of margin calls and requests for more collateral to back up loans at the banks. Bankers, brokers, clerks, messengers were almost at the end of their strength; for days and nights they had been driving themselves to keep pace with the most terrific volume of business that had ever descended upon them. It did not seem as if they could stand it much longer.

But the worst was still ahead. It came the next day, Tuesday, October 29th.

The big gong had hardly sounded in the great hall of the Exchange at ten o'clock Tuesday morning before the storm broke in full force. Huge blocks of stock were thrown upon the market for what they would bring. Five thousand shares, ten thousand shares appeared at a time on the laboring ticker at fearful recessions in price. Not only were innumerable small traders being sold out, but big ones, too, protagonists of the new economic era who a few weeks before had counted themselves millionaires. Again and again the specialist in a stock would find himself surrounded by brokers fighting to sell— and nobody at all even thinking of buying. To give one single example: during the bull market the common stock of the White Sewing Machine Company had gone as high as 48; on Monday, October 28th, it had closed at 11⅛. On that black Tuesday, somebody—a clever messenger boy for the Exchange, it was rumored—had the bright idea of putting in an order to buy at 1—and in the temporarily complete absence of other bids he actually got his stock for a dollar a share! The scene on the floor was chaotic. Despite the jamming of the communication system, orders to buy and sell—mostly to sell—came in faster than human beings could possibly handle them; it was on that day that an exhausted broker, at the close of the session, found a large wastebasket which he had stuffed with orders to be executed and had carefully set aside for safekeeping—and then had completely forgotten. Within half an hour of the opening the volume of trading had passed three million shares, by twelve o'clock it had passed eight million, by half-past one it had passed twelve million, and when the closing gong brought the day's madness to an end the gigantic record of 16,410,030 shares had been set. Toward the close there was a rally, but by that time the average prices of fifty leading stocks, as compiled by the *New York Times*, had fallen nearly forty points. Meanwhile there was a near-panic in other markets —the foreign stock exchanges, the lesser American exchanges, the grain market.

So complete was the demoralization of the stock market and so exhausted were the brokers and their staffs and the Stock Exchange employees, that at noon that day, when the panic was at its worst, the Governing Committee met quietly to decide whether or not to close the Exchange. To quote from an address made some months later by Richard Whitney: "In order not to give occasion for alarming rumors, this meeting was not held in the Governing Committee Room, but in the office of the president of the Stock Clearing Corporation directly beneath the Stock Exchange floor. . . . The forty governors came to the meeting in groups of two and three as unobtrusively as possible. The office they met in was never designed for large meetings of this sort, with the result that most of the governors were compelled to stand, or to sit on tables. As the meeting progressed, panic was raging overhead on the floor. . . . The feeling of those present was revealed by their habit of continually lighting cigarettes, taking a puff or two, putting them out and lighting new ones—a practice which soon made the narrow room blue with smoke. . . ." Two of the Morgan partners were invited to the meeting and, attempting to slip into the building unnoticed so as not to start a new flock of rumors, were refused admittance by one of the guards and had to remain outside until rescued by a member of the Governing Committee. After some deliberation, the governors finally decided not to close the Exchange.

It was a critical day for the banks,

that Tuesday the 29th. Many of the corporations which had so cheerfully loaned money to brokers through the banks in order to obtain interest at 8 or 9 per cent were now clamoring to have these loans called—and the banks were faced with a choice between taking over the loans themselves and running the risk of precipitating further ruin. It was no laughing matter to assume the responsibility of millions of dollars' worth of loans secured by collateral which by the end of the day might prove to have dropped to a fraction of its former value. That the call money rate never rose above 6 per cent that day, that a money panic was not added to the stock panic, and that several Wall Street institutions did not go down into immediate bankruptcy, was due largely to the nerve shown by a few bankers in stepping into the breach. The story is told of one banker who went grimly on authorizing the taking over of loan after loan until one of his subordinate officers came in with a white face and told him that the bank was insolvent. "I dare say," said the banker, and went ahead unmoved. He knew that if he did not, more than one concern would face insolvency.

The next day—Wednesday, October 30th—the outlook suddenly and providentially brightened. The directors of the Steel Corporation had declared an extra dividend; the directors of the American Can Company had not only declared an extra dividend, but had raised the regular dividend. There was another flood of reassuring statements —though by this time a cheerful statement from a financier fell upon somewhat skeptical ears. Julius Klein, Mr. Hoover's Assistant Secretary of Commerce, composed a rhapsody on continued prosperity. John J. Raskob declared that stocks were at bargain prices and that he and his friends were buying.

John D. Rockefeller poured Standard Oil upon the waters: "Believing that fundamental conditions of the country are sound and that there is nothing in the business situation to warrant the destruction of values that has taken place on the exchanges during the past week, my son and I have for some days been purchasing sound common stocks." Better still, prices rose—steadily and buoyantly. Now at last the time had come when the strain on the Exchange could be relieved without causing undue alarm. At 1:40 o'clock Vice-President Whitney announced from the rostrum that the Exchange would not open until noon the following day and would remain closed all day Friday and Saturday—and to his immense relief the announcement was greeted, not with renewed panic, but with a cheer.

Throughout Thursday's short session the recovery continued. Prices gyrated wildly—for who could arrive at a reasonable idea of what a given stock was worth, now that all settled standards of value had been upset?—but the worst of the storm seemed to have blown over. The financial community breathed more easily; now they could have a chance to set their houses in order.

It was true that the worst of the panic was past. But not the worst prices. There was too much forced liquidation still to come as brokers' accounts were gradually straightened out, as banks called more collateral, and terror was renewed. The next week, in a series of short sessions, the tide of prices receded once more—until at last on November 13th the bottom prices for the year 1929 were reached. Besides the figures hung up in the sunny days of September they made a tragic showing:

	High Price Sept. 3, 1929	Low Price Nov. 13, 1929
American Can	181⅞	86
American Telephone & Telegraph	304	197¼
Anaconda Copper	131½	70
General Electric	396¼	168⅛
General Motors	72¾	36
Montgomery Ward	137⅞	49¼
New York Central	256⅜	160
Radio	101	28
Union Carbide & Carbon	137⅞	59
United States Steel	261¾	150
Westinghouse E. & M.	289⅞	102⅝
Woolworth	100⅜	52¼
Electric Bond & Share	186¾	50¼

The *New York Times* averages for fifty leading stocks had been almost cut in half, falling from a high of 311.90 in September to a low of 164.43 on November 13th; and the *Times* averages for twenty-five leading industrials had fared still worse, diving from 469.49 to 220.95.

The Big Bull Market was dead. Billions of dollars' worth of profits—and paper profits—had disappeared. The grocer, the window-cleaner, and the seamstress had lost their capital. In every town there were families which had suddenly dropped from showy affluence into debt. Investors who had dreamed of retiring to live on their fortunes now found themselves back once more at the very beginning of the long road to riches. Day by day the newspapers printed the grim reports of suicides.

Coolidge-Hoover Prosperity was not yet dead, but it was dying. Under the impact of the shock of panic, a multitude of ills which hitherto had passed unnoticed or had been offset by stock-market optimism began to beset the body economic, as poisons seep through the human system when a vital organ has ceased to function normally. Although the liquidation of nearly three billion dollars of brokers' loans contracted credit, and the Reserve Banks lowered the rediscount rate, and the way in which the larger banks and corporations of the country had survived the emergency without a single failure of large proportions offered real encouragement, nevertheless the poisons were there; overproduction of capital; over-ambitious expansion of business concerns; overproduction of commodities under the stimulus of installment buying and buying with stock-market profits; the maintenance of an artificial price level for many commodities; the depressed condition of European trade. No matter how many soothsayers of high finance proclaimed that all was well, no matter how earnestly the President set to work to repair the damage with soft words and White House conferences, a major depression was inevitably under way.

Nor was that all. Prosperity is more than an economic condition; it is a state of mind. The Big Bull Market had been more than the climax of a business cycle; it had been the climax of a cycle in American mass thinking and mass emotion. There was hardly a man or woman in the country whose attitude toward life had not been affected by it in some degree and was not now affected by the sudden and brutal shattering of hope. With the Big Bull Market gone and prosperity going, Americans were soon to find themselves living in an altered world which called for new adjustments, new ideas, new habits of thought, and a new order of values. The psychological climate was changing; the ever-shifting currents of American life were turning into new channels.

The Post-war Decade had come to its close. An era had ended.

ECONOMICS OF THE GUARANTEED WAGE

Seymour E. Harris

Organized labor has won many victories in its efforts to better wages and working conditions. Will the next big advance be the guaranteed annual wage? Certain to influence the thinking of labor and business are the economic factors involved. Here a noted economist provides a thoughtful analysis of the problem and, incidentally, a good example of documented business writing. Professor Harris teaches at Harvard.

The guaranteed annual wage, guaranteed employment, guaranteed wages, or whatever the appropriate term, promises to become one of the major economic issues of the next few years. Many explanations can be adduced for the recent vogue for the guaranteed wage. Dissatisfaction with the unemployment compensation (UC) program is surely one reason. This program covered only one-quarter of the cost to labor of unemployment in a year of modest unemployment even after almost 10 years of unparalleled prosperity. (That is, in 1949, when 3.4 million persons were unemployed, wage losses amounted to about $7.6 billion, and unemployment benefits, $1.9 billion.) [1] Even in 1953, the average maximum benefit was $27 per week; the average weekly benefit, $23.58; the average potential duration, 22 weeks; the average duration of benefits, 10 weeks; and the duration for persons who exhausted their benefits, 19 weeks. [2]

A second reason for the increased interest in the guaranteed wage is the greater importance attached to fringes. This emphasis on fringes may be explained by the fact that the basic wage has risen to a level where much more than minimum needs are being met. Thus, from 1939 to 1953, wages per employee (exclusive of supplements, etc.) rose by 57 percent; real per capita *disposable* income (after taxes) of the entire population, by 46 percent. In

[1] Figures from National Income, 1954 Edition (U.S. Department of Commerce, Office of Business Economics, 1954, published as a supplement to the Survey of Current Business); Social Security Bulletin, September 1954; and Economic Report of the President transmitted to the Congress, January 28, 1954.

[2] U.S. Department of Labor, 1953 Supplement to Handbook of Unemployment Insurance Financial Data, September 1954; cf. Hearings on Unemployment Insurance, House of Representatives, Ways and Means Committee, June 1954 (pp. 101–102); averages calculated.

Excerpted from a paper read at the annual meeting of the Industrial Research Association in Detroit, December 1954. Reprinted from the *Monthly Labor Review*, February 1955, by courtesy of the author.

this same period, the number of jobs rose by more than 19 million, or about 40 percent, and, in relation to population 14 years and over, from 46 to 56 percent. All these figures point to much higher living standards.[3]

On the issue of the effects of economic adjustments on the factory worker, there is much truth in the position that factory workers suffer more than others. This was evident, for example, in 1929–32, 1937–38, and 1948–49, when the relative decline in employment for manufacturing was greater than that in the services or in trade.

THE CASE FOR THE GUARANTEED WAGE

Much can be said for the guaranteed wage. On the assumption that the guaranteed wage involves management in no additional wage costs, i.e., that labor asks for a guaranteed wage rather than for a rise in pensions or an increase in the basic wage rate, the program can be supported on the grounds that X percent of costs thus incurred yield higher returns in the estimate of the worker than alternative forms of wage increases. The fact that workers seek their gains in this manner supports this position. Of course, trade union leaders may want the guaranteed wage partly because they can achieve a higher wage increase in this manner than through orthodox approaches. The explanation of this fact may be that employers can afford to pay more under a guaranteed wage program because, under the pressure of higher outlays charged to instability, the incentive to reduce costs would be increased; or it may simply be that bargaining for a guaranteed wage program may be more effective than for a rise in the basic wage

[3] Figures computed from Economic Report of the President, op. cit.

rate. For example, in periods of inflationary pressure it is easier to win public approval of a program that does not add to inflationary pressures currently. In fact, the large growth of pension programs in the postwar years may be associated partly with this consideration. In this connection, it should be observed that, as Chancellor Clark Kerr and others have argued, trade unionism has not succeeded in increasing the share of income going to wages (the stability of proportions over the years has been remarkable),[4] and hence the gains under a guaranteed wage program may merely represent a changed pattern in the manner of obtaining wages, the overall rise itself being associated with gains of productivity. This generalization applies, of course, to income taxes. There is much evidence of substantial changes toward equality in recent years when income after taxes is considered.[5] But the gains in distribution relate, to a considerable extent, to increased amounts of employment and the improvement in the relative position of low-income workers.

Undoubtedly a guaranteed wage program, as it spread, would increase the pressure to improve the unemployment compensation program, for employers affected by the introduction of guaranteed wages might feel under a competitive disadvantage, either vis-a-vis competitors in their industry, or in competition with producers or sellers of competing products. Since payrolls vary from 10 to 90 percent of costs, it is obvious that any program which im-

[4] For excerpts from Dr. Kerr's paper on Trade Unionism and Distributive Shares, presented at the IRRA 1953 annual meeting, see Monthly Labor Review, February 1954 (p. 146).

[5] See, especially, Goldsmith, Jaszi, Kaitz, and Leibenberg, Size Distribution of Income Since the Mid-Thirties, in The Review of Economics and Statistics, February 1954 (p. 26, in particular).

poses costs upon the basis of payrolls would greatly affect the competitive position of different products and firms. Even when one union has exclusive jurisdiction in an industry, costs of different firms may be affected unevenly. Thus, according to one estimate, a limitation of applicability of guaranteed wages to workers with 3 years' seniority would cover 94 percent of the workers in one company of an industry and 51 percent in another.[6]

The trade unions consider the guaranteed wage, in part, as a weapon for improving unemployment compensation and hence contend that the introduction of guaranteed wages would increase the pressure to improve unemployment compensation. But I am inclined to believe that the parallel with Old Age and Survivors Insurance is not so great as they often assume, nor am I convinced that they played as large a part in improving OASI as they claim. It is well to remember that, under OASI, in the early years in particular, large subsidies are involved, and the improvement of benefits lightens the burden on private pensions. Also relevant is the fact that under OASI taxes are levied on both employers and employes, whereas under unemployment compensation, the tax is imposed on employers only (with unimportant exceptions), and hence there is less incentive among employers to urge expansion of the unemployment compensation program than there was to urge liberalization of OASI with the surge of pension programs. Indeed, should unemployment compensation become a burden on the general taxpayer in part—as it well might—employers, seeking to shift the burden of the guaranteed wage from one on payrolls to one on all taxpayers, may be more

[6] J. W. Garbarino, Guaranteed Wages, Berkeley, University of California, 1954 (p. 42).

disposed to seek alleviation through an improved unemployment compensation tax.

In discussions of this aspect of the problem, another issue has escaped attention. The guaranteed wage scheme would apply presumably to all regions where unions operate on a national basis and therefore costs would be roughly equal in all regions. This would be an important advantage for the guaranteed wage over unemployment compensation wherever unions operate on a national basis and enforce roughly equal demands (e. g., the United Steelworkers and the United Automobile Workers, both CIO), for under unemployment compensation there is a strong and unfortunate tendency for States to compete in keeping benefits and taxes down.

Trade union leaders support the guaranteed wage in part because they believe that it would reduce the rate of technological improvement. Undoubtedly just as the economist far from the smoke of the factory underestimates the significance of the costs of change, so the trade-union leader may overestimate the damage done. Yet the trade unions may have a case here. There is something to be said for slowing down technological change when the costs of adjustment are heavy. By imposing upon the employer part of the costs to the displaced worker and thus forcing him to bear part of the costs of change, the proponents of the guaranteed wage support the view that change may be too rapid. One result of the guaranteed wage may well be fewer improvements in depression periods when employers would have to include as costs the wages of displaced workers; and more improvements in prosperous periods when the potentially displaced workers would be absorbed in jobs created by the growth in demand. In the same vein, labor contends that, though a guaranteed wage equal to 100 percent of wages may slow up the transfer of workers into growing industries, mobility may be excessive. Further, they take the position that there is a case, on both economic and noneconomic grounds, for eschewing excessive mobility because, first, in depression, high mobility may be of little use and, second, in prosperous periods, there is a reservoir of workers in the expanding labor force. Further, all workers in an industry have a stake in a guaranteed wage reserve and would resent excessive use (and hence unjustifiable immobility) by a minority. But I hasten to add that a guaranteed wage unwisely formulated might interfere with required mobility.

In this connection, it is well to consider the possibility of slowing up migration of firms from one region to another in response to lower wage costs and tax concessions—migrations which may well destroy, and in fact have destroyed, the entire industry of some towns. The guaranteed wage might well make some of these migrations unprofitable; and I would be inclined to support it on these grounds. The employer has some responsibility to his workers, their families, and the community.

Another appeal of the guaranteed wage may well lie in its effects upon the distribution of income among workers. The incidence of unemployment is felt especially by the younger workers, for seniority rights protect the older worker, and the younger workers would especially gain from the protection of a guaranteed wage program. Therefore, it would follow that if (say), instead of a 5-percent rise in basic wage rates, a new contract provided a guaranteed wage clause costing 5 percent of wages, then the younger workers (exclusive of probationary workers, who would not generally be eligible) would gain dispropor-

tionately vis-a-vis contributions, and other workers would lose relatively. Undoubtedly in order to restrict the resultant redistribution of rewards, the UAW proposes that employers, in the absence of notice, guarantee a full week's work and that funds in the guaranteed wage reserves be rationed, once declines become serious and it becomes apparent that those laid off first might exhaust all or a large part of the available funds, leaving older workers unprotected. The first measure would especially profit probationary workers, who might otherwise be the first to lose employment, and would also protect all workers against losses through a reduced working week; the second would assure the older workers of some part of the total payments on account of lost time.

SOME QUESTIONS RAISED BY GUARANTEED WAGES

On the assumption that wages are determined by marginal productivity, there should be no opposition to guaranteed wages on the part of employers. But there seems to be much opposition.

First, employers are fearful of the costs. Their fears are greater the more uncertain the obligation assumed—for example, a program which would limit payments (e. g., 10 cents an hour as proposed by the Steelworkers) would meet less opposition from all but the highly stable industries than would one with uncertain obligations. Indeed, if management fails to compensate for the increased costs out of a rise of productivity, a reduction in other rewards to workers, or a rise of prices, then the additional costs must come out of profits. Even so, when profits are high, the introduction of a guaranteed wage may be consistent with reasonable returns. It is conceivable that with profits at about one-third of wages and salaries, as they were in 1946–53[7] part of the costs of guaranteed wages might be financed out of profits. (But the historical trends already mentioned suggest somewhat different conclusions.)

In orthodox theory, the payroll "tax" will ultimately be borne by the worker, but, in the short run, capital may pay. Ultimately, however, on the assumption that returns on capital are reduced as a result of the guaranteed wage, new investment will be discouraged in the industries subject to guaranteed wages and this will create pressure for passing the new burden on by reducing wages or raising prices.[8] When the coverage of guaranteed wages is thus limited through reduced capital entry, the returns on capital in the guaranteed wage industries would tend to return to their previous relative level—a tendency which would be subject to all kinds of opposing forces. When the guaranteed wage is widely established, workers or (and) consumers would pay—but returns for management and capital may be cut to some extent.

No one can really estimate the costs of a guaranteed wage, for they would depend upon the benefits offered, the amount of unemployment, taxes saved, and resultant reduction of costs.[9] But, on the assumption that unemployment would not exceed the low levels (average) of the last 15 years and that the guaranteed wage would provide benefits equal to wages, a very rough guess of the cost would be three times

that of unemployment compensation, or about 4½ percent of payrolls—somewhat more if allowance is made for the fact that wages of the unemployed when they were employed were probably less than for all workers. (Unemployment compensation provides benefits equal only to one-third of wages.) To this must be added additional costs related to the longer period of idleness covered under the guaranteed wage, less strict disqualifications, elimination of waiting periods, etc. But even if workers are covered for a year, the costs will not necessarily be raised by 52/19 (the numerator being the number of weeks covered by the guaranteed wage and the denominator, the average number of weeks covered prior to exhaustion of benefits under unemployment compensation in 1953), but some allowance must be made for the longer period covered under guaranteed wage. In 1953, the exhaustion rate (the ratio of exhaustions to new claims filed) was 20 percent and would be much higher in periods of substantial unemployment. Perhaps 1 percent additional should be allowed for this factor, and hence total costs might be 6 percent (4½ plus 1 plus ½ for the other items mentioned). But this 6 percent is an overall figure based on the assumption of light unemployment.[10]

The most careful survey of costs yet made, in the Latimer report, was based on estimates for the period 1937–1941, derived from analyses of 47 cases under various benefit schedules. For example, under a guarantee of 40 hours for 52 weeks covering all workers with 3 months' service, according to the report, costs varied from 0.4 to 33 percent of

[7] Profits of corporations before taxes and income of unincorporated enterprise (in part not profits) amounted to $472 billion. Wages and salaries added up to $1,267 billion. Calculated from National Income, 1954, op. cit.

[8] S. E. Harris, Economics of Social Security, New York, McGraw-Hill Book Co., Inc., 1941.

[9] Cf. Guaranteed Wages, Report to the President by the Advisory Board, Office of War Mobilization and Reconversion, Washington, 1947 (ch. VIII).

[10] I have made no allowance for the fact that part of the workers would not be covered under the guaranteed wage. This is roughly offset by noncoverage of part of wages under unemployment compensation.

payrolls per year, the average being 10 percent and the highest costs accruing to plants in unstable industries. Even a long secular decline without a severe cyclical decline and without large seasonal fluctuations may not result in high costs. The report says: "By selecting the limitations which will meet the particular conditions out of which the excessive costs arise, moreover, the costs will be reduced to reasonable levels, while maintaining guarantee benefits at the maximum level feasible under all conditions . . . the gross cost was reduced, by appropriate limitations, to less than an average of 6.0 percent annually even in the highest cost cases." [11]

When the economist associates wages with productivity, he does not mean that wages in excess of a level determined by productivity may not be paid; rather, he implies that the continuance of such a policy would mean the eventual liquidation of the business. When wages are high relative to prices, the employer may be able to reduce wages, raise productivity, or increase prices. The troublesome feature of the guaranteed wage program for the employer lies in the fact that here he is committed to a substantial additional cost, largely fixed, which may continue for a long period, and that this is an element of cost which is intractable. It therefore becomes necessary for the employer to reduce the rigidity of the system if he is to find it acceptable and workable. This may be done by setting a ceiling on the costs (e. g., 10 percent of payrolls), by limiting the guarantees (e.g., a reduced number of weeks, a payment less than 100 percent of wages), and by allowing a reduction in numbers covered in the midst of a secular decline (that is, a worker may

lose rights to guaranteed wages after the lapse of a designated period). The workability of the guaranteed wage would be enhanced if a period of accumulation were required, as under unemployment compensation. Finally, as payrolls decline, insofar as costs are based on payrolls, they too would decline.

Obviously in growing industries it is much easier to carry the burden of unemployment than in declining industries. For example, this is indicated by the trends in employment from 1899 to 1951. Obviously, it would be much easier, other things being equal, to support the guaranteed wage in chemicals, petroleum and rubber, metals, machinery, and instruments than in textiles, apparel, and shoes. In the last group, the imposition of additional charges as a penalty for reducing the numbers of workers attached to the existing firms might well accelerate the decline.[12] In textiles, a continuation of losses in employment at the rate prevailing in 1951–54 would result in the disappearance of the industry from New England in 9 years, and from the United States in 15 years.

In industries subject to great cyclical instability or secular declines, it may be especially necessary to set a limit of payments as a percentage of payrolls. (The average annual cost of the whole cycle would be considerably less than the ceiling set for any one year.) Special provisions may also have to be made in industries that are strongly seasonal, in which the worker is often compensated to some extent by higher pay for the losses involved in seasonality.[13]

[11] Guaranteed Wages: Report to the President, op. cit. (p. 75).

[12] S. E. Harris, Interregional Competition, Proceedings of the American Economic Association, May 1954 (p. 375).
[13] Professors Samuelson and Hansen raised some doubts on this issue in Guaranteed Wages: Report to the President, op. cit. (pp. 422–424).

RELEVANT UNEMPLOYMENT COMPENSATION FAILURES

One argument used against the guaranteed wage is that concentration on it would weaken the movement to strengthen unemployment compensation, which is greatly in need of improvement. Of course, unemployment compensation is much more important than the guaranteed wage, and it would be unfortunate if the campaign for the latter greatly reduced interest in the former. It would undoubtedly be a long time before as many as 10 million workers were covered by guaranteed wages, but at the end of 1953, unemployment compensation covered more than 70 percent of all wage and salary payments. As a result of new legislation in 1954 affecting employers in small establishments and Federal employees, the number of workers covered rose by 4 million, only 10 million not now being covered. However, only about one-half the unemployed (even in a period of light unemployment, as in 1954) received benefits under unemployment compensation—and those at but one-third of wages. In fact, in the first half of 1954 (prior to passage of the legislation referred to), unemployment averaged 3.5 million, but the unemployed receiving compensation under the State unemployment laws and the Railroad Unemployment Insurance Act averaged less than 2 million or 56 percent.[14] The need for improvement stems in part from the following important failures of unemployment compensation.

First, contributions have been disappointing. Whereas they amounted to 2.72 percent of taxable payrolls in 1938–40, they were down to 1.40 percent in 1946–53 and 1.30 percent in 1953. Reduced rates under experience

[14] Figures from Survey of Current Business, November 1954, and Social Security Bulletin, September 1954.

rating account for this decline. One unfortunate result has been an unhealthy competition among States to keep both benefits and contributions low. Another has been the accumulation, after 15 years of unprecedented prosperity, of a reserve of but $9 billion—an amount that could be wiped out in a brief period of heavy unemployment. With the uneven incidence of unemployment, the reserves of vulnerable States have several times fallen to dangerously low levels; but the Federal Government has shown no disposition to provide reinsurance or even an adequate loan system. (The legislation of 1954 is a gesture in this direction.)

Second, even after more than 15 years of unemployment compensation and despite the advances in 1954, about one-fifth of all workers are still uncovered. What is more, whereas taxable covered wages equaled 96 percent of total covered wages in 1939, by 1953 the ratio was only 72 percent.

Third, there has been a serious decline in the proportion of the average weekly benefit to the total wages: 41.1 percent in 1938–40 to 32.5 percent in 1951–53, as compared with a goal, according to the able long-time Administrator of the Social Security Board, Mr. Arthur Altmeyer, of 50 percent. In a period during which wages tripled, the average weekly benefit rose only from $10.72 (1938–40) to $22.82 (1951–53). This decline in the ratio of benefits to wages is the more serious in that, in relation to total compensation (both wages and fringe benefits, the latter having risen greatly), benefits have been reduced even more than is suggested above.

THE GUARANTEED WAGE AND EMPLOYMENT

The guaranteed wage is suspect for an important reason: it may cut down employment. One of the most frequent complaints made against the guaranteed wage holds that if, in employing a worker, the employer assumes the responsibility not only of paying him when he is at work but also when he is idle, he will be most reluctant to hire additional workers. Moreover, once the employer is confronted with outlays to support idle workers and especially when demand is declining, he will reduce outlays in all possible directions, thus contracting demand (and employment) of his suppliers.

Is there any reply to this criticism? There are some protective devices. Thus, the guaranteed wage contract may restrict the program to workers with some seniority and thus not confront the employer with this additional liability at the time of hiring workers. Other safeguards may include the following: Limitations on the guaranty in terms of employer costs in cents per hour of work or percentage of payrolls, the number of workers to be covered (e. g., only those with 1 year of service or more), the period to be covered, the number of weeks of guaranty, and the percentage of weekly pay to be guaranteed; the recourse to accumulation of reserves and hence reduced dependence on charges on payrolls in periods of declining demand; built-in protection related to the reduced payrolls as demand declines; introduction of the plan after a building-up period; and reinsurance. It is especially important to make the guaranteed wage responsive to secular declines related to technological change and declines in demand. Otherwise the guaranteed wage, in contrast to unemployment compensation, may hamper movement required in a dynamic economy.

The advantage of reinsurance lies in reducing the charge on payrolls needed to accumulate reserves when they are pooled. Management will have to weigh these savings against the unwillingness to assume responsibilities for the unemployment of rival firms. Possibly a reinsurance provision by government would solve this problem, but this is not to be expected until the guaranteed wage is widely used.

The guaranteed wage raises another important issue: Is it safe to pay the worker as much or almost as much when unemployed as when employed? In some unions, there seems to be a disposition to demand, as a matter of principle, 100 percent of wages under the guaranteed wage. But actually, when allowance is made for the nontaxation of income received under unemployment compensation (assuming integration) and the savings of outlays when unemployed (lunches, transportation, etc.), it would be possible to maintain income with a guaranty of 80–90 percent of wages. I am inclined to believe that a guaranty of, say 85–90 percent of wages would be preferable when adjustments are made for tax relief under unemployment compensation, etc. This is not because I believe that workers are happy being paid for idling. In fact, in some States low-income workers seem to receive as much as 90 percent of wages under unemployment compensation. Nor am I convinced by the many charges made by employers that the workers drawing unemployment compensation do not seek work and prefer to be idle at 30–40 percent of their customary wages. Once jobs became available not only did the 10 million or more persons who were unemployed in the 1930's find jobs in the 1940's and 1950's, but several million additional (aside from normal accretions) joined the labor market. But nevertheless it is my opinion that the American people object to equal payments to workers irrespective of whether they work or are idle.

Exercises

"Alexandrian Commercialism," by Miriam Beard

1. In a paragraph of about 200 words sum up Alexandria's preëminence in trade.
2. Write a description of some modern city in the same vein as this passage.
3. The author writes: "The role of the business man in binding together and expanding empire has been overshadowed in written history by the deeds of military heroes." Write a paper enlarging upon this idea.
4. After the necessary library research, write a report on the role of businessmen during the Revolutionary War, or during some other period suggested or appoved by your instructor.
5. In what ways does business contribute to knowledge? Discuss.
6. Using "commercialism" in a derogatory sense, write a theme on commercialism in modern American life.
7. Explain one of the following allusions, which you will find in Miss Beard's text. Name your sources of information.
   a. The world geography of Ptolemy.
   b. Rhodian maritime law.
   c. Phoenician bookkeeping.
   d. Egyptian skill in documentation.
   e. Babylonian banking methods.

"Of the Division of Labor," by Adam Smith

1. Write a paragraph in which you analyze Adam Smith's writing style.
2. Write a paper in which you apply Adam Smith's views on the division of labor to modern instances.
3. Write a theme in a light or satirical vein on the division of labor in your household.
4. From your own observation and thought, write a theme on the possible deleterious effects of the division of labor on the workman. In what ways may the harm be offset? Discuss.
5. Sum up in 75–100 words the fourth paragraph beginning, "In every other art and manufacture. . . ."
6. From library sources find out more about Adam Smith. Write a short biography.

"Report on Manufactures," by Alexander Hamilton

1. Sum up in a few paragraphs this portion of Hamilton's report.
2. Do you detect Hamilton's borrowings from Adam Smith? (See the selection just preceding.) Write a paragraph on the similarities.
3. Discuss Hamilton's language and his organization and presentation of ideas.
4. Write a letter to Alexander Hamilton, telling him what has happened with respect to this country's manufactures since he submitted his report.
5. From library sources, write a paper on Hamilton's contributions as first Secretary of the Treasury.
6. From library sources write a brief biography of Alexander Hamilton.
7. Through reference to both this report and Carl Crow's "They Had No Carriage Trade" (see Sec. 4), establish the conditions under which Hamilton proposed the encouragement of manufactures.

"The Merchant of Prato," by Iris Origo

1. From this brief excerpt, can you detect any qualities that account for Datini's success as a merchant? Write a short paper on the subject, supporting your answer by specific references to the text.
2. After the necessary research on the subject, write a report on the merchant of the Middle Ages. Include footnotes and a bibliography.
3. Write a brief history of insurance, such as an insurance broker might put in a leaflet to distribute to his customers.
4. Write a paper on present-day business hazards.
5. Write a light theme built around the idea that life these days presents hardly any risk at all, what with all the types of insurance protection a person can buy.

"A Time of Great Prosperity," by Washington Irving

1. Do you see in Irving's essay any parallel to recent Wall Street behavior? Write a theme on the subject.
2. Discuss Washington Irving's use of figurative language.
3. Compare Washington Irving's treatment of his subject with that of Frederick Lewis Allen in the following selection.
4. Considering his style, what chance do you think Washington Irving would have for employment as a business writer for the *New York Times* or in some business office? Support your views.

"Crash!" by Frederick Lewis Allen

1. Abbreviate Mr. Allen's account of the crash to about 500 words.
2. Write a piece on America at this moment. Follow the style of the first several paragraphs of Mr. Allen's description of September, 1929, but use the present tense.
3. From a study of the financial pages of the newspapers, write an estimate of America's present financial health.
4. In a paragraph describe the difference between a "bull market" and a "bear market" and indicate the kind that is now operating.
5. In a current stock market table (see the financial pages of your newspaper), look up the status of five of the stocks listed by Mr. Allen, and write a paragraph describing their performance this year.
6. Obtain the annual report of a large company, and from the information it contains, write a statement of the company's general condition.
7. If you have ever visited the New York Stock Exchange or any of the other large financial marketplaces in this country, write a theme on your experience. If you have not made such a visit, perhaps you can describe an auction of any kind.

"Economics of the Guaranteed Wage," by Seymour E. Harris

1. Define "guaranteed wage."
2. Put the substance of this paper in language adapted to the average factory worker.
3. Discuss the organization of this part of Professor Harris' paper.
4. Discuss this paper as an example of objective analysis of a controversial question.

5. Write an argument for (or against) the guaranteed wage, choosing your language deliberately to affect the reader's views.

6. Define the following terms (all of which can be found in this paper) and use each correctly in a sentence or paragraph of your own composition: incidence, liquidation, cyclical, productivity, rigidity, alleviation, orthodox, *vis-à-vis*, proponent.

7

Moral Values in Business

Unlike the physician or teacher or other men in the professions, the businessman has worn the mantle of guilt for centuries. For trade has not always been regarded as honorable and many tradesmen still make profit at the expense of the innocent, the ignorant, and the gullible. Newer ideologies, too, question even the individual's right to profit. In truth, the idea that stature is measured by worldly goods has seldom had a firm foundation. Most businessmen seek satisfaction beyond money. Above all, they desire to live at peace with their Maker and to know the respect of their neighbors. But the quest is not always easy. Competition imposes battle conditions. Customers make impossible demands. Even one's own government sometimes takes opposing sides.

How should the businessman act? What are his obligations to his workers and to society? What are his obligations to himself? The authors of the following selections seek the answers to these urgent questions.

ETHICS IN A BUSINESS SOCIETY

Marquis W. Childs and Douglass Cater

Are people able to love their neighbors in the way the Bible teaches and still earn a profitable living in a business civilization? This is the question posed by a study undertaken by the Federal (now the National) Council of Churches of Christ on a grant by the Rockefeller Foundation. In the book from which the following excerpts are taken, Messrs. Childs and Cater have tried to interpret some of the churches' effort to relate two seemingly unrelated parts of our society: religion and economics. Mr. Childs is a noted commentator on public affairs and author of *Sweden, the Middle Way.* Mr. Cater is Washington correspondent of the *Reporter* Magazine.

THE AGE OF CERTITUDE

The suggestion that religion was in any sense irrelevant to the immediate concerns of daily life would have seemed strange in the Middle Ages. Such a suggestion might even have sounded heretical in an age when the embrace of the Church included man's every thought and action. We are so much the children of our time, the result of the long process of rationalizing, liberalizing thought, of Reason applied to Nature, progressing from Hume and Locke to Jefferson and the pragmatism of the American outlook, that it is difficult for us to comprehend that earlier era when men lived so largely within a closed circle described by the Church and its canons.

In the Middle Ages the primary concern of rich and poor alike, the feudal lord and the peasant-serf, was the salvation of the soul. Man's time on earth was brief and for the most part filled with trials and tribulations. He expected little else in the short interlude before eternity. By the beginning of the fourteenth century the Schoolmen had prepared a comprehensive body of theological law covering every phase of life.

The economic life of the time, certainly in the initial phase, was on a narrow and restricted basis. And even as the beginnings of a more extensive commerce appeared, the ethical dictates of the Church were a widely influential force. As R. H. Tawney puts it in his brilliant and erudite "Religion and the Rise of Capitalism":

Hence all activities fall within a single system, because all, though with different degrees of immediateness, are related to a single end, and derive their significance from it. The Church in its wider sense is the Christian Common-wealth, within which that end is to be realized; in its narrower sense it is the hierarchy divinely commissioned for its interpretation; in both it embraces the whole of life, and its authority is final. Though practice is perpetually at vari-ance with theory, there is no absolute division between the inner and personal life, which is "the sphere of religion," and the practical interests, the external order, the impersonal mechanism, to which, if some modern teachers may be trusted, religion is irrelevant.

Usury was a sin. Trade itself was dubi-ous in the ethical view of the Church. As one authority expressed it, "who-soever buys a thing, not that he may sell it whole and unchanged, but that it may be a material for fashioning something, he is no merchant. But the man who buys it in order that he may gain by selling it again unchanged and as he bought it, that man is of the buy-ers and sellers who are cast forth from God's temple." This was the view of the master theologian, St. Thomas Aquinas, and it was expressed in even sharper terms by St. Antoninus, a spe-cialist in the economic life of the Middle Ages. Because trade and usury were considered sinful, these functions, as the sluggish current of commerce began to quicken a little, were left largely to those outside the Church whose souls, in the view of the time, could not be further jeopardized.

Through the intervening centuries a complete reversal has taken place. Ac-quisition, increase of money, mercantile achievement, considered in the Middle Ages vices comparable to lust and glut-tony, became in the era of capitalism major virtues.

The society of the Middle Ages was, of course, a static society, based largely on an agricultural economy. It was a poor society in which, while the ex-tremes of power and wealth, as between the feudal lord and serf, were great, the total supply of goods from outside the manors was limited to what the few guilds and traders could furnish. There was, it is scarcely necessary to say, no understanding of commerce and trade in the sense they have come to have in our time.

In this poor society even if all the incomes had been made equal the pov-erty of the poor would scarcely have been relieved one whit. As Professor Boulding points out in "Goals of Economic Life," we have learned in our time that the increase of productivity is a precondition to the abolition of pov-erty. Such a concept was wholly alien to the Middle Ages. Under the hier-archical system of that era prices were to be established at such a level, prefer-ably by official action, that each man would "have the necessaries of life suitable for his station." In the ban on usury, Tawney points out, the emphasis was on taking a payment for money which was fixed and certain as between borrower and lender. The crime was in the kind of pact specifying that the usurer should get his money back with an increase whether the borrower gained or lost.

But while every man was fixed in his station from lowest to highest, they were all enclosed within the same care-fully defined circle of values. Under the eye of God, to the end of the salvation of the soul, they were the same even though the peasant was little better than a slave working out his tribute to the lord of the manor. But the powers of the lord of the manor were after all only earthly powers.

Within the unity of the Church all kinds and classes were one, and it was the continuing concern of the Church to protect the humble and the helpless from the rich and avaricious. Those guilty of avarice were made to do pen-ance by giving large alms. Punishment was meted out not only to usurers for taking what we would now call interest, but to those who were able to buy cheaper and with the passage of time to sell dearer. In practice, of course, at one level and another these canons were violated. There remained nevertheless into the late Middle Ages, when the rising tide of trade from city to city was breaking down the old barriers, the fundamental belief of priests and people alike that traffic in money and goods endangered the soul.

Looking back from our own time of confusion to this era when the walls of faith encompassed man's every act whether mean or noble, we undoubtedly exaggerate the sense of oneness that this brought. Yet the great cathedrals could scarcely have risen had they not come out of a common devotion to the glory of God. With their infinity of detail, their imaginativeness, the evidence of devotion and dedication in craftsmanship and artistry, they could not have been ordered into being, as were the pyramids, by a despot.

Romanticized as this epoch has been, one may nevertheless see in the cathedrals proof of rewards and satisfactions in a way of life that had this magnificent flowering. Here was the visible sign of men's love of God made manifest. That the cathedrals should have been the supreme achievement of a Christian society was no accident. Nor was it any happenstance that artisans and craftsmen from the whole country round contributed their labors through months and years to the common purpose of a community inseparably bound together. . . .

THE CREDO OF INDIVIDUALISM

Adam Smith is generally credited as being the founder of the laissez-faire school of economy, even though phrases with the same meaning were current long before he published his book. But he would be startled at the way the concept has been strained and stretched. Translated roughly laissez faire means permission to do as you will. It was the disciples following after the master who invented much of the dogma that today in popularized, vulgarized form passes under his name. It became part of the soaring optimism of the nineteenth century, that extraordinary epoch when, as had never happened before in recorded history, the population of the earth was doubled in a period of unprecedented peace and prosperity.

One of the most enthusiastic of the disciples was Claude Frédéric Bastiat, a popularizer whose "Economic Harmonies" was published posthumously in 1850. Economic laws, as understood by Bastiat, were translated into bright homilies that caught the popular fancy. For Bastiat "the acquisition of riches is of providential creation, natural, and consequently moral." This was ideally suited to the temper of the era which for all its surface smugness wanted to be assured that the great wealth derived from the mills spreading like a rash over the countryside was a part of God's purpose.

As Bastiat in France, so Henry Carey in this country spread the doctrine of complete laissez faire. This was reinforced in Carey's view by an unquenchable optimism over the boundless prospects for American prosperity. The outlook in the new continent with its still largely untouched resources was such as to refute the pessimistic conclusions of old-world philosophers. Carey ruled out the gloomy view of Malthus that an ever expanding population would constantly overtake technical progress and resources in such a way that hunger and misery would always catch up or run ahead of the human race. And Carey added another device to the laissez faire of Adam Smith. This was a protective tariff to safeguard developing industry. In America there need be no class conflict since labor's share of the total product would constantly increase and there would be a complete harmony of interest. While men must associate with other men this would only strengthen individualism.

With some slight variations here and there this is the doctrine that still permeates much of the business community in America. A century after such apostles of optimisim as Carey, the speeches at any service club luncheon could be taken almost literally out of the literature of a time when the transcendent virtues of individualism were first being proclaimed. In 1850 the new creed won ready response from eager and industrious individuals who were pushing back new frontiers not only in industry and finance but in every department of life. They wanted to be told that what they were doing was right and good, in the interests of both heaven and earth.

It seems to many today that the credo of individualism has worn a little thin; that its constant reiteration may arise from doubt as to its current validity. This is discussed by the contributors to "Goals of Economic Life." Thus Clark C. Bloom, Associate Professor of Economics at the University of Iowa, shows how even those who are most likely to preach "perfect competition" and the market mechanism rely on one form of government intervention or another. Professor Bloom concludes that we can no longer count on reaching economically correct results automatically, as a by-product of what individuals do in pursuit of their private interests. The element of practical ethics, he finds, has become an indispensable "factor of production."

Yet it is to the "dynamic" of the economics of Adam Smith that business men and many economists are more and more inclined to attribute the extraordinary gains in productivity of the American system. The Twentieth Century Fund underwrote a 777-page study, "Employment and Wages in the United States," by Professor W. S. Woytinsky and associates, published in 1953, which has this as its introductory note: "The economics of competition and the free market refute those who once argued that the American economy had reached a plateau." Professor Woytinsky finds that the rise of real wages in this country over the past century has carried the American living standard to top place in the world with an average increase of between one and two per cent a year. This has meant a real wage level today at least four times as great as that of a century ago. And there is no reason, in the view of the Woytinsky team, why average real earnings cannot rise over the next decade or two at an average of 2.5 to 3 per cent a year. "Euge! Belle! Dear Mr. Smith!"

Although many of today's most passionate preachers of individualism are hardly aware of it, a great deal of the religious and ethical framework out of the past has been carried over into the present. How important this heritage is to the order and stability in our own day the disciples of individualism sometimes almost willfully refuse to see. The conviction of a century ago was that pure self-interest and nothing else would make society run at the peak of greatest efficiency for the greatest good of all concerned. In "Social Responsibilities of the Businessman" Howard R. Bowen quotes the following from the London Economist of 1847:

It may be hurtful to the pride of statesmen to discover how little they can really do . . . to eradicate misery, to alleviate suffering, and improve society. Yet—so it is—the progress of civilization shows more and more how few and simple are the real duties of a government; and how impossible it is to add to those duties without inflicting permanent mischief on a community . . . But the aim of all statesmen who have acquired a higher reputation has been to remove regulations and restrictions imposed by others—to remedy the errors of former statesmen by removing old regulations, and not by *imposing new* ones. All that can be said of the great statesman is that he discovered error and removed it; that he found a country harassed by restrictions and regulations, and that he freed it.

But even when the credo of individualism was being heralded as the ultimate triumph of the human mind, the conviction of laissez faire was not actually lived up to to the fullest extent. The successful functioning of the system clearly required reasonable adherence to a moral code. Beginning early in the nineteenth century there were restrictions put on the rights of the individual in the conduct of his own business. The early factory laws attempted to ameliorate somewhat the harsh lot of the working class. It was forbidden to employ children under six or seven for more than ten hours a day.

This has been consistently the direction with a complicated and voluminous body of law growing up to safeguard not only life and limb but liberty and the pursuit of happiness. Sometimes it has come only after a fierce struggle between opposing powers. But the process has been greatly helped by the example of moral men who felt themselves bound to do unto others as they would have others do unto them. It was greatly helped by the evangelical movement in the churches offering stern resistance to rampant individualism which would walk roughshod over the weak and the lowly. Without the frame of reference afforded by the religious and ethical inheritance of the past the laissez-faire system might well have degenerated into chaos and violence. This is a profoundly important truth which those who today repeat the shibboleths of individualism too often do not understand or prefer to ignore.

THE CONDITION OF THE WORKING CLASSES
Pope Leo XIII

In the following passage from one of the great Papal encyclicals, Leo XIII argues the justice of private property and the responsibility of the owner to use his wealth in the public good.

. . . It is surely undeniable that, when a man engages in remunerative labor, the impelling reason and motive of his work is to obtain property, and thereafter to hold it as his very own. If one man hires out to another his strength or skill, he does so for the purpose of receiving in return what is necessary for sustenance and education; he therefore expressly intends to acquire a right full and real, not only to the remuneration, but also to the disposal of such remuneration, just as he pleases. Thus, if he lives sparingly, saves money, and, for greater security, invests his savings in land, the land, in such case, is only his wages under another form; and, consequently, a working-man's little estate thus purchased should be as completely at his full disposal as are the wages he received for his labor. But it is precisely in such power of disposal that ownership obtains, whether the property consist of land or chattels. Socialists, therefore, by endeavoring to transfer the possessions of individuals to the community at large, strike at the interests of every wage-earner, since they would deprive him of the liberty of disposing of his wages, and thereby of all hope and possibility of increasing his stock and of bettering his condition in life.

What is of far greater moment, however, is the fact that the remedy they propose is manifestly against justice. For every man has by nature the right to possess property as his own. This is one of the chief points of distinction between man and the animal creation, for the brute has no power of self-direction, but is governed by two main instincts, which keep his powers on the alert, impel him to develop them in a fitting manner, and stimulate and determine him to action without any power of choice. One of these instincts is self-preservation, the other the propagation of the species. But both can attain their purpose by means of things which lie within range; beyond their verge the brute creation cannot go, for they are moved to action by their senses only, and in the special direction which these suggest. But with man it is wholly different. He possesses, on the one hand, the full perfection of the animal being, and hence enjoys, at least as much as the rest of the animal kind, the fruition of things material. But

Quoted from the *Great Encyclical Letters of Leo XIII* translated by Father John Wynne, S.J., Benziger Brothers, Inc. Publishers and Copyright owners.

animal nature, however perfect, is far from representing the human being in its completeness, and is in truth but humanity's humble handmaid, made to serve and to obey. It is the mind, or reason, which is the predominant element in us who are human creatures; it is this which renders a human being human, and distinguishes him essentially and generically from the brute. And on this very account—that man alone among the animal creation is endowed with reason—it must be within his right to possess things not merely for temporary and momentary use, as other living things do, but to have and to hold them in stable and permanent possession; he must have not only things that perish in the use of them, but those also which, though they have been reduced into use, remain his own for further use.

This becomes still more clearly evident if man's nature be considered a little more deeply. For man, fathoming by his faculty of reason matters without number, and linking the future with the present, becoming, furthermore, by taking enlightened forethought, master of his own acts, guides his ways under the eternal law and the power of God, whose providence governs all things. Wherefore it is in his power to exercise his choice not only as to matters that regard his present welfare, but also about those which he deems may be for his advantage in time yet to come. Hence man not only can possess the fruits of the earth, but also the very soil, inasmuch as from the produce of the earth he has to lay by provision for the future. Man's needs do not die out, but recur; although satisfied today they demand fresh supplies for tomorrow. Nature accordingly owes to man a storehouse that shall never fail, affording the daily supply for his daily wants. And this he finds solely in the inexhaustible fertility of the earth.

Neither do we, at this stage, need to bring into action the interference of the State. Man precedes the State, and possesses, prior to the formation of any State, the right of providing for the sustenance of his body. Now to affirm that God has given the earth for the use and enjoyment of the whole human race is not to deny that private property is lawful. For God has granted the earth to mankind in general, not in the sense that all without distinction can deal with it as they like, but rather that no part of it has been assigned to any one in particular, and that the limits of private possession have been left to be fixed by man's own industry, and by the laws of individual races. Moreover, the earth, even though apportioned among private owners, ceases not thereby to minister to the needs of all, inasmuch as there is no one who does not sustain life from what the land produces. Those who do not possess the soil, contribute their labor; hence it may truly be said that all human subsistence is derived either from labor on one's own land, or from some toil, some calling which is paid for either in the produce of the land itself, or in that which is exchanged for what the land brings forth.

Here, again, we have further proof that private ownership is in accordance with the law of nature. Truly, that which is required for the preservation of life, and for life's well-being, is produced in great abundance from the soil, but not until man has brought it into cultivation and expended upon it his solicitude and skill. Now, when man thus turns the activity of his mind and the strength of his body towards procuring the fruits of nature, by such act he makes his own that portion of nature's field which he cultivates—that portion on which he leaves, as it were, the impress of his individuality; and it cannot but be just that he should possess that portion as his very own, and have a right to hold it without any one being justified in violating that right.

So strong and convincing are these arguments, that it seems amazing that some should now be setting up anew certain obsolete opinions in opposition to what is here laid down. They assert that it is right for private persons to have the use of the soil and its various fruits, but that it is unjust for any one to possess outright either the land on which he has built, or the estate which he has brought under cultivation. But those who deny these rights do not perceive that they are defrauding man of what his own labor has produced. For the soil which is tilled and cultivated with toil and skill utterly changes its conditions: it was wild before, now it is fruitful; was barren, but now brings forth in abundance. That which has thus altered and improved the land becomes so truly part of itself as to be in great measure indistinguishable and inseparable from it. Is it just that the fruit of a man's own sweat and labor should be possessed and enjoyed by any one else? As effects follow their cause, so is it just and right that the results of labor should belong to those who have bestowed their labor.

With reason, then, the common opinion of mankind, little affected by the few dissentients who have contended for the opposite view, has found in the careful study of nature, and in the laws of nature, the foundations of the division of property, and the practice of all ages has consecrated the principle of private ownership, as being preeminently in conformity with human nature, and as conducing in the most unmistakable manner to the peace and tranquillity of human existence. The same principle is confirmed and enforced by the civil laws—laws which, so long as they are just, derive from the

law of nature their binding force. The authority of the divine law adds its sanction, forbidding us in severest terms even to covet that which is another's:— *Thou shalt not covet thy neighbor's wife; nor his house, nor his field, nor his man-servant, nor his maid-servant, nor his ox, nor his ass, nor anything which is his.*[1] . . .

The great mistake made in regard to the matter now under consideration is to take up with the notion that class is naturally hostile to class, and that the wealthy and the workingmen are intended by nature to live in mutual conflict. So irrational and so false is this view, that the direct contrary is the truth. Just as the symmetry of the human frame is the resultant of the disposition of the bodily members, so in a State is it ordained by nature that these two classes should dwell in harmony and agreement, and should, as it were, groove into one another, so as to maintain the balance of the body politic. Each needs the other: Capital cannot do without Labor, nor Labor without Capital. Mutual agreement results in pleasantness of life and the beauty of good order; while perpetual conflict necessarily produces confusion and savage barbarity. Now, in preventing such strife as this, and in uprooting it, the efficacy of Christian institutions is marvellous and manifold. First of all, there is no intermediary more powerful than Religion (whereof the Church is the interpreter and guardian) in drawing the rich, and the poor breadwinners, together, by reminding each class of its duties to the other, and especially of the obligations of justice. Thus Religion teaches the laboring man and the artisan to carry out honestly and fairly all equitable agreements freely entered into; never to injure the property, nor to outrage the

[1] Deuteronomy v. 21.

person, of an employer; never to resort to violence in defending their own cause, nor to engage in riot or disorder; and to have nothing to do with men of evil principles, who work upon the people with artful promises, and excite foolish hopes which usually end in useless regrets, followed by insolvency. Religion teaches the wealthy owner and the employer that their work-people are not to be accounted their bondsmen; that in every man they must respect his dignity and worth as a man and as a Christian; that labor is not a thing to be ashamed of, if we lend ear to right reason and to Christian philosophy, but is an honorable calling, enabling a man to sustain his life in a way upright and creditable; and that it is shameful and inhuman to treat men like chattels to make money by, or to look upon them merely as so much muscle or physical power. Again, therefore, the Church teaches that, as Religion and things spiritual and mental are among the workingman's main concerns, the employer is bound to see that the worker has time for his religious duties; that he be not exposed to corrupting influences and dangerous occasions; and that he be not led away to neglect his home and family, or to squander his earnings. Furthermore, the employer must never tax his work-people beyond their strength, or employ them in work unsuited to their sex or age. His great and principal duty is to give every one a fair wage. Doubtless, before deciding whether wages are adequate, many things have to be considered; but wealthy owners and all masters of labor should be mindful of this—that to exercise pressure upon the indigent and the destitute for the sake of gain, and to gather one's profit out of the need of another, is condemned by all laws, human and divine. To defraud any one of wages that are his due is a crime which cries to the avenging anger of Heaven. *Behold, the hire of the laborers . . . which by fraud hath been kept back by you, crieth aloud; and the cry of them hath entered into the ears of the Lord of Sabaoth.*[2] Lastly, the rich must religiously refrain from cutting down the workmen's earnings, whether by force, by fraud, or by usurious dealing; and with all the greater reason because the laboring man is, as a rule, weak and unprotected, and because his slender means should in proportion to their scantiness be accounted sacred.

Were these precepts carefully obeyed and followed out, would they not be sufficient of themselves to keep under all strife and all its causes?

But the Church, with Jesus Christ as her Master and Guide, aims higher still. She lays down precepts yet more perfect, and tries to bind class to class in friendliness and good feeling. The things of earth cannot be understood or valued aright without taking into consideration the life to come, the life that will know no death. Exclude the idea of futurity, and forthwith the very notion of what is good and right would perish; nay, the whole scheme of the universe would become a dark and unfathomable mystery. The great truth which we learn from Nature herself is also the grand Christian dogma on which Religion rests as on its foundation—that when we have given up this present life, then shall we really begin to live. God has not created us for the perishable and transitory things of earth, but for things heavenly and everlasting; He has given us this world as a place of exile, and not as our abiding-place. As for riches and the other things which men call good and desirable, whether we have them in abundance, or lack them altogether—so far as eternal happiness is concerned—it matters

[2] St. James v. 4.

little; the only important thing is to use them aright. Jesus Christ, when He redeemed us with *plentiful redemption*, took not away the pains and sorrows which in such large proportion are woven together in the web of our mortal life. He transformed them into motives of virtue and occasions of merit: and no man can hope for eternal reward unless he follow in the blood-stained footprints of his Saviour. *If we suffer with Him, we shall also reign with Him.*[3] Christ's labors and sufferings, accepted of His own free-will, have marvellously sweetened all sufferings and all labor. And not only by His example, but by His grace and by the hope held forth of everlasting recompense, has He made pain and grief more easy to endure; *for that which is at present momentary and light of our tribulation, worketh for us above measure exceedingly an eternal weight of glory.*[4]

Therefore those whom fortune favors are warned that freedom from sorrow and abundance of earthly riches are no warrant for the bliss that shall never end, but rather are obstacles;[5] that the rich should tremble at the theatenings of Jesus Christ—threatenings so unwonted in the mouth of Our Lord[6]—and that a most strict account must be given to the Supreme Judge for all we possess. The chief and most excellent rule for the right use of money is one which the heathen philosophers hinted at, but which the Church has traced out clearly, and has not only made known to men's minds, but has impressed upon their lives. It rests on the principle that it is one thing to have a right to the possession of money, and another to have a right to use money as

one wills. Private ownership, as we have seen, is the natural right of man; and to exercise that right, especially as members of society, is not only lawful, but absolutely necessary. "It is lawful," says St. Thomas of Aquin, "for a man to hold private property; and it is also necessary for the carrying on of human existence."[7] But if the question be asked, How must one's possessions be used? the Church replies without hesitation in the words of the same holy Doctor: "Man should not consider his outward possessions as his own, but as common to all, so as to share them without hesitation when others are in need. Whence the Apostle saith, Command the rich of this world . . . to offer with no stint, to apportion largely."[8] True, no one is commanded to distribute to others that which is required for his own needs and those of his household; nor even to give away what is reasonably required to keep up becomingly his condition in life; "for no one ought to live other than becomingly."[9] But when what necessity demands has been supplied, and one's standing fairly taken thought for, it becomes a duty to give to the indigent out of what remains over. *Of that which remaineth, give alms.*[10] It is a duty, not of justice (save in extreme cases), but of Christian charity—a duty not enforced by human law. But the laws and judgments of men must yield place to the laws and judgments of Christ the true God, who in many ways urges on His followers the practice of almsgiving—*It is more blessed to give than to receive;* [11] and who will count a kindness done or refused to the poor as done or refused to Himself—*As long as you did it to one of My least brethren,*

[3] 2 Tim. ii. 12.
[4] 2 Cor. iv. 17.
[5] St. Matt. xix. 23, 24.
[6] St. Luke vi. 24, 25.

[7] 2a 2æ Q. lxvi. Art. 2.
[8] Ibid. Q. lxv. Art. 2.
[9] Ibid. Q. xxxii. Art. 6.
[10] St. Luke xi. 41.
[11] Acts xx. 35.

you *did it to Me*.[12] To sum up, then, what has been said: Whoever has received from the divine bounty a large share of temporal blessings, whether they be external and corporeal, or gifts of the mind, has received them for the purpose of using them for the perfecting of his own nature, and, at the same time, that he may employ them, as the steward of God's providence, for the benefit of others. "He that hath a talent," says St. Gregory the Great, "let him see that he hide it not; he that hath abundance, let him quicken himself to mercy and generosity; he that hath art and skill, let him do his best to share the use and the utility thereof with his neighbor." [13]

As for those who possess not the gifts of fortune, they are taught by the Church that in God's sight poverty is no disgrace, and that there is nothing to be ashamed of in seeking one's bread by labor. This is enforced by what we see in Christ Himself, who *whereas He was rich, for our sakes became poor;* [14] and who, being the Son of God, and God Himself, chose to seem and to be considered the son of a carpenter—nay, did not disdain to spend a great part of His life as a carpenter Himself. *Is not this the carpenter, the son of Mary?* [15] From contemplation of this divine exemplar, it is more easy to understand that the true worth and nobility of man lies in his moral qualities, that is, in virtue; that virtue is moreover the common inheritance of men, equally within the reach of high and low, rich and poor; and that virtue, and virtue alone, wherever found, will be followed by the rewards of everlasting happiness. Nay, God Himself seems to incline rather to those who suffer misfortune; for Jesus Christ calls the poor "blessed";[16] He lovingly invites those in labor and grief to come to Him for solace;[17] and He displays the tenderest charity towards the lowly and the oppressed. These reflections cannot fail to keep down the pride of those who are well to do, and to embolden the spirit of the afflicted; to incline the former to generosity and the latter to meek resignation. Thus the separation which pride would set up tends to disappear, nor will it be difficult to make rich and poor join hands in friendly concord. . . .

[12] St. Matt. xxv. 40.
[13] St. Gregory the Great, Hom. ix. in Evangel. n. 7.
[14] 2 Cor. viii. 9.

[15] St. Mark vi. 3.
[16] St. Matt. v. 3: Blessed are the poor in spirit.
[17] St. Matt. xi. 28: Come to Me, all you that labor and are burdened, and I will refresh you.

CREDO

Frank W. Abrams

As former chairman of the board of the Standard Oil Company (New Jersey), Frank W. Abrams has contributed as much as any man to the industrial growth of modern America and to peaceful trade relations with the rest of the world. A firm advocate of business freedom, he also preaches the creed of business responsibility. The following article summarizes his business faith.

Every American businessman knows he does not earn his living in an isolated compartment somehow separated from the rest of the life of the nation. He is not just "a businessman." He is first of all a man and an American citizen. His livelihood depends upon his ability, sometimes alone but usually in association, to make a profit out of competing with others who serve the needs of his fellow men. He succeeds most when he serves best the interest of the largest number of people.

For business is but part of a whole— one of the many great threads that make up the fabric of American life. It is the process by which a democratic nation attends to its material well-being and strength. Business has demonstrated the reciprocal benefits of the incentives of freedom: how the dignity and worth and well-being of the individual can be enhanced; how the general welfare can be served; and how business succeeds in the process.

The responsible businessman knows that a free flow of innovation, new technology, and improved products is an indispensable requirement of a dynamic society. It is part of his job to stimulate that flow.

He considers competition in products and prices a basic tool of progress. He looks upon limitations and regulations that dull the sharp edge of competition —for whatever reason, by whatever means—as potential or immediate hazards to progress.

He notes that improved transportation and communication are resulting in a shrinking world and he sees an expansion of the business community beyond national boundaries, to the point where national well-being is tied to the well-being of the rest of the world. This requires, in his view, attitudes toward international trade that recognize the necessity for lifting the barriers against an increased flow of trade and for the stimulation of more liberal trade and investment arrangements among nations. Indeed, he begins to feel that perhaps gradual relief from international trade and investment restrictions may be an essential part of the worldwide development of democratic political institutions.

Since business is an activity volun-

From the *Saturday Review*, January 23, 1954. Reprinted by permission.

tarily engaged in by many people for their common benefit, he looks and works toward a better understanding of the mutuality of interest—among owners of business, its managers, its other employes. It seems to him clear that as this understanding is achieved the allegation of class conflict in our society falls to the ground, and with it the fallacious propaganda claims of our authoritarian foes.

He recognizes that mutuality of interest calls for a diligent attention to the security of those associated with an enterprise and for constructive measures to achieve that security within the limits determined by the nature of a business and by factors of personal initiative and effort.

He looks upon voluntary action beyond that of earning a living or taking a profit as a characteristic of free people and a hallmark of American society. He puts a high value on those self-starting activities that result in organizations, committees, and councils to do things that in other countries might be left to government, or left undone. He knows that business benefits by this tradition of voluntary action and sees it as a great bulwark against the encroachment of big government. It seems to him appropriate that business should support, through contributions and otherwise, such voluntary efforts to meet the valid needs of people.

As an American citizen he shares the hope that the United States will always deserve to be regarded as a showcase of the free society in action, moving from achievement to fresh achievement. He sees business as an exhibit in this showcase which displays the superiority of competitive enterprise over any other economic system ever devised for spreading the material benefits of freedom over a whole nation.

He sees business as a means toward an end—in the same way that political institutions, education, and professions are means to an end. That end is making life in a free society better. In fulfilling the functions of business as the means toward the end of a just and decent society he believes that business managers meet their obligations to the ever-growing number of people who are the owners of business.

THE GOLDEN RULE IS STILL GOLDEN

J. C. Penney

Born in 1875, venerable James Cash Penney has lived through some crucial periods in the moral history of American business, but his belief in fair dealing has remained steadfast. With no more than a high school education he built a retail empire, only to have it crumble in the depression of the thirties. Following a fresh start, he is now board chairman of a chain of over 1600 dry goods stores that bear his name.

It is my belief that Golden Rule principles are just as necessary for operating a business profitably as are trucks, typewriters, or twine. Many will deny this and will cite examples seeming to prove that it doesn't pay out. I can do that too.

When I was in my 20's, I purchased a butcher shop in Longmont, Colorado, for $300, which I had saved while going to school and while working at my first job in a store. The best and most profitable customer of the shop was the leading hotel of the city. My meat cutter advised me, "If you want to keep the hotel trade, you will have to buy the chef a bottle of whisky each week. He does the buying."

I accepted the advice, without much thought, and bought the customary bottle of liquor. But after I had done so, a strange feeling came over me. I asked myself, "Were he living today, what would my father say?" Very well I knew the answer—for Father was opposed to the use of intoxicating liquors. And was it fair to my other customers to do for one what I would not do for

them? Obviously not—so I determined then and there that never again would I bribe that cook, or anyone else, to get business.

I lost the trade of the hotel and because of that I also lost the butcher shop and the $300 I had saved penny by penny. Up to that point, practicing the Golden Rule apparently didn't pay out. But I have always been thankful that I did not yield to questionable expediency. Had I done so I might have become a successful butcher, but I would probably never have found my lifework in a wider field.

But I take no credit for that crucial decision. My father was responsible for it. He was a farmer and a preacher. As a very young boy, I had understood that he worked at two different callings, but only gradually did I come to see that my father, in his own mind, did not recognize any real difference between them. He plowed, he planted, he harvested, and he applied his industry with just the same earnestness that he preached his sermon. Thereby he im-

From *The Rotarian*, February, 1947. Reprinted by courtesy of the publisher.

pressed me with the fact that he had one ministry: *to serve.*

That lesson was further impressed on my mind when I got my first job in a retail store. I had an inborn liking for handling and selling things, and my father, just before he passed on and realizing death was near, said, "Jim will make it. I like the way he has started out." I had occasion to think of his words later when other salesmen were taking customers away from me because they could make special prices for a favored few—fixed prices to one and all were not then the custom. I had to deal with men to whom thumb-on-the-scale manipulation was a fine art, misrepresentation of products was cleverness, and dishonest advertising and labelling were "tricks of the trade."

But if "let the buyer beware" was the motto practiced by some businessmen, it was not characteristic of the majority. In these days when so many look to Government to regulate trade practices, we easily forget that businessmen themselves led the way. For every example of shady or fraudulent dealing that has come to my attention in a long career, I can cite scores of examples of manufacturers, wholesalers, and retailers who voluntarily put the Golden Rule to work in their relations with employees, competitors, and customers.

Rotary has reinforced this concept, terming it Vocational Service, but long before Paul Harris founded our organization in 1905, most businessmen both large and small were trying to operate on the principle of "he profits most who serves best." They knew that the fly-by-night, chiseling, fraudulent operators were unfair both to legitimate business and to the public. That is why businessmen have organized into trade groups and why they have taken the lead in creating protective legislation.

A typical example of the latter is the U.S. Pure Food and Drug Act. It was promulgated and urged by businessmen more than 40 years ago. It has had an increasing influence as manufacturers have learned that they must establish a reputation for consistency of quality in pure and unadulterated products, not because it is the law, but because it is to their own self-interest to serve their customers honestly. And they have found the value of advertising such products honestly.

We have made great progress in business practices. If we are to consolidate past gains and to advance, we who are in business must give time and effort, which are not always immediately productive of profits, to the training of our successors. We have this responsibility to the vocation which gives us our livelihood—but we should be glad to do it for the sake of the young men themselves. I sincerely believe that we who employ should build something into a man instead of constantly taking something out of him. So I shall offer this advice:

Do not primarily train men to work. Train them to serve willingly and intelligently.

Do not train men merely to obey orders that they may or may not fully understand. Train them to study the job, to develop perception of what is to be done, then to turn loose upon it their understanding, initiative, and effort.

Do not train men merely to be as your shadow. Train them to bring as much of their ability into action as they can reach, deep down in themselves. Encourage them to believe that there is in themselves a mine pocket full of riches. You can, by your careful and thoughtful training of them, make them wealthy in developed ability.

Countless thousands of men are stranded in business routine. In each one of them may be a latent ability which when developed would be of immeasurable profit to the employer. There seems to be a fatal impression with many businessmen that to hire a man as he is means to keep the man on as he is. But it is wrong to look upon any man as being an immovable, unimprovable human being.

I was fortunate, as a young man, in getting employment with a retail store that advertised itself to be responsible to the customer, not in a general way, but in the specific spirit of the Golden Rule. This was to me inspiring. It generated energies and developed talents which I was called upon to exercise when, after an apprenticeship, I was considered worthy to take over the managership of a store. When I was given the privilege of buying a one-third interest in the store, I discovered that management opened responsibilities that I welcomed as a challenge. I began to take count of my new responsibilities, mastering them as I could. As a result of my study, I reached the conviction that I could master them only in accordance with Golden Rule principles I had seen practiced by my father.

Young men today should have similar opportunities to prove and improve themselves. Employers should train them with a view toward partnership participation in the business they help to create. It is my experience that employees will respond to the stimulus of fairness and liberality. Partnership participation makes a man dig into himself to qualify. He becomes eager to master the technique of a job greater than the one he has.

Developing men brings as much—even more—satisfaction as making profits. H. G. Wells, the late distinguished English author, puts it this way:

"Success has absolutely nothing whatever to do with a man's reputa-

tion, or material possessions, or social prominence.

"True success is the relation between what a man is today (that is what he has finally become) and what he could have become had he made the most of his ability and opportunity through all the years of his working life."

It is an astonishing contrast that Mr. Wells makes in the two conditions: (1) not what any one of us is in the later years of life, but (2) what we *could* have become had we done the utmost with all our ability, understanding, and control directed upon a worth-while ultimate purpose.

This means that a young man starting out can so increase and direct his effort that it will carry him far beyond the usual time of men's retirement. Let me say this of retirement: No man should live a business life of 20 or 30 years and then retire into *nothing*. Along the way he should have provided for himself *something* into which to retire; something worth while as an adventure in benefits and service.

Success in business does not depend upon genius. Any young man of ordinary intelligence who is morally sound and not afraid to work should succeed in spite of obstacles and handicaps if he plays the game fairly and keeps everlastingly at it. When I see a youngster identifying himself so closely with his work that the closing hour passes unheeded, I recognize the beginnings of success. He is doing more than is required of him—that is, more than his employer requires of him, but not more than his conscience requires.

Here are six searching principles which I believe form the essentials of business success. I offer them in the hope that they will be passed on to young men and women just starting their business careers:

1. *Be prepared.* Know all about your business—a little more than anyone else

knows. You will, as a rule, achieve what you are prepared for.

2. *Work hard.* The only kind of luck that you are justified in banking on is that based on hard work. This means sacrifice, persistent effort, and dogged determination. Growth is never by chance; it is the result of effort.

3. *Be honest.* By this I mean the finer honesty of purpose that will not allow you to give less than your best; that will make you count not your hours, but your duties and opportunities; that constantly urges you to enlarge your information and to increase your efficiency.

4. *Have confidence in men.* A man's value increases when he receives responsibility and feels that he is being relied upon. One must exercise commonsense and good business judgment, of course, but believing in your self and trusting in your fellowman pay off.

5. *Appeal to the spirit in man.* One of the wisest men who ever lived said, "The letter killeth, but the spirit giveth life." Every organization in which I have been associated has proved that if its members are motivated by an indomitable desire to succeed, the organization will succeed.

6. *Practice the Golden Rule.* It sums up all I have said—and here it is as it was enunciated on the hillsides of Judea nearly 2,000 years ago: "*Therefore all things whatsoever ye would that men should do to you, do ye even so to them.*"

Exercises

"Ethics in a Business Civilization," by Marquis W. Childs and Douglass Cater

1. Sum up briefly the attitude of the Church toward the businessman in the Middle Ages.
2. Discuss the modern attitude toward moneylending.
3. Discuss the present attitude toward the middleman as opposed to that which prevailed in the Middle Ages.
4. Write a humorous theme about the small-loan business. You may call it, "Do You Need Money?"
5. Take a moral position on installment buying and build a theme on it. Treat the subject lightly if you wish.
6. Explain the phrase, ". . . the credo of individualism has worn a little thin." Can you give any current examples such as those Professor Bloom (page 264) might have had in mind?
7. Explain the statement, made near the end of this article, "Without the frame of reference afforded by the religious and ethical inheritance of the past, the laissez-faire system might well have degenerated into chaos and violence."
8. What is a shibboleth? With the help of your dictionary and the Bible, write a theme on the subject. Give some modern examples.

"The Condition of the Working Classes," by Pope Leo XIII

1. Write a paragraph summing up Leo XIII's justification of private property.
2. What is the Papal argument against socialism?
3. Define and discuss the proper relationship between laborer and employer as stated in this paper.
4. Explain the distinction made between the right to possess wealth and the right to use it. What responsibilities does private property entail?
5. What consolation does the Pope offer the worker? Explain briefly.

"Credo," by Frank W. Abrams

1. Define and explain the term "credo."
2. State Frank Abrams' credo in a single sentence.
3. The author states that competition in products and prices is a basic tool of progress. Discuss this point, contributing your own examples.
4. Discuss some of the obstacles to the fulfillment of the author's wish for relief from restrictions on international trade.
5. What does the author mean by his statement (seventh paragraph) about "mutuality of interest"? Explain.
6. Discuss Mr. Abrams' theory of voluntary action (eighth paragraph).
7. Discuss Mr. Abrams' credo as an expression of democratic thought.
8. From what you have observed of business and businessmen, would you say that the business credo expressed by Mr. Abrams is generally observed? Explain and support your position.
9. Write a credo for the worker.
10. Write a credo for the college student.

"The Golden Rule Is Still Golden," by J. C. Penney

1. See the last sentence in this article. Restate the Golden Rule in simple, modern English.

2. Do you believe, as Mr. Penney does, that "he profits most who serves best"? Suppose honesty did not pay? Express your views in a theme on the Golden Rule.

3. Select examples of ethical business or advertising practices that have especially impressed you. Write a theme of commendation.

4. Describe some of the questionable business practices of today.

5. Write an indictment of shady advertising, making specific references to current publication advertisements or television commercials.

6. From your reading and observation, would you say that modern business as a rule does develop its people and give them opportunities for advancement? Discuss.

7. Mr. Penney quotes H. G. Wells's definition of success. Would the same definition apply to success in college? Explain your views.

8. Mr. Penney says, "Any young man of ordinary intelligence who is morally sound and not afraid to work should succeed in spite of handicaps if he plays the game fairly and keeps everlastingly at it." Do you agree? Write a theme on the subject. You may wish to consult the articles in Section 1.

9. Write a theme giving your views of the six "searching principles" Mr. Penney considers essential to business success.

10. With the advantage of the brief biography in this article and in the editor's introduction, try to explain how Mr. Penney came by various parts of his business philosophy.

11. Find out what you can about the National Better Business Bureau and write a report on the subject.

8

The Businessman in American Literature

Whatever hero the businessman may be in the pages of the *Wall Street Journal*, he has—deservedly or not—suffered outrageously at the hands of American novelists. William Dean Howells, it is true, was able to avoid the stereotypes and depict Silas Lapham as a flesh-and-blood businessman, although a financial failure in the end. But Howells set no fashion. Frank Norris, Sinclair Lewis, and John Dos Passos are only a few of his successors who show businessmen at their materialistic worst.

Lately, however, the fictional businessman has had a change of fortune. Perhaps the reason is that businessmen themselves have taken to writing novels. Cameron Hawley, Richard Bissell, W. H. Prosser, Louis Auchincloss, and Lawrence Schoonover belong in this category. Their business people consistently move as human beings against realistic business backgrounds. In the following pages the reader will meet four well-known businessmen in American literature.

THE RISE OF SILAS LAPHAM
William Dean Howells

William Dean Howells will probably never achieve stature as a major American novelist, but he has the distinction of being among the first to treat the American businessman with realism. Silas Lapham is not vulgar perhaps, but commonplace. Yet, as the story unfolds, he proves to be—in spite of his social aspirations—honest, and even sensitive. In the part that follows, the reader sees Lapham before family and business troubles have come to test his character.

When Bartley Hubbard went to interview Silas Lapham for the "Solid Men of Boston" series, which he undertook to finish up in *The Events*, after he replaced their original projector on that newspaper, Lapham received him in his private office by previous appointment.

"Walk right in!" he called out to the journalist, whom he caught sight of through the door of the counting-room.

He did not rise from the desk at which he was writing, but he gave Bartley his left hand for welcome, and he rolled his large head in the direction of a vacant chair. "Sit down! I'll be with you in just half a minute."

"Take your time," said Bartley, with the ease he instantly felt. "I'm in no hurry."He took a note-book from his pocket, laid it on his knee, and began to sharpen a pencil.

"There!" Lapham pounded with his great hairy fist on the envelope he had been addressing. "William!" he called out, and he handed the letter to a boy who came to get it. "I want that to go right away. Well, sir," he continued, wheeling round in his leather-cushioned swivel-chair, and facing Bartley, seated so near that their knees almost touched, "so you want my life, death, and Christian sufferings, do you, young man?"

"That's what I'm after," said Bartley. "Your money or your life."

"I guess you wouldn't want my life without the money," said Lapham, as if he were willing to prolong these moments of preparation.

"Take 'em both," Bartley suggested. "Don't want your money without your life, if you come to that. But you're just one million times more interesting to the public than if you hadn't a dollar; and you know that as well as I do, Mr. Lapham. There's no use beating about the bush."

"No," said Lapham, somewhat absently. He put out his huge foot and pushed the ground-glass door shut between his little den and the book-keepers, in their larger den outside.

"In personal appearance," wrote Bartley in the sketch for which he now

From *The Rise of Silas Lapham* by William Dean Howells. First published in book form in 1885.

studied his subject, while he waited patiently for him to continue, "Silas Lapham is a fine type of the successful American. He has a square, bold chin, only partially concealed by the short reddish-grey beard, growing to the edges of his firmly closing lips. His nose is short and straight; his forehead good, but broad rather than high; his eyes blue, and with a light in them that is kindly or sharp according to his mood. He is of medium height, and fills an average arm-chair with a solid bulk, which on the day of our interview was unpretentiously clad in a business suit of blue serge. His head droops somewhat from a short neck, which does not trouble itself to rise far from a pair of massive shoulders."

"I don't know as I know just where you want me to begin," said Lapham.

"Might begin with your birth; that's where most of us begin," replied Bartley.

A gleam of humorous appreciation shot into Lapham's blue eyes.

"I didn't know whether you wanted me to go quite so far back as that," he said. "But there's no disgrace in having been born, and I was born in the State of Vermont, pretty well up under the Canada line—so well up, in fact, that I came very near being an adoptive citizen; for I was bound to be an American of some sort, from the word Go! That was about—well, let me see!—pretty near sixty years ago: this is '75, and that was '20. Well, say I'm fifty-five years old; and I've lived 'em too; not an hour of waste time about me, anywheres! I was born on a farm, and—"

"Worked in the fields summers and went to school winters: regulation thing?" Bartley cut in.

"Regulation thing," said Lapham, accepting this irreverent version of his history somewhat dryly.

"Parents poor, of course," suggested the journalist. "Any barefoot business? Early deprivations of any kind, that would encourage the youthful reader to go and do likewise? Orphan myself, you know," said Bartley, with a smile of cynical good-comradery.

Lapham looked at him silently, and then said with quiet self-respect, "I guess if you see these things as a joke, my life won't interest you."

"Oh yes, it will," returned Bartley, unabashed. "You'll see; it'll come out all right." And in fact it did so, in the interview which Bartley printed.

"Mr. Lapham," he wrote, "passed rapidly over the story of his early life, its poverty and its hardships, sweetened, however, by the recollections of a devoted mother, and a father who, if somewhat her inferior in education, was no less ambitious for the advancement of his children. They were quiet, unpretentious people, religious, after the fashion of that time, and of sterling morality, and they taught their children the simple virtue of the Old Testament and Poor Richard's Almanac."

Bartley could not deny himself this gibe; but he trusted to Lapham's unliterary habit of mind for his security in making it, and most other people would consider it sincere reporter's rhetoric.

"You know," he explained to Lapham, "that we have to look at all these facts as material, and we get the habit of classifying them. Sometimes a leading question will draw out a whole line of facts that a man himself would never think of." He went on to put several queries, and it was from Lapham's answers that he generalised the history of his childhood. "Mr. Lapham, although he did not dwell on his boyish trials and struggles, spoke of them with deep feeling and an abiding sense of their reality." This was what he added in the interview, and by the time he had got Lapham past the period where risen Americans are all pathetically alike in their narrow circumstances, their sufferings, and their aspirations, he had beguiled him into forgetfulness of the check he had received, and had him talking again in perfect enjoyment of his autobiography.

"Yes, sir," said Lapham, in a strain which Bartley was careful not to interrupt again, "a man never sees all that his mother has been to him till it's too late to let her know that he sees it. Why, my mother—" he stopped. "It gives me a lump in the throat," he said apologetically, with an attempt at a laugh. Then he went on: "She was a little, frail thing, not bigger than a good-sized intermediate school-girl; but she did the whole work of a family of boys, and boarded the hired men besides. She cooked, swept, washed, ironed, made and mended from daylight till dark— and from dark till daylight, I was going to say; for I don't know how she got any time for sleep. But I suppose she did. She got time to go to church, and to teach us to read the Bible, and to misunderstand it in the old way. She was good. But it ain't her on her knees in church that comes back to me so much like the sight of an angel as her on her knees before me at night, washing my poor, dirty little feet, that I'd run bare in all day, and making me decent for bed. There were six of us boys; it seems to me we were all of a size; and she was just so careful with all of us. I can feel her hands on my feet yet!" Bartley looked at Lapham's No. 10 boots, and softly whistled through his teeth. "We were patched all over; but we wa'n't ragged. I don't know how she got through it. She didn't seem to think it was anything; and I guess it was no more than my father expected of her. He worked like a horse in doors and out—up at daylight, feeding the stock, and groaning round all day with his rheumatism, but not stopping."

Bartley hid a yawn over his note-book, and probably, if he could have spoken his mind, he would have suggested to Lapham that he was not there for the purpose of interviewing his ancestry. But Bartley had learned to practice a patience with his victims which he did not always feel, and to feign an interest in their digressions till he could bring them up with a round turn.

"I tell you," said Lapham, jabbing the point of his penknife into the writing-pad on the desk before him, "when I hear women complaining nowadays that their lives are stunted and empty, I want to tell 'em about my mother's life. I could paint it out for 'em."

Bartley saw his opportunity at the word paint, and cut in. "And you say, Mr. Lapham, that you discovered this mineral paint on the old farm yourself?"

Lapham acquiesced in the return to business. "I didn't discover it," he said scrupulously. "My father found it one day, in a hole made by a tree blowing down. There it was, lying loose in the pit, and sticking to the roots that had pulled up a big cake of dirt with 'em. I don't know what give him the idea that there was money in it, but he did think so from the start. I guess, if they'd had the word in those days, they'd considered him pretty much of a crank about it. He was trying as long as he lived to get that paint introduced; but he couldn't make it go. The country was so poor they couldn't paint their houses with anything; and father hadn't any facilities. It got to be a kind of joke with us; and I guess that paint-mine did as much as any one thing to make us boys clear out as soon as we got old enough. All my brothers went West, and took up land; but I hung on to New England, and I hung on to the old farm, not because the paint-mine was on it, but because the old house was— and the graves. Well," said Lapham, as if unwilling to give himself too much credit, "there wouldn't been any market for it, anyway. You go through that part of the State and buy more farms than you can shake a stick at for less money than it cost to build the barns on 'em. Of course, it's turned out a good thing. I keep the old house up in good shape, and we spend a month or so there every summer. M'wife kind of likes it, and the girls. Pretty place; sightly all round it. I've got a force of men at work there the whole time, and I've got a man and his wife in the house. Had a family meeting there last year; the whole connection from out West. There!" Lapham rose from his seat and took down a large warped, unframed photograph from the top of his desk, passing his hand over it, and then blowing vigorously upon it, to clear it of the dust. "There we are, all of us."

"I don't need to look twice at you," said Bartley, putting his finger on one of the heads.

"Well, that's Bill," said Lapham, with a gratified laugh. "He's about as brainy as any of us, I guess. He's one of their leading lawyers, out Dubuque way; been judge of the Common Pleas once or twice. That's his son—just graduated at Yale—alongside of my youngest girl. Good-looking chap, ain't he?"

"She's a good-looking chap," said Bartley, with prompt irreverence. He hastened to add, at the frown which gathered between Lapham's eyes, "What a beautiful creature she is! What a lovely, refined, sensitive face! And she looks good, too."

"She is good," said the father, relenting.

"And, after all, that's about the best thing in a woman," said the potential reprobate. "If my wife wasn't good enough to keep both of us straight, I don't know what would become of me."

"My other daughter," said Lapham,

indicating a girl with eyes that showed large, and a face of singular gravity. "Mis' Lapham," he continued, touching his wife's effigy with his little finger. "My brother Willard and his family—farm at Kankakee. Hazard Lapham and his wife—Baptist preacher in Kansas. Jim and his three girls—milling business at Minneapolis. Ben and his family—practising medicine in Fort Wayne."

The figures were clustered in an irregular group in front of an old farmhouse, whose original ugliness had been smartened up with a coat of Lapham's own paint, and heightened with an incongruous piazza. The photographer had not been able to conceal the fact that they were all decent, honest-looking, sensible people, with a very fair share of beauty among the young girls; some of these were extremely pretty, in fact. He had put them into awkward and constrained attitudes, of course; and they all looked as if they had the instrument of torture which photographers call a head-rest under their occiputs. Here and there an elderly lady's face was a mere blur; and some of the younger children had twitched themselves into wavering shadows, and might have passed for spirit-photographs of their own little ghosts. It was the standard family-group photograph, in which most Americans have figured at some time or other; and Lapham exhibited a just satisfaction in it. "I presume," he mused aloud, as he put it back on top of his desk, "that we sha'n't soon get together again, all of us."

"And you say," suggested Bartley, "that you stayed right along on the old place, when the rest cleared out West?"

"No-o-o-o," said Lapham, with a long, loud drawl; "I cleared out West too, first off. Went to Texas. Texas was all the cry in those days. But I got enough of the Lone Star in about three months, and I come back with the idea that Vermont was good enough for me."

"Fatted calf business?" queried Bartley, with his pencil poised above his note-book.

"I presume they were glad to see me," said Lapham, with dignity. "Mother," he added gently, "died that winter, and I stayed on with father. I buried him in the spring; and then I came down to a little place called Lumberville, and picked up what jobs I could get. I worked round at the saw-mills, and I was ostler a while at the hotel—I always did like a good horse. Well, I wa'n't exactly a college graduate, and I went to school odd times. I got to driving the stage after while, and by and by I bought the stage and run the business myself. Then I hired the tavern-stand, and—well to make a long story short, then I got married. Yes," said Lapham, with pride, "I married the school-teacher. We did pretty well with the hotel, and my wife she was always at me to paint up. Well, I put it off, and put it off, as a man will, till one day I give in, and says I, 'Well, let's paint up. Why, Pert,'—m'wife's name's Persis,—'I've got a whole paint-mine out on the farm. Let's go out and look at it.' So we drove out. I'd let the place for seventy-five dollars a year to a shif'less kind of a Kanuck that had come down that way; and I'd hated to see the house with him in it; but we drove out one Saturday afternoon, and we brought back about a bushel of the stuff in the buggy-seat, and I tried it crude, and I tried it burnt; and I liked it. M'wife she liked it too. There wa'n't any painter by trade in the village, and I mixed it myself. Well, sir, that tavern's got that coat of paint on it yet, and it hain't ever had any other, and I don't know's it ever will. Well, you know, I felt as if it was a kind of harum-scarum experiment, all the while; and I presume I shouldn't have tried it, but

I kind of liked to do it because father'd always set so much store by his paint-mine. And when I'd got the first coat on,"—Lapham called it cut,—"I presume I must have set as much as half an hour, looking at it and thinking how he would have enjoyed it. I've had my share of luck in this world, and I ain't a-going to complain on my own account, but I've noticed that most things get along too late for most people. It made me feel bad, and it took all the pride out of my success with the paint, thinking of father. Seemed to me I might 'a taken more interest in it when he was by to see; but we've got to live and learn. Well, I called my wife out,— I'd tried it on the back of the house, you know,—and she left her dishes,—I can remember she came out with her sleeves rolled up and set down alongside of me on the trestle,—and says I, 'What do you think, Persis?' And says she, 'well, you hain't got a paint-mine, Silas Lapham; you've got a gold-mine.' She always was just so enthusiastic about things. Well, it was just after two or three boats had burnt up out West, and a lot of lives lost, and there was a great cry about non-inflammable paint, and I guess that was what was in her mind. 'Well, I guess it ain't any gold-mine, Persis,' says I; 'but I guess it is a paint-mine. I'm going to have it analysed, and if it turns out what I think it is, I'm going to work it. And if father hadn't had such a long name, I should call it the Nehemiah Lapham Mineral Paint. But, any rate, every barrel of it, and every keg, and every bottle, and every package, big or little, has got to have the initials and figures N. L. f. 1835, S. L. t. 1855, on it. Father found it in 1835, and I tried it in 1855.'"

"'S.T.—1860—X.' business," said Bartley.

"Yes," said Lapham, "but I hadn't heard of Plantation Bitters then, and I hadn't seen any of the fellow's labels. I set to work and I got a man down from Boston; and I carried him out to the farm, and he analysed it—made a regular job of it. Well, sir, we built a kiln, and we kept a lot of that paint-ore redhot for forty-eight hours; kept the Kanuck and his family up, firing. The presence of iron in the ore showed with the magnet from the start; and when he came to test it, he found out that it contained about seventy-five per cent. of the peroxide of iron."

Lapham pronounced the scientific phrases with a sort of reverent satisfaction, as if awed through his pride by a little lingering uncertainty as to what peroxide was. He accented it as if it were purr-ox-eyed; and Bartley had to get him to spell it.

"Well, and what then?" he asked, when he had made a note of the percentage.

"What then?" echoed Lapham. "Well, then, the fellow set down and told me, 'You've got a paint here,' says he, 'that's going to drive every other mineral paint out of the market. Why,' says he, 'it'll drive 'em right into the Back Bay!' Of course, I didn't know what the Back Bay was then; but I begun to open my eyes; thought I'd had 'em open before, but I guess I hadn't. Says he, 'That paint has got hydraulic cement in it, and it can stand fire and water and acids'; he named over a lot of things. Says he, 'It'll mix easily with linseed oil, whether you want to use it boiled or raw; and it ain't a-going to crack nor fade any; and it ain't a-going to scale. When you've got your arrangements for burning it properly, you're going to have a paint that will stand like the everlasting hills, in every climate under the sun.' Then he went into a lot of particulars, and I begun to think he was drawing a long-bow, and meant to make his bill accordingly. So I kept pretty cool; but the fellow's bill didn't amount to anything

hardly—said I might pay him after I got going; young chap, and pretty easy; but every word he said was gospel. Well, I ain't a-going to brag up my paint; I don't suppose you came here to hear me blow—"

"Oh yes, I did," said Bartley. "That's what I want. Tell all there is to tell, and I can boil it down afterward. A man can't make a greater mistake with a reporter than to hold back anything out of modesty. It may be the very thing we want to know. What we want is the whole truth; and more; we've got so much modesty of our own that we can temper almost any statement."

Lapham looked as if he did not quite like this tone, and he resumed a little more quietly. "Oh, there isn't really very much more to say about the paint itself. But you can use it for almost anything where a paint is wanted, inside or out. It'll prevent decay, and it'll stop it, after it's begun, in tin or iron. You can paint the inside of a cistern or a bathtub with it, and water won't hurt it; and you can paint a steam-boiler with it, and heat won't. You can cover a brick wall with it, or a railroad car, or the deck of a steamboat, and you can't do a better thing for either."

"Never tried it on the human conscience, I suppose," suggested Bartley.

"No, sir," replied Lapham gravely. "I guess you want to keep that as free from paint as you can, if you want much use of it. I never cared to try any of it on mine." Lapham suddenly lifted his bulk up out of his swivel-chair, and led the way out into the wareroom beyond the office partitions, where rows and ranks of casks, barrels, and kegs stretched dimly back to the rear of the building, and diffused an honest, clean, wholesome smell of oil and paint. They were labelled and branded as containing each so many pounds of Lapham's Mineral Paint, and each bore the mystic devices, *N. L. f.* 1835–*S. L. t.* 1855. "There!" said Lapham, kicking one of the largest casks with the toe of his boot, "that's about our biggest package; and here," he added, laying his hand affectionately on the head of a very small keg, as if it were the head of a child, which it resembled in size, "this is the smallest. We used to put the paint on the market dry, but now we grind every ounce of it in oil—very best quality of linseed oil—and warrant it. We find it gives more satisfaction. Now, come back to the office, and I'll show you our fancy brands."

It was very cool and pleasant in that dim wareroom, with the rafters showing overhead in a cloudy perspective, and darkening away into the perpetual twilight at the rear of the building; and Bartley had found an agreeable seat on the head of a half-barrel of the paint, which he was reluctant to leave. But he rose and followed the vigorous lead of Lapham back to the office, where the sun of a long summer afternoon was just beginning to glare in at the window. On shelves opposite Lapham's desk were tin cans of various sizes, arranged in tapering cylinders, and showing, in a pattern diminishing toward the top, the same label borne by the casks and barrels in the wareroom. Lapham merely waved his hand toward these; but when Bartley, after a comprehensive glance at them, gave his whole attention to a row of clean, smooth jars, where different tints of the paint showed through flawless glass, Lapham smiled, and waited in pleased expectation.

"Hello!" said Bartley. "That's pretty!"

"Yes," assented Lapham, "it is rather nice. It's our latest thing, and we find it takes with customers first-rate. Look here!" he said, taking down one of the jars, and pointing to the first line of the label.

Bartley read, "THE PERSIS BRAND," and then he looked at Lapham and smiled.

"After *her*, of course," said Lapham. "Got it up and put the first of it on the market her last birthday. She was pleased."

"I should think she might have been," said Bartley, while he made a note of the appearance of the jars.

"I don't know about your mentioning it in your interview," said Lapham dubiously.

"That's going into the interview, Mr. Lapham, if nothing else does. Got a wife myself, and I know just how you feel." It was in the dawn of Bartley's prosperity on the *Boston Events*, before his troubles with Marcia had seriously begun.

"Is that so?" said Lapham, recognising with a smile another of the vast majority of married Americans; a few underrate their wives, but the rest think them supernal in intelligence and capability. "Well," he added, "we must see about that. Where'd you say you lived?"

"We don't live; we board. Mrs. Nash, 13 Canary Place."

"Well, we've all got to commence that way," suggested Lapham consolingly.

"Yes; but we've about got to the end of our string. I expect to be under a roof of my own on Clover Street before long. I suppose," said Bartley, returning to business, "that you didn't let the grass grow under your feet much after you found out what was in your paint-mine?"

"No, sir," answered Lapham, withdrawing his eyes from a long stare at Bartley, in which he had been seeing himself a young man again, in the first days of his married life. "I went right back to Lumberville and sold out everything, and put all I could rake and scrape together into paint. And Mis'

Lapham was with me every time. No hang back about *her*. I tell you she was a *woman!*"

Bartley laughed. "That's the sort most of us marry."

"No, we don't," said Lapham. "Most of us marry silly little girls grown up to *look* like women."

"Well, I guess that's about so," assented Bartley, as if upon second thought.

"If it hadn't been for her," resumed Lapham, "the paint wouldn't have come to anything. I used to tell her it wa'n't the seventy-five per cent. of purr-ox-eyed of iron in the *ore* that made that paint go; it was the seventy-five per cent. of purr-ox-eyed of iron in *her.*"

"Good!" cried Bartley. "I'll tell Marcia that."

"In less'n six months there wa'n't a board-fence, nor a bridge-girder, nor a dead wall, nor a barn, nor a face of rock in that whole region that didn't have 'Lapham's Mineral Paint—Specimen' on it in the three colours we begun by making." Bartley had taken his seat on the window-sill, and Lapham, standing before him, now put up his huge foot close to Bartley's thigh; neither of them minded that.

"I've heard a good deal of talk about that S. T.—1860—X. man, and the stove-blacking man, and the kidney-cure man, because they advertised in that way; and I've read articles about it in the papers; but I don't see where the joke comes in, exactly. So long as the people that own the barns and fences don't object, I don't see what the public has got to do with it. And I never saw anything so very sacred about a big rock, along a river or in a pasture, that it wouldn't do to put mineral paint on it in three colours. I wish some of the people that talk about the landscape, and *write* about it, had to bu'st one of them rocks *out* of the landscape with

powder, or dig a hole to bury it in, as we used to have to do up on the farm; I guess they'd sing a little different tune about the profanation of scenery. There ain't any man enjoys a sightly bit of nature—a smooth piece of interval with half a dozen good-sized wineglass elms in it—more than *I* do. But I ain't a-going to stand up for every big ugly rock I come across, as if we were all a set of dumn Druids. I say the landscape was made for man, and not man for the landscape."

"Yes," said Bartley carelessly; "it was made for the stovepolish man and the kidney-cure man."

"It was made for any man that knows how to use it," Lapham returned, insensible to Bartley's irony. "Let 'em go and live with nature in the *winter*, up there along the Canada line, and I guess they'll get enough of her for one while. Well—where was I?"

"Decorating the landscape," said Bartley.

"Yes, sir; I started right there at Lumberville, and it give the place a start too. You won't find it on the map now; and you won't find it in the gazetteer. I give a pretty good lump of money to build a town-hall, about five years back, and the first meeting they held in it they voted to change the name,—Lumberville *wa'n't* a name,—and it's Lapham now."

"Isn't it somewhere up in that region that they get the old Brandon red?" asked Bartley.

"We're about ninety miles from Brandon. The Brandon's a good paint," said Lapham conscientiously. "Like to show you round up at our place some odd time, if you get off."

"Thanks. I should like it first-rate. Works there?"

"Yes; works there. Well, sir, just about the time I got started, the war broke out; and it knocked my paint higher than a kite. The thing dropped perfectly dead. I presume that if I'd had any sort of influence, I might have got it into Government hands, for gun-carriages and army wagons, and may be on board Government vessels. But I hadn't, and we had to face the music. I was about broken-hearted, but m'wife she looked at it another way. 'I guess it's a providence,' says she. 'Silas, I guess you've got a country that's worth fighting for. Any rate, you better go out and give it a chance.' Well, sir, I went. I knew she meant business. It might kill her to have me go, but it would kill her sure if I stayed. She was one of that kind. I went. Her last words was, 'I'll look after the paint, Si.' We hadn't but just one little girl then,—boy'd died, —and Mis' Lapham's mother was livin' with us; and I knew if times did any-ways come up again, m'wife 'd know just what to do. So I went. I got through; and you can call me Colonel, if you want to. Feel there!" Lapham took Bartley's thumb and forefinger and put them on a bunch in his leg, just above the knee. "Anything hard?"

"Ball?"

Lapham nodded. "Gettysburg. That's my thermometer. If it wa'n't for that, I shouldn't know enough to come in when it rains."

Bartley laughed at a joke which be-trayed some evidences of wear. "And when you came back, you took hold of the paint and rushed it."

"I took hold of the paint and rushed it—all I could," said Lapham, with less satisfaction than he had hitherto shown in his autobiography. "But I found that I had got back to another world. The day of small things was past, and I don't suppose it will ever come again in this country. My wife was at me all the time to take a partner—somebody with capital; but I couldn't seem to bear the idea. That paint was like my own blood to me. To have anybody else concerned in it was like—well, I don't know what.

I saw it was the thing to do; but I tried to fight it off, and I tried to joke it off. I used to say, 'Why didn't you take a partner yourself, Persis, while I was away?' And she'd say, 'Well, if you hadn't come back, I should, Si.' Always did like a joke about as well as any woman I ever saw. Well, I had to come to it. I took a partner." Lapham dropped the bold blue eyes with which he had been till now staring into Bart-ley's face, and the reporter knew that here was a place for asterisks in his interview, if interviews were faithful. "He had money enough," continued Lapham, with a suppressed sigh; "but he didn't know anything about paint. We hung on together for a year or two. And then we quit."

"And he had the experience," sug-gested Bartley, with companionable ease.

"I had some of the experience too," said Lapham, with a scowl; and Bartley divined, through the freemasonry of all who have sore places in their memories, that this was a point which he must not touch again.

"And since that, I suppose, you've played it alone."

"I've played it alone."

"You must ship some of this paint of yours to foreign countries, Colonel?" suggesterd Bartley, putting on a profes-sional air.

"We ship it to all parts of the world. It goes to South America, lots of it. It goes to Australia, and it goes to India, and it goes to China, and it goes to the Cape of Good Hope. It'll stand any climate. Of course, we don't export these fancy brands much. They're for home use. But we're introducing them elsewhere. Here." Lapham pulled open a drawer, and showed Bartley a lot of labels in different languages—Spanish, French, German, and Italian. "We ex-pect to do a good business in all those countries. We've got our agencies in

Cadiz now, and in Paris, and in Hamburg, and in Leghorn. It's a thing that's bound to make its way. Yes, sir. Wherever a man has got a ship, or a bridge, or a dock, or a house, or a car, or a fence, or a pig-pen anywhere in God's universe to paint, that's the paint for him, and he's bound to find it out sooner or later. You pass a ton of that paint dry through a blast-furnace, and you'll get a quarter of a ton of pig-iron. I believe in my paint. I believe it's a blessing to the world. When folks come in, and kind of smell round, and ask me what I mix it with, I always say,

'Well, in the first place, I mix it with *Faith*, and after that I grind it up with the best quality of boiled linseed oil that money will buy.' "

Lapham took out his watch and looked at it, and Bartley perceived that his audience was drawing to a close. " 'F you ever want to run down and take a look at our works, pass you over the road,"—he called it rud,—"and it sha'n't cost you a cent."

"Well, may be I shall, sometime," said Bartley. "Good afternoon, Colonel."

"Good afternoon." . . .

BABBITT

Sinclair Lewis

Sinclair Lewis gave the language a new word when he wrote this novel of a hustling real-estate broker who by his own wistful admission never accomplished anything "except just get along." The American College Dictionary defines *Babbitt* as "a self-satisfied person who conforms readily to middle-class ideas and ideals, esp. of business success." The following excerpt from the book describes Babbitt's philosophy before the hint of doubt began to trouble him.

Babbitt's virtues as a real-estate broker—as the servant of society in the department of finding homes for families and shops for distributors of food— were steadiness and diligence. He was conventionally honest, he kept his records of buyers and sellers complete, he had experience with leases and titles and an excellent memory for prices. His shoulders were broad enough, his voice deep enough, his relish of hearty humor strong enough, to establish him as one of the ruling caste of Good Fellows. Yet his eventual importance to mankind was perhaps lessened by his large and complacent ignorance of all architecture save the types of houses turned out by speculative builders; all landscape gardening save the use of curving roads, grass, and six ordinary shrubs; and all the commonest axioms of economics. He serenely believed that the one purpose of the real-estate business was to make money for George F. Babbitt. True, it was a good advertisement at Boosters' Club lunches, and all the varieties of Annual Banquets to which Good Fellows were invited, to speak sonorously of Unselfish Public Service, the Broker's Obligation to Keep Inviolate the Trust of His Clients, and a thing called Ethics, whose nature was confusing but if you had it you were a High-class Realtor and if you hadn't you were a shyster, a piker, and a fly-by-night. These virtues awakened Confidence, and enabled you to handle Bigger Propositions. But they didn't imply that you were to be impractical and refuse to take twice the value of a house if a buyer was such an idiot that he didn't jew you down on the asking-price.

Babbitt spoke well—and often—at these orgies of commercial righteousness about the "realtor's function as a seer of the future development of the community, and as a prophetic engineer clearing the pathway for inevitable changes"—which meant that a real-estate broker could make money by guessing which way the town would grow. This guessing he called Vision.

In an address at the Boosters' Club

he had admitted, "It is at once the duty and the privilege of the realtor to know everything about his own city and its environs. Where a surgeon is a specialist on every vein and mysterious cell of the human body, and the engineer upon electricity in all its phases, or every bolt of some great bridge majestically arching o'er a mighty flood, the realtor must know his city, inch by inch, and all its faults and virtues."

Though he did know the market-price, inch by inch, of certain districts of Zenith, he did not know whether the police force was too large or too small, or whether it was in alliance with gambling and prostitution. He knew the means of fireproofing buildings and the relation of insurance-rates to fire-proofing, but he did not know how many firemen there were in the city, how they were trained and paid, or how complete their apparatus. He sang eloquently the advantages of proximity of school-buildings to rentable homes, but he did not know—he did not know that it was worth while to know—whether the city schoolrooms were properly heated, lighted, ventilated, furnished; he did not know how the teachers were chosen; and though he chanted "One of the boasts of Zenith is that we pay our teachers adequately," that was because he had read the statement in the *Advocate-Times*. Himself, he could not have given the average salary of teachers in Zenith or anywhere else.

He had heard it said that "conditions" in the County Jail and the Zenith City Prison were not very "scientific"; he had, with indignation at the criticism of Zenith, skimmed through a report in which the notorious pessimist Seneca Doane, the radical lawyer, asserted that to throw boys and young girls into a bull-pen crammed with men suffering from syphilis, delirium tremens, and insanity was not the perfect way of educating them. He

had controverted the report by growling, "Folks that think a jail ought to be a bloomin' Hotel Thornleigh make me sick. If people don't like a jail, let 'em behave 'emselves and keep out of it. Besides, these reform cranks always exaggerate." That was the beginning and quite completely the end of his investigations into Zenith's charities and corrections; and as to the "vice districts" he brightly expressed it, "Those are things that no decent man monkeys with. Besides, smatter fact, I'll tell you confidentially: it's a protection to our daughters and to decent women to have a district where tough nuts can raise cain. Keeps 'em away from our own homes."

As to industrial conditions, however, Babbitt had thought a great deal, and his opinions may be coördinated as follows:

"A good labor union is of value because it keeps out radical unions, which would destroy property. No one ought to be forced to belong to a union, however. All labor agitators who try to force men to join a union should be hanged. In fact, just between ourselves, there oughtn't to be any unions allowed at all; and as it's the best way of fighting the unions, every business man ought to belong to an employers'-association and to the Chamber of Commerce. In union there is strength. So any selfish hog who doesn't join the Chamber of Commerce ought to be forced to."

In nothing—as the expert on whose advice families moved to new neighborhoods to live there for a generation—was Babbitt more splendidly innocent than in the science of sanitation. He did not know a malaria-bearing mosquito from a bat; he knew nothing about tests of drinking water; and in the matters of plumbing and sewage he was as unlearned as he was voluble. He often referred to the excellence of the bathrooms in the houses he sold. He was fond of explaining why it was that no European ever bathed. Some one had told him, when he was twenty-two, that all cesspools were unhealthy, and he still denounced them. If a client impertinently wanted him to sell a house which had a cesspool, Babbitt always spoke about it—before accepting the house and selling it.

When he laid out the Glen Oriole acreage development, when he ironed woodland and dipping meadow into a glenless, orioleless, sunburnt flat prickly with small boards displaying the names of imaginary streets, he righteously put in a complete sewage-system. It made him feel superior; it enabled him to sneer privily at the Martin Lumsen development, Avonlea, which had a cesspool; and it provided a chorus for the full-page advertisements in which he announced the beauty, convenience, cheapness, and superogatory healthfulness of Glen Oriole. The only flaw was that the Glen Oriole sewers had insufficient outlet, so that waste remained in them, not very agreeably, while the Avonlea cesspool was a Waring septic tank.

The whole of the Glen Oriole project was a suggestion that Babbitt, though he really did hate men recognized as swindlers, was not too unreasonably honest. Operators and buyers prefer that brokers should not be in competition with them as operators and buyers themselves, but attend to their clients' interests only. It was supposed that the Babbitt-Thompson Company were merely agents for Glen Oriole, serving the real owner, Jake Offutt, but the fact was that Babbitt and Thompson owned sixty-two per cent. of the Glen, the president and purchasing agent of the Zenith Street Traction Company owned twenty-eight per cent., and

Jake Offutt (a gang-politician, a small manufacturer, a tobacco-chewing old farceur who enjoyed dirty politics, business diplomacy, and cheating at poker) had only ten per cent., which Babbitt and the Traction officials had given to him for "fixing" health inspectors and fire inspectors and a member of the State Transportation Commission.

But Babbitt was virtuous. He advocated, though he did not practise, the prohibition of alcohol; he praised, though he did not obey, the laws against motor-speeding; he paid his debts; he contributed to the church, the Red Cross, and the Y.M.C.A.; he followed the custom of his clan and cheated only as it was sanctified by precedent; and he never descended to trickery—though, as he explained to Paul Riesling:

"Course I don't mean to say that every ad I write is literally true or that I always believe everything I say when I give some buyer a good strong selling-spiel. You see—you see it's like this: In the first place, maybe the owner of the property exaggerated when he put it into my hands, and it certainly isn't my place to go proving my principal a liar! And then most folks are so darn crooked themselves that they expect a fellow to do a little lying, so if I was fool enough to never whoop the ante I'd get the credit for lying anyway! In self-defense I got to toot my own horn, like a lawyer defending a client—his bounden duty, ain't it, to bring out the poor dub's good points? Why, the Judge himself would bawl out a lawyer that didn't, even if they both knew the guy was guilty! But even so, I don't pad out the truth like Cecil Rountree or Thayer or the rest of these realtors. Fact, I think a fellow that's willing to deliberately up and profit by lying ought to be shot!"

EXECUTIVE SUITE

Cameron Hawley

When Avery Bullock drops dead, there develops a battle for the succession to the presidency of the Tredway Corporation. In the scene that is reprinted below, Don Walling wins, but not before engaging in an illuminating discussion of what men and corporations work for. Cameron Hawley—himself a former business executive—conveys in these pages something of his own enthusiasm for the creativeness and fierce competition that characterize the business life.

MILLBURGH, PENNSYLVANIA
2.05 P.M. EDT

Mary Walling was acutely conscious of the atmosphere of hair-trigger apprehension that hung over the stiffly seated group in the library of the old Tredway mansion. The conversation that had filled these first few minutes was forced and aimless, without point or purpose. There had been, of course, no open acknowledgment by anyone of what would be decided here this afternoon— and she sensed that there would be no such acknowledgment, even after the decision was made—yet she was sure that all of the others secretly shared her awareness that, before they left this room, the new president of the Tredway Corporation would be selected.

There had been no lessening of Mary Walling's earlier fear that her own happiness would be jeopardized if her husband moved up to the presidency, but that threat had been overbalanced by the later-rising and even more terrifying fear of what the effect on Don might be if he were to lose what he now so clearly regarded as the fulfillment of his own destiny. She knew that he could never be happy now without it—and his happiness was a prerequisite of her own.

The moment she and Don had entered the room, Mary Walling's apprehension had been aroused by the way that Loren Shaw had already preempted a seat beside the desk, as close to Julia Tredway Prince as it was possible for anyone to be. When, a moment later, George Caswell had come in with Erica Martin, Shaw had adroitly maneuvered Caswell into a chair between his own and Dudley's. Thus—partly by accident and partly, she was sure, by Shaw's design—Don now sat alone facing the shoulder-to-shoulder solidarity of Shaw, Caswell and Dudley. She knew that the three had lunched together and it was only too clear that the addition of Julia Tredway Prince's vote was all they needed to make Loren Shaw president. Don had said he was sure of Mrs.

Prince's support, but Mary Walling found it difficult to share her husband's certainty. There had been nothing beyond simple courtesy in the way that Mrs. Prince had greeted Don when they arrived and, during these past few minutes, Loren Shaw had been making the most of his strategic position at Julia Tredway Prince's side.

Feeling herself an outsider—almost an observer with no right of participation—Mary Walling had slipped back into the corner behind her husband. She realized too late that his face was hidden from her view—by then Erica Martin had already taken the chair in the opposite corner—but there was the compensating advantage of being able to watch the room from his viewpoint and to see every glance that was sent in his direction by any of the others.

Of one thing she was now certain—Loren Shaw wasn't thinking of Don as his competitor in the battle for the presidency. The way that Shaw's eyes stabbed toward her husband when Alderson's name had been mentioned by George Caswell made it clear that Shaw regarded Don as only the lieutenant of his real adversary.

"I, too, am sorry that Mr. Alderson isn't here," Julia Tredway Prince said. "You weren't able to locate him, were you, Mr. Walling?"

Don shook his head in silence and Mary Walling wished that she could see his eyes, wondering whether he was aware as she was that Julia Tredway Prince's remark had been the first admission, even by indirection, that there was a purpose behind the invitation that had brought them together—and aware, too, of the implications of Shaw's glance.

If Julia Tredway Prince's remark had really been purposeful, the purpose was quickly abandoned. She turned to George Caswell and again asked a question that seemingly had no point except

to force conversation. "I understand that you flew over, Mr. Caswell?"

"Yes—and quite luxuriously. A friend of mine was good enough to give me the use of his company's plane for the day."

"You know that's getting to be quite a thing," Dudley burst out as if he had withstood the restraint of silence as long as possible, "—all these presidents of big companies having their own private planes. I was on this NAM committee last year—had a meeting down at New Orleans—and three of the big boys came down in their own planes. Man, that would really be the life, having your own plane!"

Shaw cleared his throat. "I should think it might be an extravagance that would be a little difficult to justify to the stockholders."

"Oh, I don't know," Caswell said in mild rebuttal. "There has to be some way to compensate a corporation president adequately these days. It's hardly possible to do it with salary alone, income taxes being what they are."

Julia Tredway Prince looked up at her husband who was lounging against the doorframe. "Dwight and I met a man in Jamaica last winter who had flown down in his own plane. He was the president of some steel company—remember, Dwight?"

Dwight Prince's long face contorted in a forced grin. "Yes, he'd traded a duodenal ulcer for a DC 3—which hardly makes me think he'd gotten the best of it. As a matter of fact—" he hesitated as if he were enjoying the attention he was receiving, "—it's a little difficult for me to understand why any man would want to be the president of a large corporation these days. As far as I'm concerned it's one of the least rewarding forms of suicide."

Mary Walling was not surprised to see Shaw's head snap up and her husband's shoulders square, but she was puzzled by George Caswell's squinting frown.

"Oh, hardly as bad as that," Caswell said, his poise quickly recovered. "In a properly organized corporation, with adequate delegation of authority, there's no reason why the right man should be under too great a strain."

"The right man," Shaw repeated as if it were a point to be driven home. "And it does take the right man these days—a very different type of man than was required in the past."

There was a warning in Shaw's purposeful tone and Mary Walling glanced anxiously at the back of her husband's head. His shoulders were hunched and he seemed to have no interest in anything except his clasped hands.

"I'm not certain that I understand you, Mr. Shaw," Julia Tredway Prince said.

Shaw seemed surprised. "It's the point that I made last evening."

There was something close to shock in Caswell's quick side glance, but Shaw was looking at Mrs. Prince and didn't see it.

"Oh, yes," Mrs. Prince said. "It's quite an interesting theory. You see— well, suppose you explain it to the others, Mr. Shaw."

There was the stillness of tense expectancy and Mary Walling saw Loren Shaw shake out a fresh handkerchief. It was the second time that she had seen him do the same thing during the bare five minutes they had been in the room.

"Well, it's a bit more than a theory," Shaw said. "The point I was making was that—well, there was a time, of course, when most of our company presidents came up on the manufacturing side of the business. In those days that was excellent preparation for general executive responsibility, because most of the problems that came to the president's desk were concerned with

manufacturing. Later, as distribution problems became more important, we sometimes saw a president rise from the sales organization—and again that was quite appropriate. Today, however, we have a very different situation. The problems that come to the president's office are predominantly *financial* in character. Matters concerning manufacturing and distribution are largely handled at lower levels in the organization. The president—who we must always remember is the agent of the stockholders—must now concern himself largely with the primary interest of the stockholders."

"And the typical stockholder isn't interested in anything but dividends?" Julia Tredway Prince asked, more as a prompt than a question.

"Exactly," Shaw said. "Of course you're an exception, Mrs. Prince. You still have what we might call a sense of *ownership*. The average stockholder doesn't think of his stockholdings as ownership—any more than he thinks of himself as the part owner of the bank where he has a savings account—or the part owner of the government because he has some Defense bonds. When he buys Tredway stock he makes an *investment*. The only reason he makes it is to get a return. Thus, at the top level, the corporation must now be governed to be what its owners want it to be—a *financial institution* in which they can invest their money and receive a safe return with the emphasis on *safety*. As a matter of fact—well, you know this, Mr. Caswell—there isn't one stockholder out of ten who could even name the cities where we have our principal factories."

"You're absolutely right," George Caswell said—and the strength of the support that he offered Shaw made Mary Walling feel the hard clutch of despair. "There's no doubt that the emphasis in corporation management has gone over on the financial side. I'm sure that's why it has become so common during these last few years for men to step from investment or banking into corporation management."

Loren Shaw hesitated as if his caution had been aroused, but then quickly went ahead. "Yes, there have been cases like that—where a corporation was so unfortunate as to find itself without a major executive who was trained in financial control and modern management methods. More typically, of course, there's such a man available right within the organization."

It was a direct bid, a challenge, a throwing down of the gauntlet, and Mary Walling's heart sank as she saw that her husband wasn't going to respond. She leaned far forward attempting to see the expression on his face and, looking up, her eyes met Julia Tredway Prince's.

"Oh, Mrs. Walling, you aren't very comfortable there, are you?" Mrs. Prince said quickly. "Won't you come up here?"

It was an invitation that could not be denied and as Mary Walling moved forward Julia Tredway Prince rose from the chair behind the desk and she sat down beside her on the sofa in front of the window.

"I don't know that I get you completely, Loren," Walt Dudley said in a petulant grumble. "I can see that we have to keep the stockholders happy—got to earn a profit—but I don't see how you can say that selling isn't important—or manufacturing either."

"Of course they're important," Shaw said, his voice tinged with the forbearance of a teacher for a not-so-bright pupil. "But don't you see, Walt, they're not ends in themselves, only the means to the end. Then, too, it's a matter of management levels. As I said a moment ago, by the time you get to the presidential level, the emphasis must be pre-

dominantly financial. Take income tax as only one example. To a far greater degree than most people realize, income tax has become a primary governing factor in corporation management. In our own case—well, over the past year I've devoted a substantial amount of time to the development of a new relationship between the parent company and some of our wholly owned subsidiaries in order to give us a more favorable tax situation. Here's the point—that one piece of work, all purely financial in character, will contribute more to our net earnings than the total profit we'll make from one of our smaller factories.

"Take another example—one that I'm sure will interest Mr. Walling. Don and his associates have done a very capable job of reducing cost on our finishing operation at Water Street—producing some very nice savings—but, unfortunately, it will add little to our net earnings, less than a quarter as much as we will gain from a new accounting procedure that I was fortunate enough to get the government to approve in connection with the depreciation of the assets of our lumber company. Do you see what I mean, Walt—that top management has to be largely financial these days?"

Dudley said something and Shaw went on talking, but Mary Walling's ears were blocked with the realization that Don's hopes were blasted. What Shaw said was true. The world was changing. The Bullards were defeated and the Shaws were inheriting the earth. The accountants and the calculators had risen to power. The slide rule had become the scepter. The world was being overrun with the ever-spawning swarm of figure-jugglers who were fly-speckling the earth with their decimal points, proving over and over again that nothing mattered except what could be

proved true by a clerk with a Comp-
tometer.

Julia Tredway Prince cleared her
throat. "Are you suggesting, Mr. Shaw,
that there's no place any more for corporation presidents of Mr. Bullard's
type?"

It was the first mention of Avery
Bullard's name and it came like an unexpected clap of thunder. Every eye in
the room was on Loren Shaw. Even
Don Walling, as Mary noticed gratefully, was watching him sharply.

Shaw was balling his handkerchief in
the palm of his right hand but his voice,
when he spoke after a moment's hesitation, carried no trace of the nervous
tension that his fingers betrayed. "I was
speaking in general terms, of course—
not specifically about the Tredway
Corporation."

"I'd still be interested in having your
viewpoint," Julia Tredway Prince said
pleasantly. "I'm sure the others would,
too."

The handkerchief was a hard ball,
tight-clutched in Shaw's hand, but his
voice was still carefully casual. "No one
can deny that men of Mr. Bullard's type
played a great part in our industrial
past. They belonged to an important
phase of our commercial history. I
would be the first to acknowledge the
great debt that we owe Mr. Bullard for
his leadership in the initial formation
and early development of the Tredway
Corporation."

The way in which Shaw had rele-
gated Avery Bullard to the distant past
was so purposeful that Mary Walling
was certain that Don couldn't have
missed it. She glanced at him and
caught the fading of an odd half-smile
that seemed to recall some memory in
her mind, yet despite the quick frantic
racking of her brain she could not remember when she had seen it before,
nor what special meaning it had in the
lexicon of their intimacy. Then, sud-

denly, she forgot everything else in the
realization that Don was about to speak,
that he was going to fight back. Hope-
less or not, he would make the try! She
knew that the effort might make his
defeat all the more bitter, but that
realization could not dim the elation
that made her heart pound wildly as
she waited for his first words.

"As I get your point, Loren," Don
said, "you're maintaining that Avery
Bullard was the right man to build the
company, but now that the company
has been built we need a different type
of management in order to make the
company produce the maximum
amount of profit for the stockholders."

Mary Walling watched her husband
intently, surprised at his composure.
She had been expecting the flare of
half-anger but his voice was cleanly dis-
passionate.

Shaw, too, seemed surprised, his hesi-
tance betraying his search for a hidden
trap. "I don't know that I'd express it
in exactly those terms—but, yes, that's
substantially what I mean."

An expectant hush had fallen over
the room and George Caswell broke it
by saying nervously, an undertone of
near-embarrassment shading his voice.
"I don't know that this is anything we
have to thresh out here today—too soon
for any of us to see the situation clearly.
After all—" He had glanced at his wrist
watch and suddenly stiffened, his eyes
fixed and staring, and there was a long
pause before he said in a low voice.
"Coincidence, of course—happened to
look at my watch—exactly two-thirty."

Mary saw other blank looks that
matched her own.

"Just twenty-four hours," Caswell
said in whispered explanation. "He died
yesterday at two-thirty."

Mary Walling's heart sank—afraid
that Don had lost his chance, afraid
that the cloud of grief that now shadowed the room could not be broken.

Then she heard Julia Tredway Prince say, "Avery Bullard is dead. Nothing can change that, no matter how long we wait to talk about it."

There was strength in her voice but when she turned Mary saw, in puzzling contrast, that there was a mist of tears in her eyes. She knew now what Julia had done—that she had purposefully saved the situation for Don—and she felt the warmth of a gratitude that was chilled only by the sensing of her own failure in not having been able to do for her husband what another woman had done.

But one thing was now clear. Don had been right about Julia Tredway Prince's support. With her vote and Alderson's, he needed only one more. Where would it come from? Her eyes polled the faces of the three men who sat facing him . . . Shaw, Caswell, and Dudley . . . close-shouldered and resolute. What could Don possibly do to break through the barrier of their tight-woven opposition?

Unexpectedly, it was Dwight Prince who spoke. "I've often wondered about men like Mr. Bullard. He was a great deal like my father, you know—willing to give his whole life to a company—lay everything on the altar like a sacrifice to the god of business. I've often asked myself what drives them to do it—whether they ever stop to ask themselves if what they get is worth the price. I don't suppose they do."

"It's accomplishment that keeps a man going," Dudley said in his sales-meeting voice. "That's what I always tell my boys—it isn't the money that counts, it's that old feeling of accomplishment."

An enigmatic smile narrowed Don Walling's eyes as he looked intently at Loren Shaw. "Going back to this question of the kind of a management that you think the company ought to have from here on out, Loren—the kind of

a management that measures its accomplishment entirely in terms of return to the stockholders. We'd need a strong man to head up that kind of a management, wouldn't we?"

A faint flush warmed Loren Shaw's neck. "Of course."

"And it would be a big job, even for an able man? He'd have to throw himself into it—make a good many personal sacrifices in order to do a job?"

Shaw hesitated, wary and unblinking. "If he were the right man there'd be no worry on that score."

"What incentive would he have?" Don Walling demanded, and for the first time there was the sharp crackle of attack in his voice. "You will grant that there'd have to be an incentive?"

Loren Shaw forced a cold smile. "I'd say that sixty thousand a year might be considered something of an incentive."

"You would?" Don Walling's voice was whiplashed with astonishment. "Do you really think a man of that caliber would be willing to sell his life for money—for what would be left out of sixty thousand a year after tax?"

Dwight Prince's tongue-in-cheek voice cut in unexpectedly. "You could always give him his own plane as a bonus."

The flush on Shaw's neck spread like a seeping stain. "Of course there's more than money involved."

"What?" Don Walling demanded. "What Walt just called a sense of accomplishment? Would that satisfy you, Loren? Just suppose that you were the man—that you were the president of the Tredway Corporation."

Mary Walling's heart stood still as her body stiffened to the shock-wave of what Don had said. She had not expected this . . . that it would be brought out in the open . . . and the taut silence made it plain that the others hadn't expected it either.

Don Walling leaned forward. "Suppose that you were to spend the next twenty years—all the rest of your working life—in doing what you say needs to be done. Would you be satisfied to measure your life's work by how much you had raised the dividend? Would you regard your life as a success if you'd managed to get the dividend up to three dollars—or four—or five or six or seven? Is that what you want engraved on your tombstone when you die—the dividend record of the Tredway Corporation?"

The blood-color had crept out over the mask of Shaw's face, but Mary Walling saw that it was not the flush of an embarrassment that acknowledged defeat, but the stain of an anger born out of desperation.

Like a fighter at bay, Shaw tried to escape the attack with a diversion. "That's all very well, Mr. Walling—to take the high-minded attitude that money isn't important—but how far do you think you'd get next month if you offered the union negotiators a sense of accomplishment instead of the six cents an hour they're demanding?"

George Caswell grimaced, shifting uneasily in his chair. Mary Walling could sense his disappointment at Shaw's weak evasion of the issue. Had Don seen it, too? Did he realize that Caswell might be split away from Shaw—that Caswell might give him the one vote that was all he needed?

Don Walling's eyes were still on Shaw. "What sense of accomplishment would you offer them—the wonderful hope that if they passed up a raise and sweated their guts out to make that production line run a little faster, that we might be able to raise the dividend from two dollars to two dollars and ten cents?"

There had been a smile in his voice, dulling the edge of his sarcasm, but now as his eyes left Shaw and fanned the whole room his words were soberly

measured. "I don't want to be facetious about this—it's too serious for that. Loren's right when he says that we have an obligation to our stockholders—but it's a bigger obligation than just paying dividends. We have to keep this company *alive*. That's the important thing —and a company is like a man. No man can work for money alone. It isn't enough. You starve his soul when you try it—and you can starve a company to death in the same way. Yes, I know— sometimes our men in the factories give us the impression that all they want is another raise in wages—and then another and another and another. They make us think that getting more money is all that matters to them. But can we blame them for that? God knows, we've done our best to try to make them believe that money is the only measure of accomplishment that matters to us.

"Look at what we did this last year with what we called a 'communications program.' We put out a movie that analyzed our financial report and had meetings in all the plants. The men weren't much interested in our financial report—we knew that to begin with, it was the premise we started from—so what did we do? We tried to *force* them into being interested. We disguised the dollars as cartoons—little cartoon dollars that jumped into workers' pocketbooks—other little cartoon dollars that dragged in piles of lumber and built factories—and a big fat dollar that took a trip to Washington and was gobbled up by Uncle Sam. Oh, it was all very clever—even won some kind of an award as an outstanding example of how to promote industrial understanding. Understanding? Do you know what it forced our men to understand? Only one thing—the terrible, soul-killing fact that dollars were all that mattered to the management of this company—dollars—dollars—and nothing else."

"But that program was Mr. Bullard's

own idea," Shaw cut in like a quick knife thrust.

Mary Walling had been so completely swept along that her guard had dropped and Shaw's interruption came as a shocking surprise. Her eyes flashed to her husband. Had he been caught off guard, too?

"No, I don't think we can call that Mr. Bullard's idea alone," Don Walling said. "It's something that's in the air today—the groping of a lot of men at the top of industry who know they've lost something, but aren't quite sure what it is—nor exactly how they happened to lose it. Mr. Bullard was one of those men. He'd been so busy building a great production machine that he'd lost sight of why he was building it—if he ever really knew. Perhaps he didn't."

Julia Tredway Prince's voice, so close to Mary Walling's ears that even a whisper seemed like an explosion in the silence, asked, "Do you know, Mr. Walling?"

Mary Walling held her breath through the moment of silence. Could he answer that question? A smile flickered on his face . . . that same tantalizingly familiar smile that she hadn't been able to identify before. Now suddenly, she remembered when she had seen it before . . . that night when he had finally designed their house . . . when, after all of his groping and fumbling had frightened her almost to the point of losing faith in him, he had suddenly made everything come right and clear.

"Yes, I think I do," he said. "You see, to Mr. Bullard, business was a game—a very serious game, but still a game—the way war is a game to a soldier. He was never much concerned about money for its own sake. I remember his saying once that dollars were just a way of keeping score. I don't think he was too much concerned about

personal power, either—just power for power's sake. I know that's the easy way to explain the drive that any great man has—the lust for power—but I don't think that was true of Avery Bullard. The thing that kept him going was his terrific pride in himself—the driving urge to do things that no other man on earth could do. He saved the company when everyone else had given up. He built a big corporation in an industry where everyone said that only small companies could succeed. He was only happy when he was doing the impossible—and he did that only to satisfy his own pride. He never asked for applause and appreciation—or even for understanding. He was a lonely man but I don't think his loneliness ever bothered him very much. He was the man at the top of the tower—figuratively as well as literally. That's what he wanted. That's what it took to satisfy his pride. That was his strength—but of course that was his weakness, too."

Mary Walling listened in amazement. Where were those words coming from . . . those words that he could never have said before but were now falling so easily from his lips? Was that actually Don who was talking . . . the same man who had never been able to answer those dark-of-night questions before?

She watched him as he rose from his chair and in the act of standing he seemed a giant breaking shackles that had held him to the earth . . . shaking loose the ties that had bound him to the blind worship of Avery Bullard. He stood alone now . . . free.

"There was one thing that Avery Bullard never understood," Don Walling went on. "He never realized that other men had to be proud, too—that the force behind a great company had to be more than the pride of one man —that it had to be the pride of thousands of men. A company is like an army—it fights on its pride. You can't win wars with paychecks. In all the history of the world there's never been a great army of mercenaries. You can't pay a man enough to make him lay down his life. He wants more than money. Maybe Avery Bullard knew that once—maybe he'd just forgotten it—but that's where he made his mistake. He was a little lost these last few years. He'd won his fight to build a great company. The building was over—at least for the time being. There had to be something else to satisfy his pride— bigger sales—more profit—something. That's when we started doing things like making the sixteen-hundred series."

He turned and confronted Dudley. "Are your boys proud when they sell the sixteen-hundred series—when they know that the finish is going to crack and the veneer split off and the legs come loose?"

"But that's price merchandise," Dudley said in fumbling defense. "There's a need for it. We're not cheating anyone. At that price the customers know that they can't get—"

"How do you suppose the men in the factory feel when they make it?" Don Walling demanded. His eyes shifted from Dudley to Shaw. "What do you imagine they think of a management that's willing to stoop to selling that kind of junk in order to add a penny a year to the dividend? Do you know that there are men at Pike Street who have refused to work on the sixteen-hundred line—that there are men who have taken a cut of four cents an hour to get transferred to something else?"

"No, I wasn't aware of that," Shaw said—and the weakness of his voice signaled the first thin crack in his armor. "I don't suppose it would hurt too much if we dropped that line. After all, it's a small part of our business."

A voice in Mary Walling's mind wanted to shout out at her husband,

urging him to drive in for the kill that would clinch his victory. Couldn't he see that Shaw was defeated . . . that Caswell was nodding his approval . . . that Walt Dudley was waiting only to be commanded?

But Don Walling turned, looking out of the window, and his voice seemed faraway as if it were coming from the top of the distant white shaft of the Tredway Tower. "Yes, we'll drop that line. We'll never again ask a man to do anything that will poison his pride in himself. We'll have a new line of low-priced furniture someday—a different kind of furniture—as different from anything we're making now as a modern automobile is different from an old Mills wagon. When we get it, then we'll really start to grow."

His voice came back into the room. "We talk about Tredway being a big company now. It isn't. We're kidding ourselves. Yes, we're one of the biggest furniture manufacturers but what does it mean? Nothing! Furniture is close to a two-billion-dollar industry but it's all split up among thirty-six hundred manufacturers. We have about three per cent of the total—that's all, just three per cent. Look at other industries —the percentage that the top manufacturer has. What if General Motors had sat back and stopped growing when it had three percent of the automobile industry? We haven't even started to grow! Suppose we get fifteen per cent of the total—and why not, it's been done in a dozen industries? Fifteen per cent and the Tredway Corporation will be five times as big as it is today. All right, I know it hasn't been done before in the furniture business, but does that mean we can't do it? No—because that's exactly what we are going to do!"

His voice had built to a crescendo, to the moment that demanded the shout of an answering chorus—and then in the instant before the sound could have broken through the shock of silence, Mary Walling saw a tension-breaking smile on her husband's face. In the split second that it took her eyes to sweep the room, she saw that the smile was mirrored in all the faces that looked up at him . . . even in the face of Loren Shaw.

She had sensed, a few minutes before, that Shaw was defeated, but she had expected a last struggle, a final flare of resistance. It had not come. Instinctively, she understood what had happened. In that last moment, Loren Shaw had suddenly become aware that his brain had been set aflame by a spark from Don Walling's mind—a spark that he himself could never have supplied. Now he was fired to accomplishments that had been far beyond the limits of his imagination. Mary Walling understood the faintly bewildered quality of Shaw's smile, because she, too—long ago—had found it mysteriously strange that Don's mind was so unlike her own.

George Caswell was standing, extending his hand. "We're all behind you, Don. I can promise you that."

"Yes sir, Don, you bet we are!" Walt Dudley boomed.

Shaw shook hands silently but it was a gesture that needed no words to make it a pledge of loyalty.

THE MAN IN THE GRAY FLANNEL SUIT
Sloan Wilson

Tom Rath, wearing the gray flannel suit, is an anomaly in business fiction. He wants to work—but not too hard. In the hands of another author, Tom might have been portrayed as lazy or unambitious. Here he wins sympathy and reaps reward as a sensitive publicity man whose life has been deeply affected by his war experience. His boss, who might have been a hero in a Cameron Hawley novel, becomes an object of pity as he cries, "Somebody has to do the big jobs!" Sloan Wilson has written for *The New Yorker* and other magazines.

The next morning Tom got to the airport before Hopkins did. He waited at the gate where Flight 227 was posted. In a few moments he saw Hopkins walking toward him. Hopkins looked small—a short, almost frail-appearing man hurrying across the terminal, holding a huge hard leather briefcase in his hand. "Good morning, Tom!" he said briskly. "It's good of you to come on such short notice as this!"

"No trouble at all," Tom replied, still avoiding the use of Hopkins' name, because he couldn't make up his mind whether to call him "Ralph" or not. They walked aboard the plane, and Hopkins politely resisted the efforts of a stewardess to put his briefcase in the luggage compartment—it was so big that she thought it was a suitcase. No one aboard the plane recognized Hopkins. Tom had grown so used to seeing him deferred to in the United Broadcasting building that it was a shock to see him treated like anyone else. Hopkins obviously didn't mind—if anything, he appeared more diffident and more anxious to be polite than anyone else on the plane. He meekly allowed himself to be jostled away from the seat he was heading for, and when the stewardess offered him some chewing gum, he said, "Thank you—thank you very much, but I think not. I don't chew gum," and smiled apologetically, being almost absurdly careful not to hurt her feelings. She smiled back at him. What a nice little man, she thought.

Tom sat next to Hopkins. Even before the plane took off, Hopkins opened his briefcase, took out a thick report in pale-blue covers, and started to read. When the plane's engines roared, and they taxied toward the runway, he glanced up briefly. "This might interest you, Tom," he said, leaned over, and took another report from his briefcase. "This is something Bill Ogden roughed out on our plan for a subsidiary company to put programs on film—it's still just in the tentative planning stage, of course."

"Thanks," Tom said, accepting the document. As the plane rushed down the runway and lunged into the air, he opened the report. "On the basis of all available data, which is as yet incomplete, there might be considerable advantage in organizing an affiliated company, rather than trying to do the job directly ourselves," he read. He glanced out the window of the plane. Already they were at an altitude of about a thousand feet. He flexed his shoulder muscles, unconsciously trying to see if the parachute harness were strapped tight enough, then realized what he was doing, and smiled at himself. Sitting back, he tried to concentrate on Ogden's report.

After reading for two hours, Hopkins placed his briefcase on his lap and started writing memoranda with a pencil. He worked steadily throughout the long trip. When the plane finally landed in Hollywood, Tom felt tired, but Hopkins seemed energetic as ever. "We're right on time," he said with satisfaction, glancing at his watch. "Let's go to the hotel and wash up. Then we've got some meetings scheduled."

At the hotel a suite of large rooms had been reserved for Hopkins with an adjoining private room and bath for Tom. It was late, but Hopkins didn't mention dinner. They left their bags and hurried to the executive offices of the United Broadcasting Corporation's Hollywood building. Hopkins introduced Tom to a succession of men, all of whom talked fast and with apparent urgency about matters Tom could hardly understand at all. He was glad when they went into a private dining room adjoining one of the offices and sat down around a long table. In all, there were eight men present, and they all kept talking to Hopkins at once. A pretty waitress brought cocktails.

"I'll tell you, Ralph," a tall but rather paunchy man with the oddly apt name of Potkin said. "Like it or not, live shows are going out. In another ten years, the whole television business will be right here. You ought to be thinking in terms of moving your whole operation. If you don't, it's not going to be long before the tail out here starts wagging the dog in New York."

"I'm not convinced of that yet," Hopkins said. "And that's not the only consideration involved in setting up a subsidiary company. There are some legal angles to this. . . ."

On and on the conversation went. It was nine o'clock in the evening before it was over. "Come on over to my house for a drink," Potkin said.

"No," Hopkins replied. "I'm a little tired. I think I'd better go back to the hotel and get some rest. Want to come, Tom?"

"Sure," Tom said.

A taxi took them to the hotel. In the elevator Hopkins said, "Want to stop in for a nightcap before you turn in?"

"That would be fine," Tom replied.

When they entered Hopkins' suite, Tom saw that someone in the company's Hollywood office had made all the arrangements he had made at Atlantic City the month before. On a table was a large vase of long-stemmed roses, and in the bedroom was an electric refrigerator and a cabinet holding a small bar. Tom suspected suddenly that Hopkins had never asked for such elaborate fixings, that they were all the idea of Ogden or someone else trying to please him, and that Hopkins was simply too polite to object. He wished he could find out, but there didn't seem to be any way to ask. Hopkins fixed two glasses of bourbon on the rocks and sprawled out on a sofa the way he had the night he and Tom had talked in his apartment. To his increasing discomfort, Tom found that Hopkins was staring at him again. There was the same mixture of tiredness and kindness on his face, the same steady gaze. Tom sipped his drink nervously.

"Well, what do you think?" Hopkins asked suddenly.

"About what?"

"About this whole operation we've been talking about. Do you think we ought to set up a separate but affiliated organization?"

"I don't know," Tom said. "There's so much involved. . . ."

"Of course—we can't make a decision yet. How would you like to move out here and work on this end of things for a year or so?"

"What?" Tom asked in astonishment.

"You could work with Potkin. He's right about one thing—this end of the business is going to get increasingly important. If you put in a year or two on it, I think you might pick up a lot that would be useful when you came back to New York."

Several thoughts immediately flamed up in Tom's mind. This is his way of getting rid of me, he suddenly knew—this personal assistant business is making him as uncomfortable as it's made me. But he's still trying to do something for me—now he just wants to do it at a distance, by remote control. It's a great opportunity, he thought, but what would happen to our housing project? He was suddenly filled with the confusion of moving, putting his grandmother's house on the market to sell the quickest way possible, and looking for a place to live in Hollywood. Out of this welter of impressions came one word: no. He didn't say it. Instead, he said, "Gosh, that's a pretty big step. . . ."

"Don't you like the idea?"

Wait a minute, Tom thought. If I say no, he's going to wonder what the devil to do with me in New York. I'll be upsetting his whole scheme. If I

buck him, he's liable to turn on me. This is like petting a tiger. "I don't know," he said carefully. "I'd like to have a little time to think it over."

"Don't you want to learn the business?" Hopkins asked quietly, but with obvious import.

"Of course . . ." Tom began. Then he paused and took a sip of his drink. The hell with it, he thought. There's no point in pretending. I've played it straight with him so far, and I might as well keep on. Anyway, he's a guy who can't be fooled. He glanced up and saw that Hopkins was smiling at him with great friendliness. Here goes nothing, Tom thought, and the words came with a rush. "Look, Ralph," he said, using the first name unconsciously, "I don't think I do want to learn the business. I don't think I'm the kind of guy who should try to be a big executive. I'll say it frankly: I don't think I have the willingness to make the sacrifices. I don't want to give up the time. I'm trying to be honest about this. I want the money. Nobody likes money better than I do. But I'm just not the kind of guy who can work evenings and week ends and all the rest of it forever. I guess there's even more to it than that. I'm not the kind of person who can get all wrapped up in a job—I can't get myself convinced that my work is the most important thing in the world. I've been through one war. Maybe another one's coming. If one is, I want to be able to look back and figure I spent the time between wars with my family, the way it should have been spent. Regardless of war, I want to get the most out of the years I've got left. Maybe that sounds silly. It's just that if I have to bury myself in a job every minute of my life, I don't see any point to it. And I know that to do the kind of job you want me to do, I'd have to be willing to bury myself in it, and, well, I just don't want to."

He paused, out of breath, half afraid to look at Hopkins. And then it happened—Hopkins gave a funny, high, indescribable little laugh which rose in the air and was cut off immediately. It was a laugh Tom never forgot, and it was followed by a moment of complete silence. Then Hopkins said in a low voice, "I'm glad you're honest. I've always appreciated that quality in you."

It was Tom's turn to laugh nervously. "Well, there it is," he said. "I don't know what I do now. Do you still want me to work for you?"

"Of course," Hopkins said kindly, getting up and pouring himself another drink. "There are plenty of good positions where it's not necessary for a man to put in an unusual amount of work. Now it's just a matter of finding the right spot for you."

"I'm willing to look at it straight," Tom said. "There are a lot of contradictions in my own thinking I've got to face. In spite of everything I've said, I'm still ambitious. I want to get ahead as far as I possibly can without sacrificing my entire personal life."

Hopkins stood with his back turned toward Tom, and when he spoke, his voice sounded curiously remote. "I think we can find something for you," he said. "How would you like to go back to the mental-health committee? That will be developing into a small, permanent organization. I'm thinking of giving my house in South Bay to be its headquarters. That would be quite nice for you—you wouldn't even have any commuting. How would you like to be director of the outfit? That job would pay pretty well. I'd like to think I had a man with your integrity there, and I'll be making all the major decisions."

"I'd be grateful," Tom said in a low voice.

Suddenly Hopkins whirled and faced him. "*Somebody has to do the big jobs!*" he said passionately. "This world was built by men like me! To really do a job, you have to live it, body and soul! You people who just give half your mind to your work are riding on our backs!"

"I know it," Tom said.

Almost immediately Hopkins regained control of himself. A somewhat forced smile spread over his face. "Really, I don't know why we're taking all this so seriously," he said. "I think you've made a good decision. You don't have to worry about being stuck with a foundation job all your life. I'll be starting other projects. We need men like you—I guess we need a few men who keep a sense of proportion."

"Thanks," Tom said.

Hopkins smiled again, this time with complete spontaneity. "Now if you'll pardon me, I think I'll go to bed," he said. "It's been a long day."

Exercises

"The Rise of Silas Lapham," by William Dean Howells

1. Point out the means by which Howells establishes Lapham's bourgeois characteristics.
2. Write a paragraph on Bartley Hubbard as a newspaperman.
3. If Silas Lapham were a modern executive, what would his biography read like? Rewrite this interview in terms of present-day probabilities. (Reference to Sec. 1 may help you.)
4. Discuss Silas Lapham's defense of outdoor advertising.

"Babbitt," by Sinclair Lewis

1. Discuss Sinclair Lewis' prejudices as revealed by his characterization of Babbitt.
2. Adhering to the facts in this passage, write a description of Babbitt in such terms that he emerges as a sympathetic character.
3. Outside of *Babbitt's* merits as a novel, how do you account for the satisfaction so many readers have found in the author's exposure of George F. Babbitt? Write a theme on the subject.
4. Compare Silas Lapham and George Babbitt as examples of American businessmen. Who is truer to type? Discuss.

"Executive Suite," by Cameron Hawley

1. Discuss Don Walling's creed as a businessman.
2. Discuss the justice of Loren Shaw's position.
3. To what extent is this narrative an idealization of modern business? Discuss.

"The Man in the Gray Flannel Suit," by Sloan Wilson

1. William H. Whyte, Jr., author of *The Organization Man* (an excerpt will be found in Sec. 1) has expressed concern over the trend toward paternalism in business. Discuss the evidences of such paternalism in this passage.
2. Contrast the treatment of executive Ralph Hopkins at the hands of the author with that received by Babbitt and Silas Lapham.
3. Do you believe that the job philosophy expressed by Tom Rath is winning converts among young people going into business? To what extent does the older ideal of hard work and financial success prevail among your set? Discuss.

9

How, What, and Why: The Art of Exposition

In a sense, business is one of the great educational forces of our time. Through its journalism, advertising, and public relations literature, it teaches science, history, management, economics, finance, fashion, interior decoration, kitchen skills, and the social graces. Specialists in many fields of knowledge often join with designers, artists, and photographers to communicate their subjects clearly and interestingly. The office writer can learn much from their efforts. For whether he is dictating specifications, giving instructions, or outlining the company's profit-sharing plan, he needs to employ similar skill in exposition.

Most of the readings in the preceding sections rely heavily on expository treatment. In the following miscellany are several more examples of exposition especially selected for their interest to business students.

THE STORY OF FIGURES

Burroughs Corporation

Between the curvilinear numerals on a Sumerian clay tablet and the figures served up by electronic tape lie six thousand years of business history. In *The Story of Figures*, told in part below, a leading business machines manufacturer adds to its own good will and to popular knowledge at the same time.

INTRODUCTION OF NUMBERS

When man first began to figure he wrote out words to illustrate his numbers. Then the Greeks devised the plan of having the first letter of the word illustrate the number. Thus D (Δ) comes from the Greek word for ten (deka) from which we get "decimal." The Roman numeral system followed a similar principle.

The Syrians and Hebrews used the twenty-two letters of their alphabet to represent numbers. The Phoenicians had two methods. They either wrote out numbers in words or used vertical marks for units and horizontal marks for tens.

The Arabs abandoned the use of number words in the eighth century and adopted the system used by the Hindus, who shortened their number words down to the first letters. The Western Arabs modified this even further and devised what are known as the Gubar (dust) numerals which are the ancestors of our modern numerals.

Our system of placing our numbers —so that we read 55 as fifty-five, not 5 plus 5—owes its origin to the Hindus.

The Babylonians wrote their numerals with a pointed stick or stylus on soft clay tablets. The marks made by the point of the stylus are like arrowheads or wedges. The numerals thus written are called "cuneiform" numerals from the Latin "cuneus" (a wedge). The mark made by the other end or blunt end of the stylus formed a circle, just as it would if you pressed the wrong end of a pencil into the clay. By pressing with only one side of the blunt end, a crescent was formed. These circles and crescents are called "curvilinear" numerals. When the Babylonians kept accounts they used cuneiform numerals to denote debits and curvilinear numerals to denote credits, somewhat as we use red and black ink in account books today.

PRIMITIVE METHODS OF FIGURING

Necessity drove man to figuring. As families grew into tribes and tribes into nations a system of trade sprang up. One tribe or nation might have wonderful clay for making pottery; another might grow herbs for dyestuffs

Reprinted from *The Story of Figures* by courtesy of Burroughs Corporation.

or medicine. They would trade clay for herbs. As nations grew and the volume of trade increased, they felt the need of selling on credit. A nation raising grains or herbs might need clay for pottery, but the harvest might be some time away. So it bought clay, giving its promise to pay in grain when the harvest came in. Written records became necessary; and accounting was born. Coins or tokens were made to represent certain definite values.

The first writing of numerals probably was done by scratching on soft clay with a pointed stick. Clay tablets, inscribed by the Sumerians 5000 years ago, show that these merchants were familiar with bills, receipts, notes, accounts and systems of measures. A Babylonian tablet, deciphered after more than 5000 years, was found to record payments made by draft and by clay check.

In a tomb near the Great Pyramids of Gizeh in Egypt, recent explorers have found very ancient numerals painted on the walls in which 1 is represented by a vertical line, 10 by a kind of horseshoe, 100 by a corkscrew shape, 10,000 by a pointing finger, 100,000 by a frog and 1,000,000 by a man looking astonished.

About 4000 years ago Ahmes the Moon-born, an Egyptian temple scribe wrote a handbook on arithmetic. It is now in the British Museum. Written in ink on papyrus, a paper made from reeds, this book contains examples of linear equations, unit fractions and mensuration. The occasional use of red ink suggests that a teacher corrected the work.

The Egyptians became so accurate in figuring that their architects, who measured the base for the Great Pyramid of Gizeh across a rocky mound they could not see over, completed their work with an error in the sides of only 1/27000 part of a right angle.

Once man began to write down figures it was not long before he began to calculate.

ADDITION

Primitive man picked up a skin and said, "One skin," He picked up another and said, "Two skins." That was about the limit of his arithmetic. Some, perhaps, counted as high as five and then said, "Five skins and one skin," when they meant six. This was the first addition. The Niues of the Southern Pacific still say "One fruit, two fruits, many fruits." Australian savages can rarely count above two. The Veddahs, or wild men of the Island of Ceylon, have words for only 1 and 2. For any number over two they say "Two and one more, and one more, and one more, and one more, and one more, etc." Addition was the base of all figuring. It still is the only method of computation with primitive tribes all over the world.

As trade grew, systems were devised for larger numbers. The decimal system was one of these. It was the general favorite because it has as its basis the fact that man has ten fingers and ten toes and that he used these in his early counting. Some systems such as the Babylonian had sixty as their basis while the Aztecs used twenty. So the Eskimos and the American Indians of the West Coast today count by twenty, using the sum of their fingers and toes as a basis. In this way large sums can be represented by simple addition.

The Israelites, though rated as unusually intelligent people, confined their counting to low numbers, using addition to denote larger numbers. Thus they spoke of the average life of a man as three score years and ten, because it was easier to count twenty (a score) three times and then add half a score (10) than it was to count up to seventy. This was plain addition.

SUBTRACTION—MULTIPLICATION—DIVISION

Subtraction links itself directly with addition in primitive methods of figuring. Since subtraction is merely taking away something, primitive man even today in subtracting three from five holds up five fingers and then turns down three of them leaving two. This solves the problem quite effectively.

The Roman numeral system, believed to have been inherited from the Etruscans, embraces the principle of subtraction. It uses letters for symbols; for instance, X means 10, C means 100. If a letter is placed before another of greater value, it is subtracted. If it follows the larger one, it is added. IV means $V-I=4$; XC means $C-X=90$; VI means $V+I=6$; CX means $C+X = 110$. As an old eighteenth century book on arithmetic has it: "Note that IV signifies four as IX signifies nine; which takes as it were by stealth or pulls back one from 10. So that in fact I stands behind X and picks his pockets, and I stands behind V and picks his."

The Roman system indicates multiplication by horizontal and vertical bars. Thus $\overline{\text{XVIII.}}$ is $18 \times 1000 = 18,000$. Vertical bars at the side and a horizontal bar above denote multiplying by 100,000. Thus $\boxed{\text{X}} = 10 \times 100,000 = 1,000,000$, or one million.

Ancient multiplication was a matter of repeated addition. In multiplying two by four, the ancients merely added two and two and two and two and got eight. Later they compiled long and complicated tables giving the results of multiplication. These were used extensively.

Division, even in the early times, probably was done by means of repeated subtractions. To divide nine by three the ancients were believed to have subtracted three from nine giving six; then three from six leaving three; and three from three leaving nothing. They found that three goes into nine three times. This method and the addition methods of multiplication are complicated and tedious. While there remain in ancient works no well defined rules for division it is assumed that this is the theory on which arithmetical processes were developed.

FRACTIONS AND DECIMALS

The word "fraction" is derived from the Latin word "fractum" which means "broken." Ancient man in his trade dealings had little need to resort to fractions. When ancient peoples encountered difficulties in handling parts of a broken object they created various measuring systems for designating subunits. Our word "inch" is a relic of the Roman system. The Romans clung to 12 as a basis of their division of measures because it is easily divisible by 2, 3, 4 and 6. This permitted the taking of simple fractional parts. They divided the foot into twelfths, each twelfth being called an "uncia" whence comes our "inch." They also used the same fractional part "uncia" for the twelfth of pound whence we get our word "ounce." Counting commercially by twelfths, their "duodecim" meaning twelve, gives us our "dozen."

Every system of counting has its radix or base. Ten was the one most often used and formed the basis of the decimal system through the primitive method of counting by tens from the ten fingers and ten toes. The Babylonian system, as has been noted before used sixty as the radix. From this we get our minutes and seconds both in time and angles.

BIRTH OF MECHANICAL FIGURING

Ages ago man's inventive genius

turned to ways and means of saving head work in the tedious process of figuring. The ancient Arabs and Romans were just as eager to find ways of saving time and labor as are our inventors today.

As trading and shopkeeping grew more and more complicated some lazy genius invented a way to avoid keeping figures in his head or having to scratch them on tablets of clay. He invented a board, covered with dust, on which he could trace figures, draw columns and work with pebbles. Perhaps he was a Greek, as this dust board was called the abacus, from the Greek word "abak" (pronounced abacue) meaning "dust." The blackboard of the modern schoolroom possibly is derived from the old primitive dust board.

The early Greek bankers and the early Romans made an abacus of stone provided with grooves in which small stones called "calculi" moved up and down. From their "calculi" we derive our word "calculate."

The Chinese developed and even today use the wooden abacus as you may see in almost any Chinese laundry. The proprietor does his figuring on it and keeps his books with the familiar ink brush.

Even earlier than the abacus were the "sangi" or number rods still used for computing by the Koreans and Japanese.

These rods, though not used in the same way, are a reminder of the tally system in vogue in England from the time of William the Conqueror to as late as Charles II. When a man owed money he would record the amount by cutting notches in a stick called a tally stock. He would give the stick to his creditors.

Sometimes dishonest creditors would cut extra notches before they presented the tally stock for payment. So the system was changed. After the notches were made the tally was split down the middle. The notches on the creditor's half then had to correspond to the notches on the debtor's half. Hence the verb "to tally" and its use in such examples as: "His figures don't tally" and "Your idea tallies with mine."

Banks kept records of deposits by the tally system. Their depositors held tally stocks corresponding to those in the bank. From this came the modern word "stockholder."

Up to 1543, the British Government also kept records of transactions by the tally system. After the system ceased, the basement of the House of Commons remained cluttered with vast accumulations of these dry sticks for nearly two centuries. Finally it was decided to burn them. The stove became overheated and a fire ensued which burned down both the House of Commons and the adjacent House of Lords.

THE STORY OF PAPER

The Champion Paper and Fibre Company

The blank sheet that drives the businessman to dictation and the budding author to despair is the product of an industry almost two thousand years old. The history of paper is briefly told in this introduction to a brochure detailing the progress of a leading producer.

Mankind learned to write (in a manner of speaking) many thousands of years ago. He used the things at hand: stones, flat bones, the walls of caves. In Egypt, two thousand years before the birth of Christ, he was using thin sections of a tough reed, papyrus, cemented together, to record his work. The British Museum today has an example thought to be more than 3000 years old. It is known as The Great Harris Papyrus and is in the form of a scroll 133 feet long by sixteen and three-quarters inches wide.

Parchment and vellum made from the skins of animals were probably used a thousand years and more before the beginning of the Christian Era, as were bamboo and silk.

But it was not until the Divine Event in Bethlehem—more than a hundred years after—that paper as such was invented.

This great discovery is generally credited to a Chinese court official, Ts'ai Lun. The year is 105 A.D. The paper which Ts'ai Lun presented to his Emperor was made from cellulose fibres by the same basic principles of maceration, hydration and mechanical matting which are used to this day.

New ideas moved infinitely more slowly in that ancient civilization than they do in ours. It took more than a thousand years for the discovery of the principles of papermaking to get from China into Europe by way of Samarkand and Bagdad. And then it took several more centuries before it was used for the education of the people.

In 1390, the first paper mill was built in Germany. England's first paper mill was built about a hundred years later.

Movable type provided the impetus which forced the development of papermaking in Europe. The Gutenberg Bible is believed by many to be the first book printed from type. It was produced during the middle of the 15th Century. That stimulated the making of paper so that books could be multiplied by the printing process.

Another 200 years passed before the new American Colony was producing paper at the Rittenhouse mill, built in Germantown, Pennsylvania, in 1690. All paper in those early days was made by

Reprinted from *This Is Champion* by courtesy of the Champion Paper and Fibre Company.

hand of the cellulose fibre derived from rags. A good worker might make as many as 750 sheets per day.

If we had to depend upon rags as the source of raw materials for papermaking, it is safe to say there would be no paper bags, no paper food containers, no national magazines and very few books. There just aren't enough rags available to keep the paper industry operating for even a single day.

Civilization owes much to a French scientist named Reaumur, for it was he who first advanced the idea that wood fibre could be the basic material in the paper making process. About the middle of the 19th Century, paper was being made by using ground-up wood as the source of the fibrous material. It must have been a pretty poor product by present-day standards, but it still stands as the foundation upon which the industry was built.

Then during the years between 1867 and 1874, came the invention of a chemical process by which the cellulose fibre in the wood could be separated to be reconstituted in the form of thin sheets suitable for printing purposes. The originator of the sulphite method of pulping wood was Benjamin Tilghman.

The sulphate process, another chemical method of making wood pulp, was developed in 1884—and papermaking was on its way to becoming one of the leading industries of the world.

For example: By 1889, the United States alone produced more than a million tons of paper. And in the short space of the next decade, the annual production had nearly tripled.

Without such a spectacular increase in the availability of paper and paper products, it is doubtful indeed if printing, publishing, advertising and merchandising could have attained their 20th Century stature and it is even more doubtful if modern civilization, culture and education could have ever reached their highly developed stage.

PHANTOM PROFITS
Roger M. Blough

The word "profit" is so much the victim of semantics that business finds it necessary to explain the term again and again. Roger M. Blough, board chairman of the United States Steel Corporation, put the matter in plain language before a meeting of shareholders.

When a machine is used to produce steel—or anything else—it wears out a little each year. In other words, it "depreciates." So if we buy a machine that will last for 25 years, and if the machine costs us 25 million dollars, it will wear out at the rate of a million dollars' worth each year. Thus the Federal tax laws permit us to recover a million dollars a year, on the average, on this machine as a cost of doing business. And at the end of the 25 years, when the machine wears out, we have got our 25 millions back through this process of "normal depreciation." So theoretically we can buy a new machine with it. . . .

But that's where Old Man Inflation steps in. During the past ten years alone, our plant and equipment costs have more than doubled. So 25 million dollars won't begin to pay for the new machine. Let me give you an actual example of this problem as we face it today:

Back in 1930 we built an open hearth plant which cost about 10 million dollars. Today it will cost us about 64 million dollars to replace that plant. Through depreciation we have recovered the original 10 millions that we spent on this facility. The remaining 54 millions, however, will have to come out of our profits . . . our profits after taxes.

But in order to earn 54 millions in profits after taxes, we have to earn 112½ millions before taxes. And, last year, it took the profit on six hundred million of the dollars we received from our customers—about one-seventh of our total sales—to pay for that one open hearth plant.

So every penny of profit we made on one-seventh of our total sales last year will be wiped out in replacing this open hearth. And that, of course, is only one facility. We have many other furnaces, mills and machines which must be replaced each year.

In this connection, however, I should point out that many new facilities we buy today are better and more productive than the old ones they replace; and the new open hearth shop I have just described will produce about one-third more steel than the present one does. But taking this into full account, it will still cost more than 4½ times as much, per ton of capacity, as the original facility did.

As printed in the First National City Bank *Monthly Letter*, July, 1956.

Thus you see that a substantial part of our profits are not real profits in the sense that they can be used to pay dividends, or to provide for expansion and growth, or to serve any of the other functions that a profit is supposed to perform. They are what I would call phantom profits destined for replacement, profits which are eaten up by inflation, almost before we get them. They cannot finance progress. We must use them just to stand still.

WHAT *IS* AUTOMATION?
John Diebold

Automation has been hailed as both a herald of Utopia and a messenger of doom. What *is* automation? The lucid answer that follows was written by a graduate of the Harvard Business School who, as head of his own management consulting firm, ranks as an expert in the installation of automatic factories.

. . . Automation is a means of analyzing, organizing and controlling our production processes to maintain continuous optimum use of all our production resources—human as well as material.

For a simple illustration, take the development of a mattress factory. A mattress was produced originally by hand by a single craftsman. In the nineteenth century, however, mattress making was divided into a number of separate steps, according to the skills of individual workers. Thus, the springs might have been made on one floor of a factory, the frame on another, the cloth material on still a third and the whole assembled on yet another. Mechanization did not change this basic division; machines to make springs were introduced into the spring department, machines to manufacture frames into the frame department, and so on.

But to automate such a factory, the entire process would have to be revised into an integrated, self-regulating system. How could this be done?

The first step would be to analyze the manufacturing operation, to question not only the way things are being done, but why they are being done that way. We would have to "rethink" the product. Every phase of production, even the product itself, would have to be studied to determine what degree of automation would achieve the greatest economies. This might lead, for example, to a decision to redesign the mattress frame completely to permit the use of automatic machines, or the substitution of a new material for mattress padding—say foam rubber, which is easier to handle than cotton or wool. It might involve the design of special machinery to attach the springs and other parts to the frame in a single operation. This, of course, is an oversimplification of the complex management and engineering decisions that would have to be made, but it illustrates the broad nature of such changes.

The second phase in the automation of the mattress factory would be to organize the actual production facilities into an integrated system—to "rethink" the manufacturing process, to combine or eliminate production steps and possibly rearrange them in a more efficient order. Once the ideal sequence had been determined, the machines could be linked together to keep production

From *Collier's*, March 16, 1956. Reprinted by permission.

moving in a continuous flow. Wherever possible a part, once gripped, should not be released until its manufacture and placement were complete. Then in the automated mattress factory the end product would flow out as one, long continuous strip of finished bedding, to be sliced off automatically in appropriate sizes.

The linking phase of automation is the form most familiar to the public, largely because of the publicity accorded its development in the automotive industry. Often referred to as "Detroit automation," it is fundamentally a new method for handling products between various steps in the mass-production assembly line.

Not long ago, for example, an automobile engine block was milled at one machine, removed by a worker and put on a conveyer, again removed by another worker and bored at the next machine, and so on as the engine moved spasmodically down the line. Today, complex handling devices, often as large as the production machines themselves, automatically remove the parts from the milling machine, turn and position them as necessary and hold them in place for the next machine's operation. Thus, an engine block goes from a rough casting to finished product—which may involve as many as 530 distinct operations—in a continuous, automatic journey. One such line, at the Ford Motor Company's Cleveland plant, performs the entire process in less than 15 minutes.

Detroit automation may profitably be applied wherever repetitive operations are to be performed on long production runs of identical parts. It has spread to large areas of the metalworking, electrical, electronic, meat-packing and food-processing industries.

Is there more to automation than this process of continuous production? Yes, there is the element of control.

Automation seeks to make the production system as self-regulating as possible. Actually, we are now leaving the push-button era and entering an era in which buttons push themselves.

What, for example, would happen to our continuous process if a single machine began to turn out parts slightly off-sized because of tool wear? It would be possible, of course, to station workers at each machine to gauge the parts as they are made and adjust the machine's performance accordingly. But then we should lose all the advantages of our continuous process. Obviously we must provide a machine or device capable of performing the same inspection and correction functions as the human operator—and without interrupting the production flow.

Behind the complex new self-regulation devices lies a simple principle. It is called "feedback." It was employed in James Watt's flyball governor to maintain his steam engine at constant speed, and by the Dutch to keep windmills facing into the wind. But it was not until World War II, when many of our best scientific minds were directed toward the development of radar and antiaircraft-fire control, that an organized and generally useful theory of feedback control was developed.

The human nervous system may be described as a complex feedback system. When you reach for a glass of water, the way you guide your hand to the glass is quite similar to the way a feedback control system directs the fire of an antiaircraft gun: your hand actually "zeroes in" upon the glass, first perhaps tending to overshoot, then falling short, and constantly being corrected according to the information provided by your senses. Similarly, in an industrial feedback system, information concerning the actual performance of an operation is continually compared with the desired result. Performance is continually corrected to minimize the difference. Thus, truly automatic operation, independent of changing conditions, is achieved.

How is a feedback system of automation different from what is commonly called "automatic" operation?

Consider, for example, an "automatic" street-lighting system. Typically, such a system turns on the electric lights at a certain hour and shuts them off again at another fixed time. Though the system starts and stops automatically, it cannot be said to be self-regulating. To make it self-regulating we would have to introduce feedback—in the form of a device which would operate the lights according to actual light conditions. Such a device would consist of a light-sensitive instrument, such as the light meter used in photography, which could be set to activate the lighting system whenever the natural light fell below a certain point, regardless of the time of day.

Is automation practicable for small as well as large-scale operations?

Thanks to the application of feedback, the answer once again is yes. But because so much of the discussion of automation has dealt with the more obvious achievements of the automotive and chemical-process industries (including oil refining and papermaking), it is often mistakenly assumed that the advantages of automation are limited to industries producing large volumes of a single product.

It is true that the huge special-purpose transfer devices and conventional "automatic" machine tools typical of Detroit automation cannot be changed from one product specification to another without costly and time-consuming adjustments. Therefore, they are of little use to the small manufacturer or "jobber," who may be machining an order of valves this week and an order of brake pedals next week. But

feedback automation promises to alter this situation by making machines versatile as well as automatic. Such flexible control can be achieved by a number of means, but that most highly developed is "tape instruction." One of the most publicized of the tape-instructed machines is a large milling device designed at Massachusetts Institute of Technology; it has served as inspiration for many commercial machines. Today, a number of firms throughout the country are manufacturing and marketing a wide variety of tape-controlled milling machines, lathes, drill presses and the like.

These machines can be made to vary their operations over a wide range through the use of punched paper cards or tapes—or even magnetic tapes, much like those used for sound recording—upon which operating instructions have been coded in a series of dots which the machine translates into electric impulses. The control device "reads" its instructions—just as a teletype machine "reads" the news, or a player piano "reads" the music on a roll—and, in effect, produces a finished part direct from the original blueprint.

With such "tape-instructed" machines, it no longer is necessary to turn out a six-month supply of a product in order to make a job-lot production run worth while. Two or three pieces can be machined as required and the tape stored until further parts are needed. Since most of this country's production is in the form of job-shop runs, this is an important accomplishment.

Although until recently feedback control has been used most extensively in such process industries as chemical manufacturing and oil refining, it is now being introduced into metalworking and, through the medium of the electronic computer, into offices as well. In fact, entire industrial and commercial enterprises actually are large feedback systems, containing the means of their own regulation and correction. All that is needed is to organize all parts of the process—production, pricing, advertising, sales, design and so on —in such a way that the control centers have continuous and accurate information concerning the operation of every part.

That's where the automatic high-speed information-processing machines come in. Of all the machinery of automation, these great computers have most strongly aroused the curiosity of the public, perhaps because of the seeming incredibility of their performance. They're at the heart of the complex network of instruments and controls that exemplify the feedback-system approach to automation.

Modern computers deal with words as well as with numbers, and can solve simple logical problems as well as complex mathematical questions. Every major advance in the speed, accuracy or storage capacity of electronic computers makes possible the solution of problems that were previously considered insoluble.

At Harvard University, the Mark IV, an electromechanical machine, has been used to compare thousands of Biblical manuscripts in order to discover the chronological sequence in which they were written; the machine uses the gradual changes in text from one era to the next as the basis for classification. The 701, a large-scale scientific machine built by the International Business Machines Corporation, is being used by the United States Weather Bureau at Suitland, Maryland, for experimental weather forecasting.

Less spectacular, perhaps, but no less significant, are the roles computers have played in solving the problems of engineering and industry. The machines are used daily to find the answers to questions involved in the design and testing of aircraft, guided missiles and warships. (Use of an "electronic brain" enabled the DC-7 airliner to fly six months sooner than would have been possible if conventional methods had been used to make all the necessary calculations.) Computers also have been used extensively in atomic research, by the Army Ordnance Department in ballistics studies, by public utilities and by a number of government agencies engaged in statistical work.

But surely the most significant application of computers has been to modernize and speed up office paper work in American business. The changes have only just begun, but for some time now Bell Telephone has been operating an Automatic Message Accounting system which records calls, assigns them to the right subscriber, and computes and prints bills—all automatically. American Airlines is keeping track of ticket reservations on a central magnetic-drum "memory" unit. The Toronto Stock Exchange handles bid and asked quotations by a similar device. And a number of large department stores have begun to record their sales with electronic "tag readers," eventually to become part of central data-processing systems.

Another important development in this field was revealed recently when the Bank of America announced that it has tried out and intends to install a $750,000 electronic computer named ERMA (Electronic Recording Machine —Accounting), capable of handling all the records for some 50,000 checking accounts. This machine, being installed at the San Jose, California, branch, credits individual accounts with deposits, debits withdrawals, stores details of all transactions, maintains correct balances, accepts stop-payment and hold orders, warns if an account is overdrawn, and sorts checks.

Actually, electronic computers of all

sizes are being used today by hundreds of corporations for payroll computations, market analysis, billing, inventory control and similar jobs. Yet the revolution has scarcely begun. Where a little more than a year ago no more than a dozen large-scale computers were on order for business use, today orders for more than 200 are waiting to be filled.

Most of today's machines are dinosaur-sized. They are the room-filling forebears of small, transistorized low-power-consuming data-processing machines of tomorrow. In another ten years today's computers will be regarded with much the same nostalgia and curiosity with which we now look back on the Model T car. . . .

WHAT A SECURITY IS—AND WHY

Merrill Lynch, Pierce, Fenner and Beane

Affectionately called "We the People" because of the number of names in its title, the Wall Street firm of Merrill Lynch, Pierce, Fenner and Beane has for many years proclaimed to the common man the advantages of investing in corporate securities. The explanation that follows is part of a booklet that continues the program of education.

When a man owns stock in a company, that means he is a part owner of the company. When he owns one of the company's bonds, that means he has loaned the company money.

Every corporation is wholly owned by its stockholders, and nobody else. The terms and conditions of ownership are all set forth in detail in the law of the state in which the company is incorporated and in the charter and by-laws of the company. The common stockholders have a right, generally, to vote for the election of directors, to examine the books of the company, and to share in the distribution of assets— whatever property the company owns— if the corporation is dissolved. But most importantly, if the company makes money it is expected to pay out a part of its profits regularly as dividends to the stockholders.

The size of most publicly-owned corporations makes it impractical for the individual stockholders to take an active part in management. An individual stockholder may be the owner, but he is seldom the boss. Instead, he exerts his influence by voting. The members of the board of directors of a corporation are the representatives of the stockholders. They are voted into power and they can be voted out of power by the stockholders.

The directors of a company select the officers who run the company. The president, vice-president, secretary, and treasurer, together with all of the managers, department heads, supervisors, foremen and workmen are the employees. The directors hold the power to hire and fire the president and other top officers. The directors and the officers work for the stockholders.

Some corporations, like some individual businessmen, manage to get along on what they have without borrowing. Many companies, however, need more capital to expand their business. Banks, of course, are a common source of short-term money (that is, money which is to be repaid in a matter of months), but if the corporation needs long-term or permanent

Reprinted from How to Invest by courtesy of Merrill Lynch, Pierce, Fenner and Beane.

capital, the most common practice is either to issue additional stock or sell bonds. Stockholders of a company are owners, but bondholders are *creditors*. They do not own the business, but lend money to it—money which the company borrows at a set rate of interest and which it agrees to repay at a specified date.

Investing in securities has one big difference from the investment one makes in his own business. The individual businessman who puts his capital to work in his own business is relying on his own ability as a business manager for any return on his investment.

When you invest in corporate securities you invest in a business that is managed by someone else—the directors, the president, vice-president and other officers of the corporation. Day-by-day business decisions are not made by the investor. This is a fundamental difference, but it does not mean for an instant that wise investment does not call for decision on the part of the investor.

The investor's decision is of a different kind. It is his task to pick the industry, then the company, and finally, the security that best fits his need. It is his continuing job to keep an eye on the industry and the company so that he can withdraw his investment if economic conditions or inept management threaten the company's future.

PLANNING YOUR INVESTMENT PROGRAM

Detailed planning of your investment program is a fascinating and scientific business.

The first and most important step is to get your investment purpose clearly in mind. Here are three broad possible objectives—growth, income, and safety.

These classifications are not to be thought of as excluding one another because many times they overlap. They are not the only possible objectives, but at the outset they do represent three prominent landmarks for you to use in plotting your course.

Growth might well be the objective you have principally in mind. If you are comparatively young and can normally look forward to many more years of productive work, you probably will feel free to take some risk in the expectation of seeing your estate grow in value over the years. The young businessman, who can look forward to increased earning power in the years to come, will not normally be satisfied with static savings, nor should he be. New industries, vigorous companies, and managements with young ideas abound in America. Some fall by the wayside, to be sure, and that introduces an element of risk. Many succeed, however, and with them lies the opportunity for dynamic savings—for investing in growth.

Although growth stocks might be of primary interest to young men, it must be remembered that "young" is a relative term. Anyone who, because of present earnings, is not dependent upon income from his investments and is willing to assume risks is "young" enough to make growth his primary investment objective.

Income might be termed the middle-ground objective of investment planning. About the time that the children start going away to college, when a man feels more inclined to reach for an easy chair than for the lawn mower, most investors are also more acutely interested in income than they are in growth. Aggressive companies that look good for the future often pay little or nothing in dividends now because they need to reinvest their earnings in order to grow. When looking for steady income, the investor must place less emphasis on the opportunity for growth, more on present earnings.

Safety is the third reference point. If your primary consideration is safety of principal, your investment plan has to be built with this clearly in mind. The emphasis that you place on safety will be determined by your personal outlook and family considerations. Investors who are dependent for all of their income upon their security holdings naturally will demand a high degree of safety. Also, if you are setting up a fund for some particular purpose, such as the education of your children, you normally will be willing to sacrifice both growth and income to the greater need of preserving the principal of the fund.

In investment planning, that old bromide—"You can't have your cake and eat it too"—is especially true. You can't expect to get the best in growth, income, and safety all at the same time.

DIVERSIFICATION FOR SAFETY, INCOME, GROWTH

Diversification is the device you can use to balance these three somewhat divergent objectives in building an investment program. The notion of diversification is often misinterpreted through oversimplification. All too many investors have the idea that if they own several securities they automatically have a diversified portfolio. On the other hand, many noninvestors feel that because their funds are small they cannot afford to diversify and hence should not become investors at all. Both of these ideas are wrong. Diversification must be considered in terms of the different kinds of securities that are available as they relate to the three different investment objectives.

In the first place, here are two big major classes of securities in which one may invest—equities and debt instruments—(or in more common terms—Stocks and Bonds). We may further divide stocks into common and preferred. Common stock, as we have said, represents simple ownership. Common stock does not carry a fixed dividend. The directors of the corporation do not have to declare dividends even when there are large profits, and if they fail to declare a dividend, they do not have to make up the payment later.

Preferred stock, however, falls in a different class. On preferred stock a specific dividend is fixed in advance. A $5 preferred stock, for instance, is one on which the company is to pay five dollars a year. There are many varieties of preferred stock, but dividends are almost always "cumulative." This means that if the company is unable to pay the dividend when due, it "accumulates" and the company must pay up all unpaid preferred dividends before it can pay anything on the common stock.

Bonds, as we have explained, are evidences of debt. Not only does the company promise to pay a stated amount of interest each year, but it also promises to pay back the principal on maturity or when it is due. "Principal" means simply the amount of the loan, usually $1,000 per bond. (If a bond is quoted at 98, it means that the bond is selling at $980 per $1,000 of face value. Bonds are quoted at a percent of their face value. There are very few corporate bonds in $100 denominations.) Because interest, principal, and maturity date are fixed, bonds of good companies tend to be much more stable in price than stocks.

Here is the way the three major kinds of securities relate to the three major objectives.

	Growth	Income	Safety
Common stock	best	variable	least
Preferred stock	variable	steady	good
Bonds	generally none	very steady	best

That simple summary is largely self-explanatory, but some additional notes may be in order.

COMMON STOCK

Common stocks are best for growth because they reflect the earning power and the prospects of a company. On a bond or preferred stock only a fixed return is paid. You are relatively sure of getting that, but just that and nothing more, regardless of how much money a company earns. Only the common stockholder stands to benefit in terms of increased dividends if the company grows and prospers. On the other hand, of course, he's the one who stands to lose most heavily if the company loses money or fails.

Although about 90% of the companies whose stocks are bought and sold on the New York Stock Exchange have paid dividends in each of the last ten years, and although those dividends have averaged above 5% of the prices at which these stocks were selling at each year-end, any generalization about the income you can expect to realize on a common stock is apt to prove dangerous. About the only safe observation any one can make is that income is likely to be variable.

Some common stocks have paid regular dividends for decades; some have *averaged* good returns over a period of years; some have *averaged* low returns, and some have paid no dividends at all. Actually, of course, many a common stock that has never paid a dividend could be considered a good buy when the prospects for growth are judged against price. But the important thing for the investor to remember is that each common stock is different from every other; income is one of the great variables.

Although of the three kinds of securities, common stocks are rated least attractive as far as safety is concerned, that rating definitely requires some explanation. The term "safety" is used here in a limited sense and refers strictly to the investor's expectation of getting back as many dollars from his investment if he sells as he put into it when he bought. He runs less risk as far as that kind of safety is concerned, if he buys preferred stocks or bonds, for their prices don't fluctuate as much.

But from another point of view, common stocks can properly be considered the safest kind of long-term investment. Here's why: Historically, the prices of food and clothing and other necessities have moved pretty steadily upward in this country. Now when that happens, stock prices on the average are likely to rise too, because a share of stock represents part ownership of a company, and when prices of goods generally increase—including prices of the company's own products—investors quite properly consider the company itself worth more. That's why dollars invested in common stocks are not so likely to lose their purchasing power in a period of inflation as dollars which are invested in preferred stocks or bonds that have a fixed dollar value.

Over 60 years, stock prices have scored an average advance of about 3.2% a year, but there has been nothing regular or consistent about this program upward. Quite the contrary, it has been characterized by wide fluctuations up and down.

Now if you paid $100 for a stock and had to sell out at the bottom of one of the big dips, perhaps at a price of $50 or $60, in order to raise cash, it would be small comfort to you to know that your stock should have increased about 3.2% a year on the basis of historical averages. That's why we've always said no one should invest in stocks unless he has adequate savings and insurance.

One last point: Although the pretty steady decline in the purchasing power of the dollar has had a lot to do with making common stocks worth more, that's not the whole story by any manner or means. Average stock prices have increased because business in this country has grown steadily more productive and more profitable. That's a basic trend that isn't likely to stop.

PREFERRED STOCK

Since a preferred stock usually pays only a fixed dividend, regardless of how much money a company earns, the preferred stockholder obviously doesn't stand nearly as good a chance to share in the growth of that company as the common stockholder does. However, there are many different kinds of preferreds, and some of them do offer the owner virtually an equal opportunity to participate in the company's growth because they are "convertible." This means that they can be exchanged for common stock within a certain period at some stated price.

For example, if the common stock of a company is selling at $15 a share, a preferred stock issued at a par value of $100 might be convertible, at the owner's option, into five shares of common for five years. If the price of the common were to rise above $20 a share during that five years, it would be profitable for the owner to convert his preferred into common, provided he could figure on getting as good a dividend return from the five shares of common as from the one share of preferred.

While preferred stock assures the owner a pretty steady income, that is true only so long as the company operates profitably. If the company gets in the red, dividends may stop. Most preferred stocks, however, provide that dividends shall be cumulative. This means that all back dividends on the preferred must be paid up before common dividends can be paid. In short, a temporary suspension of payment on the preferred dividend does not mean that the income is necessarily lost. Arrears may be paid up when business improves. Some preferred stocks give the preferred stockholders a vote in company affairs if dividends are not paid. And some preferreds stipulate that dividends are to be paid only if earned. The investor should ask for a full description of any preferred stock before he buys.

Because preferred stocks have a prior claim on earnings and assets, they tend to be more stable in price than common stocks and are not as sensitive to minor changes in earnings as common stocks. Of course, preferred stock prices are also subject to the psychological influences that produce booms and depressions. Prices of preferred stocks vary both with the fortunes of the company and in accordance with rights they give to the holder.

BONDS

Most bonds have no opportunity to reflect growth because the interest rate is fixed and so is the dollar value at maturity. Occasionally, bonds are issued that are convertible into common stock, in which case, of course, they have the same possibility of reflecting growth that is shown by convertible preferred stocks. Such bonds are unusual, however.

Although a company occasionally fails to meet interest on its bonds, the income from bonds can generally be regarded as very steady.

As for safety, there is more likelihood that you can sell a good bond tomorrow for approximately what you paid for it yesterday than is the case with any other type of security. This is true because a company pledges that the money will be repaid, and it backs up that pledge by posting collateral of various kinds. Thus a "first mortgage bond" is backed by a first mortgage on certain physical assets of the company. A "debenture" is backed only by the general credit of the company. So long as the credit of the company or the collateral behind the bond remains sound, its price does not generally fluctuate greatly. Prices will change, of course, as the credit of the company changes and they will vary as interest rates vary.

COMPANIES KEEP SCRAPBOOKS, TOO
Alexander R. Hammer

Much of the information businessmen obtain as a guide to action comes from the business pages of their newspaper. *The New York Times* does an especially fine job in making business news as interesting as it is informative. The following story, treating a little-publicized phase of business routine, was done by a staff writer.

Not long ago, press clippings were collected chiefly by Hollywood stars, would-be stars and other publicity-hungry celebrities. Times have changed.

Today, these notices are bought and utilized by business men as well—and not to flatter their egos. Companies have found them a valuable means to spur sales, stimulate promotion, discover leads for new business, and so on. In fact, some 90 per cent of all press clippings—more than 20,000,000 a year—are pasted in corporate scrapbooks.

Although the nation's thirty recognized clipping bureaus gross only about $5,000,000 a year (their fees average about 15 cents a clipping plus reading charges), they are opening the door to millions, if not billions, of dollars' worth of trade to business concerns.

THE BEST CUSTOMERS

Many business men, especially since World War II when competition became more intense, have discovered that good sales prospects can be found in a wide variety of unrelated newspaper items—a fire story, an account of a prison break, or a letter to the editor, to name a few. To tap these sources fully they have become the press clipping bureaus' best customers.

For instance, construction and engineering concerns and their major suppliers use the clipping services to learn when and where new schools, churches, bridges, roads and sewers are contemplated.

Manufacturers of fire alarms, extinguishers, life nets, fire-fighting apparatus and similar equipment check the clippings for fire stories. Where a residential or commercial structure has been destroyed, builders try to anticipate what rebuilding or repair work needs to be done. Producers of home furnishings, office equipment and industrial machinery also can get sales leads from such stories.

A jail break clipping may indicate to jail manufacturers or contractors the need for a new alarm or lock system, new building construction, or perhaps such seemingly unrelated items as new

From *The New York Times*, April 6, 1957. Reprinted by permission of *The New York Times* and the author.

recreational and kitchen equipment to quiet unrest among the prisoners.

BUDGET STORIES A SOURCE

Budget stories are another major source of leads for the enterprising salesman, manufacturer and contractor. For example, school budgets totaling several billion dollars a year are reported in the public press. Each school system must purchase a wide range of articles and equipment, ranging from pencils and textbooks to new buildings.

One of the biggest aids to business men is found in the letters-to-the-editor columns. Whenever a neighborhood needs a new fire station, road, traffic light, bridge or other improvement, someone usually makes this want known in a letter to the local newspaper. These letters provide clues to possible new customers.

Besides the clients who are looking for new customers, press-clipping subscribers include investors interested in bond issues, companies that want to check on competitive advertising and companies that want to build good-will among customers or prospective customers.

In the last category is a large pharmaceutical concern with a standing order for clippings about doctors, dentists and druggists. The company mails these clippings along with congratulatory notes to the persons involved.

One large manufacturing company maintains good employe relations by collecting clippings about the social and civic activities of its workers and sending the news items to those mentioned in the write-ups. Employes are delighted to find that executives of the company can take time out for this recognition.

Hundreds of companies regularly use promotional montages of their press clippings for salesmen to show customers. Others include similar publicity collections in annual reports.

KEEPING UP WITH PRICES

Companies also utilize press clippings to keep tabs on price increases or decreases of their competitors to see if their own products are in line competitively. They also use the clippings to plan or revise their advertising campaigns on the basis of their competitors' actions.

One of the largest and oldest press-clipping bureaus in the United States is the Luce Press Clipping Bureau, which was founded in 1888. It has offices in New York, Topeka, Kan., and Kansas City, Mo. Luce has 100 readers poring over the editorial and advertising matter in 1,834 daily newspapers, 8,000 weekly newspapers and 3,500 magazines and business publications. Two other leading press-clipping bureaus are Henry Romeike, Inc., and Burrelles Press Clipping Bureau, both in New York.

John P. French, manager of Luce's New York office, said yesterday that about 75 per cent of all press bureau clippings came from newspapers and the rest from magazines and periodicals. He said that Luce's bill for newspapers and magazines amounts to nearly $100,000 a year.

Mr. French said that about two-thirds of his company's subscribers were permanent, having been customers for years. One of the company's oldest subscribers is the International Silver Company, which ordered its first clipping from Luce in 1906.

Luce mails its clippings every other day to its clients, according to Mr. French. Most press-clipping bureaus, he said, charge from $12 to $20 a month for reading plus from 12 to 15 cents a clipping. About 50 per cent of a bureau's operation, he said, consists of the actual reading of the newspaper or magazine, while the rest entails the clipping, captioning, editing and mailing of the clipping.

Luce Press Clipping Bureau also has an affiliate, Luce, International, with offices in Amsterdam, the Netherlands, which supplies clients with press and magazine clippings from all countries in the world, including those behind the Iron Curtain. Many American companies with overseas branches use both domestic and overseas press-clipping services.

THE SEA AROUND OUR CABLES

Eldon Nichols

One often speaks of the romance of modern business but cannot always summon the language to make the point convincing. The following article is a well-written reminder that business and adventure are not alien to each other as it adds a captivating chapter to the story of communication. Its author is the project manager of Alaskan and Pacific Cables, Long Lines Department, American Telephone and Telegraph Company.

Between the sunlit surface waters of the open sea and the hidden hills and valleys of the ocean floor lies the least known region of the sea. These deep, dark waters, with all their mysteries and their unsolved problems, cover a very considerable part of the earth. The whole world ocean extends over about three-fourths of the surface of the globe. If we subtract the shallow areas of the continental shelves and the scattered banks and shoals, where at least the pale ghost of sunlight moves over the underlying bottom, there still remains about half the earth that is covered by miles-deep, lightless water, that has been dark since the world began.[1]

The air and the earth are two of nature's elements which have long received the bearers of man's spoken messages: the air since open-wire telephone lines were first strung from roof-top to roof-top in the earliest days of Bell's "speaking telegraph"; and the earth from the time when cables were taken down from poles and buried in the ground.

Now telephone cables are being entrusted to still another element: the sea. The arduous task of laying twin telephone cables between North America and Great Britain has been successfully accomplished, and conversations flash back and forth beneath the Altantic's waves in smooth routine. The Alaskan cables followed, and were opened for service on last December 11. The Pacific has already been plumbed and charted in another direction, and twin cables to the Hawaiian Islands are to be laid this year.

With the first two of these elements —air and earth—telephone people are rather familiar. They know how to deal with them to best advantage: what the principal hazards to their circuits are, and how to guard against them.

Not so with water—the ocean. This is pretty much a new medium to them, and while there is a great and historic

[1] From *The Sea Around Us*. Copyright 1951, Rachel L. Carson. Published by Oxford University Press, New York.

Reprinted from the *Bell Telephone Magazine* for Winter 1956–57 by courtesy of the American Telephone and Telegraph Company.

body of information about Oceanus and all his seven seas, and even some experience applicable to submarine telephone cables, deep water is still strange to telephone men. It is natural, then, that since the transatlantic submarine telephone cable became a real probability, we have been learning all we can about conditions in the oceans: particularly what may cause damage to cables and interrupt service, and how to avoid or overcome the causes.

Such information we have been gaining from a variety of sources. There is the history of submarine telegraph cables, which first came into use more than a hundred years ago, and the experience of the officers of present-day cable ships. There are the published works of oceanographers and other scientists, and the discussions we have had with a number of these gentlemen. There is our own experience, still rather slight but rapidly increasing, with the planning and laying of the new cables and, of course, with older but shorter submarine cables—particularly those between Key West, Florida, and Havana, Cuba. Some of the things we have learned have proved not only important but interesting to those of us who have sought them out. Perhaps you will find them so too.

A convenient way to cover our subject is to begin at the cable terminal building (near where the cables come ashore—or put to sea, if you will), and continue down to the shore and on through the water to the deep ocean floor, stopping to consider each of the possible hazards we find along the route.

The terminal building is usually located quite close to the shore, in part to keep the cables as short as possible but principally because any damage to them by construction workers or others could result in a power surge that might destroy the nearest sub-

marine repeater. The cables are buried deeply all the way from the terminal building down to the shore, across the beach, and to a point below the low tide line.

FROM LAND TO WATER

Ideally, the cables should enter the water from a sandy beach in a sheltered location where there is little or no surf. In some cases however, the only sheltered waters available are frequented by vessels, which may damage the cables with their anchors; or they are at the mouths of streams, where masses of silt, or floating logs borne by spring floods, might cause trouble. Consider, for example, the California coast, where the cables to Hawaii will land. Here, the best landing site is an exposed beach where the prevailing northwest winds cause heavy surf. Fortunately, divers who checked the bottom for us found there are no rocks against which the cables might be chafed by the waves. It is expected that the shifting sand will soon cover the cables, but that at times they may again be uncovered by storms. To strengthen and protect the cables, they will be covered by two layers of heavy galvanized-steel armor wires.

In some areas, icebergs may drift over a cable and run aground in shallow water, grinding the cable against the bottom. During the laying of the west-to-east transatlantic telephone cable in 1955, an iceberg appeared unexpectedly in Trinity Bay, Newfoundland—an area previously free from them—and it was necessary to detour around it. Fortunately, the water was deep enough to float the iceberg away without causing any damage.

Where land and ocean come together there is in most places a broad, slightly sloping, flat plateau, called the continental shelf, over which the water is less than 100 fathoms deep. (A fathom is six feet.) On our Atlantic Coast this shelf is some two hundred miles wide; on the Pacific Coast it is more likely to be twenty—both figures varying considerably with the location.

Wherever the continental shelf is smooth and free from rocks, we are likely to find commercial fishermen operating "beam" or "otter" trawlers. These are sturdy, powerful vessels which drag large nets equipped with weights to hold them down close to the ocean bottom. (On the Pacific Coast beam trawlers are generally called "draggers.") At the outer corners of a trawler's net are two large "otter boards" made of planks and weighted with steel shoes which slide along on the bottom. The otter boards are rigged like kites, so that they tend to pull away from each other, holding the net wide open. Cables, particularly old ones weakened by corrosion, are often damaged when an otter board is dragged over them; even a strong new cable may be caught on the end of an otter board and pulled up to the surface—where the fisherman may cut the cable to free his tackle.

Wherever possible, we route our cables through areas where trawlers cannot operate because the bottom is too irregular or rocky. Although we must avoid rocks in rough shallow water, where waves would scrape the cables against them, there is little or no wave motion at depths of more than 18 or 20 fathoms, so that rocks are not particularly harmful under these conditions. Additional measures to guard against trawlers are being studied and an active program is being planned. This will include efforts to inform all operators of trawlers of the locations of our cables and to enlist their coöperation.

Marine borers, particularly teredos or "shipworms," are potential enemies of our cables in water of shallow and moderate depth. The shipworm, which is not a worm at all but a relative of the clam, attaches itself to a submerged object, usually wood, and drills a deep hole which is used as a home or shelter. Since teredos might drill holes into our cables between the armor wires, we use a "teredo tape" of copper around the return tapes which form the outer conductor. The teredo tape is wrapped on tightly, with overlapping joints, and is expected to give complete protection.

Another enemy from the animal world, on rare occasions, is the whale. The sperm whale has a peculiar habit of diving to depths as great as half a mile and burrowing into the soft bottom. In several instances, cable ships dispatched to repair a broken cable have found the remains of a whale entangled in it.

TO GREATER DEPTHS

When the gradually sloping continental shelf finally reaches a depth of between one hundred and two hundred fathoms below sea level, the bottom begins to descend at a much steeper angle. This region is called the continental slope. In routing our cables here, we try to avoid the steepest places; because here the cables may be under excessive strain, or great quantities of mud or sand may have accumulated, in readiness for a submarine landslide that will carry away any cables that are in its path.

Cutting through the continental shelf and slope are many submarine canyons which, if they were exposed to our view, would rival or surpass the great canyons of our western states. We avoid these sea canyons, since the cables might be exposed to abrasion from currents carrying silt. There is also the danger of sharp rocks at points where the cables are suspended.

It is easy to picture a submarine landslide of sand or mud slumping down a steep underwater slope. Not quite so simple in concept is the "turbidity current." If silt consisting of particles of sand, which are much heavier than water, begins to tumble down a submarine slope, the result may be quite different from the slide which our experiences above water would lead us to expect. The heavy particles of silt, instead of sticking together, may be separately suspended in the water, forming a mixture much heavier than water but not at all sticky, and behaving more like mercury than like mud. A turbidity current of this kind may flow initially at a speed as high as sixty miles an hour, and may travel several hundred miles out across the nearly flat ocean floor before finally coming to rest.

It is pretty well established that it was such a current as this, starting on the Grand Banks of Newfoundland on November 18, 1929, and sweeping into the Atlantic, which carried away all the transatlantic telegraph cables. In some instances as much as two hundred miles of cable could not be found and had to be replaced.

Those whose work is involved with ocean deeps sometimes encounter two questions that seem to trouble people. First, does a cable or other object really sink all the way to the bottom, or does it somehow reach a state of balance part of the way down, and remain suspended there? The answer to this is that any object that is heavier than an equal volume of water will sink, and since the density of water changes very little with depth, practically any object which sinks beneath the surface will go all the way to the bottom. In fact, many objects will be crushed together into smaller volumes by the pressure of the water after they have sunk part of the way, after which they will sink faster. Of course an object that is lighter than an equal volume of water will float, part of it projecting above the surface.

The second question is, how do we know the depth of the ocean, since divers and submarines can descend only a few hundred feet below the surface? The depth of the ocean was once measured by lowering a weight at the end of a line until an abrupt reduction in the tension on the line indicated that the weight had touched bottom. Each measurement made in this manner in deep water took an hour or more. Now a sonic depth measuring set, or echo sounder, does the job in a few seconds. A very loud "ping" of sound is shot downward from a device in the bottom of the ship's hull. The sound travels to the ocean bottom at a speed of about 800 fathoms per second and part of it returns to the ship as an echo. The time required for the round trip is measured and recorded automatically on a chart. Since "pings" are sent at short intervals, a profile of the ocean bottom along the course followed by the ship is traced upon the chart.

MOUNTAINS OF THE DEPTHS

Rising from the deep ocean floor are many isolated submarine mountains, called sea-mounts, and numerous long ranges. There is, for example, a continuous mountain chain in the Atlantic extending from the Arctic Ocean to the Antarctic, breaking the surface at intervals to form islands. This range had to be crossed by the transatlantic cables, of course. The route of the cables to be laid between California and Hawaii next summer crosses the Murray Fracture Zone. This is a little-explored submarine ridge extending westward across the Pacific from the California coast. Present indications are that this great seam may prove to be even grander in scale than the better known Mendocino Fracture Zone, farther north, which contains a steep slope or escarpment a mile high and a thousand miles long. However, crossing points have been found at which the slope will not be excessively steep.

In addition to the many ridges and sea-mounts, there are, particularly in the Pacific, odd cone-shaped mountains with flat tops, called guyots. Apparently these guyots once were volcanoes which rose above the surface of the sea to form volcanic islands. Through ages of exposure to wind, rain, and waves, the part above the surface eroded until the island was quite flat. Then finally the whole volcanic cone and the nearby ocean bottom sank, submerging the island completely.

We detour our cables around submarine mountains and ridges wherever we can, because of the danger of breakage on their steep, rough slopes. Another reason is the possibility that they may contain outcroppings of copper or other metals which, in salt water, might set up an electrolytic action that would cause the cables' armor to corrode and disappear rapidly.

Not all of the ocean floor is mountainous, however; a great deal of it is deeply covered with sediment, forming great flat areas called abyssal plains. This sediment, which has been settling down through the water for millions of years, consists mainly of silt from rivers, dust from volcanic eruptions and other sources, and the shells and remains of countless tiny plants and animals, called plankton. This kind of ocean bottom furnishes an ideal bed for a cable, and its smooth, undisturbed surface gives evidence that there has been no volcanic activity in the recent past.

The possibility of a volcanic erup-

tion occurring on the ocean bottom under or near a cable has been studied recently because of several reports from pilots of aircraft in the vicinity of the Hawaiian Islands. These observers reported seeing masses of brown, yellow, and green material on the surface of the ocean. In one case it was first thought that a new island had risen from the ocean floor at a point about 750 miles northwest of Honolulu. After a few days, however, this "island" disappeared, and it is now believed to have been floating material, possibly volcanic mud or ashes.

In the most recent case of this kind, it was later reported that the floating material was not of volcanic origin at all but was a floating mass of marine plants known as algae. At any rate, the probability of an eruption occurring close to any particular cable route is exceedingly remote.

EARTHQUAKE HAZARDS

Submarine earthquakes have occurred frequently in some areas, notably along the route of the Alaskan cables, according to calculations based on seismograph records obtained at a number of observatories. Seismologists have told us that the centers of most of these disturbances are several miles below the bottom of the ocean floor, and that it is unlikely that many of them result in cracks or fractures on the ocean floor that would break a cable. Nevertheless, we avoid earthquake areas wherever we can.

In addition to these earthquakes beneath the ocean floor, the possibility of damage near the shore had to be considered in one instance. This was the selection of the landing site in California for the cables to Hawaii. The site finally chosen is on the western, or seaward, side of the only fault line in the vicinity, which is known as the San Andreas Fault, and so a slippage along this line would not be likely to break our cables. Incidentally, the San Francisco earthquake of 1906 was caused by a sudden major slippage along the San Andreas Fault. It runs parallel to the coast line north of San Francisco, and at present the land and the nearby ocean bottom west of the fault—which will include our cable landing and terminal building site—is moving northwestward about two inches a year with respect to the rest of the United States.

Any object submerged in the ocean is constantly pressed on all sides by the weight of the water above. The pressure in pounds per square inch is equal to the weight of a column of water one inch square extending all the way up to the ocean's surface. The significance of this rather dull statement is that in some parts of the Pacific, where our cables will be laid in water as deep as three thousand fathoms, the pressure on every square inch of the surface of the cable and repeaters will be about 8000 pounds. This great pressure has made it necessary to enclose the vacuum tubes and other delicate components of each repeater in a very strong cylinder made of overlapping steel rings, and to seal the ends of the cylinder with extreme care.

WEIGHT, DEPTH, TENSION

When cable is being laid in very deep water, the tension at the upper end becomes quite high because of the cable's own weight. And if it becomes necessary to pick up the cable later for repairs, the tension is generally about twice as high as the laying tension. Along the deeper parts of the route to Hawaii the picking-up tension will be around 25,000 pounds, with an additional surge of two or three thousand pounds whenever the cable ship is

lifted by a wave. To keep the cable from breaking under such high tensions, the armor wires used in the deep-sea sections are being made of special high-strength steel. Little could be gained by increasing the diameter of the armor wires, for this would increase the weight as well as the strength. When a splice must be made in the cable, it is essential that the armor wires be overlapped and wrapped in such a way that the splice is as strong as the cable itself.

The ocean's greatest depths are found not in the middle, as we might expect, but in deep trenches near chains of islands. The deepest spot now known, the Marianas Trench, has a depth of 5,940 fathoms, or nearly six nautical miles. Other deep trenches lie near the Aleutians, the Philippines, and the West Indies. Although we have no need at present to lay cables across or around any of these trenches, they affect our plans in a peculiar way. The ocean floor at the bottoms of trenches seems to be in a state of unrest, and at times it suddenly rises or sinks. When this happens, the displacement of the vast quantity of water above generates a series of great waves. These waves, known by the Japanese name "tsunami" but often miscalled tidal waves, rush across the ocean for great distances at speeds as high as five hundred miles an hour. When such waves arrive at a distant shore, they cause the water to rise and fall to levels far above and below the normal tides, sometimes causing great destruction. The Hawaiian Islands have experienced tsunamis from several of the island trenches in the Pacific. In 1946 a particularly severe one rushed in from the Aleutian Trench and the sea rose as much as fifty feet above normal at some parts of the coast line. To guard against damage from this source, the cable terminal building in Hawaii is being built on a hillside 130 feet above sea level, far higher than any tsunami ever experienced there.

Getting our feet wet is a relatively new experience. Still unknown problems may lurk in the depths—and we are quite certain that we haven't found all the answers to the hazards we face. But we have the utmost confidence in our submarine telephone cables—in service, a-building, and to come—and they form an incalculably important addition to the telephone networks by which people everywhere may speak with one another and hear one another's words and tones. That is why we have reported here something of our progress in the search for ways to protect the new submarine cable systems.

MODERN SUBMARINE TELEPHONE CABLE SYSTEMS

In each system, the main span consists of two one-way cables, like the two separate roadways in a modern superhighway. Each cable has only a single central conductor, surrounded by polyethylene insulation and an outer return conductor made of copper tapes. However, thirty-six telephone conversations may be carried on at the same time by the use of carrier techniques. This is another way of saying that at each end of the cable system there are thirty-six small transmitters, each operating on its own frequency assignment like a tiny radio broadcasting station. The radio signals from these transmitters, instead of being broadcast, are directed into one of the cables and travel through it to the distant end, where there are thirty-six receivers. Each of these receivers is tuned to the frequency of one of the distant transmitters. In this way thirty-six separate two-way voice channels are obtained.

Since the signals weaken rapidly during their trip through the cable, vacuum tube amplifiers or repeaters are inserted in the cable during manufacture at intervals of about 40 miles and are laid on the ocean floor. The amplifiers have vacuum tubes designed for very long life, and are housed in flexible copper tubes supported on the inside by steel rings which are little larger than the cable itself.

Power for the vacuum tubes is transmitted through the cables from terminal stations on shore at both ends; these stations also contain the carrier equipment which prepares the 36 voice currents for transmission through the cables and separates them from each other again at the other end.

Exercises

"The Story of Figures," Burroughs Corporation

1. Condense "The Story of Figures" to 500 words, slanting it to eighth-grade students.
2. Write a theme on the origin of words used in arithmetic. Take your information both from this article and from an unabridged dictionary.
3. Study the sales literature of some manufacturers of calculating machines; then write a paper describing in simple terms what modern calculating machines can do.
4. Write a short piece based on the idea that business without figures is inconceivable. Assume that this piece will form the introduction to "The Story of Figures" reproduced here.

"The Story of Paper," Champion Paper and Fibre Company

1. With the help of your dictionary, write a sentence or two establishing the connection between the words "papyrus" and "paper."
2. What is "maceration"? Is vellum still made exclusively from animal skins? See your dictionary.
3. With the help of library sources, write as interestingly as you know how a similar brief history of one of the following:
   a. The alphabet
   b. Printing
   c. Writing instruments

"What Is Automation?" by John Diebold

1. Starting with Mr. Diebold's first sentence and expanding the idea in your own words, write a paragraph explaining the meaning of automation.
2. In a paragraph define one of the following terms related to automation:
   a. Rethinking a manufacturing process
   b. The linking phase
   c. Feedback
   d. Tape instruction
3. Write an explanation of some process or procedure that you have observed in a factory, home, or shop. If you wish, you may explain in detail one of the following:
   a. Ways to bind a report
   b. Simonizing a car
   c. Making a typewriter erasure
   d. Rewiring a lamp
   e. Drawing a pie chart
   f. Replacing a typewriter ribbon
4. Discuss the expository methods (e.g., definition, illustration, analogy, contrast) used by Mr. Diebold.

"What a Security Is—and Why," Merrill Lynch, Pierce, Fenner and Beane

1. In a paragraph establish clearly the respective identities and roles of the owners of a corporation and the managers.
2. Translate into a paragraph the essence of the table in the section headed, "Diversification for Safety, Growth, Income."

3. Discuss the language and organization of this piece. What qualities do you believe you can well apply to your own writing?

4. Consult, in a newspaper that prints it, the daily table of transactions on the New York Stock Exchange; then write an explanation of the various column headings.

5. After investigation, write a report on the comparative advantages of putting money in a savings bank and investing it in United States Savings Bonds.

6. Write a theme on the subject, "How Much Should One Save?"

"Phantom Profits," by Roger M. Blough

1. Sum up Mr. Blough's point in a single sentence.

2. Write a critique of Mr. Blough's statement as an example of down-to-earth English.

3. Write a simple statement analyzing the disposition of your allowance or salary, at the same time arguing its inadequacy in terms of your needs.

"Companies Keep Scrapbooks, Too," by Alexander R. Hammer

1. Write a report on the ways in which a job-seeker can use news articles to secure leads for application letters. Base your report on actual study of business news stories.

2. Cut out three news stories that suggest job potentialities, and write an application letter opening (the first paragraph or two) utilizing the information in each story. Paste up the news stories and attach them to your paper.

3. Cut out a newspaper story about a marriage, promotion, new appointment, or the like, and write a letter of congratulation to the subject. Assume that you are an acquaintance.

4. After studying the financial section of a good morning newspaper, write an advertisement designed to get more of the newspaper's present readers to turn to that section. Describe the sort of information the readers will find there every day.

"The Sea Around Our Cables," by Eldon Nichols

1. Condense this article for use in a leaflet to be enclosed with telephone bills. Keep the copy down to about 300 words.

2. Analyze the means by which the author has tried to make his story clear to the lay reader.

3. Study the author's use of topic sentences and his methods of paragraph development and write a theme on your findings.

10

The Office

Except for those in sales and factory jobs, most business people are destined to spend half their waking hours in offices. There one finds an institutionalized way of life complete in its attention to both business and social needs. The office has changed mightily since women took to the typewriter. Gone are the spittoon, Spencerian penmanship, flat filing, and the high bookkeeper's chair. Newly arrived are punch-card systems, electric copying machines, air conditioning, the catered coffee break, and Muzak.

Sometimes office life tends to regimentation; sometimes it affords genuine creative opportunities. In any case, it houses human beings of many different temperaments and backgrounds who must learn to work together.

ITS MONOTONOUS CLICK

Richard N. Current

"Five years ago the typewriter was simply a mechanical curiosity," the *Penman's Art Journal* observed in 1887. "Today its monotonous click can be heard in almost every well-regulated business establishment in the country. A great revolution is taking place, and the typewriter is at the bottom of it." The invention of the typewriter is generally attributed to Christopher Latham Sholes, who put together his first crude model in 1867. The revolution that followed is described below. Richard N. Current is Professor of History at the University of Illinois.

. . . When the businessman said, "Take a letter," he usually said it to a woman. Men typists held all the speed championships, and male clerks and amanuenses traditionally had pre-empted all kinds of office work, yet even before 1890 women occupied a great and growing majority of secretarial positions. These "competent young ladies" were "bringing into our business offices, lawyers' offices, editorial sanctums, etc., an element of decency, purity, and method." They were "working a perceptible change" in the old atmosphere of profanity and spittoons. Not that they were crowding out the young men. Instead, the whole field was widening, new clerical jobs opening every day. But nine out of every ten new employees were women.

A girl who wanted to work had motive enough for trying to obtain a clerical job. In the 1880's she had few other attractive opportunities. The New York working girl, for example, could slave in a dressmaker's sweatshop or a cigar factory for a few dollars a week, but her reputation, if not her morals, would suffer, and she would be considered as fair game for predatory youths of the leisure class. The respectable woman, if forced to earn a living, might properly make and sell preserves or pies, illustrate seashells or paint china, give music lessons or teach school, but that was about all until clerical positions began to open up. In 1886, when a saleswoman in a dry goods store earned only six dollars a week, a proficient woman typist in a business office earned fifteen. Money, however, was not the only object: office work was more pleasant and less fatiguing than work in a factory, store, or even school. And that was not all. "It is curious," the anonymous head of a large insurance firm was quoted in 1891, "but during the past year five of our best women clerks have married men of means and are now living in ease and leisure." Certainly the ambitious and self-respecting girl had every reason for wanting to become a "type-writer"—as she herself was likely to be called.

And the businessman had his reasons for hiring her in preference to her brother. Very likely she was better at the job, though this was a hotly debated point, a phase of the larger controversy over women's rights which was raging in the 1880's. Those taking the negative argued that a woman simply could not produce consistently as much and as good work as a man because of unblinkable facts of nature: every four weeks she lost temporarily a fifth of her "vital power." Affirmative spokesmen, or rather spokeswomen, replied that men were "more frequently absent because of their vices," and they cited the example of stenography and typewriting to clinch their case. "Here it is admitted that women are superior to men, their greater quickness of perception and motion giving them obvious advantages," a feminist declared in 1886. Another added in 1891: "Business men tell me they prefer women as shorthand amanuenses for one particular reason. It is because, contrary to tradition, women are less likely than men to disclose the business secrets of their employers. Then, too, they are more faithful and more apt to remain for a long period in the service of one employer." That is, presumably, the woman would remain if she did not happen to meet a man of means who would support her in a life of ease and leisure.

Whatever the merits of the feminist and antifeminist debate, the woman had one clear and undisputed advantage in the eyes of her employer. She cost less. Businessmen, having spent good money on typewriters, usually sought to compensate by cutting down on operating expenses. At first they hired untrained boys, who were cheap. The operators presumably needed no special skill; the machine would do the work. It did not, of course, and so employers turned increasingly to women with training and experience. These had to be paid more than the mere boys but not so much as good men typists. In 1886, when top pay for women was fifteen dollars a week, most men were getting twenty.

This differential in pay, with other facts of the matter, casts some doubt on the assumption, which came to be widely held, that "women achieved economic emancipation through the writing machine." The truth is that the women most in need of emancipation—the sweatshop slaves, for instance—were the ones least affected by the office revolution. The business employer looked for the daughters of decent middle-class families, living at home, in preference to girls from the slums or even the farms. "Unfortunately," as a woman reporter said in 1891, "respectable relations cannot be manufactured to order. Most clerks have comfortable homes with their parents. As a rule, the clerk's entire salary is at her disposal for her personal requirements."

The independent, self-supporting girl could make her way as a "typewriter," but only with difficulty. In New York the Young Women's Christian Association, to overcome the prejudice against the career girl and help her find work, sponsored typing and shorthand classes as early as the 1870's. According to a historian of the Y.W.C.A., the education committee of the association discussed seriously the danger that "the female mind and constitution would be certain to break under the strain of a six months' course in stenography and typewriting"—an apprehension that was rather absurd in view of the backbreaking chores American women had done from time immemorial in household and mill.

The fact that women were working outside the home was not new in the 1880's. What was new was the fact that, in tremendous numbers, they were getting respectable, white-collar jobs. And they were doing more than taking dictation and running typewriters. They were also working as cashiers, bookkeepers, filing clerks, even telegraph operators. In telegraphy they got their start by serving as strikebreakers early in the decade. In all these various occupations they were at least as efficient as men, and they were willing to work for lower wages. The spirit of the time, influenced by the women's rights agitation, demanded that they be given a chance. And so, even without the advent of the typewriter, even without any basic change in office practice, they very likely would have replaced male clerks sooner or later, for they could have pushed pens and pencils equally well and for less pay.

That is not to deny that the coming of the typewriter affected the office revolution and thereby the role and status of women. It helped to unsettle the established routine, shake businessmen out of their fixed habits, and wake them to the feasibility of new ways. If it did not free all women wage slaves, it nevertheless hastened the entry of thousands upon thousands of women workers into what had always been a preserve for men and what, in the absence of technological change, might have remained one for years to come. It provided a catalyst for the process by which the sphere of female activity was considerably widened.

There were other consequences. Together with the new duplicating devices it inspired, the writing machine swelled tremendously the output of recorded words. Duplicating in earlier days, except of course on the printing press, was tedious, slow, and altogether unsatisfactory. Anyone wanting to keep copies of his outgoing correspondence could do no better than use the letter-press. This squeezed together the original letter, written in indelible ink, and a wet second sheet, thin enough that the impression would show through it. Once dried, the copy made a record that afterward could be referred to—and even deciphered if blurs and blots were not too numerous. In the 1870's Thomas A. Edison tried to improve upon the letter-press with his combination of a waxed stencil and an electric pen. This pen, with a vibrating needle for a point, wrote directly on the stencil, which then could be used to make an indefinite number of duplicates. The idea never amounted to much until the typewriter replaced the electric pen for cutting stencils. Meanwhile duplicates of typewritten material were being made by means of the old letter-press, or a gelatine pad, a lithographic stone, or carbon paper. The carbon paper was sometimes coated on both sides (the reversed copy being readable through thin oiled paper), and in that way as many as thirty copies could be produced at once.

The ready multiplication of documents saved time and labor, but it also added to labor and wasted time. As early as 1885 a judge complained that typewritten papers were clogging the courts. Formerly, when attorneys themselves wrote what they had to submit, they were mercifully brief, he said. Now that they could dictate to a typist, they were much wordier than they needed to be, and the poor judge found it harder and harder to keep up with his docket. No doubt the postman had cause to complain also, as the general increase in correspondence stuffed his mailbags and made heavier his weary load.

Certainly the historian in years to come would view with mixed feelings what was happening in those days. He might even be inclined to divide history into two epochs: B.T. and A.T., that is, before and after the introduction of the typewriter. Before, records were relatively scarce. After, they piled up by the thousands of tons, and the historian's problem became not how to find them but how to find his way through them.

The multiplication of records not only measured but also made possible a growing complexity of life. In particular, it facilitated the rise of both Big Business and Big Bureaucracy, which together have furnished a central theme of American history since the Civil War. That war meant more than a conflict over slavery, more than a struggle for what men South or North thought right. It was, as it has been aptly called, a Second American Revolution. It marked the passage of the United States from an agrarian to an industrial economy and from a Federal Union to a New Nation conceived in profit-seeking and dedicated to the proposition that business is supreme. The emerging corporate enterprise required for its life and growth vastly more sheer paper work than any number of old-time clerks, equipped with pencil or pen, could efficiently handle. So did the leviathan government that followed. For businessman and bureaucrat alike, the typewriter arrived just in the nick of time.

Great things from small inventions grow. From the typewriter rose a new industry, eventually producing office appliances of all kinds. From it came a change in the atmosphere and the procedures in office and bureau. A new class of white-collar women appeared, and new job opportunities at least indirectly raised the status of women in general. Facilities for mass communication were multiplied. Indeed, from the typewriter, one of the comparatively unsung inventions of the machine age, stemmed in large part not merely big business and big government but big civilization as well.

Americans of the 1880's sensed that a quiet revolution was under way, and they knew that a mechanical invention was back of it. They were technology conscious. Throughout the nineteenth century one innovation after another had affected ways of living so strikingly that they could not fail to take notice. They thought of the steam engine, the reaper, the sewing machine, the telegraph, the telephone, the dynamo, and so on. And they readily added the typewriter to their list.

"Type writing is as great an improvement on long-hand writing as steam locomotion is upon the stage coach of olden times," the Milwaukee *Evening Wisconsin* declared in 1887. "In the face of its general use and great utility, it is astonishing how few people know who the inventors were or how great was their labor in bringing it to a state of usefulness."

THE NEW OFFICE

C. Wright Mills

The mechanization of the office is, indeed, a fact. Some argue that this has freed employees from the drudgery of dull and routine jobs. Others, like C. Wright Mills, hold that the new office is stultifying. Anyone who has worked in a large office has his own view, but he cannot fail to be aroused by the following account of the white collar world by one of its most literate critics. Dr. Mills is Professor of Sociology at Columbia University. He also wrote *The Power Elite*.

The modern office with its tens of thousands of square feet and its factory-like flow of work is not an informal, friendly place. The drag and beat of work, the 'production unit' tempo, require that time consumed by anything but business at hand be explained and apologized for. Dictation was once a private meeting of executive and secretary. Now the executive phones a pool of dictaphone transcribers whom he never sees and who know him merely as a voice. Many old types of personnel have become machine operators, many new types began as machine operators.

1. The rise of the office manager, from a 'chief clerk' to a responsible executive reporting directly to the company treasurer or vice president, is an obvious index to the enlargement of offices and to the rise of the office as a centralized service division of the entire enterprise. It is under him that the factory-like office has been developing. Specializing as he does in the rational and efficient design and service of office functions, the office manager can obviously do a better job than a detached minor supervisor.

The office manager had begun to appear in the larger companies by the late 'twenties. Many early office managers were 'detail men' holding other positions, perhaps in the accounting department, but at the same time 'handling' the office force. But as the office increased in importance and in costs, it grew into an autonomous unit and the office manager grew with it. He had to know the clerical work and the routing of all departments; he had to be able to design and to adapt to new administrative schemes and set-ups; he had to train new employees and re-train old ones. The all-company scope of his domain gave room for his knowledge and prestige to increase, or at least his claims for prestige *vis à vis* 'other department heads.' By 1929, about one-third of one large group of office managers came from non-office executive positions, whereas half worked up through the office, and some

17 per cent came up through other offices, so that one may assume the position already had a recognized status.

II. As office machinery is introduced, the number of routine jobs is increased, and consequently the proportion of 'positions requiring initiative' is decreased. 'Mechanization is resulting in a much clearer distinction between the managing staff and the operating staff,' observed the War Manpower Commission. 'Finger dexterity is often more important than creative thinking. Promotions consequently become relatively rare. . . . Some large office managers actually prefer to hire girls who are content to remain simply clerks, who will attempt to rise no higher than their initial level.'

As we compare the personnel of the new office with that of the old, it is the mass of clerical machine-operatives that immediately strikes us. They are the most factory-like operatives in the white-collar worlds. The period of time required to learn their skills seems steadily to decline; it must, in fact, if the expense of introducing machines and new standardized specializations is to be justified. For the key advantages of most mechanical and centralizing office devices are that, while they permit greater speed and accuracy, they also require cheaper labor per unit, less training, simpler specialization, and thus replaceable employees.

These interchangeable clerks often punch a time clock, are not allowed to talk during working hours, and have no tenure of employment beyond a week or sometimes a month. They typically have no contact with supervisors except in the course of being supervised. In large offices these people are the major links in the system, but in their minds and in those of their managers, there is rarely any serious thought of learning

the whole system and rising within it. Even in the middle 'twenties 88 per cent of the office managers questioned in one survey indicated that they definitely needed people 'who give little promise of rising to an executive status,' and 60 per cent stated that there was 'very little opportunity' in their offices to learn, and hence rise, by apprenticeship.

The rationalization of the office, on the one hand, attracts and creates a new mass of clerks and machine operators, and their work increasingly approximates the factory operative in light manufacturing. On the other hand, this new office requires the office manager, a specialized manager who operates the human machinery.

III. The bookkeeper has been grievously affected by the last half century of office change: his old central position is usurped by the office manager, and even the most experienced bookkeeper with pen and ink cannot compete with a high-school girl trained in three or four months to use a machine. It is like a pick and shovel against a power scoop.

The bookkeeping or billing machine posts, enters, totals, and balances; from the accumulated postings control accounts are made up. And such a machine is a simple sort of apparatus, although it is still second only to the typewriter in offices today. Other new machines displace ten of the old, and their operatives, at one stroke. Just as the high-school girl with her machine has displaced the pen-and-ink bookkeeper, so the big new machines promise, in due course, to displace the high-school girl. At the top of the new 'bookkeeping' world are the professional accountants and electronic technicians. But their predominance on any practical scale is still largely to come. In the meantime, the stratum of older bookkeepers is demoted to the level of the clerical mass.

'When recruiting new employees for this operation,' says the manager of a bookkeeping operation in a large company, 'we seek girls about seventeen years minimum age, at least two years' high school or its equivalent, with no previous business experience and good personal qualifications. We prefer inexperienced girls and those who have some economic incentive to work as we have found they make the steadiest workers; so we select from our recruits what we classify as the semi-dependent or wholly dependent applicant. . . .'

iv. The secretary has been the model of aspiration for most office girls. The typewriter has, of course, been the woman's machine, and in itself it has not led to factory-like effects. In and out of the office world, it has been a highly respectable machine. Its operator, equipped with stenographer's pad, has managed to borrow prestige from her close and private contact with the executive.

The standard girl-hierarchy in offices has been formed around the typewriter in the following way: (1) The private secretary, as someone's confidential assistant, in many cases can actually act for him on many not always routine matters. She takes care of his appointments, his daily schedule, his check book—is, in short, justifiably called his office wife. If her boss's office warrants it, she may even have stenographers and typists working for her. (2) The stenographer is a typist who also takes dictation. (3) The typist works only with the machine; because her work is a straight copying matter, her most important traits are speed and accuracy at the keyboard. Unlike the secretary, and to a lesser extent the stenographer, she is usually closely supervised.

In the new, rationalized office, this hierarchy—graded in income, skill, degree of supervision, and access to important persons—has begun to break down. There is now a strong tendency to limit the number of secretaries; many $15,000-a-year executives do not have private secretaries and never see a shorthand stenographer. Instead they dictate to a machine, whose cylinders go to a pool of typists. Although this pooling of stenographic services took place in many big offices before dictaphone equipment was installed, usually the two went together. Systematic studies clearly revealed the wastefulness of individually assigned stenographers, the alternate periods of slack and of frenzy rather than a smooth and efficient flow.

Since its beginnings in the 'twenties, the centralization of the stenographic operation has spread continuously, being limited only by size of office and inertia. The trend is for only the senior executives to have private secretaries and for both stenographers and typists to become pooled as transcribing typists. In one large insurance company's home office less than 2 per cent of the employees are assigned as secretaries to persons above the rank of Division Manager. The junior executive has his stenographer on his desk in a metal box, or may even dictate directly to the transcribing pool via inter-office telephone.

The centralized transcribing pool has further advantages: for the 'poor dictator,' the machines allow adjustments in audibility; they eliminate over-time imposed by late afternoon dictation, and also the strain of reading hurriedly written notes. 'They hear it automatically and have only to punch the keys to get the results,' the managerial literature states. 'Girls with speed and accuracy' are what are wanted in the new office.

The skill of shorthand becomes obsolete; the white-collar girl becomes almost immediately replaceable; work in offices becomes increasingly a blind-alley. The new white-collar girl cannot know intimately some segment of the office or business, and has lost the private contact that gave status to the secretary and even the stenographer. The work is regulated so that it can be speeded up and effectively supervised by non-executive personnel. In short, the prized white-collar spot for women is becoming more and more the job of a factory-like operative. By the early 'thirties, Amy Hewes was observing, 'The shadowy line between many . . . clerical tasks and *unskilled* factory occupations is becoming more and more imperceptible.'

The new office is rationalized: machines are used, employees become machine attendants; the work, as in the factory, is collective, not individualized; it is standardized for interchangeable, quickly replaceable clerks; it is specialized to the point of automatization. The employee group is transformed into a uniform mass in a soundless place, and the day itself is regulated by an impersonal time schedule. Seeing the big stretch of office space, with rows of identical desks, one is reminded of Herman Melville's description of a nineteenth-century factory: 'At rows of blank-looking counters sat rows of blank-looking girls, with blank, white folders in their blank hands, all blankly folding blank paper.'

•

THE TESTIMONIAL LUNCH

Corey Ford

A business institution, along with the baseball pool and the gossip at the water cooler, is the testimonial lunch. This account by an accomplished American humorist does not add to anyone's knowledge of the subject, but it helps to revive some of the libels fondly perpetuated by everyone on the payroll.

In contrast to the carefree spirit of the Bridal Shower, the Testimonial Lunch for Mr. Murgatroyd is a rather formal affair. It is held in the private dining room of the Stafford Hotel, following a suggestion by Mr. Twitchell's credit manager that this might be a good way to collect some of that back bill which Mr. Stafford has owed the firm for a couple of years. At the head table, appropriately decorated with ferns and a bowl of olives and celery, Mr. Murgatroyd occupies the place of honor between Mr. Twitchell and Mr. Twitchell's brother-in-law, the first vice-president, and is flanked on either side by the assistant vice-presidents, department heads, and other members of Mr. Twitchell's immediate family. The rest of the staff is seated at the lower table, where there aren't any olives and the service is at least two courses behind. Some of them never get to dessert at all.

The luncheon gets under way promptly, since Mr. Twitchell has a golf date at two o'clock, and the rest of the brass want to get back to the office as soon as possible to watch the base-ball game on television. Mr. Twitchell glances at his watch from time to time and drums his fingers impatiently, while Mr. Murgatroyd bolts his chicken à la king in nervous silence. The employees at the lower table have barely started on the entrée when Mr. Twitchell rises, taps on his water glass with the blade of a knife, and announces that he would like to say a few words about the guest of honor, a man whose name we all know, Mr. Merganthrop.

Amid the ensuing polite patter of hands, Mr. Murgatroyd gazes down at his plate with a sheepish smile. He is wearing a shiny blue serge business suit, a bachelor's button from the garden which Mrs. Murgatroyd fastened in his lapel when he started to work this morning, and a celluloid collar which hops up and down over his adam's apple whenever he swallows. Mr. Twitchell frowns at his watch, and holds up his hand to terminate the brief applause.

"I want to take this opportunity," he begins, "of expressing our appreciation to Mr. Morganthau for the co-operation and loyalty which he has shown during the past seventeen years. No one has done more to put the L. C. Twitchell Company where it is today, and we all regret that, due to certain unavoidable changes in the organization, the firm will no longer be able to avail itself of the privilege of his services. And so we say gratefully, from the bottoms of our hearts: 'So long, Mr. Mortimer, and good luck to you wherever you go.'"

Mr. Twitchell beams at the members of the audience, who smile back at him uneasily. Mr. Twitchell's son is graduating from Yale next month, and each of them is wondering to himself privately how much longer the firm will be able to avail itself of *his* services too. Mr. Twitchell clears his throat, shattering the silence like a rifle shot, and turns to Mr. Murgatroyd.

"As a slight token of our esteem and affection, Mr. Merton," he concludes, "I therefore wish to present you with this solid gold bill clip as a slight token of our affection and esteem. I'm sorry we didn't have time to get it engraved, due to all the haste and confusion, but if you will take it back to the jeweler any time he'll put your initials on it free of charge."

Mr. Murgatroyd, blinking tears of gratitude, climbs nervously to his feet, puts on his spectacles, and takes from his pocket the typewritten speech of thanks which he has been practicing in front of Mrs. Murgatroyd every night for the past two weeks. As he opens his mouth to speak, Mr. Twitchell grasps his hand hurriedly and explains that unfortunately he has an important business conference coming up and he knows Mr. Merk will understand if he has to duck out now. The remaining vice-presidents and department heads file past Mr. Murgatroyd, shake his hand, and follow Mr. Twitchell through the door. The office manager remarks pointedly to the rest of the staff that it is almost two o'clock and he certainly wouldn't want to get back to the office and find a lot of empty desks. As Mr. Murgatroyd sinks back into his chair at the deserted head table, a waiter sidles toward him, places a scribbled computation upside down on a saucer at his elbow, and tiptoes away.

Mr. Murgatroyd is left alone with his bill clip, and the bill.

BUSINESS MANNERS
Robert Sheehan

Whether he is receiving visitors or ejecting them, the business executive finds his deportment governed by conventions which he cannot learn about in books, but which he is nevertheless expected to observe. Robert Sheehan, an associate editor of *Fortune*, has made a study of executive gloss. In this article he imparts the results in the urbane manner the subject suggests.

As any old-timer competent to testify will tell you, sometimes nostalgically, business manners in the U.S. are vastly better than they used to be. They have been improving so much, indeed, that now they appear to be superior to the manners encountered in ordinary social intercourse—say, at cocktail parties and dinners, in restaurants, Parent-Teacher Association meetings, clubs, and common carriers. Even in the supposedly genteel academic world, it is not unusual for opposing theorists to attack each other in the most personal kind of way, and in the arts, of course, the studied slur and the vituperative feud are a way of life for some practitioners. Some areas of business are still pretty rough and tumble too, but so far as corporation life is concerned, businessmen seem to have developed the capacity to disagree as pleasantly as they agree.

These days, they have to. Certain patterns of courteous and considerate business behavior have grown up that are de rigueur the country wide, and it takes an executive of rare genius or

prodigious power to ignore them with impunity. These things are rarely spelled out in books or training courses. But the very fact that business manners have not been formally articulated—that they are something a man gathers by instinct and observation—makes them all the more important to the executive career. However it may be in baseball, in business nice guys finish first—or, at least, guys who seem to be nice.

The manners of the businessman when he is off the job may be something else again. At a private cocktail party there is nothing to restrain him from being as big a boor as the next fellow, and he sometimes is. But not in the office; sheer ritual forbids it. For all one knows, some of the rituals observed in business intercourse today may have no more substance than that convention of the Middle Ages called Courtly Love, in which the knights and their ladies were as much interested in the exaggerated gallantries and swoonings of the courtship as in the actual pleasures of the bedchamber. Business-

Reprinted by Special Permission from the January 1957 issue of *Fortune* Magazine; © by Time Inc.

men, to be sure, have not yet lost their love of profits, but there is a certain fascination in the formalities preceding the deal, and it does often seem that the ritual is enjoyed for itself.

Take, for example, the method of receiving visitors that many a corporation president practices today. No longer does he merely rise from his chair, shake hands, indicate your chair, and proceed crisply with the business at hand. Instead, he sweeps out from behind his desk and greets you warmly at the threshold of his office. More often than not, he deserts his desk entirely, and pilots you to a nook on the opposite side of the room. As you loll back on a couch, he draws up a chair and begins to talk to you from across a coffee table, and not necessarily, for the moment, about the business at hand. Conceivably this may serve some ulterior purpose, but conceivably it's also a refreshing little break in his own routine.

This is all very charming, but is it practical? For a businessman to tread such stately measures throughout the working day, often suffering fools gladly the while, takes time, and time is expensive. Few executives, in truth, ever give much thought to the cost of acting out these rituals. It's simply expected of you, so you do it, and perhaps you like to kill a little time talking fishing or golf. But most executives are quick to rationalize their behavior in terms of self-interest and ultimate profits. Good manners, they reflect, constitute a necessary lubricant to business. A few moments spent on the amenities erase doubts and hostility, and establish a climate for the free exchange of facts and ideas. "An ingratiating manner," says a top management consultant, "often tips the scales in a business transaction, and an exhibition of rudeness can be absolutely fatal." He cites a scandalous case in point.

Not so long ago, a rather unprepossessing shareholder of a middling-sized West Coast Company presented himself to the president and politely suggested that his holdings might entitle him to a place on the board. "We do not have the time," the president replied, "to educate an outsider in this business." As it turned out, however, the shareholder had the time, and the money, to acquire effective control of the company, and his first order of business, understandably, was to force out the president.

THE OBLIGATIONS OF OFFICE

Actually, it is the topmost officers who are usually most meticulous about their manners, and most prodigal with their time for the sake of the amenities. Nearly 40 per cent of some 150 company presidents interviewed for this report claimed they answer their own telephones without any screening whatsoever. People who call from the other end of the line might well be astonished at this claim, but in any event presidents can give good reasons why the practice *should* be followed. The president of a large midwestern insurance company who does answer his phone (and also dials his own numbers) says, "I find that 95 per cent of the calls coming in are ones I want to take. Why screen out the 5 per cent of nuisance calls at the risk of irritating the other 95 per cent?"

The president of a utility company who answers his own phone asks, "What has the amount of my salary got to do with my telephone manners? My time is no more valuable to me than that of the caller is to him, whoever he may be." The head of an architectural firm whose executives are required to take calls direct says, "Our customers are busy and important people, and we want them to get through to us quickly. So what if an occasional insurance salesman gets hold of us? That's his gain and our worry."

But it was the president of an aircraft company who put the problem most vividly. "Suppose," he says, "I lose ten or fifteen minutes a day taking fruitless calls. But then Captain Eddie Rickenbacker urgently phones me long distance from a pay station to hell-and-gone somewhere. Do I want him juggled around from secretary to secretary, or quizzed on who he is and what he wants?" Somehow, the picture of Eddie Rickenbacker sweating it out in a phone booth, his face aglower under those fierce eyebrows, seems to clinch the case for accepting the unscreened call.

The majority of executives, however, still feel the need for screening if for no other reason than to divert calls that properly should go to other people in the organization. Even so, most such executives insist that they are never inaccessible, or as one president phrased it, "No one who calls, and requests to speak to me personally, is ever refused." At the very least, they want the screening process to be as subtle and painless as possible. For a secretary to ask, "Who's calling?" or "What did you wish to speak to him about?" is now considered a criminal offense. "May I tell him who's calling?" is just about the limit of allowable inquisitiveness.

Some executives, nevertheless, foolishly hide behind the skirts of their secretaries, a breach of business etiquette on a par with the table ostrich who explores his teeth under cover of his napkin. The genuinely perfect secretary, of course, is one who never permits a breath of suspicion that she is deciding whether or not the caller shall be connected with her boss. A secretary's words can kill. It is amusing to learn, for instance, that the phrase "He's in conference" is now regarded

as utterly cornball, and in fact offensive, though the equally elusive "He's in a meeting" is permissible. But the best practice of all, it is agreed, is for the secretary to give the caller a precise idea of what the executive is doing, e.g., "He's holding a budget session with the divisional vice presidents right now. May he call you when he's free?" Such candor is disarming and preserves the caller's self-esteem. Of course, it's important that the executive does call back when he's free, else the fraudulence of the whole routine is exposed, and the sting of the rebuff compounded.

But the supreme telephone insult, virtually all executives agree, is to place a call through your secretary, and make the party at the other end of the line hold the connection until you're ready to come on. Says an otherwise uncholeric executive, "When I answer my phone, and a female voice says, 'Please hold on a minute, Mr. Zilch is calling,' I promptly hang up. Let Mr. Zilch call back, and let his be the voice that speaks when I say 'Hello.'" Peculiarly, this breach is often committed by those who get most indignant when it is done to them.

On the whole, telephone manners in business are pretty tidy. It is the one phase of business etiquette, incidentally, that is frequently set out by corporations in rule-book form. Also, the practice of calling in the telephone company to monitor calls and instruct personnel in the courteous and efficient use of the telephone is quite widespread. (Though secretly monitoring a call for bad manners would seem to be a case of setting a thief to catch a thief.)

There is one point, however, that the rule books usually do not discuss. Should an executive accept telephone calls while visitors are present? On the one hand, it is embarrassing to a visitor, and an imposition on his time, to be required to sit and gawk while the host-executive takes call after call, some of them of an obviously confidential nature. On the other hand, it may be practically essential for the executive to answer some of the calls, or if the visit is a lengthy one his secretary may stack up more deferred calls than he is able to handle adequately. Some executives merely offer a brief "Beg pardon," and brazen it out. A better practice is for the executive to anticipate, if possible, such calls as are critical, and by pre-arrangement with his secretary have them put through. At the outset of the interview, he can then say to his visitor, "I am expecting an important call, which with your permission, etc." If the call does come, some executives prefer to excuse themselves and take the call in an anteroom. If done gracefully, it is more comforting to the visitor, who doesn't then have to go through a foolish pantomime to prove he's no eavesdropper. If feasible, of course, the best behavior is to quench all calls. But here again some subtlety is in order. The overt command to "Hold all calls, Miss Bettersby" may be flattering to the visitor, but more likely it makes him edgy and apprehensive. It's a puzzlement. Said one executive, "I'm damned if I know just what to do in some situations. I wish business could settle on an accepted practice."

THE DROPPER-INNER

But the severest test of business manners is occasioned by the appearance of unscheduled visitors. Is it not, to begin with, a breach of etiquette to present oneself in the office of an important executive without an appointment? Maybe so, but the practice is widespread, and executives are remarkably tolerant in their reactions.

Of course, it helps to be a customer, or a potential customer, but in the case of banks, department stores, and consumer-goods manufacturers, that classification takes in a lot of territory. And as one bank president phrased it, "A customer is never an interruption of my work; he is the purpose of it."

At any rate, "accessibility," or at least the appearance of it, is a fetish among top officers today. They feel it necessary to say such things as, "I never turn anyone away entirely"; "I try to see everyone with a legitimate reason for calling on me"; "I'll see anybody so long as it's not to the detriment or inconvenience of the people who've gone through the effort to make an appointment."

Therefore, all over the U.S., as you read this, thousands of executives and their unscheduled callers are executing a business ballet that might be called "the Fast Shuffle." After identifying himself to the lobby receptionist, the visitor is dispatched or perhaps escorted to the executive's anteroom, where he is received by a personable secretary. The secretary jots name and purpose of visit on a piece of paper and dissolves through a door to the inner office. In a moment the executive emerges and gives the visitor the big but brief hello. After that, one of several gambits may be followed. The executive apologizes for his crowded schedule, and may invite his visitor to return later in the day, next day, or next week. Sometimes it is suggested that another officer of the company is really better qualified to handle the mission. In that case the executive may summon a subaltern, linger long enough to introduce him to the visitor, and wish them both Godspeed and success. "It only takes a couple of minutes," explains one executive. But never, he warns, make the mistake of bringing them into your office.

A western banker, quite without cynicism or conceit, offers the rationale of this routine: "The fact that he has to wait, or be bucked along to another officer, is not so irritating to him as the fact he's not recognized by the head man. A few words of personal greeting from me makes all the difference in the world to him."

GET LOST, PLEASE

What happens, though, when a host-executive is so extravagantly charming that a visitor simply will not get up and leave of his own accord? At this point most executives stop playing games and take the simple, short route out of the dilemma. "I have one of those *rising voice* techniques," one executive pridefully explains, "and I use it to make a summarizing or concluding statement." Others insinuate such goodby-please phrases as "Next time you're in town, we'll pursue it further," or "When we're not so pressed for time, let's etc., etc." Executives of a more conspiratorial nature press a hidden button, which brings in a secretary with a little note, at which the executive frowns and says, "Tell him I'll be with him in a few minutes."

A sly fellow in Los Angeles has two clocks in his office, one facing him, the other facing the visitor. When he looks pointedly at clock A, the caller involuntarily looks at clock B, and gets the message. As a last resort, most executives find that the "rise and remain standing" technique is effective, though a construction-company president reports that he also puts on his hat just to make sure. And one of those retired Army generals who took over a command in private enterprise used to clap his hands together smartly and cry, "Well now, does that answer all your questions?" Finally, there is an executive in Texas who, when visitors overstay, is said to take an electric razor out of his drawer and begin to shave.

ARE SALESMEN PEOPLE?

Significantly, the grade-A treatment is not confined to distinguished visitors. In one veteran's opinion, "The major development in business manners in the past quarter-century has been the growth of the idea that a man who is trying to sell you something should be treated courteously." This change was vastly stimulated by conditions during World War II, when many salesmen suddenly became suppliers of critical materials, and it was good business to coddle them. But the wartime attitude endures, and the old practice of "softening up" salesmen by keeping them waiting an hour or two has a lot fewer adherents.

The purchasing vice president of a major electronics company says, "We go out of our way to be pleasant to salespeople. As a matter of fact, I've never had a salesman call on me that I didn't learn something from him. There's no better carrier of information than a wide-awake salesman who eats and breathes the industry he serves." This executive even goes so far as occasionally to write a note to a salesman thanking him for a particular presentation. "If we can't give him an order," he says, "at least we can help him prove to his boss that he called on us and did his best. After all, the major thing he's selling is his time."

The president of another company strikes the same note. "I try to see most salesmen, because I want my own salesmen to be received wherever they go. If I don't do it, how can I expect it of others?" Perhaps this kind of thinking —this recognition of mutuality—is at the root of the improvement in business manners generally.

NO PRIVACY FOR PRESIDENTS

"I try to treat my business visitors," the platitude runs, "as I would a guest in my house." But when one turns from the treatment of outsiders to the broad field of intramural office manners, the principles and practices are not so simple or explicit. A fellow worker—whether subordinate, superior, or coequal—is not a guest in one's house. He is a member of a hierarchy, and however friendly the organization may be, the question of status is inescapable. But aside from the more obvious rites and taboos that turn on status, there are a few interesting and relatively new points of protocol that bear reporting.

Office manners are both more considerate and more democratic than they used to be, and as in the case of external or public relations, the burden of performance is on the president. He must make the same show of accessibility to his employees as he does to his customers, and to this end there has been established the shibboleth of the "open door." A bookkeeper, a draftsman, or a correspondence clerk can shut his door, if he has one, to the noise and traffic of the office, but not the president or the chief of an important department. An exception, of course, is a conference with a visitor. But if an employee is within and the door is closed, the usual inference is that the fellow is getting a raise, or a dressing down, or perhaps the pink slip.

As a symbol, the boss's open door may score a point, but that it actually aids communication or raises the general level of manners is rather dubious. Do the employees really come streaming through that open door? "Thank God, no," is probably what most bosses would say in the moment of truth.

Sometimes the symbol is completely hollow. There is an insurance-company president, for example, who is particularly proud of his open door. But the fact is that the executive offices are in haughty isolation on a floor on which 99 per cent of the help would fear to be caught dead. About once a month a female personnel officer takes new employees on an indoctrination tour through those hallowed chambers. As she approaches the president's office, she turns, with finger to her lips, and whispers, "Shhh. If we're real quiet, I think Mr. X's door is open a crack, and perhaps we'll be able to see him at work!"

SUMMONING SUBORDINATES

More to the point is the manner in which the boss approaches or summons his subordinates, and here there has been a creditable advance in democracy and gentility.[1] The cryptic command, submitted through a secretary, is less and less in favor. And ditto with buzzer systems. The preferred method is to telephone the subordinate in person, invite, not order, him to drop by, and explain at least in general terms the reason for the conference. Better still, when the geography of the office permits, is for the ranking officer on occasion to trot down to the subordinate's quarters. A bank president says, "I like to pop into the other fellow's office at least once a week—often enough, anyway, to take the curse off the summons when I have to issue it." Another chief executive says, "It relaxes me to get away from my desk, and I think it bucks up a junior executive when I

[1] The rude executive "squawkbox," so often seen in motion pictures about business, seems to be on its way out. The new intercom systems feature signal lights and soft chimes, and calls can be made and received with privacy. One manufacturer advertises its product as "the intercom with built-in courtesy."

make the gesture of coming to him. You can often get your business done quicker that way, too."

This, in turn, poses a little etiquette problem for the junior executive. Should he rise when a senior officer enters his office? Certainly he shouldn't "snap to" and suck in his gut. But despite some company presidents' protestations that the gesture is quite unnecessary, an ambitious junior probably does himself no harm by coming to his feet. A revealing comment comes from a hearty New England executive. "When they give me that routine," he said, "I simply tell them, 'Relax.'" But then he adds, "I suppose it's only the courtesy paid an older man by a young man, and perhaps the young executive who doesn't possess that kind of everyday, natural manners isn't apt to have other desirable business qualities."

DON'T CALL ME MISTER

When it comes to the use of first names in business, however, the old standards have been rudely shattered, though no conscious discourtesy has been involved in the process. An executive who gets around said this is now a first-name country, and the practice extends throughout most business with the occasional exception of the president and the chairman of the board.

Of the 150 businesses queried for this article, 85 per cent could be said to operate on a first-name basis, and the list seems to cut across all regions and all types of businesses and industries. The usage, of course, varies in degree. There's a Texas oil company where the president admonishes the veriest newcomer to "call me Harry." There is a West Coast utility which says that "equals and near equals deal with each other on a first-name basis. The newest or youngest is immediately called by his first name, and if he feels

comfortable about it, replies similarly." There's one curious instance where the president is called "Jim" by all employees except the top executives, who cling to "Mr." And there is an on-the-fence company (insurance) where, as they put it, "a second-line officer wouldn't be the first to offer a first name to a first-line officer." But in all of them familiarity breeds, and the few barriers that exist are gradually breaking down.

But now for a strong word of caution. The 15 per cent that stick to "Mr." feel strongly about it. A mortgage-company official bit off his answer to the question in one sentence: "I don't call people in business by their first names." A life-insurance president said, "That fast jump to the first name —I don't know if it irritates, but it gives you pause, makes you wonder if he has the balanced judgment you're looking for." A tobacco-company president (with heat): "Permitting the use of first names by every Tom, Dick, and Harry destroys the dignity and respect that the head of a company has to maintain with his staff." A Chicago banker (with a pooh-pooh): "Oh, I suppose a first-name basis is legitimate, but there's an artificial tendency to overdo it. I got a letter this morning signed 'Joe.' I don't know him from Adam."

So for newcomers and juniors, the consensus of advice is, obviously, to wait for the veterans and seniors to offer the first name, and then, playing it by ear, find the moment when a first-name response comes naturally and comfortably. The sensitive junior will not, of course, overlook the danger in waiting too long; in a first-name country, a forty-year-old who persists in calling his fifty-five-year-old boss "Mr." might seem to be implying that the poor old fellow is about through.

WINING AND DINING

Finally, a few new turns in the etiquette of entertainment are worthy of report. Businessmen are tending toward more restraint in this area, and more finesse in the execution of such gestures when they are deemed necessary.

Now that the expense account and the tax allowance are so thoroughly and universally understood, there is no longer any genuine sentiment to be expressed, or regard to be gained, by the big blowout or the extravagant gift. (Nor is there any point in fatuously bickering over who picks up the check.) Not untypical is the executive who reports that a bottle of Scotch at Christmas might be acceptable, but if given so much as a case he returns it with a polite note of regret. Also, many executives declare that the night on the town for visiting firemen has lost its lure, and that the only impressive gesture one can make is to invite them to one's home.

Now, if the burden of this reportage on the manners of the modern American businessman seems too good to be true, readers are entitled to take a small discount. Obviously, in answering a query on good manners, most men are under a compulsion to muster their own best manners and temper their views with charity. Nevertheless, the consensus was remarkable, and such dissent as was expressed was not from the finding that good manners prevail, but was concerned with the danger of overdoing the thing.

Said a utility-company president of a neighboring oil company notable for its politesse, "For my money, they are too bloody servile. They act like an overanxious shopgirl trying to make a sale." And there was the Chicago banker who said, "I'm afraid most of us conform too much. We run the chance that we'll all be mice, and there'll be no rats to lead us." Perhaps the spirit of the American Tobacco Co.'s late George Washington Hill, who always wore his hat in the office and liked to hurl flowerpots on the floor for emphasis, will yet rise again.

Exercises

"Its Monotonous Click," by Richard N. Current

1. Discuss the contributions of the typewriter to the "office revolution."
2. Discuss the extent to which the typewriter contributed to the economic emancipation of women.
3. What factors account for the present preference for women in office jobs? Discuss.
4. Discuss some communication problems created by the typewriter. Feel free to contribute your own ideas.
5. Find out about some of the office copying machines that followed the typewriter and are in current use. In a report, describe what they can do and how they do it.
6. Explain what the author means when he says that the multiplication of records facilitates the rise of both Big Business and Big Bureaucracy.

"The New Office," by C. Wright Mills

1. Draw up a topical outline of this selection.
2. Explain in a paragraph the author's view of "The New Office."
3. If you have had any office experience, write a theme describing the conditions of work in the light of Dr. Mills' findings.
4. Let some friend or relative who works in an office, or who recently worked in one, read this article; then discuss the subject matter with him. Write a report on what he says.
5. Write an analysis of this piece, from the point of view of the author's objectivity, selection of details, and language.
6. What is a stenographic pool? Explain in a paragraph.
7. From the stenographer's point of view, what are the arguments for and against machine dictation?
8. With mechanization of the folding operation, would Melville's description (last paragraph) hold true? How apt is the quotation here?

"The Testimonial Lunch," by Corey Ford

1. Why does the mispronunciation and misspelling of proper names so often cause laughter? Write a theme discussing your theory.
2. What is the humor in Corey Ford's obviously stereotyped characters? Explain.
3. Discuss the relation of Corey Ford's characters and situations to office reality.
4. Write a humorous piece on one of the following:
   a. The Senior Prom
   b. Class Elections
   c. The Class Politician
   d. Orientation
   e. Commencement

"Business Manners," by Robert Sheehan

1. As gleaned from this article, list five rules that govern the manners of executives.

2. Write a theme on the value of good manners in business.
3. Discuss the manners of business people you have observed.
4. Write a theme on one of the following:
a. Manners in the Classroom
b. Entertaining Visitors
c. "The Dropper-Inner"
d. Train (or Bus or Plane or Subway) Manners
e. Salespersons' Manners
5. The following terms appear in this article: nostalgically, vituperative, de rigueur, articulated, amenities, prodigious, rationalize, uncholeric, fetish, gambits, protocol, creditable, politesse. Define each term and use it correctly in a sentence or short paragraph of your own composition.
6. Discuss Mr. Sheehan's manner of writing.